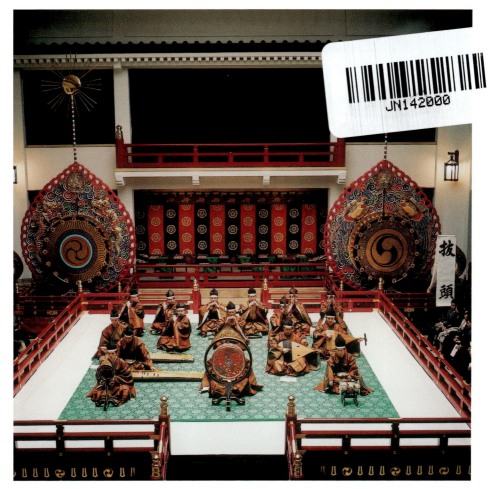

1. *Gagaku kangen* "Battō"
　(Courtesy of The Board of the Ceremonies of Imperial Household Agency)

2. *Sankyoku gassō*
　From left, Fukuda Tanehiko, koto; Tomiyama Seikin I, shamisen; and Nohtomi Haruhiko, shakuhachi.
　(Photo: Tomiyama Seijin)

3. *Noh* **"Okina"** (at Otsuki Nogakudo, June 1966)
Ando Takejiro, shite (Courtesy of Ando Nobumoto)

4. **Wearing** *Noh* **costume**

5. *Noh* **mask "Shōjō"**

6. Noh costume (Courtesy of Sasaki Noh-robes)
Clockwise from top left, "Karaori", "Chōken", "Ōkuchi", "Nuihaku".

7. *Kabuki* "Otokodate Kichirei Soga" (at National Theatre, January 1973)
Onoe Shōroku II as Kobayashi Asahina Yoshihide, left, and Onoe Shōroku III as Soga Goro Tokimune, right. (Photo: National Theatre)

8. Scene of *hōe* (Courtesy of Nishidaiji)

Traditional Japanese Music at a Glance

Traditional Japanese Music at a Glance

The New Edition

Kenji Tanaka &
Takashi Koto

Academia Music Ltd.

Tokyo, Japan 2016

Published by Academia Music LTD.
28-21 Hongo 1-chome, Bunkyo-ku, Tokyo, 113-0033 JAPAN
www.academia-music.com

Kenji Tanaka and Takashi Koto
Traditional Japanese Music at a Glance

ISBN 978-4-87017-089-6

Copyright © 2016 by Kenji Tanaka and Takashi Koto

All rights reserved. No part of this publication may be reproduced, stored in a retrieval system, or transmitted, in any form or by any means, electronic, mechanical, photocopying, recording, or otherwise, without the prior permission of the Publisher.

First Edition, February 2016
Printed in Japan

Cover design by Shukuro Habara and Katsuya Kato

Easy Access to the Story of Japanese Music

Because of their great variety, it is extremely difficult, even for Japanese people, to grasp the essence of traditional Japanese musical genre, or to easily learn some details. Prof. Kenji Tanaka has tried to solve this task, and has succeeded very admirably in his Japanese book, using diagrams and flowcharts. The book is unique and contributes greatly to the literature of Japanese music. It is appreciated and widely read.

The book has now been translated, edited, and transformed into a new English edition by Dr. Takashi Koto. I am very glad, and am delighted that with this new book which gives non-Japanese speakers easy access to the story of Japanese music. They can learn about and digest our national music both historically and systematically. The final benefit is a more profound acquaintance with the wide range of our beautiful *hōgaku* (Japanese music).

Both scholars have been my students many years ago, when I was President and Professor of Musicology at Kunitachi College of Music, Tokyo. Accordingly, I am so happy and feel so honored to write this short recommendation.

Tokyo, July 10. 2015
Bin Ebisawa 海老澤敏

Ex-President/ Professor emeritus,
    Kunitachi College of Music, Tokyo
Ex-President, Musicological Society of Japan
Honorary Member, Reale Accademia
    Filarmonica di Bologna
Honorary Member, International Mozarteum
    Foundation Salzburg
Member, Academy for Mozart Research, ditto.

Well-thought Ideas in This Book

This book is full of well-thought ideas that will help readers understand the wide variety of music genres of Japanese traditional music through time and place in details. One of the most impressive resources embedded in this book as a whole is no doubt that it is full of conceptual diagrams that are based upon deep understanding of the historical facts of Japanese music in general, indeed so much full of information of complicated nature that any normal verbal description often would result in thick volumes of books as found in normal bibliographies.

Both authors studied at the Kunitachi College of Music in Tôkyô, where I used to teach for several years shortly after finishing my graduate studies in the United States. I remember well the enthusiastic activities of the young promising students. Therefore, I now understand that they can make contributions of a kind such as found in this book. Particularly, Dr. Kenji Tanaka, who much later became a doctorate candidate under my supervision at Osaka University in the 1990s, wrote his dissertation on music industry in Japan, which impressed me highly by way of unique ideas. I was wishing that he would make use of his talent in the field of traditional music of Japan in general.

Dr. Takashi Koto, who accomplished his doctoral studies at Harvard University, translated and edited the entire book. Therefore, the present book can be recommended for international readership.

        May 23. 2015　Chiayi, Taiwan
        Osamu Yamaguti 山口修

        Professor emeritus, Osaka University
        Presently Visiting Professor, Nanhua University in Southern Taiwan

Contents

Preface xii

Acknowledgments xiv

About This Book xv

Chapter 1: Evolution of Music in Japan 1
   Corpus of Various Genres—Genealogy of Japanese Music 2
   Classification by the Hierarchy of the Audience 4
   Melodic and Narrative Songs—Characteristics of Japanese Music 6
   The Role of Public Entertainment—Early Modern Music and Immorality 8
   Theory and *Ma* (Space)—Unique Esthetics of Japanese Art 10
   Various Japanese Music Notation Systems 12
   Schools and *Iemoto* (School Heads) in the Japanese Patriarchal System 14

Chapter 2: *Gagaku* 17
   What is Ancient *Gagaku* Music? 18
   Gagaku as a Melting Pot 20
   Native Japanese Dance and Songs—Ancient Japanese Music 22
   Globalization of Ancient Music—Foreign Culture from the Continent 24
   A Hundred-Year Reform—Musical Adaptation in the Heian Period 26
   Thousand-Year Old Music and Dance—*Gagaku* Today 28
   Three Friends, "Ensemble, Dance, and Songs" 30
   Arcana, Which the General Public Can Not See—*Kuniburi no Utamai* 32
   Heian People's Trendiest Culture—Foreign Music, *Bugaku* 34
   Heian Nobles' Culture—*Kangen* and *Gagaku* Songs 36
   Eternal Sound of Eurasia—The Musical Instruments of *Gagaku* 38
   The Exotic Masks and Costumes 40
   Musical Terms of *Gagaku* 42
   Tradition of the Past—Notation of *Gagaku* 44
   1300 Year Old Music School—Tradition of *Gagaku* 46
   Fusion of *Shōmyō* and *Gagaku*—*Gagaku* outside Imperial Court 48
   The Ōnin War and Civil Wars—The History of *Gagaku* 50

Chapter 3: *Shōmyō* 53
   Introduction of *Shōmyō* 54
   Hon-shōmyō and *Zatsu-shōmyō* 56
   Adaptation of *Shōmyō* 58
   Hōe and *Hōyō*—Buddhist Ceremonies 60
   Structure of *Shōmyō*—*Hakase* passed down its 1200-year history 62
   30-Year Ascetic Practice for the Full Initiation 64
   From Paean to Funeral Hymns 66

    Shōmyō and Buddhist Music as the Roots of Japanese Music 68

Chapter 4: *Noh* **71**
    Inseparable *Noh* and *Kyōgen* 72
    Development Process of *Noh* and *Kyōgen* 74
    Like Father and Son: Kan'ami and Zeami 76
    Mugen-noh and *Jo-ha-kyū* 78
    Patronage from Shogun 80
    Noh Performance All Day Long 82
    Abbreviated Performances of *Noh* 84
    Noh Actors: *Shite* and *Waki* 86
    A Stage without Curtains 88
    Delicate and Mysterious *Noh* Masks 90
    Noh Costume and Fashion 92
    Kakegoe (Yells): the Essence of *Noh* Music 94
    Yōkyoku: Restrained and Monotonous Melodies...96
    Hayashi, Instrumental Ensemble in the Middle Ages..98
    Kyōgen: Sophisticated Humor 100
    Music of *Kyōgen*..102
    Masks, Costume and Props of *Kyōgen*...104
    Noh and *Kyōgen* Preserved in Local Regions 106

Chapter 5: *Biwa* and *Shigin* **109**
    Origin of *Biwa* and Family of Plucked String Instruments 110
    Biwa-hōshi: The Earliest Minstrel of Narrative Music 112
    Heikyoku and "The Tale of the Heike" 114
    Structure of *Heikyoku* 116
    Genealogy of Modern *Biwa* 118
    Biwa Music in Transition 120
    Shigin and *Gin'ei*: Recitation of Poems 122
    The Nature of *Kanshi* 124

Chapter 6: *Shakuhachi* **127**
    The Roots of *Shakuhachi* 128
    Legends of Japanese *Shakuhachi* 130
    Mysterious Cult: Fuke Sect and *Komusō* 132
    Legends of Fuke Sect 134
    Kurosawa Kinko, Father of *Shakuhachi* Music, and Other Schools 136
    Splendid Transformation and New World of *Shakuhachi* 138
    Shakuhachi World Reflecting Times: *Honkyoku* and *Gaikyoku* 140
    Shakuhachi Notation Systems: From Timbres to Methods 142
    Shakuhachi: Oldest and Newest Instrument 144

Chapter 7: *Koto* 147
Koto with or without Bridges 148
What is *Sōkyoku*? 150
Transformation of *Tsukushi-goto* and Genius Yatsuhashi Kengyō 152
Transformation of Yatsuhashi Kengyō's *Sōkyoku* 154
Varieties of Early Modern *Sōkyoku* 156
Differences between Ikuta and Yamada 158
Pedigree of Early Modern *Sōkyoku* 160
Sōkyoku of Modern Times 162
Sōkyoku Blooming in the Edo Period: Summary of *Koto* Music History ... 164
Other Members of *Koto* Family 166

Chapter 8: *Shamisen (1) Jiuta* 169
Tōdōza: Blind Men's Guild 170
Shamisen: Flower of Edo Culture 172
Guns, *Shamisen* and Xavier 174
Birth of *Jiuta* and Schools of *Shamisen* Music 176
Versatility of *Jiuta* 178
Two Wheeled Vehicle: *Jiuta* and *Sōkyoku* 180
Tracing the History of *Jiuta* 182
Kokyū, Bowed String Instrument 184
Sankyoku 186

Chapter 9: *Shamisen (2) Jōruri* 189
What is *Jōruri*? 190
Birth of *Ningyō-jōruri* 192
Ko-jōruri in Transition 194
Takemoto Gidayū, an Epoch-making *Jōruri* Chanter 196
Chikamatsu Monzaemon 198
Bold *Gidayū-bushi* 200
Birth of *Uta-jōruri* 202
Lineage of *Bungo-bushi* 204
Jōruri vs. *Kabuki* 206
Buddhist Sermons: *Sekkyō-bushi* 208

Chapter 10: *Shamisen (3) Kabuki* 211
Kabuki: Japanese Counterpart of Western Revue 212
Kabuki: Hodgepodge Performing Arts 214
The Birth of *Kabuki* 216
Music of *Kabuki* 218
Diversified *Nagauta* 220
Nagauta: Orchestra of Japanese Instruments 222

Jōruri in Kabuki 224
  Geza Music: Sound Effects for Snowfall 226
  Modern Nagauta as Pure Music..228
  Japanese Dances 230

Chapter 11: Shamisen (4)—Short Songs... 233
  Popular Songs at the End of the Edo Period 234
  Refined Aesthetic Sense of Edo 236
  Evolution of Shamisen Music...238
  Music of Townspeople: Brief History of Shamisen Music 240

Chapter 12: Folk Songs... 243
  Songs of the Countryside 244
  Work Songs 246
  Folk Songs of Early Modern Age 248
  Accompaniments for Folk Songs...250
  Diffusion of Folk Songs 252
  Haiyabushi: Main Body of Folk Songs 254
  Esashi Oiwake: More Than a Folk Song 256
  Children's Songs...258
  New Folk Songs..260
  Instrumental Music Derived From Folk Songs..262
  Songs since the Age of Gods: Summary of Folk Songs 264

Addendum: Japanese Musical Instruments 267
  Classifications of Japanese Musical Instruments...268
  Types of Shamisen 270
  Types of Koto: Ever Changing Music for Unchanged Instruments 271
  Types of Biwa 272
  Varieties of Shakuhachi 273
  Varieties of Pipes 274
  Varieties of Percussion 275

Index 276

About the Authors 294

Preface

Kenji Tanaka

This book is an introduction to Japanese traditional music with flowcharts. It is formatted for easy and intuitive understanding of the wide variety of music genres of Japanese music.

The range of traditional Japanese music is wide, from ancient court music with a fifteen-hundred-year history to '*gendai hōgaku* (contemporary traditional Japanese music)'. Each genre has been individually developed and still coexists today. In other words, Japanese traditional music is an enormous corpus composed of various genres. Moreover, it is extremely complicated and diversified like intertwined threads since each genre was developed, interrelated and influenced each other in a long history and process.

I am not a performer or a scholar of Japanese traditional music and used to be one of the learners. I needed to learn the basics of Japanese traditional music as an educator. That is why I thought of writing an introductory book for novices to gain a fundamental knowledge in a short time without reading a mountain of books.

In this book, each genre in a category is placed in facing pages so that readers can get a whole picture at a glance. Also readers can correctly and directly access the item which he/she searches for.

To understand the content at a glance, charts are used for every genre. Since these charts visually illustrate the relationship and influences of genres with a single arrow or line, the verbal descriptions are substantially simplified.

As a result, the whole book has been simplified with condensed contents and a wide range of categories and genres is covered. For example, '*shigin*' (narrative singing) or folk song which is closely related to the formation of many genres and often omitted in other books is treated as an independent genre.

I use the most general terms for genres, titles of works, and musical instruments and terms which can be referred to in multiple ways.

This book is written for learners as a guidepost which demonstrates the whole picture of Japanese traditional music at a glance. Therefore, the readers can use it as an illustrated reference book rather than a reader. I hope it is helpful and used like an encyclopedia by the interested reader.

Takashi Koto

It is difficult, even for Japanese, to grasp the whole history of traditional Japanese music. Located in the Far East, Japan absorbed various cultures from other Asian countries. Western cultures were also introduced to Japan, even before the Meiji Restoration. Many musical instruments and styles originated from foreign imports. Old and new musical forms were juxtaposed and influenced each other. We would need a multi-volume encyclopedia to cover everything.

When I read "Illustrated History of Traditional Japanese Music" written by my colleague Dr. Tanaka, I immediately knew that it would be my duty to introduce it to the world. The book effectively splits the complicated history into simple units of facing pages. The units are independent, and at the same time, the parts of the whole. The international edition of the book should be very beneficial to both general readers and also professional scholars and teachers in the ethnomusicology.

I felt that the book had to be rewritten for international readers. The original book targeted Japanese people and contained many social and linguistic matters that might only seem to interest Japanese people. With a professional background as a composer, critic, writer and translator, I believed I was well qualified for the project. I hope all my efforts till now will pay off.

Acknowledgments

Kenji Tanaka

This book, a new English edition of my "Illustrated History of Traditional Japanese Music", was completed in cooperation with Dr. Takashi Koto. He not only translated Japanese into English but also appropriately revised the contents of the book for the English readers.

I would like to express my very great appreciation for the generous of this project. I thank the Tokyodo Shuppan, the publisher of the original Japanese book. They understood the importance of the publication of the English edition and waived the copyright of the English edition. Without their understanding, this book would never be made possible. I thank the president and the editor of Academia Music Ltd. They appreciated the value of this book and made it possible. Last but not least, I am grateful for the support of my teacher, Dr. Osamu Yamaguchi.

Takashi Koto

In translating this book into English, which is my second language, I would need a reviewer of my translation. The reviewer had to be a native English speaker. No financial aid or budget was expected when I started this project. It was Dr. Sidney Feinleib who volunteered to take the important but unrewarded role. Now residing in Japan he used to live in the same district in Boston where I have lived for more than thirty years. He is an author and taught at universities in Tokyo. He is knowledgeable about music as well as the Japanese culture.

Many other people contributed to the development of this book. Firstly, I am grateful to my ethnomusicology teacher Dr. Osamu Yamaguchi. He had studied in the United States and authored several books and articles in ethnomusicology. He gave me a lot of useful advice about terminology and other aspects of music. When I started translating the book a few years ago, he sent me a long facsimile and encouraged me to go on. Secondly, I thank Dr. Bin Ebisawa, one of the best teachers I have ever had. He praised the book and wrote a foreword for us. Thirdly, I wish to thank the photographers and owners of the photos for permission to use them in this book. All photos in the original book were replaced with new ones and with new captions.

Lastly, I thank the president Mr. Kazuo Sakuma and the editor Tomoko Muraoka of Academia Music Ltd. Academia Music has been famous as an importer and a distributor of classical and academic music books in Japan. They recognized the importance of this book and decided to extend the academic knowledge about traditional Japanese music to the world. Foreigners are interested in Japanese culture, more than ever, due to the upcoming Tokyo 2020 Summer Olympics. I hope the world will appreciate Academia Music's decision to publish this book.

About This Book

This book is a new English edition of "Illustrated History of Traditional Japanese Music" (Kenji Tanaka, Tokyodo Shuppan, 2008). The original Japanese book contains some chapters related only to the Japanese language or specific areas of the Japanese society which do not generally interest the international readers. The translated edition has removed such chapters and also appropriately added or revised some parts or expressions in various places for international readers. Furthermore, all the photos of the original Japanese book had to be replaced due to the copyright and the captions of the new photos had to be written. Since this edition is not a simple translation, we decided to call it a new English edition co-authored by Kenji Tanaka, the original author, and Takashi Koto, the translator and reviser.

Because the land of Japan spans from north to south in great distance, it creates room for significant variation in the traditional music from region to region. Particularly, Okinawa, an island once called 'Ryukyu Kingdom' and later became Japan's southernmost prefecture in the 19th century, has developed its own unique social system and culture. Due to the geographical distance, the traditional music in the mainland and Okinawa did not affect each other so much. This book focuses on the traditional music in the mainland. The topic of traditional music in Okinawa will be covered in another research.

The readers must read this "About This Book" before opening any chapter and understand the followings:

(1) Name conventions: In English, the given name comes first followed by the family name while in Japanese the order of the family and given names, if any, is reversed. However, it is a common practice in the Western society that the names of the historical figures are written 'as is' in Japanese, not in the reversed order. Using only one style, either the Japanese or Western style, is not appropriate. We decided that the names of those who were born after the Meiji Restoration (1829) are written in the Western style, and all other names of the historical figures are written in the Japanese style. Examples: Michio Miyagi (given + family names), the father of the modern *koto* music, and Tokugawa Ieyasu (family + given names), the founder of the Tokugawa shogunate.

(2) Spellings in *romaji*: The Revised Hepburn system familiar to English readers is employed. We use sha, shi, sho, cha, chi, chu, tsu, fu, ji, and zu, and so on. Examples: *shamisen* (instrument), Chidori (title), *tsuzumi* (instrument), Meiji (era) and so on. The long vowels are written as ā, ī, ū, ē, ō. Examples: Hōryū-ji (temple). Geminate consonants are written with double consonants. Examples: *kakko* (instrument). Nasal vowels are written with a single 'n'. If it is followed by a vowel or one of na, ni, nu, ne, or no, an apostrophe is added. Examples: Kan'ami (name, different from Kanami) and *shin'nai* (musical style, different from *shinai*). The proper nouns such as titles are written in roman (upright) and general Japanese words are written in italics. Examples: "Rokudan" (work title), and *koto*

(instrument). Compound nouns are not clearly defined in general but whenever possible, they are written with a hyphen '-' between nouns. Examples: *tsukushi-goto* (instrument).

(3) *Romaji* or translation: Titles of works and books can be written in untranslated *romaji* or English translation. For English readers, the untranslated *romaji* spellings have no meaning and hard to distinguish, especially if it is long. We translated the title whenever possible. Examples: "The Moon Over the Ruined Castle" (spelled "Kōjō no Tsuki" in *romaji*). However, short titles are often spelled in *romaji*. Examples: "Rokudan" (title, meaning 'six steps' or 'six variations').

(4) Japanese loan words in English: If the words or proper nouns have been established in English, they are used and do not follow the convention above. Examples: Tokyo (location, Tōkyō in the above convention), and *noh* (musical genre, *nō* in the above convention).

Takashi Koto

Chapter 1: Evolution of Music in Japan

Corpus of Various Genres—Genealogy of Japanese Music

The flowchart on the next page describes most Japanese musical types. It organizes the complicated flow of relationships chronologically, from ancient times to the present, based on the style. The condensed chart may be difficult to read but it clearly shows the background of the formation, the process of interactive development, and the characteristics of Japanese music.

The characteristics of Japanese music can be classified by many factors. Firstly, there is a wide range of musical types. Generally speaking, old things in society become obsolete when new ones emerge. However, Japanese music is a little different. When a new type emerges because of new influences, such as when old styles of public entertainment change to newer, the old musical type can coexist with the new comer and does not disappear. As a result, there are numerous types and variations.

Secondly, the names of musical types and variations are multi-structured. For example, there is a genre called '*jōruri*' that accompanies or narrates plays or stories. When *jōruri* is influenced by other styles or even by choice of a different scene in a play, or a new episode of a story, it becomes a new school. Then, although it is still *jōruri*, the new school name is used as a new type. As an example, we use the names '*nagauta* and *tokiwazu*' and not '*nagauta* and *jōruri*'.

Thirdly there is another classification over the type and the genre, such as '*katarimono* (narrative songs)' vs. '*utaimono* (melodic songs)' or 'theatrical music' vs. 'parlor music'. Moreover, if we minutely examine this classification, any musical genre, for example, a public entertainment, may be manifold corresponding to both groups.

Fourthly, because many types are the total artwork encompassing literature, poetry, drama, dance, folkloric performing arts, religion, ritual and so on, we cannot limit only the musical element in classifying the musical type.

Fifthly, appreciation of musical types can be hierarchical. In other words music is classified by the hierarchy of the audience, such as the noble class, priests, warriors, merchants, civilians, and so on. The social rank of the listeners determines the process of the development and the social rank of a musical type.

There are further influences on classifications based on the historical era, such as the Middle Ages or modern times, and classifications based on musical instruments, as well. This complexity may be one of the reasons why modern people are unfamiliar with Japanese music.

Traditional Japanese Music at a Glance

■ Genealogy of Japanese Music

- **Foreign music**
  - Ancient ritual music
  - Ancient primitive songs → Utagaki, Tōka
  - Chinese music → Tōgaku → Sahō dance → Kangen
  - Korean music → Komagaku → Uhō dance
  - **Gagaku**: Saibara, Rōei
  - Mikagura, Azuma-asobi, Yamatouta
  - Ancient public entertainment → Gigaku, Sangaku → Various folklore, Sarugaku, Dengaku/noh

- **Buddhist Music**
  - Hōe-gagaku
  - Shōmyō → Rongi, Wasan
  - Temple songs
  - Shakuhachi
  - Tsukushi koto
  - Mōsō-biwa
  - Kōshiki, Sekkyō, Saimon

- **Noh**
  - Kusemai → Kōwaka-mai
  - Medieval songs
  - Yamato/Sarugaku → Noh, Kyogen

- **Melodic songs / Tōdō music**
  - Heikyoku
  - Sōkyoku, Jiuta
  - Jiuta-sōkyoku
  - Gaikyoku shakuhachi
  - Edo kouta

- **Narrative songs**
  - Sekkyō-bushi → Uta-saimon → Sekkyō-saimon → Sekkyō-za
  - Chongare → Rōkyoku

- **Kabuki music**
  - Nagauta → Geza, Uta-jōruri

- **Jōruri**
  - Ko-jōruri → Bungo-bushi
  - Tokiwazu-bushi
  - Kiyomoto-bushi
  - Gidayū-bushi

- **Uta-jōruri**
  - Shin'nai-bushi
  - Miyazono-bushi

- **Modern instrumental music**
  - Modern koto music
  - Modern shakuhachi
  - Modern nagauta
  - Ogie-bushi

- **Shamisen songs / Melodic songs**
  - Hauta, Utazawa, Kouta
  - Ballads → Zokkyoku → Vaudevillian music

- Satsuma-biwa
- Tsukushi-biwa
- Sankyoku
- Shin hōgaku (New Japanese Music) → Modern Japanese music

Classification by the Hierarchy of the Audience

Let us examine the relationship between the genre and the school of traditional Japanese music. *Gagaku, jiuta, koto* music (*sōkyoku*), *nagauta*, and *jōruri* are genres. *Gidayū* (or *gidayū-bushi*) and *tokiwazu* (or *tokiwazu-bushi*), and *shin'nai* (or *shin'nai-bushi*) are styles within a genre called *jōruri*. However, these styles are treated like genres because they depict different scenes of a play, or a new episode of a story and the musical characteristics are significantly different from the original *jōruri*. In case of *koto* music, two major schools, Ikuta and Yamada, remain as schools in the genre since they share many common characteristics and are basically similar.

Traditional Japanese music is roughly divided into vocal music and instrumental music, which is further divided into the narrative songs, or *katarimono*, and melodic songs, or *utaimono*. Traditional Japanese music is 85 percent vocal music and the rest instrumental music.

Traditional Japanese music can be classified chronologically as well: *gagaku* in ancient times, *shōmyō, heikyoku*, and *noh* music in the Middle Ages, *shamisen, koto*, and *shakuhachi* music in early modern times, and modern Japanese music in the Meiji period during which Western music was introduced. It was the time of the qualitative transformation and modernization of traditional music, rather than the birth of new genres. These are not only merely chronological divisions but they clearly depict who were the dominant groups in society at the time as well.

Music was closely related to the society and the hierarchy of the audiences. Elegant *gagaku* became a part of the culture of the nobles who adapted music introduced from Asia during the foundation of the nation. People who were impoverished by the long lasting wars during the Middle Age embraced Buddhism and its music. *Heikyoku* and *noh* favored by the *samurai* (warriors) class during the Warring State Period depict that everything was evanescent. The townsmen, mostly merchants, abandoned old '*wabi-sabi*' esthetics (beauty that is imperfect, impermanent, and incomplete) and enjoyed the stage entertainment and the amusement quarters during the peaceful Tokugawa shogunate era. The "gay and chic" culture and early modern music flourished.

Thus, the history of traditional Japanese music is the history of the society and people as well.

Traditional Japanese Music at a Glance

■Classification of Japanese Music

●Genres, Styles, and Schools

- *Heikyoku, jiuta, sōkyoku, nagauta, jōruri*-------Genres
- *Gidayū, tokiwazu, kiyomoto, shin'nai*-------Originated from style names ➡ Styles
- *Yamada, Ikuta, Kinko, Tozan*-------Schools

●Vocal Music (85% of total)

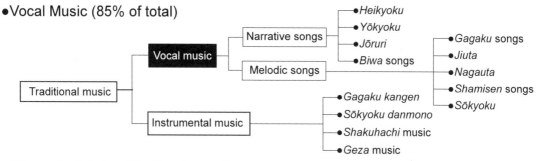

●Chronological classification by audiences

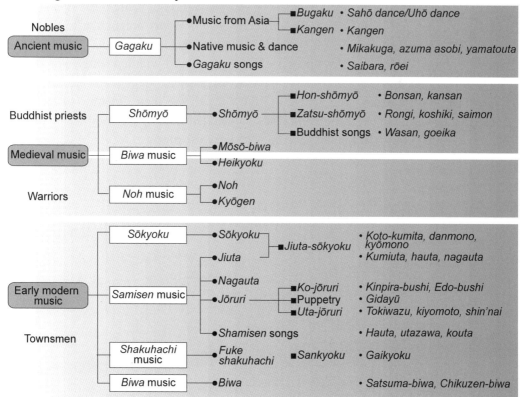

Melodic and Narrative Songs—Characteristics of Japanese Music

Since time immemorial, people sang during rituals or while laboring. Also, in ancient times before writing, a storyteller conveyed real or imagined events in words, sung with a melody-like intonation.

Two subgenres in vocal music gradually evolved from these songs and melody-like intonation (sung narration) and were affected by various styles, tunes, and instrumental skills of each period. They are the melodic songs called '*utaimono*' and the narrative songs called '*katarimono*'. These subgenres form the general primary classification of traditional early modern music. The major types of the melodic songs are *jiuta*, *sōkyoku* (*koto* music), *nagauta* and *shamisen*-accompanied songs. The major types of the narrative songs are *jōruri*, *uta-saimon*, *sekkyō-bushi*, and *biwa* music.

The table on the right page summarizes the melodic and narrative songs as well as the differences between them. Simply put, the difference is on which is the main element: melody or lyrics. The melodic songs resemble the art songs of the West, while the narrative songs are primarily composed of recitation or recitative.

However, the border between the two genres is not so clear. For example, the most typical type of narrative *jōruri* is *gidayū* (or *gidayū-bushi*) but some other styles, such as *shin'nai* (or *shin'nai-bushi*) and *kiyomoto* (or *kiyomoto-bushi*), are similar to the melodic songs. On the other hand, *ōzatsuma-bushi*, a type of melodic *nagauta*, is similar to the narrative songs. Also, a part of the opposite type is placed within a song. For example, songs of narrative *jōruri* or *gidayū* have melodic parts called '*kudoki*' and '*sawari*' respectively. These parts make good contrast to the body of the song. In spite of the unclear borderline between the two genres and dual characteristics, the division of the melodic and narrative songs is important in the genealogy of Japanese music.

■Melodic Songs and Narrative Songs

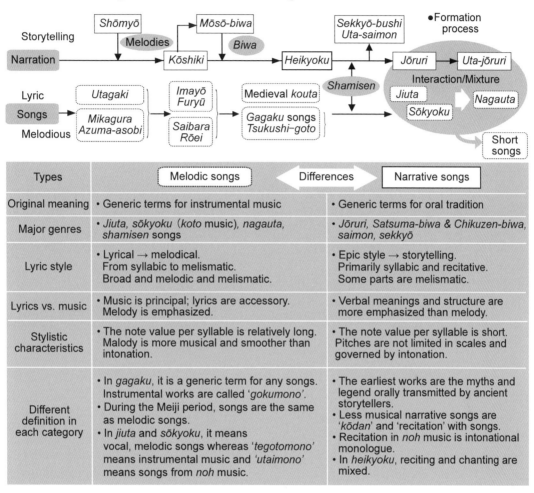

Types	Melodic songs ⇔ Differences ⇒	Narrative songs
Original meaning	• Generic terms for instrumental music	• Generic terms for oral tradition
Major genres	• *Jiuta, sōkyoku* (*koto* music), *nagauta*, *shamisen* songs	• *Jōruri, Satsuma-biwa* & *Chikuzen-biwa*, *saimon, sekkyō*
Lyric style	• Lyrical → melodical. From syllabic to melismatic. Broad and melodic and melismatic.	• Epic style → storytelling. Primarily syllabic and recitative. Some parts are melismatic.
Lyrics vs. music	• Music is principal; lyrics are accessory. Melody is emphasized.	• Verbal meanings and structure are more emphasized than melody.
Stylistic characteristics	• The note value per syllable is relatively long. Malody is more musical and smoother than intonation.	• The note value per syllable is short. Pitches are not limited in scales and governed by intonation.
Different definition in each category	• In *gagaku*, it is a generic term for any songs. Instrumental works are called '*gokumono*'. • During the Meiji period, songs are the same as melodic songs. • In *jiuta* and *sōkyoku*, it means vocal, melodic songs whereas '*tegotomono*' means instrumental music and '*utaimono*' means songs from *noh* music.	• The earliest works are the myths and legend orally transmitted by ancient storytellers. • Less musical narrative songs are '*kōdan*' and 'recitation' with songs. • Recitation in *noh* music is intonational monologue. • In *heikyoku*, reciting and chanting are mixed.

●Ambiguous differences

		Melodic songs Types	Narrative songs Types
Melodic songs	●*Gagaku* songs	• Saibara, rōei	—
	●Buddhist songs	• Wasan, goeika	—
	●*Jiuta*	• Kumiuta, nagauta, hauta	• *Jōruri*
	●*Nagauta*	• Nagauta, ogie-bushi	• *Uta-jōruri, Ōzatsuma-bushi*
	●*Shamisen* songs	• Hauta, utazawa, kouta	—
	●*Sōkyoku*	• Kumiuta	—
Narrative songs	●*Zatsu-shōmyō*	—	• Kōshiki
	●*Heikyoku*	—	• Heikyoku
	●*Sekkyō-bushi*	• *Uta-sekkyō*	• Sekkyō-bushi
	●*Jōruri*	• Tokiwazu, kiyomoto, shin'nai	• Gidayū-bushi
	●*Biwa* music	—	• Mōsō, Satsuma & Chikuzen

The Role of Public Entertainment—Early Modern Music and Immorality

The development of most Japanese music was closely related to public entertainment such as shows and dances of each period. In this book, sections about *kabuki* and puppet *jōruri* devote a great deal of space to explain public entertainment because it is inseparable from the music.

In the beginning, music accompanied ritual and folk events in which people participated. Then, in the Middle Ages, certain music and entertainment prospered under the protection of upper-circle patrons such as the nobles and the *samurai* class. This entertainment and music artistically developed reflecting the aesthetic sense and taste common to the class.

During the early modern times, music of commoners flourished as performing arts. Such entertainment was basically a business for profit from admission fees. Therefore, what people liked won popularity and the rest disappeared. As always, as people were the audience, their interests were always changeable. During the early modern times, the common people accelerated the diversification of public entertainment, replacing the old with the new. The fertile soil for public entertainment was theaters and houses of gay quarters, called the big two notorious places. Lured by the entertainment districts, many townsmen ruined their lives. Inspired by shows at the houses, many double suicides and adultery with actors or actresses occurred. The criticism of the establishment in *sewamono* (play dealing with the lives of ordinary people) angered the Tokugawa shogunate.

The two notorious places were entertainment districts to attract common people. They are where music was indispensable and many new songs and dances were produced. Theatrical music such as *nagauta* and *jōruri* was derived from performing arts while *zashiki* music (private or non-theatrical music) was derived from *shamisen* songs such as *jiuta* and *hauta* in Japanese-style rooms at houses of gay quarters. However, the two styles were not clearly divided. For instance, *shin'nai-bushi*, one of the types of *jōruri*, won popularity at the entertainment districts and was later taken up by strolling musicians. *Ogie-bushi*, one of the types of *nagauta*, was sung not on a stage but in parlors of gay quarters.

Performing Arts and Japanese Music

Genres and Audience

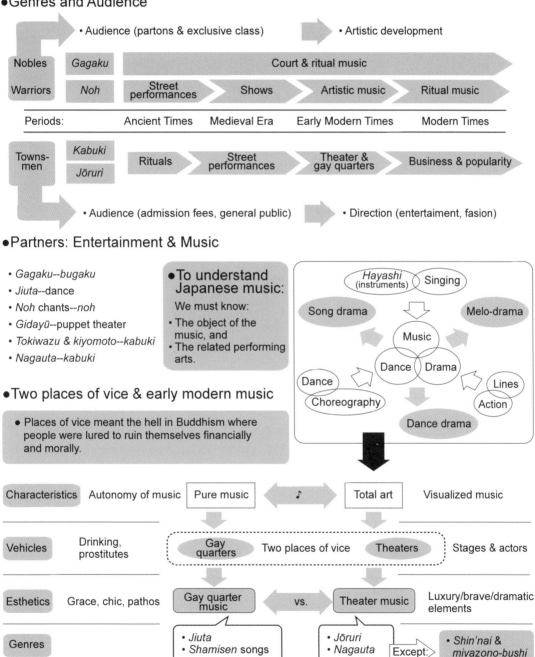

Partners: Entertainment & Music

- *Gagaku*--*bugaku*
- *Jiuta*--dance
- *Noh* chants--*noh*
- *Gidayū*--puppet theater
- *Tokiwazu* & *kiyomoto*--*kabuki*
- *Nagauta*--*kabuki*

- To understand Japanese music:
  We must know:
  - The object of the music, and
  - The related performing arts.

Two places of vice & early modern music

- Places of vice meant the hell in Buddhism where people were lured to ruin themselves financially and morally.

Theory and *Ma* (Space)—Unique Esthetics of Japanese Art

Japan adapted music theory from China into its own theory. *Gagaku* and *shōmyō* were based on it but music afterwards deviated from it and was not systematic or logical. In traditional music, particularly when vocal music was dominant in early modern times, individual expression was more emphasized than theory.

Rokushiro Uehara (1848 - 1913) found that traditional Japanese music was made of pentatonic scales which could be grouped into two modes: '*In*' (or *miyakobushi*) and '*Yō*' (or *inakabushi*). He also pointed out that there were ascending and descending scales that differed.

Fumio Koizumi, a modern ethnomusicologist, who researched folk song melodies, discovered the existence of core tones and tetrachords in the pentatonic scales. The tetrachords are made of two core tones in a perfect fourth interval and one auxiliary tone between them. There are four basic Japanese pentatonic scales based on this theory as shown in the table on the right page: the *min'yo*, the *miyakobushi*, the *ritsu*, and the *okinawa* scales. Though some scholars raise an objection to it, the Koizumi theory is the most common at present regarding traditional Japanese musical scales.

In addition, Koizumi classified beats of folk song rhythm into two groups: the *yagibushi* and *oiwake* styles. The *yagibushi* style is syllabic (one pitch per syllable) and the *oiwake* style is melismatic (multiple pitches per syllable). Today this classification is applied not only to folk songs but also to whole traditional Japanese music.

A beat is the basic time unit in music and when a series of beats is periodically repeated, the pattern is called 'meter'. Japanese rhythm is characterized by the two-beat structure made of '*ura* and *omote*' which is equivalent to English words, 'face-up and face-down' or 'head and tail'. Unlike Western music, they do not mean accented downbeat and unaccented upbeat. This two-beat structure is called '*hyōshi*'. Each beat of *hyōshi* is elastic, very different from that of steady rhythm of Western music. The elastic beat is governed by a unique sense called '*ma*' which is equivalent to an English word, 'space' in arts. *Ma* is not a rest of Western musical notation but is a temporal empty space between two musical sounds. *Ma* is not written in musical scores. It is an important esthetics in Japanese arts.

■Musical Characteristics
●Scales and Koizumi Theory
■Pentatonic scales: *Ryo* and *Ritsu*

■*Yō* and *In* modes defined by Rokushirō Uehara

■Four basic tetra chords by Fumio Koizumi

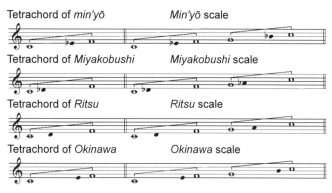

●Rhythm
■Example of the *oiwake* style: A typical melismatic song

"Esashi Oiwake"
(from NHK "Japanese Folksong Collection")

■Example of the *yagibushi* style: A typical syllabic song

"Yagibushi"
(from NHK "Japanese Folksong Collection")

●*Ma* (space)

There is a pause between tones.
The space is not a rest of Western music.
This *ma* is more important than tones.

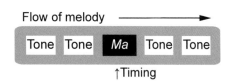

Various Japanese Music Notation Systems

The belief that traditional Japanese music is transmitted orally, without any written scores is incorrect. Every genre and school uses written scores but do not share a common system. "The Tenpyo Biwa-fu", a score for *biwa*, was created in ca. 738. The oldest printed score "Shōmyō-shū (Collection of Shōmyō)" was published in 1472, one year earlier than the publication of the Gregorian chant. Since most traditional Japanese music consists only of a melody line without accompanying harmony or played by ensembles, as is often the case for Western music, there was no need to develop a common notation system for genres and musical instruments. In addition, since a genre often equated a musical instrument, a specific notation system was invented for each genre or each school.

Although written scores were used, they were just memoranda. The learner studied music through an oral tradition, one-to-one with a master. Traditional Japanese music was not a hobby to enjoy and studying it was more like ascetic practice. The master taught the pupil not only the performance technique but also the manners and disciplines of the school.

At the end of the Edo period music lovers emerged from common people and wanted more convenient practice. As a result, easy-to-understand, written scores for everyone were contrived and published. A notation system was exclusively developed for a specific genre, and moreover, a specific school. If a learner of *koto* or *shamisen* music, for instance, began to study at another school, he had to familiarize himself with a new notation system.

The table on the right page lists the notation systems. The instrumental music is separated from vocal music in the table.

Since there was no such music theory as modern musical education, the pitches, note values, and other musical elements could not be logically taught. Instead, the oral transmission or *shōga* (syllabic mnemonic) such as '*ten*, *ton*, and *shan*' was developed.

It should be noted that whenever or wherever they lived, people in the West and East used similar devices. For instance, the Medieval neumatic notation in the West and its Eastern counterpart, *hakase* notation (see "Chapter 3: *Shōmyō*"), and the solmization (a system of attributing a distinct syllable to each note in a musical scale) in the West and its Eastern counterpart, syllabic mnemonic.

■Notation of Japanese Music

● Voices and instruments

Japanese vocal music is primary and instrumental music secondary. They are inseparable. Traditional Japanese music is monophonic and linear.

No harmony
No large ensemble No common notation system was needed.

● Music learning is:

Not a hobby, but Ascetic practice.

Requirement for students:
- Manners
- Desciplines
- Loyalty.

● Respective notation system for:

- Singing and performing
- Genres (or instruments)
- Schools in the genre.

Direct one-to-one lessons with master. Written scores were just memoranda. **Oral transmission** is essential.

● Major notation systems of Japanese music

Instrumental music — Written scores for instruments show how to play with numbers, letters, and symbols.

System	Genre/Instrument	Description
Syllabic system	*gagaku, shamisen*	Similar to Western solmization. Syllabic mnemonic shows pitches, etc.
Hole number system	*hichiriki, yokobue*	Also called *kanmei-fu*. For *shakuhachi*, finger numbers instead of hole numbers.
String name system	*koto*	String numbers/names are written.
Location system	*shamisen, biwa*	Shows where to press with fingers. Does not show pitches.
Rhythmic notation	percussion	Rhythm is writen with smallest units of notes.

Vocal music — For voice only. Most of them show lyrics only without melodic lines.

System	Genres	Description
Hakase	*shōmyō, saibara*	Like neuma system, marks next to lyrics visually show the ups and downs of melody.
Dot system	*sōka, heikyoku, utai* (noh chants)	Dots, or bars, next to lyrics are used for syllabic songs. Occasionally with note names.
Pattern system	*jōruri, nagauta*	Named melodical patterns are written with dots and note names.
Mixed	*koto* music, *nagauta*	Instrumetal and vocal systems are juxtaposed.

Schools and *Iemoto* (School Heads) in the Japanese Patriarchal System

It is not an exaggeration to say that the Japanese traditional performing arts owe their long dignified history to a system based on heads of schools. This organizational structure is fundamentally that of a patriarchal family. It exists in many areas such as religion, politics, economy and culture, in addition to music.

In performing arts, if someone begins a new and unique technique or style and attracts a group of followers and is inherited by a successor in the group, the group is a school and the grand master is *iemoto* or a school head.

In general, the school is inherited and the successor to the position of head of the school is a member of the household. Depending on the genre, a person without blood relationship may become the school head. As the school grows, improved techniques and development of new ideas results in the birth of an offshoot of the school. An excellent pupil, who is allowed to learn everything, becomes the school head of the offshoot and is given a certificate by the original school head. As this process is repeated, the school proliferates.

In the second half of the Edo period, performing arts became very popular. Schools grew bigger and amateur music lovers increasingly studied performing arts at the schools. The '*iemoto*' system, a management system with the division of labor, evolved in which the middle manager, called a natori master, gave lessons to novices and only the grand master taught high level disciples and also controlled certificates. Since a huge amount of money, such as from lesson and certificate fees, was involved with this management system, inter-factional strife concerning authority occurred and the schools were frequently split. As a result, there are now more than one hundred school heads in the genres of *kouta* and dance. In contrast, the school heads of some genres such as *ogie-bushi* and *miyazono-bushi* are desperately seeking ways to survive.

In *gagaku*, for hundreds of years the music of each instrument has been preserved as property that can be inherited. In *noh*, the *iemoto* system was very strict. Lead roles were inherited by one family which was not allowed to have offshoots or even to change the roles.

The inheritance system of the school head has a benefit of preserving the dignity of the art. But in order to maintain it, some schools have prohibited exchange with other genres and schools and have kept an exclusive organization. As a result, they are unable to adjust to today's society.

Traditional Japanese Music at a Glance

■Schools and *Iemoto* (School Heads)

●Power of *iemoto* (school heads)
- Autocrat with monopoly.
- Top of a pyramid.
- Patriarchal family system.
- Hereditary system (with adoption).

●Heads of Sects
- Elite pupils who become the heads of a sect, as powerful as grand master in hereditary system.
- Offshoots (certified or broken off caused by inevitable power struggles).

Iemoto is a commander of a school of family.

- **School**: A group of pupils who follow the founder.
- **Sects**: Offshoots from the original school, almost identical.

Grand master — Sect → *Iemoto* Sect (×6)

●*Natori* System
- Excellent pupils become '*natori*' certified and given a stage name by a school head.
- *Natori* can teach but can not certify others.
- His pupil pays certification fee to the school head, not the *natori*.
- The system causes many conflicts.
- It happens in koto or shamisen sects where amateur music lovers study.

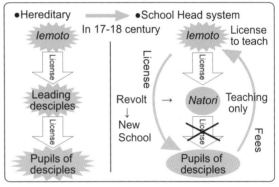

●Hereditary → ●School Head system (In 17-18 century)

Hereditary: *Iemoto* → License → Leading desciples → License → Pupils of desciples

School Head system: *Iemoto* → License → *Natori* (Teaching only, no License) → Fees → Pupils of desciples. Revolt ↓ New School. License to teach.

●*Iemoto*
- The earliest were *gagaku* musicians in the Nara period and poets in the Kamakura period.
- In the Muromachi period, leads of *noh* were school heads, such as Kanze, Konparu, Kongo, Hosho, and Kita.
- In the Edo period, *iemoto* were born in various fields such as tea ceremony, flower arrangement, incense, dance, go, painting, and calligraphy.

Genre	School/Style	Sect Name	Stage Name
Jiuta-sōkyoku	Ikuta	Seihahogaku-kai, Miyagi-kai, Sōchō-kai.	Kikusuji, Tomisuji, Nakasuji.
	Yamada	Yamato, Yamaki, Yamase	Contains 'yama'.
Shaku-hachi	Kinko	Chikuyū-sha, Kotobuki-kai, Chikumei-sha, Reibo-kai.	Mostly contains 'dō'.
	Tozan	All incorporated	Contains 'zan'.
Jōruri	Tokiwazu		Surname is Tokiwazu.
	Kiyomoto		Surname is Kiyomoto.
Bunraku (puppet theater)	Vocalists	Takemoto, Toyotake.	Surname is Takemoto, or Toyotake.
	Shamisen	Takezawa, Tsurusawa, Nozawa, Toyozawa.	Contains 'sawa'.
	Puppeteers	Yoshida	Surname is Yoshida.
Nagauta	Kineya	Kineroku-ha, Kineei-ha, Kinekatsu-ha, Sakichi-ha.	Surname is Kineya.
	Instruments	Tanaka-ya	Surname is Tanaka.
Biwa	Satsuma Chikuzen	Seiha, Kinshin-ryū, Nishiki-biwa. Asahi-kai, Tachibana-kai.	Contains 'kin' or 'sui'. Most surnames are Asahi.

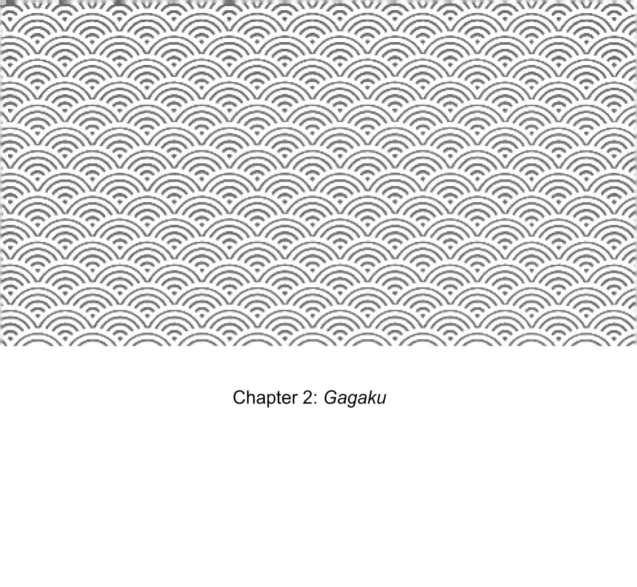

Chapter 2: *Gagaku*

What is Ancient *Gagaku* Music?

Gagaku is an intangible cultural asset that has survived for fifteen hundred years in Japan. However, only a limited number of people have heard a full live performance, and few have detailed knowledge about it.

Attendees at a wedding ceremony at a shrine rarely realize that the unfamiliar music of *shō* and *hichiriki* played there is from *gagaku*. *Gagaku* is very remote from people today. It is so esoteric that the public does not have an opportunity to see and hear the live *gagaku* performance except for the rituals held at the Imperial Household or at major Buddhist temples or Shinto shrines.

Occasionally, *bugaku*, ancient dance accompanied by *gagaku*, is televised in a special program, but the masks, costumes, dance and music are so remote from modern society that it appears (depending on the repertoire) exotic or something from the distant past and we wonder if it is Japanese art. This makes *gagaku* more incomprehensible.

Gagaku's source is the basic conventions of *yayue*, or 'elegant music' established in the Imperial Court in China during the Western Zhou Dynasty (11th-8th century BC), based on the 'ritual and music' philosophy. The Han Dynasty (206 BC-220 AD) witnessed another peak in the development of imperial court music. This music has largely been lost in China, but has survived in other parts of East Asia such as Korea and Vietnam, adapting itself to the new circumstances.

Prior to the introduction of *yayue* to Japan via various Asian countries, Japan already had its own ritual music. This native music was interwoven with foreign music during the early process of creating a nation and became Japanese *gagaku* differing from the court music of other Asian countries. Japanese *gagaku* is not in a single style, but is, as shown in the chart on the right page, composed of three kinds of music with completely different origins and cultural backgrounds. *Gagaku* is a collective name for the three kinds of music, clearly distinguished by places and purposes for presentation, and characteristics that have been preserved in Japan until today.

Traditional Japanese Music at a Glance

■ *Gagaku* in Japan

***Gagaku* is:**
- Court music for ancient ceremonies of Shintoism at the Imperial Palace.
- The oldest existing music in the world with a 1300-year history.
- Called '*utamai*' at the time and '*gagaku*' today.

● *Yayue* in China

Yayue means 'elegant music' performed in court.

- In Confucianism, the most important philosophy in China, music must not only be beautiful but also encourage our morality.

Rituals and Music — Rituals for social orders. Music for spiritual calmness.

● Musical characteristics

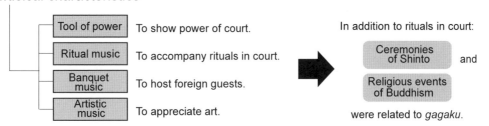

- Tool of power — To show power of court.
- Ritual music — To accompany rituals in court.
- Banquet music — To host foreign guests.
- Artistic music — To appreciate art.

In addition to rituals in court:
- Ceremonies of Shinto and
- Religious events of Buddhism

were related to *gagaku*.

● Japanese *gagaku* is integration of:

Three different types of music. *Gagaku* is the general term for those types.

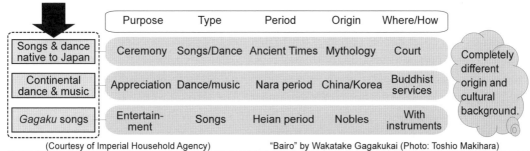

	Purpose	Type	Period	Origin	Where/How
Songs & dance native to Japan	Ceremony	Songs/Dance	Ancient Times	Mythology	Court
Continental dance & music	Appreciation	Dance/music	Nara period	China/Korea	Buddhist services
Gagaku songs	Entertainment	Songs	Heian period	Nobles	With instruments

Completely different origin and cultural background.

(Courtesy of Imperial Household Agency)

"Bairo" by Wakatake Gagakukai (Photo: Toshio Makihara)

Gagaku as a Melting Pot

In ancient Japan, native music was called '*utamai*' which meant 'song-dance'. Then, new instrumentation and music were introduced from foreign countries, especially from China.

According to the earliest records of exchange between China and Japan, Emperor Guangwu of the Eastern Han Dynasty received the envoys from the king of Wakoku (Japan) and gave them the Golden Imperial Seal in 57 A.D. Of course, there had been exchanges already, resulting in rice farming as well as the use of bronze and iron during the Yayoi period in Japan. Afterwards, there were continuous exchanges. Queen Himiko of Japan sent a tributary to the Wei Dynasty (220-265) of the Three Kingdoms as did King San to the Eastern Jin Dynasty (317-420). During the Sui and the Tang Dynasties of China (6th-10th century), the Japanese imperial embassies frequently visited China and brought back an advanced culture, including music.

At first, the foreign culture was accepted in its original form. But with social changes and aristocracy, anything that did not fit the new Japanese tastes was weeded out or changed to accommodate to them. This way for Japan to adopt foreign culture is still observed.

As for music, music from China as well as from other countries, characteristic of each country, flowed into Japan, in a burst during the Nara period (710-794). Mostly dance music for banquets was introduced, since ritual music already existed in Japan and new forms were not needed. For a while, music native to Japan and that from foreign countries coexisted and both were played and developed.

Especially during the Heian period (794-1185) when the dynastic culture thrived, aristocrats and court nobles regarded dance and music as the symbol of 'intellect' and the Emperor and court nobles willingly studied music. Many experts emerged among them and some composed new works. As a result, Japanese *gagaku,* which suited the court, inevitably formed to replace the purely foreign music. The activity of this adaptation of foreign music to Japanese court music was later known as 'the reform of the musical system'. Japanese *gagaku*, still preserved today, was established by this movement to integrate native and foreign music during the Heian period.

Traditional Japanese Music at a Glance

■ *Gagaku* as a Melting Pot

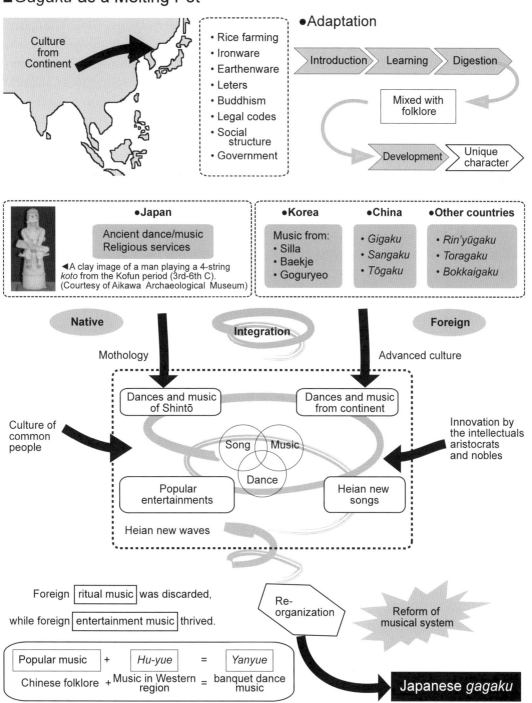

Native Japanese Dance and Songs—Ancient Japanese Music

Before foreign music was introduced from the continent, Japan had native songs and dance.

"Sānguó Zhì (Records of Three Kingdoms)", a Chinese historical book written in the 3rd century, states that in Japan "people gather for a wake and feast singing and dancing". Japanese were agricultural people and enjoyed public festivals related to agricultural rituals such as rice-planting festivals to pray for a bumper harvest. Songs and dances, for instance, *utagaki*, were closely related to these festivals.

Those customs are depicted in more than 200 poems in the oldest Japanese book "Kojiki (the Records of Ancient Matters)" and the second oldest "Nihon Shoki (The Chronicles of Japan)". Numerous ancient songs are also found in the oldest existing collection of Japanese poetry "Man'yōshū (the Collection of Ten Thousand Leaves)" and ancient records of the culture and geography "Fūdoki". Some of the poems in these books deviate from the classical Japanese verse form with thirty-one syllables, and are songs with lyrics and melodies, and even choreographic gestures (dance). For example, the beginning of one of the poems in "Kojiki" is composed of forty words in twenty verses which is punctuated exactly every two words like a dialogue between two persons. Its contents suggest that a man and woman sing the poem while dancing.

In ancient myths the "Amano Iwato" episode of a goddess and gods singing and dancing in front of a cave show that, though it is a legend, songs and dance were widely rooted in people's lives in ancient times. Also, many names of dances accompanied by songs are mentioned in the ancient chronicles and records.

Archaeologists have unearthed many ancient musical instruments along with artifacts. Such instruments include: pots of the Jōmon period (ca. 10,500-ca. 300 B.C.) probably used as drums with stretched animal skins; pipes and bells made of stone or earthenware; and ancient zithers and bronze bells of the Yayoi period (ca. 500 B.C.-300 A.D.) unearthed all over the country. A myth describes a legendary hero who holds a zither while riding with a princess. A recently unearthed ancient clay figure holding a zither, proves that a small zither existed at the time. In all parts of the world, even a myth contains some truth.

■Ancient Japanese Music

Periods	Songs	Dances/music	Instruments
Yayoi (300BC-300AD) Kofun (ca 250-538) Asuka (538-710)	• Ancient songs • *Man'yō* songs • *Fūdoki* songs • *Hōe* songs	• Amano Iwato legend • *Utagaki* • *Tōka*	• flutes (stone, earthenware, or bamboo) • *koto* (wood with 5 strings) • hand drums (earthenware in rounded body) • bells (nut shells or earthenware) • *nuride* (bronze)

Gagaku = *Utamai* = songs & dances = integral custom in ancient Japan

Amano Iwato *Kagura* in Takachiho, Miyazaki

●Legend of the Amano Iwato Cave

A legend says that sun goddes, Amaterasu, angered by the act of her brother, hid herself in a cave, Amano Iwato. This caused the darkness in the world. The other gods threw a party and goddes Uzume danced with music. Curious, Amateras peered out and was blinded by her reflection in a mirror set up outside. The cave was forced open and the world was lit again. Thus Uzume is regarded as the origin of Japanese entertainment.

●*Utagaki*

A matchmaking meeting in ancient Japan where young men and women exchanged love songs and poems. Later in court these were mixed with *tōka*, the dance introduced from China, and became the court dance and music.

Rice-planting Festival (Katori Shrine)
(From Wikipedia Commons)

●Rice planting festivals

Rice-planting songs and dances to pray for a bumper harvest as well as rice-harvesting songs and dances became public entertainment.

●Ancient songs and dances

Songs → *Azuma-uta, Kagura-uta, Miyabito buri, Shiriage-uta, Shizu-uta, Amagatari-uta, Kume-uta, Sakagura-uta, Kunishinobi-uta, Kamugatari,* etc.

Dances → *Azuma-asobi, Mikagura, Tamai, Yamatomai, Hayatonomai, Tatefushi no mai, Kishimai, Kumemai, Morogata no mai, Tsukushi-mai, Kuzu no sō,* etc.

Globalization of Ancient Music—Foreign Culture from the Continent

The first foreign musical culture was introduced from the Korean Peninsula. According to "Kojiki (The Chronicles of Japan)", a large number of performers from Silla were present at the funeral of Emperor Ingyo in the middle of the 5th century to play Silla music. Then, court music in the Korean Peninsula was continuously introduced from Baekje in the 6th century and from Goguryeo in the 7th century. It is recorded that a concert of music from the three Korean kingdoms (Baekje, Silla and Goguryeo) was held at the Imperial Court at Asuka, Nara prefecture, in 683. A little earlier, Mimashi of Baekje introduced the original music of *gigaku* into Japan, a masked drama from Wu, China, called '*utamai* from Kure (Wu)". It is unknown how Korean Mimashi of Baekje learned the Chinese masked drama. Prince Shōtoku, who utilized Buddhism to achieve a lasting peace to Japan, nourished *gigaku*. Connected with Buddhist rituals at temples during the Asuka period (5th-8th century), both 'music from Three Kingdoms' and *gigaku* were frequently performed.

By the beginning of the 8th century, sophisticated and systematic music theory and dance music as well as musical instruments and performers were introduced from the Tang Dynasty of China. "Goshōraku", "Taiheiraku" and so on were performed at the Imperial capital in Nara. Since there had already been ritual music in Japan, banquet dance music '*yanyue*', not ceremonial music, was introduced from the Tang Dynasty. During the 3rd-6th century, Chinese music was significantly influenced by music of Hu people flowing in from Central Asia via the Silk Road. New musical instruments, such as lute and double-reed oboe were adopted. Dance music of Persia and India fused with Chinese folk music into the Chinese banquet music, *yanyue* which became popular during the Tang Dynasty. This banquet music was introduced to Japan.

In the Nara period, foreign music and dance was continuously introduced from many Asian countries, including Korea and China. During the 8th century, various musical cultures flowed in from countries in all of South East Asia. For example, the original music of *rin'yūgaku* introduced by Vietnamese priest Buttetsu; music and dance from Balhae, a successor state to Goguryeo in northeast China; and the original music of *toragaku* the source country of which is still unknown.

Though so much foreign music came in, songs and dances native to Japan did not disappear and took duty as ceremonial music at the Imperial Palace until today. It is astonishing, that globalization on a large scale occurred during the process of the formation of Japanese *gagaku* hundreds of years ago.

Traditional Japanese Music at a Glance

■Music from the Continent

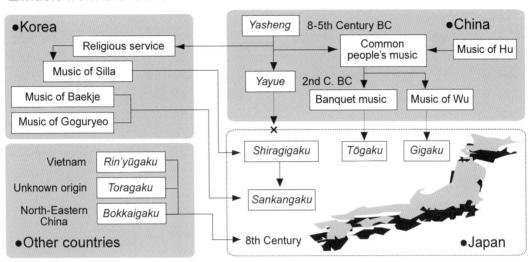

●Categories

Gigaku	612	Masked musical drama from China, also known as *Kureno Utamai*. Prince Shōtoku (573-621) nourished it to promote Buddhism. No direct relation to *gagaku*.

Name	Year introduced	Description
Sankangaku	N/A	Collective name for *Shiragigaku, Kudaragaku,* and *Kōkurigaku*. 'Sankan' stands for Samhan which comprised confederacies of Mahan, Jinhan, and Byeonhan in central and southern Korean peninsula.
Shiragigaku	453	Dance music of Silla and one of *Sankangaku*. The oldest music from the Continent in the documented history. Integrated to *Komagaku,* the right side dance, in the 9th century.
Kudaragaku	554	Dance music of Baekje and one of *Sankangaku*. Introduced a century after the introduction of *Shiragigaku*, though could be eralier. Integrated to *Komagaku,* the right side dance, in the 9th century.
Kōkurigaku	610	Music of Goguryeo. According to a study, a dancer came to Japan in the early 7th century (for Emperor Suiko's funeral). Often confused with later *Komagaku* but they are different.
Tōgaku	701	Music of Tang in China. Originated from common people's music, and also called *kogaku* (music of Hu). Later it refered to the left side music and dance.
Toragaku	731	Music of Tora. Some say Tora is present Jeju Do island in Korea but it is unknown. The name appears as a dance in "Shoku Nihongi" but what it refers to is unknown.
Rin'yūgaku	736	Music of Lin Yi. The Kingdom of Champa, present south Vietnam, was called Lin Yi in Chinese. But it might be India. The music could be introduced directly from Champa or via China.
Bokkaigaku	727 (?)	Music of Balhae (Bohai). Balhae was a kingdom in Northeastern China and North Korea in the 7th-10th century. The music was integrated into the right side dance but the original dance and music is unknown.

A Hundred-Year Reform—Musical Adaptation in the Heian Period

The import boom of foreign music ended around the early Heian period. It was probably caused by the abolishment of the Japanese envoy to the Tang Dynasty. There were other possible reasons. Gagakuryō (or Utamai no Tsukasa, the Bureau of Music), basically the first national music institute, was established and Heian aristocracy studied playing instruments and dance as their culture. Geniuses emerged, such as Emperor Ninmyō who composed, and Ōtono Kiyogami and Owarino Hamanushi, both regarded as the first professional composers in Japan. They vigorously refined foreign works and composed new ones. People tried to turn foreign music, unsuitable for the elegant court culture, into magnificent music under the musical reformation beginning in the Heian period.

    The chart on the right page summarizes the five important factors of the reform. First, foreign music flowed in, in a disorganized manner, and was grouped into *tōgaku* (music that originated in China, or the left side) and *komagaku* (that originated in Korea, or the right side). Both were organized and adapted to the Japanese culture. Some works were abandoned and some were newly composed. In this stage *gigaku*, one of the foreign types, was separated from *gagaku*. Second, foreign musical instruments were organized. Instruments duplicating timbre and range with others, rarely used, or having timbre unsuitable for Japanese taste, were discarded. Finally the types of instruments were narrowed to fourteen: five winds, three strings, and six percussive instruments. Third, complicated music theory was simplified and adapted to the Japanese climate. It was a bold reform. Sixty or so variants of Chinese scales were narrowed to six and the names of notes were translated into Japanese. Fourth, *gyoyū*, a concert under the Emperor presence at Court, was regularly scheduled. It aimed at improving the musical skills of nobles, the leaders of the reform, and making *gagaku* more refined. This reform resulted in *kangen*, a wind and string ensemble without dance.

    Lastly, two new vocal subgenres characteristic of the elegant Heian culture were born. They are *rōei*, a song over a Chinese poem accompanied by wind instruments, and *saibara*, a song arranged in the elegant *gagaku* style based on a folk song or a packhorse driver's song and accompanied by a wind and string ensemble. Under these circumstances, Japanese *gagaku* was established.

    This reform started in the Emperor Ninmyō era and took approximately 100 years to complete. It was a leisurely reform appropriate to the elegant Heian period.

■Development in Heian Period

●Reform of Music System

The music system was reformed during the period of Emperor Ninmyō reign (833-849):

(1) Grouping *gagaku* into the left and right sides.

Music from China: *Rinyūgaku* — integrated into → *Tōgaku* (Left)
Adaptation
Music from Korea: *Bokkaigaku* — integrated into → *Komagaku* (Right)

(2) Simplifying the ensemble structure.

Discarded instruments:
- Wind: *shakuhachi, makumo, ō-hichiriki*
- String: *gogen* (5-string koto), *kugo* (harp), *genkan* (lute), *Shiragi-koto*
- Percussion: *hōkyō* (suspended metallic bars)

(3) Simplifying scale systems. (Keys and note names)

Ryo scale	Ichikotsuchō (D)	Sojō (G)	Taishikichō (E)
Ritsu scale	Hyōjō (E)	Ōshikijō (A)	Banshikijō (H)

Western Key	D	D#	E	F	F#	G
Japanese Key	Ichikotsu	Tankin	Hyōjō	Shōzetsu	Shimomu	Sōjō

Western Key	G#	A	A#	H	C	C#
Japanese Key	Fushō	Ōshiki	Rangei	Banshiki	Shinsen	Kamimu

(4) Establishing *kangen* and noble's '*gyoyū*'

- Poetry and music were indispensable culture of the aristocracy and court nobles.
- Recitals and concerts of instrumental music were hosted by the aristocracy.
- These gatherings are called '*gyoyū*'.
- The instrumental music *kangen* → Japanese characteristic music

▶From the picture scroll "Kangen Emaki-shō" (Courtesy of Imperial Household Agency)

Talented court nobles
Minamoto no Hiromasa
Imperial Prince Sadayasu

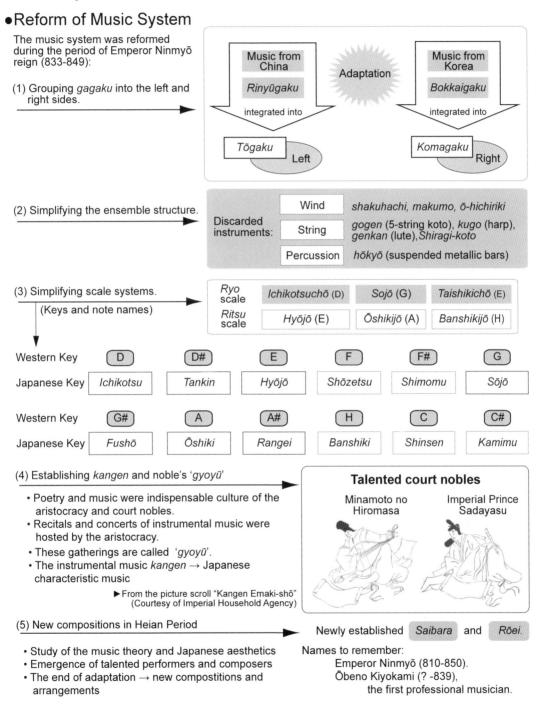

(5) New compositions in Heian Period

- Study of the music theory and Japanese aesthetics
- Emergence of talented performers and composers
- The end of adaptation → new compositions and arrangements

Newly established *Saibara* and *Rōei*.

Names to remember:
Emperor Ninmyō (810-850).
Ōbeno Kiyokami (? -839), the first professional musician.

Thousand-Year Old Music and Dance—*Gagaku* Today

The chart on the right shows the classification of Japanese *gagaku*. Since its reform in the middle of the Heian period, *gagaku* has been preserved "as is" until today, for about 1,000 years.

The music of other Asian countries, such as China and Korea, which shared the same origin with *gagaku*, became extinct or was interrupted for a certain period. Only Japanese *gagaku* has been preserved without interruption. Just its long history proves that Japanese *gagaku* is an incomparable heritage of the world.

As described already, *gagaku* is roughly divided into three subgenres based on their origins. The first, *kuniburi no utamai*, is the songs and dance native to Japan which are mainly used for the rituals related to the Imperial Household. The second, *bugaku*, is dance music introduced from China and Korea, performed during banquets. *Bugaku* is divided into two groups: *tōgaku* (the left side) and *komagaku* (the right side). Only *tōgaku* has purely instrumental ensembles called *kangen*. Unlike the songs and dance native to Japan, which are basically solemn, *bugaku* from China and Korea is characterized by its recreational, not ceremonial, nature. Masks and costumes of *bugaku* are full of exoticism and vividly colored. Dances are diversified: some are quiet and some heroic. Because of their nature, *bugaku* and *kangen* have played an important role as entertainment to cheer up solemn and sacred Buddhist and Shinto services and rites since ancient times.

The third subgenre, *gagaku kayō* (*gagaku* songs), is songs without dance. It was indispensable in the culture of the nobles who recited Chinese poems and *waka*, Japanese poetry. During the Heian period, singing a melody in the *gagaku* style over these poems became popular. Because this was younger than the other two types, the *gagaku* song was novel; for example, popular songs at the time were used. The *gagaku* songs are often called Heian new songs.

Thus, *gagaku* composed of songs, dance and instrumental music is diversified in various types.

Traditional Japanese Music at a Glance

■Classification of Today's *Gagaku*

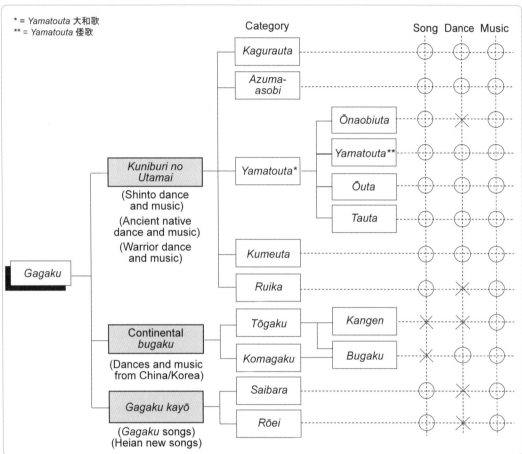

●Two Sides

Gagaku was divided into two sides based on the origin of each work:

- *Tōgaku* = from China = *Samai/Sahō no mai* (left side)
- *Komagaku* = from Korea = *Umai/Uhō no mai* (right side)

The officers of Royal Guard in the left and right sides took charge of music. That is why *gagaku* was divided into two sides.

In court, the left side was regarded higher than the right side, as opposed to the Chinese custom. But the two sides of *gagaku* were treated equally.

●*Kangen* and *Bugaku*

Kangen only belongs to *tōgaku*, while *bugaku* belongs to both sides.

Tōgaku is made up of works for:

(1) purely instrumental ensembles such as: "Etenraku", "Butokuraku", and "Senshūraku",

(2) dances such as: "Ama", "Ninomai", "Sanju", and "Ikko", and

(3) both instrumental ensembles and dances such as: "Ranryōō", "Shunteiraku", "Bairo", and "Goshōraku".

Three Friends, "Ensemble, Dance, and Songs"

Based on the presentation, *gagaku* is classified into three types: *kangen* (instrumental ensemble), *bugaku* (dance) and *gagaku kayō* (songs).

Kangen is an ensemble of 16 musicians with eight types of musical instruments: 3 winds, 2 stringed instruments, and 3 percussive instruments. Each wind part has three players. The players who sit in front are in charge of *netori*, tuning of the ensemble. All players of the ensemble face the audience. There is no conductor. The *kakko* player on the right front leads the ensemble and lets all the members know the tempo, which gradually becomes faster, by striking the *kakko*. When playing *kangen* works, all the members sit and play cross-legged on the stage in costumes of iridescent *hitatare* (a traditional men's dress) and *tateeboshi* (a cap).

Bugaku is of three types: *kuniburi no utamai* (songs with dance native to Japan), and *sahō* and *uhō* (the left and right sides, both accompanied by an ensemble). *Kuniburi no utamai* is primarily used for religious rituals and is not staged with the dance of either side. When staged, the left and right dances open with "Enbu" by two court dancers, one from each side. As illustrated on the right page, it is followed by dances: a *hiramai*, *bunomai*, *warabemai*, and *hashirimai*, in a predetermined order, with the tempos gradually becoming faster. *Hiramai* is played twice by dancers from each side, on a similar theme and in similar costume. It is called *tsugaimai*, a pair of dances. The left dance is played first and then the right dance is played. The dancer of the left side literally appears from the left side of the stage, and the one of the right side from the right side. The left dance and the right dance are well contrastive in every aspect with, for instance, reddish and greenish costume, manly and feminine choreography, and golden and silver properties. This contrast is based on the yin-yang philosophy (the balance between two extremes). Unlike *kangen*, which belongs to the *tōgaku*, the ensemble of *bugaku* of the same *tōgaku* is primarily composed of winds. The musicians of the ensemble of *bugaku* wear similar, gorgeous costumes and helmets, as do court dancers.

Rōei genre of *gagaku kayō* is antiphony-styled, elegant and gentle responsive singing. It is divided into three sections: first, recitation of Chinese poems in the Japanese way of reading Chinese; next, singing by a solo voice in a very high register, and lastly, singing in unison. In contrast, *saibara* is a rhythmical song with cheering calls based on ancient folk or popular songs. "Meiji Sentei-fu", the standard collection of *gagaku* scores compiled in 1876 and 1888, contains 90 *kangen* works, 50 *bugaku* works, and 40 *gagaku* songs though surviving repertoires are fewer than they used to be.

■Formation of *Gagaku*

Kangen — An instrumental ensemble

- 3 winds: 1. *ryūteki* 2. *hichiriki* 3. *shō*
- 2 strings: 4. *gakusō* 5. *gakubiwa*
- 3 drums: 6. *shōko* 7. *tsuritaiko* 8. *kakko*

● Stage layout

1	2	3
	4	5
6	7	8

Audience

Bugaku — A dance accompanied by instruments or songs

- *Kuniburi no utamai*: Ancient ritual song and dance in court/ Dancing over singing in unison/ Heian costume/ With no masks/ Accompaniment of a single flute, *hichiriki*, and *wagon*.
- *Uhō no mai* (right side dance): Based on music from Korean Peninsula/ Dancing over rhythm of percussion/ Greenish costume/ Masks rarely used/ 3+1 drums, *shōko*, *hichiriki*, *komabue*
- *Sahō no mai* (left side dance): Based on *tōgaku* from China/ Dancing over a melody/ Reddish costume/ Masks often used/ *kakko*, drums, *shōko*, *shō*, *hichiriki*, and *ryūteki*

●Program of *bugaku*

- *Enbu*: Opening dance to cleanse stage/ Symmetric layout of left and right dancers
- ↓ *Hiramai*: Quiet dance by four dancers/ Also called *bun'nomai*
- ↓ *Bunomai*: Heroic dance by four dancers in warrior costume with swards, spears, or shields
- ↓ *Warabemai*: Sweet dance by children in bird or butterfly costumes
- ↓ *Hashirimai*: Rhythmical dance by two dancers in exotic masks
- ↓ *Tsugaimai*: Juxtaposed pair of similar dances of left and right sides

●Dichotomy between yin-yang

	Left (yang)	Right (yin)
Music	*Tōgaku*	*Komagaku*
Style	Musculine	Feminine
Costume	Reddish	Greenish
Props	Gold	Silver
1st step	Left foot	Right foot
Symbol on drum	3 *tomoe* dragon, sun	2 *tomoe* phoenix, moon
Feet sliding	After stepping	Before stepping

Kayō — Songs in the *gagaku* style accompanied by *gagaku* instruments

Genre	Texts	Melody	Accompaniment
Saibara	Common people's songs such as popular, children's, and folk songs	Malismatic for each syllable	Clear 4/4 time. Melodic lines are more important than text meaning.
Rōei	Chinese poems pronounced in or translated into Japanese	Reciting with melodic lines	Free rhythm. Follows singing mostly in unison.

Arcana, Which the General Public Can Not See— *Kuniburi no Utamai*

Kuniburi no utamai, meaning songs with dances native to Japan, has been specially treated in *gagaku* and is distinguished from other music introduced from foreign countries. With an incredibly long history, it has been transmitted orally generation to generation as ritual music of the Imperial Palace by the families of *gagaku* musicians from foreign countries. *Mikagura no gi*, one of the most important rituals, is an all night solemn ceremony held annually in the middle of December at the front yard of the Imperial Palace Sanctuary dominated by darkness and creating tranquility. The seats for the musicians are partitioned by curtains and illuminated by the blaze of bonfires, which cleanse the ritual space.

A chief musician holds a rite to begin the performance and welcome Gods, and then "Niwabi (Bonfires)" is performed, followed by three different types of *kagura* songs: "Torimono", "Kosaibari" and "Hoshi (Stars)". *Mikagura* is performed at the Palace for Niiname-sai (a harvest festival) and the festivals of Emperors of Jinmu and Showa. By the way, we should not confuse *mikagura* with *okagura* though they share the same kanji characters. *Okagura* or simply *kagura* refers to *satokagura*, which is folk music performed at shrines, different from *mikagura* performed at the Palace. Since *mikagura* is an arcane ritual at the Palace, concealed from anyone else's eye, the general public cannot see it. Similarly, four works of *yamatouta* and *kumeuta* are performed only for the Inauguration Ceremony of a new emperor and *ruika* only for the emperor's funeral, and thus the general public seldom has the opportunity to see them.

However, the general public has an opportunity to see *azuma-asobi* among *kuniburi no utamai* at prominent shrines, because it is dance music offered to the shrine by the Imperial Household. *Azuma-asobi*, which originated from *azuma-mai*, a local entertainment in the east region, became popular in the western (Kyoto-Osaka) region and was adjusted to the court. It is more gorgeous and sophisticated than other traditional songs with dance.

Almost all works of *kuniburi no utamai* are sung in the melisma style (singing many notes for one syllable), and it is, indeed, difficult to follow the lyrics. But, we can indulge ourselves in the calm flow of time of the Heian period, while listening to the leisurely songs and watching the accompanying dances.

■Program of *Kuniburi No Utamai*

Name	Dance	Description	Occasion
Kagurauta	Ninjōmai	Performed for religious service in court. Repeatedly discontinued and revived since Heian period. The general public could not see.	The Harvest Festival, Anniversary of the Demise of the Emperor Jinmu
Azuma-asobi	Surugamai / Motomegono-mai	Warrior dance and songs in the eastern region, used for religious service. Performed in Shinto shrine outside of court. Originated from religious rituals for repose of souls, and so on.	Festival of the Vernal (or Autumnal) Equinox, Anniversary of the Demise of the Eperor Jinmu
Yamatouta*		Music performed for Inauguration Ceremony of a new emperor. Composed of 4 works.	Coronation Banquet
└ Ōnaobiuta	None	Performed as prelude for *yamatouta* on the day before Inauguration Ceremony.	Day before Coronation Banquet
├ Yamatouta**	Yamatomai	Native dance and songs in the Yamato region. Revived in the 18th century.	
├ Ōuta	Gosechinomai	The only dance by women in *kuniburi no utamai*. Five female dancers in Heian costume.	Coronation Banquet
└ Tauta	Tamai	Ritual dance and songs for bumper crop. Originated from rice planting songs. Rarely performed today.	
Kumeuta	Kumemai	Regarded as the oldest Japanese dance and song in the Emperor Jinmu era. Heroic dance.	Coronation Banquet, Anniversary of the Accession of the Emperor Jinmu
Ruika	None	Only performed for emperor's funeral. Also called 'Gosōka'. With *wagon* and *shakubyōshi*.	Emperor's funeral

●Coronation Banquet

The first "Niiname (Harvest) Festival" held by the new emperor. Niiname Festival carried out at the imperial palace and shrines throughout the country on November 23rd annually before WWII. The day has become today's national holiday "Labor Day".

◄Top: *Azuma-asobi*.
Bottom: *Gosechinomai*.
(Courtesy of Imperial Household Agency)

* = Yamatouta 大和歌
** = Yamatouta 倭歌

Heian People's Trendiest Culture—Foreign Music, *Bugaku*

Japanese native songs with dance are called *utamai* and dance with music introduced from foreign countries, *bugaku*. *Utamai* is accompanied with instruments, but singing is almost always the base. On the other hand, foreign *bugaku* has no songs (presumably, it did in the past).

The reason why *bugaku* was grouped into the left and right sides is because the Bureau of Imperial Guards, which had two divisions, the left and right sides, was in charge of *gagaku*. However, the choreography, music, costume, and masks of *bugaku* are not clearly associated with characteristics of China (the left side) and Korea (the right side). The sides can be distinguished by the titles of the work, costume colors, and sides for the entrance of dancers, but the difference between them is not as clear as that of the native Japanese and foreign style *gagaku*. It could be caused by the reform in the middle of the Heian period. The process of thoroughly adapting the foreign music to the Japanese culture might have tamed the original characteristics. Though the titles and themes still remain the same as when they were introduced, music from foreign countries might have been fairly altered due to the new works and adaptation by the nobles in the Heian period.

The important works of the left and right *bugaku* are listed on the right page. Fifty *bugaku* works were included in a collection published in the Meiji period. Presumably, three times more works existed in the Heian period. It is supposed that *bugaku* was the latest entertainment lionized by the Heian aristocracy according to many depictions about music and dance found in books written in the Heian period such as "The Tale of Genji" and "The Pillow Book". Though not included in the chart on the right page, the titles of "Genjōraku" and "Batō" are found in both the left and right dances. "Goshōraku" and "Shun'nōden" are listed in the repertoire for a concert with the presence of the Emperor. They are almost the same in both sides though the tempo of the dance and the instrumentation of the ensemble are subtly different. There are six scales in the left dance while only three in the right dance. The tunings of *koma-ichikotsu* and *koma-hyōjō* of the right side are a whole tone higher than *ichikotsuchō* and *hyōjō* of the left side. This difference is caused by the tuning of pipes, *ryūteki* of *tōgaku* (the left side) and *komabue* of *komagaku* (the right side).

The left and right *bugaku* may be alien to people today who are familiar with early modern Japanese performing arts such as *kabuki* or Japanese dance. But, for the Heian people it seemed to be the trendiest culture.

■Left/Right *Bugaku* Titles and Description

Left	Dance Type	Size	Tuning	Dancers	Costume	Description
Ryōō	*Hashiri*	Medium	*Ichikotsu*	1	*Ryōtō*	A handsome king wears a fierce mask in a battle field.
Karyōbin	*Warabe*	Medium	*Ichikotsu*	4	*Betsu*	Dance of a bird with beautiful voice in heaven performed by Sarasvati.
Seigaiha	*Hira*	Medium	*Banshiki*	2	*Betsu*	Dance by Prince Genji and his friend performed for Emperor
Taiheiraku	*Bu*	Medium	*Taishiki*	4	*Betsu*	Dance of General Xiang Yu and Liu Bang in Qin Dynasty, China. Heroic costume.
Tagyūraku	*Hira*	Medium	*Taishiki*	4	*Betsu*	Dance of players of a polo-like sport. A theory says it is a work by Huangdi (Yellow Emperor).
Genjōraku	*Hashiri*	Medium	*Taishiki*	1	*Ryōtō*	Dance of a Hu man who is pleased to find a snake, his favorite food.
Batō	*Hashiri*	Small	*Taishiki*	1	*Ryōtō*	Dance of Empress of Tang who was so jealous that she became a demon.
Ama	*Hira*	Medium	*Ichikotsu*	2	*Kasane*	A thief in a unique mask sneaks into the Palace of the Dragon King to steal a precious stone.
Shun'nōden	*Hira*	Large	*Ichikotsu*	6	*Kasane*	Dance of a bush warbler in Spring. A scene described in "The Tale of Genji".
Goshōraku	*Hira*	Medium	*Hyōjō*	4	*Ban'e*	Only work in the *Jo-ha-kyū* structure. Composed by Emperor Taizong of Tang.
Shundeiraku	*Hira*	Medium	*Sōjō*	4	*Ban'e*	A Cherry tree blossoms when Emperor Xuanzong laments for its slow bloom.

Right	Dance Type	Size	Tuning	Dancers	Costume	Description
Engiraku	*Hira*	Medium	*Ichikotsu*	4	*Kasane*	New *Komagaku* composed in Engi period (901-923). No story line.
Komaboko	*Hira*	Medium	*Ichikotsu*	4	*Betsu*	Dance of sailors who pull oars in five colors of a very old Korean ship.
Kitoku	*Hashiri*	Medium	*Ichikotsu*	1	*Ryōtō*	Dance of heroic Rizhu King (later Marquis of Guide, or 'Kitoku' in Japanese) of Xiongnu.
Hassen	*Hira*	Small	*Ichikotsu*	4	*Betsu*	Eight immortal wizards. According to one theory, it describe cranes flying about in the sky.
Nasori	*Hashiri*	Small	*Ichikotsu*	2	*Ryōtō*	Male and female dragons pleasantly dance and play.
Soriko	*Hira*	Medium	*Ichikotsu*	4	*Kasane*	Religious tune without any specific story line. Characteristic masks.
Kochō	*Warabe*	Small	*Ichikotsu*	4	*Betsu*	Cute butterflies play with yellow Japanese roses.
Bairo	*Bu*	Medium	*Hyōjō*	4	*Betsu*	Dance of heroic warriors. Characteristic rhythm.
Chikyū	*Hira*	Semi-large	*Sōjō*	4	*Kasane*	Dance for a banquet to appreciate flowers. It could be *Bokkaigaku* based on the masks.

Heian Nobles' Culture—*Kangen* and *Gagaku* Songs

In *gagaku*, *kangen* (instrumental ensemble music) and *gagaku kayō* (songs) are Japanese style music created by the Heian aristocracy. Traditional *kuniburi no utamai* and foreign *bugaku* are accompanied by dance while *kangen* and *gagaku* songs are purely instrumental and vocal music, respectively.

In the middle of the Heian period when *gagaku* was prospering, there was a garden-party style concert called *gyoyū* of *kangen* held by the Emperor and the court nobles. In the concert, *kangen* works and *gagaku* songs were alternately performed and sung. This was not a concert in which performers and audience were separated but a gathering in which all attendees, the Emperor and the court nobles, played or sang their own original compositions by turns and praised the workmanship of the work or excellence of performance of each other.

At the time, the professional musicians who performed *gagaku* for rituals and annual events at court or shrines were low ranking officers, while poetry and music were the indispensable culture of the nobles. The nobles showed off their skills and sophistication of their pastime or aristocratic *gagaku* in these garden-party style concerts. As a result, the gifted nobles, who were as good as professional musicians, became musical experts and the families of pedigree in music emerged. For example, the Tōke family which was the descendant of Minamoto no Hiromasa, and the Genke family, which was the descendant of Minamoto no Masanobu, were renowned as two big schools of *gagaku* songs.

Gagaku is classified by types, and *kangen* works number the most in the list of the *gagaku* repertoires, since most *bugaku* works are listed as *kangen*. *Bugaku* contains music for dancers entering and exiting before and after the main part of a performance. When the main part, or *tōkyoku*, is performed without these collateral parts, it is called a *kangen* work. Some works, such as the famous "Etenraku", have no dance.

Saibara and *rōei*, both *gagaku* songs, have a graceful flavor of the nobles who indulged in poetry and music. They are not simply songs, but extremely inventive and fancy music in the ornamental singing style with the skillful accompaniment of an ensemble. On the other hand, similar court songs sung at a poetry reading, such as today's New Year's Poetry Reading held at the Imperial Palace, are not so musical. That is because, though *gagaku* by the nobles still existed, the poetry reading began at the end of the Heian period, during the rise of the less elegant *samurai* (warrior) class.

■Kangen and Kayō Titles and Description

Kangen — Music for instrumental ensembles without dance and voice in slow tempo in general.

Title	Dance	Size	Tuning	Descriptions
Shun'nōden	○	Large	*Ichikotsu*	Melody suggestive of a song of a bush warbler. Regarded as luck for a new start.
Shukōshi	○	Small	*Ichikotsu*	Music for drinking. Lilting tune with nonsense refrains.
Goshōraku	○	Medium	*Hyōjō*	Five Confucian virtues (benevolence, justice, courtesy, wisdom, and sincerity) are applied to five notes.
Bairo	○	Medium	*Hyōjō*	Tune with a lively drum. Also known as *Tenjikuraku*.
Etenraku			*Hyōjō*	The most famous *gagaku* tune. According to a theory, it was composed by Emperor Wen of Han.
Ryūkaen	▲		*Sōjō*	Based on an anecdote about an immortal wizard who plucked a flower and composed a poem.
Kaiseiraku			*Sōjō*	Tune based on the improvisation by Ōtono Kiyokami and others performed at request of Emperor Ninmyō.
Senshūraku		Small	*Banshiki*	Composed for Emperor Konoe's Coronation Banquet. Since then performed as the last tune in a concert.
Sokō	○	Large	*Banshiki*	The most magnificent and important work in *tōgaku* music.
Senyūga			*Taishiki*	Since this was performed when a Princess priestess was sent to Ise Shrine, it was a taboo to use it at parting in later days.

Saibara — Singing with beats, accompanied by wind and string.

Isenoumi	Common people's labor songs such as farming or fishing songs were sophisticated in court and became *gagaku*-styled court and *gyoyū* music.
Koromogae	A song for the seasonal change of clothing with a nonsense refrain 'sa kindachi ya'.
Anatō	A song to announce the beginning of *gyoyū* with the easy-going and happy contents.

Rōei — Reciting without beats, accompanied by three solo winds.

Kashin	A song for *gyoyū* and banquets, included in "Wakan Rōeishū (Japanese and Chinese *Rōei* Collection)". Chinese poem is uttered in Japanese.
Jisei	A song of the star festival introduced from China, also included in "Wakan Rōeishū".
Kōyō	A song to appreciate red leaves and white reed catkins in the autumn, included in "Shinsen Rōeishū (New Collection of *Rōei*)".

●Two noble families in charge of *gagaku* songs: Tōke and Genke

The following two families among court-noble musicians were in charge of *gagaku* songs. Both abolished in the Kamakura (1185-1333) and Muromachi (1392–1573) periods.

- ●Tōke: Minamoto no Hiromasa (son of Prince Katsuakira and grandson of Emperor Daigo) → His son Yukimitsu → Fujiwara no Yorimune (the son of Fujiwara no Michinaga) → Fujiwara Hokke (Nakano Mikadoke)
- ●Genke: Minamoto no Masanobu (son of Prince Atsumi and grandson of Emperor Uda) → His son Tokinaka, progenitor of Uda Genji → His descendant Nobuari, progenitor of Ayanokōji

Eternal Sound of Eurasia—The Musical Instruments of *Gagaku*

During the process of the reform in the Heian period, eight instruments were abandoned and fourteen survived in *gagaku*. These surviving musical instruments have retained the same shape and timbre as when they were introduced during the Asuka period (from 6th to early 8th century) until today. The places of origin of these instruments stretch all over the regions in the Eurasian Continent, including the ones brought into Japan from Arab countries via the Silk Road.

There are five kinds of wind instruments. *Hichiriki*, one of the instruments introduced from the Persian people in Central Asia, is used in all the genre of *gagaku* including the songs with dance native to Japan except for *ruika* (funeral songs). It is a small double reed, played with an exclusively unique technique called *anbai* (portamento) producing a loud sound. *Shō* (free-reed mouth organ) is only used for *tōgaku* and songs. It can produce chords and create remarkably unique sonority in *gagaku*. The three kinds of transverse bamboo flutes, *ryūteki* with seven holes; *komabue*, originated in Korea, with six holes; and *kagurabue*, native to Japan, with six holes, can vary in size and registers. The trio of *hichiriki*, *shō* and *ryūteki* create the characteristic sound of *gagaku*.

Two stringed instruments, *biwa* (lute) and *koto* (zither), independently developed a unique music world during the Middle Ages and early modern era. In *gagaku*, they are called *gakubiwa* and *gakusō* respectively and are in charge of rhythm rather than melodies, except for performances in *kangen* (instrumental ensembles). *Wagon*, a zither native to Japan, is only used with *utamai*, the songs with dance native to Japan.

For percussion, only *kakko* and *san'no-tsuzumi* (double-headed drums) are used for the left and right dances, and *shōko* (bell) and *ōdaiko* (big drum) are used for both sides in *gagaku*. In *kangen* of *tōgaku*, *tsuridaiko* (or *gakudaiko*, hanging drum) is added to the percussion section. However, percussion such as *tsuzumi* and *kane* (gong) are not used for *kuniburi* (native *gagaku*) but instead *shakubyōshi* (clapper made of two rods), is used for all works. Percussion seems not to fit melismatic songs, which have no beat.

The early musical instruments, such as *hichiriki*, are seeing a revival in relaxing music and sound today. The sounds from time immemorial seem to fascinate the young generation of the modern age.

Traditional Japanese Music at a Glance

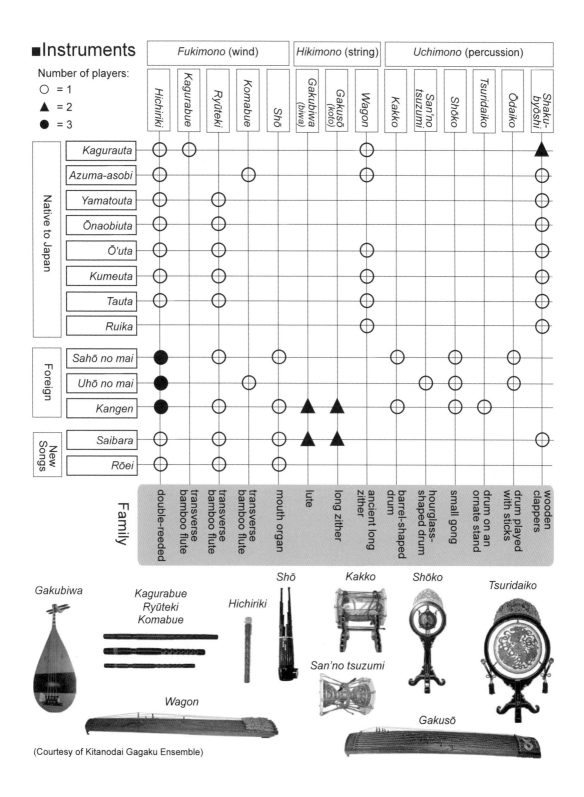

(Courtesy of Kitanodai Gagaku Ensemble)

The Exotic Masks and Costumes

If you watch the *bugaku* masterpiece "Ranryōō (King Lanling in Chinese)" without any knowledge, you must think if this is *gagaku*. I, too, had such an impression when watching *bugaku* for the first time.

The *bugaku* "Ranryōō" is based on a legend that King Lanling of Northern Qi of China (6th century) was so handsome that he wore a ferocious mask (see the right page) to avoid demoralizing his warriors in the battlefield. A mask like a beast, a red coat called *ho*, showy, brocade-woven trousers called *sashinuki*, a vest rimmed with furs called *ryōtō*. It is said that these mask and costumes were originated from the court clothing of the Tang Dynasty era. "Ranryōō" does not look like a Japanese native due to the strange mask, costumes, choreography which is reminiscent of *taichi* (Chinese martial art) to me, and the accompaniment of *hichiriki*, *shōko*, and *ōdaiko*. On the other hand, the dancers of the *utamai* (songs with dance) native to Japan such as *mikagura* and *azuma-asobi* wear more common headgear and costumes similar to what Shinto priests wear. The headgear and *hitatare* of the musicians of *kangen* are familiar to us as well. If we watch *gagaku* without knowing that the appearance of each program is significantly different from others, the person who has watched only "Ranryōō" would have a very different impression from that of the person who has watched only *azuma-asobi*. That is a story of several blind men trying to describe an elephant and drawing different conclusions based on which body part each one touched.

There are three types of costumes in *bugaku*: '*kasane-shōzoku*' (or *tsune-shōzoku*) the standard costume for the officers in the Heian period, '*ban'e-shōzoku*' with characteristic polka dots and similar to the *kasane-shōzoku*, and '*ryōtō-shōzoku*' often used for the repertoire with strange masks such as the mask of Ranryōō. In addition, '*betsu-shōzoku*' is used for specific repertoires.

The musicians use splendid headgear called *torikabuto* belonging to the *kasane-shōzoku* group when accompanying *bugaku*.

The masks of *gagaku* are not standardized, unlike *noh*. Thus, it is hard to classify them, but it is possible to group them into two types: human and animal. The characteristic exotic masks and costume of *bugaku* are representative of the ancient court culture.

■Mask and Costume

●*Bugaku* masks

Ranryōō (or Ryōō)

Nasori

Hassen

Kitoku

Batō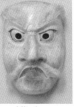

Ranryōō

(Masks and *Ranryōō*: Imperial Household Agency)

●*Bugaku* costumes

Kasane-shōzoku	'Kasane' means layers. *Hō*, *hanpi*, and *shitagasane* are layered. It originates from the dress of the officer in the Heian Period. Also called '*tsune-shōzoku*'.
Ban'e-shōzoku	Its coat (*hō*) has circular patterns, called *ban'e*, of a lion and so on. *Ban'e* is found in the costume of attendants of the Inner Palace Guards in the Heian Period.
Ryōtō-shōzoku	The dancer sticks out his head from the center hole of a sheet of fabric hemmed with fur or tassels. *Ryōtō* stands for 'both' because it has the front and back main panels.
Betsu-shōzoku	'*Betsu*' refers to a specific costume for a certain work. For instance, the 'plovers and blue whitecaps' design for "Seigaiha" and the 'carps and nets' for "Konron Hassen".

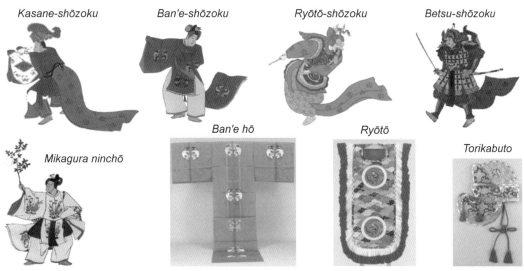

Kasane-shōzoku   Ban'e-shōzoku   Ryōtō-shōzoku   Betsu-shōzoku

Mikagura ninchō   Ban'e hō   Ryōtō   Torikabuto

(Illustration: from "Bugakuzu" published in 1905)   (*Ban'e hō*, *ryōtō*, and *torikabuto*: Imperial Household Agency)

Musical Terms of *Gagaku*

Bugaku works can be classified into *taikyoku* (large), *jun-taikyoku* (semi-large), *chūkyoku* (medium), and *shōkyoku* (small) pieces based on the size of the work. A large-scale work in several movements is called *taikyoku* and ones smaller than it are called *chūkyoku* or *shōkyoku*. *Taikyoku* is divided into two types: ones in movements of '*jo-ha-kyū* (beginning-break-rapid)' and ones in movements of '*yūsei, jo, sattō…saezuri*'. When played through all movements, the work is counted as '*ichigu*' and when only a part is played, it is called '*jun-taikyoku*'. Surprisingly, these works were classified as 'new music' and 'old music', too. The borderline between new and old is the year 754. Thus, even a 1000-year-old work is 'new music'. After Zeami (c. 1363 - c. 1443) established the *noh* theater, the concept '*jo-ha-kyū*', originating from *gagaku*, influenced various arts such as music, martial arts, tea ceremony, theater and poetry. The only existing *gagaku* work with complete '*jo-ha-kyū*', however, is "Goshōraku".

In *bugaku* (the left dance), a performance starts with '*netori* (tuning)' and dancers appear on the stage with '*chōshi*', '*bongen*', '*ranjō*', or '*ranjo*' and dance with a main piece called '*tōkyoku*'. At the end of the dance, the dancers exit the stage with '*amaranjō*' or '*shigebuki*' and then the music concludes. On the other hand, in *komagaku* (the right dance), some works do not have specific exit music and the dancers exit during the performance of *tōkyoku*. As mentioned already, most of *bugaku* works are also performed as *kangen*. More specifically, the *tōkyoku* part is played.

Hyōshi (time, meters) of *gagaku* is shown on the right page. The definition of the term is a little different from that of Western music, and broader than the time, such as 4/4 time. It defines not only the meter but also how and how many times to strike the percussion and how to control accents and ornaments. When Kibi no Makibi (a Japanese scholar and noble) introduced music theory from the Tang Dynasty of China during the Nara period, he used the term '*hyōshi*'. When Western music was introduced during the Meiji period, the term '*hyōshi*' was applied to the rhythm and beat, causing confusion, which still exists.

■Musical Terms of *Gagaku*

●Classification by size and date

Taikyoku	Large works with several movements. Among them major four are called 'Shika no taikyoku'.	Ichigu	The whole set of a large work performed at a time is called 'ichigu'.
Jun-taikyoku	Semi-large works. Exerts (the 'ha' movements) from large works.		When *ichigu* is partially performed, it is called *jun-taikyoku*.
Chūkyoku	Medium works. 'Ha' movements from large works. Most *nobe-* and *haya-hachibyōshi* are *chūkyoku*.	Kogaku	Works created before 754 are called *kogaku* (old music). *Ikko* drum is standard.
Shōkyoku	Small works. 'Kyū' movements from large works. Most *haya-shibyōsi* works are *shōkyoku*.	Shingaku	All works created after *kogaku* are called *shingaku* (new music). *Kakko* drum is standard.

●Two systems of movement:

(1)
- Jo (beginning) = Slowly without meter
- Ha (break) = Slowly with meter (*nobe-byōshi*)
- Kyū (rapid) = Fast with meter (*haya-byōsh*)

(2)

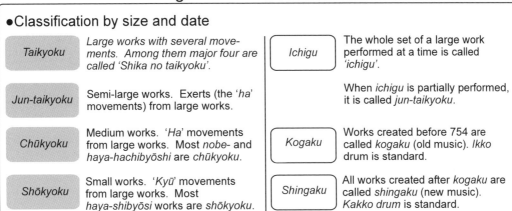

| Yūsei | Jo | Sattō | Juha |
| Kyūsei | Tesshō | Michiyuki | Saezuri |

●Types

Netori	Short work for tuning or adjusting the key. Mostly no meter.
Music for entrance or exit	Music for entrance or exit of *bugaku* dancers. Called *ranjō*, *ranjo* and so on. No meter.
Tōkyoku	The core music for dancing. For *kangen* (instrumental ensembles), it is the main movements.

●Definition of *Tōkyoku*

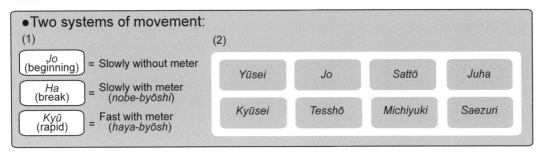

	Entrance	Dance	Exit
Tōgaku		Tōkyoku	
Komagaku		Tōkyoku	

●*Hyōshi* (meters) of *Gagaku*

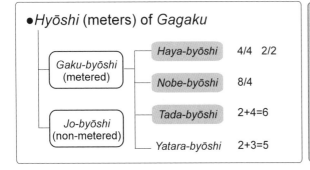

- Gaku-byōshi (metered)
  - Haya-byōshi — 4/4 2/2
  - Nobe-byōshi — 8/4
- Jo-byōshi (non-metered)
  - Tada-byōshi — 2+4=6
  - Yatara-byōshi — 2+3=5

●*Watashimono*

- Transposed works in *tōgaku*.
- Transposing to another key is called '*watasu*' in *gagaku* and the transposed works are called *watashimono*. Only applied to *kangen* music.
- Transposition modifies the mood and melody lines and even changes titles.

Tradition of the Past—Notation of *Gagaku*

The key to preserving various types of Japanese traditional music in the original form to the present is the unique methods based on the system of *gagaku*. First, the oral tradition. Though it meant secret and esoteric techniques of the family or school in the later period, it meant one-on-one mentoring with oral tradition at the times of *gagaku* formation. Second, the notation. In *gagaku*, the score was not a musical score for compositions or performances but memoranda for recording and preserving. And third, *shōga* or 'syllabic mnemonic'. Japanese characters are used to assist to memorize music. These three methods began with *gagaku* and the training in today's traditional Japanese music is based on them.

The photos on the middle column of the right page are the beginning part of the *kangen* "Etenraku" score, though it may not look like a musical score. Despite playing the same section, the notation is different for each musical instrument. We placed fragments of the same interval for each instrument and it is not equivalent to a measure in orchestral score of Western music. As mentioned already, there is no conductor.

The *hichiriki* part is made up with three lines of marks and characters. The *kanafu* written in *katakana* characters at center is used as *shōga* to denote the pitches and relative duration of notes of a melody. The black dots and circles on the right mark the end of measures and the positions for a drum to be struck. The characters (mainly numerical) on the left, called *honpu*, denotes finger holes. The players first learn the melody with *shōga*, and then how to play with *honpu*.

For *shō*, which is composed of 17 bamboo pipes, doesn't play single notes, but clusters of five or six notes, called *aitake*. The score denotes the names of *aitake*. For *gakusō* and *wagon*, a completely different notation system is used for each though they belong to the same zither family.

The music (shown at the bottom on the right page) is used for voice as well. It is neume-type notation similar to the music for *shōmyō*, in which the linear shapes placed next to the texts show the melody. Surprisingly, there is music for *gagaku* dance as well. The choreography, such as turns or waving arms, is written down on the side of the *hichiriki* notation as the music progresses.

The standard scores on the right page are excerpts from "The Meiji Sentei-fu", established by the Gagaku Bureau during the Meiji period. Amazingly, one of the oldest fragments of a musical score, "Tenpyō Biwa-fu", was jotted down created in ca. 738.

■Notation Methods of *Gagaku*

●Origin of Japanese Oral Tradition

			Influence to the later generation
Kuden	Oral tradition and one-to-one training	→	Heredity, schools, and secret
Kifu	Models of styles and memorandum as auxiliary measures	→	Notation systems specific to instruments or schools
Shōga	Onomatopoeia as notation to memorize	→	*Shamisen* oral tradition

●*Gagaku* notation samples:

Kakko part, *Biwa* part, *Gakusō* part, *Shō* part, *Yokobue* part, *Hichiriki* part

"Etenraku" (3 winds)

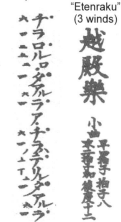

●Meiji Sentei-fu

Re-organizing the three *gagaku* centers, the Gagaku Bureau sorted out the titles and performance styles of *gagaku* and published the selected works "Meiji Sentei-fu" as models in 1888.

Works that were not selected are called '*engaku*'.

●No score but parts

Hichiriki	*Honpu* (finger holes) and *kanafu* (letters) for melody and beats.
Yokobue	*Honpu* (finger holes) and *kanafu* (letters) for melody and ranges.
Shō	*Aitake* (chord names).
Gakusō	String names.
Biwa	Finger positions.
Tsuzumi	Beats.
Wagon	How to play.
Shakubyōshi	Added to *wagon* and vocal parts.
Voice	Neuma type notation.
Dancing	Choreography.

Rōei sample

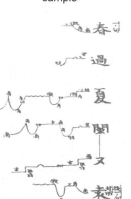

Saibara sample

Wagon sample

Chapter 2: Gagaku

1300 Year Old Music School—Tradition of *Gagaku*

In addition to the oral tradition, musical scores, and *shōga* oral notation, all of which have played an important role in preserving *gagaku*, *gakuso* (a state organization of *gagaku* performers) and *gakuke* (hereditary performers) have contributed to still hand down the skill.

When introduced from the continent, the foreign music was at first, performed by foreigners. As a result of the establishment of the Japanese legal system (based on the philosophies of Confucianism and Chinese), Gagakuryō, an organization for training performers, was installed in the Imperial ministry in 701. It was a big organization of 400 members. It is said that there had already been a training center for foreign *bugaku* in Shiten'nō-ji Temple (often called Ten'nō-ji) in Osaka. Because Shiten'nō-ji Temple, established by Prince Shōtoku, performed *gigaku* as the Buddhism ceremonial music, many foreign musicians lived nearby. One town still carries a name after *gagaku* performers. The performers at Shiten'nō-ji Temple maintain to be the posterity of Hatano Kawakatsu and their surname is Hata. In the early Heian period, the songs with dance native to Japan were exceptionally treated at Ōutadokoro (government Bureau of Song), while foreign dance music was transferred to Daidairi (Heian Palace) affiliated to the court, and Gagakuryō ended its role. *Gagaku* became closely related with Buddhist rituals and split in three: Daidairi in Kyoto, Nanto Gakuso in Nara, and Ten'nō-ji Gakuso in Osaka.

In the middle of the Heian period, *gagaku* reached the golden age in the gorgeous court culture. Soon, the feud between the Genji and Heike families began and the *samurai* class arose. After the Ōnin War from 1467 to 1477, the capital at Kyoto was ruined and *gagaku* in the Imperial Court declined. Worried about the situation, Emperor Goyōzei founded a new training center, the Sanpō Gakuso, by adding some performers from Ten'nō-ji Gakuso and Nanto Gakuso to the few remaining in Kyoto. Soon, Toyotomi Hideyoshi ruled Japan and revived *gyoyū* (a concert by nobles) under the presence of Emperor Goyōzei at Jurakudai. With this opportunity, *gagaku* revived. The third shogun, Tokugawa Iemitsu (1604-1651), built the Momijiyama Gakuso in the Edo castle that was integrated with Sanpō Gakuso under the current Imperial Palace Gagaku Department after the Meiji Restoration of 1868.

Gagaku has survived these 1,300 years and witnessed the history of Japan.

Traditional Japanese Music at a Glance

■*Gagaku* Centers and Families

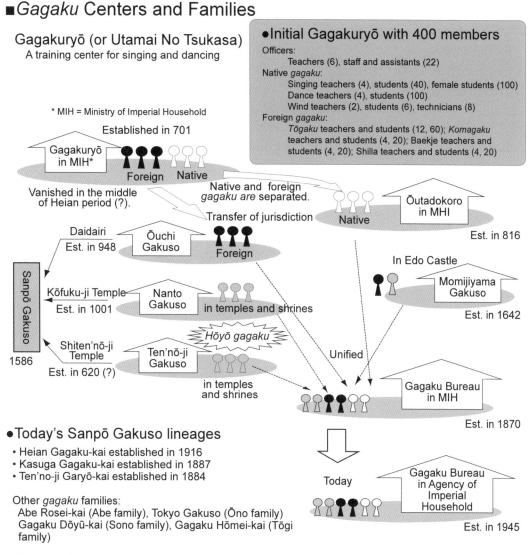

- **Today's Sanpō Gakuso lineages**
  - Heian Gagaku-kai established in 1916
  - Kasuga Gagaku-kai established in 1887
  - Ten'no-ji Garyō-kai established in 1884

  Other *gagaku* families:
  Abe Rosei-kai (Abe family), Tokyo Gakuso (Ōno family)
  Gagaku Dōyū-kai (Sono family), Gagaku Hōmei-kai (Tōgi family)

- **Gagaku lineages**

Family names are shown in ( ) followed by schools.

Genre	Ōuchi Gakuso in Kyoto	Nanto Gakuso in Nara	Ten'nō-ji Gakuso in Osaka
Shō	Bun'no (Toyohara)	Tsuji (Koma), *samai* Higashi (Koma), *samai*	Sono (Hata), *samai* Hayashi (Hata), *umai*
Flute	Yamanoi (Ōga), dance Ono (Ōno), *kagura* and *umai* Tobe (Tamate)	U'e (Koma), *samai* Shiba (Fujiwara), *samai* Oku (Koma), *samai*	Oka (Hata), *umai*
Hichiriki	Abe (Abe), *kagura* and *umai* Nakahara (Nakahara), *kagura*	Kubo (Koma), *samai*	Tōgi (Hata), flute and *samai* Tōgi (Abe), *kagura*, *hichiriki*

Fusion of *Shōmyō* and *Gagaku*—*Gagaku* outside Imperial Court

The Buddhist scripture "The Lotus Sutra" describes *gigaku* (a masked drama from Wu, China) as music for worship and of celestials. Prince Shōtoku (573–621) nourished *gigaku*, as mentioned already. *Gigaku* and other foreign dances were performed during the four Buddhist services held for the Great Buddha Inauguration Ceremony at the Tōdai-ji Temple in 752. This determined the style of Buddhist services henceforth. Afterwards, *gagaku*, arranged as elegant music and dance, flourished; while entertaining *gigaku* which lacked the solemnity that the Buddhist service sought, was regarded as being improper, and gradually declined. Soon, solemn *gagaku* was incorporated within the ceremony of the Buddhist service and became an integral part of large-scaled Buddhist services, especially for Pure Land Buddhism. In the services, a drama is performed by a priest wearing a mask to impersonate Bodhisattva. The solemn sounds along with the *shōmyō* chants reverberating in the temple unfolds glorious scenes of Amitabha Buddha in front of believers welcoming them to the Pure Land and effectively lets them experience being in paradise.

As a result of syncretization of Shinto and Buddhism in the Middle Ages, *gagaku* for Buddhist ceremonies was adopted into the Shinto rituals. This adoption spread to regional shrines built by the *samurai* class in addition to ones in big cities. Examples are the Itsukushima Shrine built by Tairano Kiyomori and the Tsurugaoka-hachimangū Shrine by Minamotono Yoritomo. Some of the shrines and temples still preserve *bugaku* and many offer it in the ritual even today. Some examples are shown in the chart on the right page. In those shrines and temples, we can appreciate the same *bugaku* that was performed in the Imperial Court.

After the takeover of administration of the shrines and standardization of Shinto ceremonies by the government during the Meiji period, the standardized rites were practiced nationally. After World War II, the situation did not change and *bugaku* can be enjoyed at the big shrines even now. Of course, all shrines and temples do not necessarily have *gakuso* or professional *gagaku* performers, and Shinto or Buddhist priests perform *bugaku* in some cases. Recently, private training organizations and performing groups have been established and they also actively perform *gagaku* at shrines and temples.

Mikagura can be appreciated at Tsurugaoka-hachimangū. At Itsukushima Shrine, we can enjoy "Ranryōō (King Lanling)", one of the most famous in *bugaku* repertoires. Watching the performance and hearing the solemn sound at the main temple building surrounded by the Seto Inland Sea and the dramatic gate of Itsukushima Shrine is very exciting for everyone.

Traditional Japanese Music at a Glance

■*Gagaku* outside the Imperial Court

"Shōwaraku" at Shiten'nōji Temple
(Photo: Yoshirō Kuramoto)

Buddhist services

- New combination of Buddhism and *gagaku*:   **Encounter**
  as seen in the Great Buddha Inauguration Ceremony (752).
- Integration of Buddhist services and *gagaku*:   **Integration**
  as seen in "Unrin'in Temple Memorial Service" (963).
- Pure Land Buddhism and *bugaku* memorial services: **Visualization**
  as seen in the drawing "Raigō of Amitābha and Twenty-five Attendants".
- Influence to *shōmyō* and Buddhist ceremony:
  as seen in *shōmyō* indoctrination and *gagaku* and *gagaku* songs for the Buddhist ceremony.
- Sponsorship from the *samurai* class:
  as seen in nationwide propagation (*gakuso* established in local temples and shrines).

"Azuma-asobi" at Kasuga-taisha Shrine
(Photo: Yoshirō Kuramoto)

Shintō services

- Syncretism of Shintō and Buddhism (the Middle Ages)
  → assimilation with Buddhist festivals
  Buddhist services (floral tribute) → Shintō services (food offering)
  Establishment of provincial governorate *gakuso*
- Anti-Buddhist movement at the beginning of the Meiji period
  → government controlled Shintō
  Regulation and unification of Shintō rituals
- Law on Religious Corporations (post WWII) → succession of practice
  Preservation of traditional arts

●*Gagaku* Performing Groups

Sanpō Gakuso lineages:
- Heian Gagaku-kai (or Heiangi-kai)
- Nanto Gakuso
- Ten'nōji Gakuso Garyō-kai

'*Gagaku* family' lineages:
- Abe Rosei-kai (Abe family)
- Tokyo Gakuso (Ono family)
- Gagaku Dōyū-kai (Sono family)
- Gagaku Hōmei-kai (Tōgi family)
- Jūnion-kai (Bun'no family)

Other lineages:
- Hōrai Gagaku-kai (Oita)
- Reigakusha (Tokyo)
- Ono Gagaku-kai (Tokyo)
- Atsuta Shrine Tōchiku-kai (Aichi)
- Chikushi Gakuso (Fukuoka)
- Nihon Gagaku Hozon-kai (Kyoto)
- Yōyū-kai (Toyama)
- Gagaku Suikō-kai (Nara)

●Temples and shrines where *gagaku* is performed

Name	Location	Group	Mikagura	Azuma-asobi	Bugaku	Buddhist gagaku
Usa Shrine	(Oita)	(priests)		●		
Kamigamo Shrine	(Kyoto)	Heian Gagaku-kai		●	●	
Shimogamo Shrine	(Kyoto)	Heian Gagaku-kai		●	●	
Iwashimizu Hachimangū	(Kyoto)	Heian Gagaku-kai			●	
Kasuga-taisha Shrine	(Nara)	Nanto Gakuso (priests)		●	●	
Shiten'nōji Temple	(Osaka)	Garyō-kai			●	●
Ise Grand Shrine	(Mie)	Jingū-shichō		●	●	
Atsuta Shrine	(Aichi)	Tōchiku-kai (priests)			●	
Itsukushima Shrine	(Hiroshima)	(priests)			●	
Tsurugaoka Hachimangū	(Kanagawa)	(priests)			●	
Nikkō Tōshōgū	(Tochigi)	Gakubu (priests)		●	●	
Sanzen-in	(Kyoto)	Heian Gagaku-kai				●
Tōshōdai-ji	(Nara)	Nanto Kōyō-kai				●
Chion-in	(Kyoto)	Heian Gagaku-kai				●
Sumiyoshi-taisha	(Osaka)	Garyō-kai			●	
Dainenbutsu-ji	(Osaka)	Gakuyū-kai (priests)			●	●
Zōjō-ji	(Tokyo)	Zōjō-ji Gagaku-kai (priests)			●	●
Hikawa Shrine	(Saitama)	Agency of Imperial Household	●			

The Ōnin War and Civil Wars—The History of *Gagaku*

The history of *gagaku* is almost as long as the historic times of Japan. During the incunabulum of the nation's foundation, when Japan actively adopted foreign culture, music along with the legal system and religious rituals was introduced from China and Korea. Soon, the imported culture was changed from the Chinese or Korean style into the Japanese-style to fit into the native society, culture and climate.

As a result of this adaptation or Japanization, Japan finally established its own style in clothing, letters, arts, music and literature in addition to the legal and social systems in the middle of the Heian period. The road of *gagaku* was eventful and reached a crisis during the Ōnin War (1467-77) in the middle of the Muromachi period. Starting in Kyoto, the ten-year long war spread to the whole country and the *gagaku* performers as well as their costumes and instruments were scattered and lost. As a result, *gagaku* was about to perish. Because the oral tradition and the pedigree were the only means to preserve *gagaku*, the absence of the performers meant its extinction. The war damage was not insignificant and quite a few works seemed to be lost forever.

The Ōnin War was followed by the unstable Warring States period, but when Hideyoshi unified Japan, the society became stable. Because of a proposal by Emperor Goyōzei (1586-1611), the musicians of Nanto Gakuso and Ten'nō-ji Gakuso were invited to revive the declined *gagaku* in Kyoto resulting in the establishment of the Sanpō Gakuso. The revived *gagaku* was performed in the presence of Emperor Goyōzei at a lavish palace Jurakudai. It was a re-creation of old-time and brilliant court culture and a historical event with Hideyoshi, who loved a luxurious life. Quite a few *bugaku* works, which were about to perish, were revived by this event.

Gagaku then reached another prime when shogun Tokugawa Iemitsu became the patron of *gagaku* and designated it as the Shogunate's ceremonial music.

After the Restoration of the Meiji Imperial rule, *gagaku* was administered by the government as court and Imperial Household ceremonial music, as it was done initially. After World War II, *gagaku* has been publicly performed and preserved as art music, in addition to the performances in the Imperial Household. By the way, the "end of the war" generally means the end of World War II for today's people, but it means the end of the Ōnin War which occurred more than 500 years ago for the people in the world of *gagaku*. This simple fact tells us how far-reaching *gagaku* tradition is.

The History of *Gagaku*

Ancient Times	Legend says goddess Ame no Uzume dances in front of the cave Amano-Iwato. Ancient entertainment: *uta* (songs), *mai* (dances), *fue* (wind), *koto*, and *tsuzumi*.
Asuka (538-710)	Shilla musicians attended the funeral of Emperor Ingyō (453). Introduction of **Buddhism** (538). 4 musicians from Baekje (554). Mimashi introduces *gigaku* (612). *Gakuso* in Shiten'nōji (620?). Shilla envoy performs music and dance in public in Osaka (673). *Sankangaku* introduced and played at Imperial Court (683). "The Records of Ancient Matters" written about then. *Gagakuryō* established in Ministry of Ceremonies (701).
Nara (710-794)	Kibi no Makibi returns from China with "Gakusho Yōroku" and musical instruments (735). Buttetsu introduces *rin'yūgaku* from Vietnam (736). *Toragaku* introduced about then. Balhae envoy plays *bokkaigaku* at the Imperial Court (740). Tōdai-ji Temple Inaugural Ceremony of Great Buddha (752). All kinds of foreign and native *gagaku* music meet together.
Heian (794-1185)	*Ōutadokoro* for native *gagaku* established (816). **Music System Reform** begins in Emperor Ninmyō's reign (833-850). New works. *Gagaku* completely established (894). Sending **Envoys to Tang** ends (894). *Gyoyū* begins (908). First performance of "Kochōraku". Fujihara no Tadafusa compiles "Saibara-fu", "Azuma-asobiuta-fu" and "Kagurauta-fu" (920). *Gakuso* established in Heian Palace (948). Talented court nobles such as Minamoto no Hiromasa and Fujiwara no Moronaga emerge. First performance of *mikagura* in the inner sanctum of Imperial Palace (1002). Taira no Kiyomori performs *bugaku* at Itsukushima Shrine (1176). Fujiwara no Kintō compiles "Wakan Rōeishū" (1012).
Kamakura (1185-1333)	*Koto* music "Jinchi Yōroku" and *biwa* music "Sango Yōroku" by Fujiwara no Moronaga (1190). "Kyōkun-shō" by Koma no Chikasane (1263). Minamoto no Yoritomo establishes *gakuso* in Tsurugaoka Hachimangū (1191).
Nanbokucho (1336-1392)	Abe no Sueuji compiles "Hichiriki-shō" (1349).
Muromachi (1336-1573)	Ōnin War (1467-77) breaks up musician groups and leaves *gagaku* in destruction state in Kyoto. Toyohara no Muneaki authors "Bukyoku-kuden" (1509) and "Taigen-shō" (1512).
Momoyama (1573-1603)	*Shamisen* introduced (around 1560). **Sanpō Gakuso** established by invited Ten'nōji and Nanto performers (1575-96). Hideyoshi holds a *bugaku* performance for Emperor Goyōzei at Jurakudai (1588).
Edo (1603-1868)	Tokugawa Iemitsu establishes Momijiyama-gakuso (1642). *Gagaku* is extensively studied. "Rosei-shō" by Koma no Mitsuatsu (1671) and "Gakka-roku" by Abe Suehisa (1690). Kamo Festival along with *azuma-asobi* is revived (1694). Yamatomai is revived in the Coronation Banquet (1748). *Gosechimai* is revived (1753). "Gakkyoku-kō" by Tayasu Munetake (1768). Revived *saibara* is formed in *gyoyū* (1809). Kumemai is revived in the Coronation Banquet (1818).
Meiji (1868-1912)	**Meiji Restoration** (1868). Gagaku Department in Ministry of Imperial Household (1871). Performers of three *gakuso* meet in Tokyo. Permission for commoners to learn *gagaku* (1873). *Gagaku* training for commoners begins at Ise Shrine (1873). "Meiji Sentei-fu" compiled (1888). Western music education for performers of Gagaku Department begins.
Taisho-Showa-Heisei (1912-)	Ministry of Imperial Household becomes Agency of Imperial Household (1947). National Theater opens and holds regularly-scheduled *gagaku* performances (1966).

Chapter 3: *Shōmyō*

Introduction of *Shōmyō*

Shōmyō are vocal music which Buddhist priests chant with melodies over sutras in the Buddhist services or other occasions. It is different from simply reciting sutras. *Shōmyō* originated from one of the five subjects which Brahman priests in ancient India had to learn, and which meant grammar and phonemics. It was introduced to China around the 1st century B.C. and then was established as the present form during the Three Kingdoms era.

Though the exact time is unknown, *shōmyō* were probably introduced into Japan as collaterals of Buddhism in the 6th century. According to the literature "Tengyōshōrei (the methods of chanting sutras)" that first described *shōmyō*, the diverse chanting styles among sects were unified by the priest Dōei from Tang Dynasty of China in 720. Also, it was stated in the literature that *sange* (scattering of lotus flowers) and *bai*, both *shōmyō*, were performed during the Great Buddha Inaugural Ceremony at Tōdai-ji in 752.

These chants were called *bonbai* or *bainoku* but after the Middle Ages they were called *shōmyō*. '*Bai*' of *bonbai* and *bainoku* stands for 'singing a sutra'. Zen, one of the Buddhist sects, still calls chants *bonbai*.

Shōmyō were called 'Nara *shōmyō* (or Nanto *shōmyō*)' until the new *shōmyō* were established. Japanese priests Kūkai and Saichō went to Tang Dynasty of China in 804 and when they returned home with *shōmyō*, they started new sects, Shingon and Tendai respectively. Great *shōmyō* masters, Kanchō of the Shingon sect and En'nin and Ryōnin of Tendai sect, emerged and established the Shingon *shōmyō* and Tendai *shōmyō* respectively. At first both *shōmyō* of Shingon and Tendai were similar but differed as the times went on, splitting into many schools. By the 11th century, 150 schools were established in the Shingon sect alone and they had to be consolidated to four schools. The reason why so many schools were established was that a sect was divided into many offshoots, each of which actively propagated.

The chart on right page lists only major schools due to the limited space. Even so, there are quite a number of unique schools. In each school, the same titled *shōmyō* chant could be sung very differently.

Traditional Japanese Music at a Glance

■What is *Shōmyō*?

General term of vocal music sung for Buddhist services and made of melodies over the texts of sutra and so on.

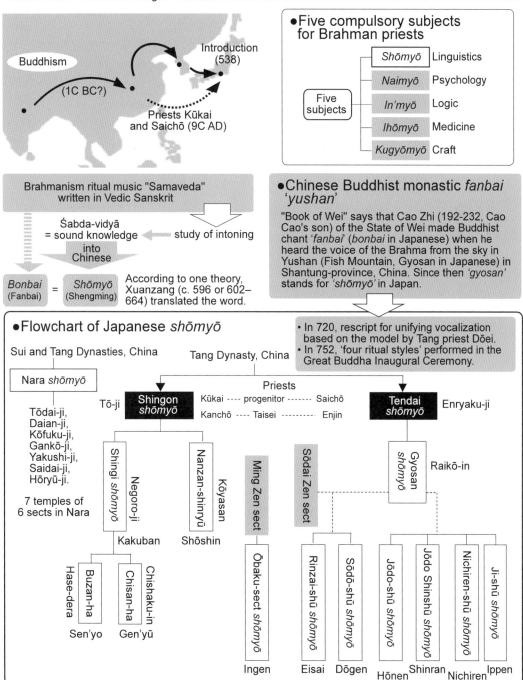

Hon-shōmyō and Zatsu-shōmyō

Shōmyō, chanted or recited for Buddhist services, are divided into two groups: *hon-shōmyō* (real *shōmyō*) and *zatsu-shōmyō* (miscellaneous *shōmyō*). In a narrow sense, only *hon-shōmyō* are called *shōmyō*. *Hon-shōmyō* are foreign *shōmyō* written in Sanskrit or Chinese as well as some chants in the same style made in Japan. Chants made in Japan after the Heian period are called *zatsu-shōmyō*. The priests chant both types of *shōmyō* while the believers chant Buddhist chants different from *shōmyō* during the services and ceremonies.

Hon-shōmyō are chants to praise the merit of Buddha and Bodhisattva, to implore the advent of deities and Buddha during a service or a training, and to cleanse and prepare the space of the services or training halls. The melodies of *hon-shōmyō* are melismatic with long-stretched syllables which vary for each sect. Even a chant with the same title is different for different sects.

The contents of *zatsu-shōmyō* are intelligible to the general public. For instance, the paean to the merit of Buddha and the high priests, the announcement of the purpose of the service they are going to perform, the explanation of the doctrine, the memorial service to the Gods and Buddha, and a wide range of prayers.

The text of Sanskrit *shōmyō* are not written in the Sanskrit characters but kanji characters (Chinese characters) as shown on the right page. That is because the phonetics of Sanskrit was written in Chinese characters when it was introduced to China, which was then introduced to Japan.

Sanskrit and Chinese paeans are shown side by side on the right page. Phonetics written in Chinese is used for the Sanskrit paean while the Chinese paean is the translation of the Sanskrit. They appear completely different but the meanings of the texts of both are the same. Though their meanings are the same, both, not only one of them, are always chanted in the Buddhist services.

From these facts, we can clearly understand that the Buddhist rituals and *shōmyō* came to Japan from China where what had originated in India was stylized and organized.

■Types of *Shōmyō*

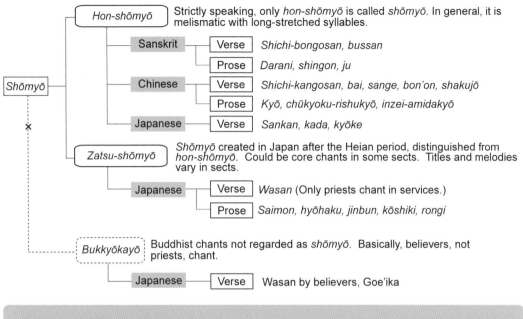

- **Sanskrit and Chinese paeans**

Bongosan	Kangosan
Phonetics of Sanskrit scripture written in Chinese characters.	Translation of Sanskrit scripture written in Chinese characters.

  * Both have the same content though they look different. Many original Chinese chants also exist.

Followings are from Shich-bongosan (Sanskrit paean, left) and Shichi-kangosan (Chinese paean, right). Though they look different, the content is the same.

- Shichi-bongosan (Sanskrit paean)

- Shichi-kangosan (Chinese paean)

Adaptation of *Shōmyō*

After it was introduced into Japan, Buddhism changed significantly in terms of its role and goal and the types of believers and supporters as the times went by. In the Nara period, when Buddhism was an integral part of the national ruling policy, the intellectual, noble and bureaucratic classes who could read and understand the sutras written in Chinese were patrons of Buddhism. For them sutras and *shōmyō* written in a foreign language were not a problem. And then, Buddhism had to adapt itself to be accepted by the general public.

The general public, mostly illiterate, who hardly understood the contents of respectful sutras and *shōmyō* with beautiful melodies written and chanted in Sanskrit and Chinese, did not accept the Buddhist worship, merits and doctrines of loanword. The sutras and *shōmyō* had to be translated into Japanese. As a result, many Japanese *shōmyō* were created by the end of the Heian period as illustrated on the right page. During the Kamakura period (1185–1333), new persuasions were established one after another and actively began to propagate using these Japanese sutras and *shōmyō*.

Since the sutras and *shōmyō* were translated on purpose to "make them easy-to-understand for the general public", they were written in plain Japanese, or, were written in Chinese and read as Japanese. Most of these newly created Japanese *shōmyō* are classified as *zatsu-shōmyō* except *sandan* which is the Japanese paean and is classified as *hon-shōmyō*.

Wasan and *goeika*, composed of verses in seven-and-five syllable meter which is the important Japanese poetry style, are not regarded as *shōmyō* but classified as Buddhist chants. Because *wasan* and *goeika* interacted with *imayō*, which were very popular contemporary songs in Japanese in the Middle Age, they were musically similar. The vulgar character of *wasan* and *goeika* was regarded as inadequate for religious rituals and was classified out of *shōmyō*. After the Kamakura period, newly established Buddhist sects such as the Jōdo Shinshū used *wasan* for the propagation and services in general. The melodies of *wasan*, similar to a lullaby in a pentatonic scale and easy-to-memorize, seem to have struck a chord with the common people in those days. Adapted to the Japanese soil, *shōmyō* had a great influence on the following Japanese musical culture.

■Adaptation of *Shōmyō*
●Background

Periods	Stages	Targets	Circumstances	Type of Priests	Purpose
Asuka	Introduction	Powers	Acceptence and adaptation	Certified or ranked	Politics
Nara	Studying	Court	Study of Buddhism	Scholars	Ruling nation
Heian	Esoteric	Priests	Factions	Illegally ordained	Secession from politics
Kamakura	Propagation	Common People	New Buddhism	Recluse	Folk religion

Propagation of Buddhism → Adaptation of *shōmyō* ⇒ Sutras translated into plain Japanese / Original Japanese sutras written in Chinese characters

●Major types of Japanese *shōmyō*

Medieval *shōmyō* formed by the mid-12th century.

Name	Style	Verse form	Purport	Description
Santan	Japanese	Prose	Paean (virtues of Buddha)	Oldest Japanese *shōmyō*, precursor of *wasan*. In prose form as well as *waka* or verse forms. "Hokkesandan", "Sharisandan".
Kada	Chinese (Chinese reading)	Verse 7-character line	Paean (virtues of Buddha)	Japan-made Chinese verse. Tendai and Shingon sects. For example, "Sōraikada" and "Kaikōkada" are sometimes accompanied by wind instruments.
Kōshiki	Chinese (Japanese reading)	Storytelling	Lecture of sutras & doctrines	Japan-made *shōmyō* as typical as *wasan*. Narrative *heikyoku* was derived from it. "Rokudōkōshiki", and "Shizakōshiki".
Rongi	Japanese	Q&A form	Lecture of sutras & doctrines	Oral exam on sutras for learned priests. Formalized with melodies, it is used for services. The style varies in each sect.
Saimon	Chinese (Japanese reading)	Verse	Paean (central figure or founder of the sect), Prayer	Prayers of yin-yang philosophy originally. Japan-made with plain melodies composed of *chi* (sol) and *kaku* (mi). Became public entertainments.
Hyōbyaku	Chinese (Japanese reading)	Verse	Announcement of services	Texts with a plain melody and a melismatic syllable at the end. Had an influence to *kōshiki* as its opening music.
Kyōke	Japanese	Quatrain single or Quatrain double or more	Teaching Buddhism	Written in plain Japanese. After the Nara period. Japan-made *shōmyō* similar to Buddhist songs.
Jinbun	Chinese (Japanese reading)	Verse	Prayer Nirvana	Praying for the coming of deities, chanting "Han'nya-shingyō", and for protection of the service. Placed before the service or before/after *hyōhaku*.
Wasan	Japanese	Seven-and-five-syllable meter, Quatrain single	Paean (virtues of Buddha)	Japan-made paean with unique poem forms and melodies different from *wasan*'s. Popular in Pure Land sects. Treated as Buddhist songs.
Goeika	Japanese	31 characters *Waka* style	Pilgrim songs	Chanting a single *waka* poem in a single melody. Integrated into today's funerals. A type of *wasan* treated as Buddhist songs.

Hōe and *Hōyō*—Buddhist Ceremonies

The main space or occasion where *shōmyō* are chanted is the Buddhist *hōe* (a mass). *Shōmyō* also plays an important role for other assemblies called Buddhist *hōyō* (a service).

The terms *hōe* and *hōyō* are confusing and will be clarified here. According to the general definition, the Buddhist *hōe* is an assembly for sermons about Buddha's teachings, usually hosted by temples, while the Buddhist *hōyō* is a gathering for reciting a special prayer or performing a memorial service for the dead, including the death anniversary. However, both are, in fact, interpreted differently by each persuasion. Some persuasions even advocate that the Buddhist *hōe* and *hōyō* are the same. Therefore, it seems difficult in reality to define both strictly.

For the Shingon Sect, a type of the esoteric Buddhism, the both terms are clearly defined. The Buddhist *hōe* means a general ritual to hold, for instance, a celebration of the completion of a temple's construction, a service for the benefit of suffering spirits, and the services during the equinoctial week. As a part of these Buddhist *hōe* services, the Buddhist *hōyō* is used to cleanse the space or adorn a Buddhist statue with decoration. *Hōyō* includes *bai*, *sange* and other *shōmyō* chants.

In the exoteric Buddhist sects other than the esoteric Buddhism, the definitions and practice of the *hōe* and *hōyō* are considerably different. Even the repertoires of *shōmyō* and sutras as well as the procedures and manners of the rituals performed by the exoteric Buddhist priests vary, depending on the sect which they belong to.

The procedure of *hōe* can generally be divided into four sections. In the introduction, the priests enter the place, bow three times, and offer the offerings. They then chant the paean to praise the merits of Buddha and the Bodhisattva, and then plead that Buddha and the Bodhisattva descend to the place where they are performing the *hōe*. In the second section, they perform the ritual, which is *hōyō*, to cleanse the place of *hōe*. In the third section, the central part of the *hōe*, the contents based on the intention of the *hōe* are announced and prayers are recited in the predetermined orders. In the closing, they pray that Buddha and Bodhisattva bless the attendance as well as all other people. The predetermined and prepared *shōmyō* chants are used for each step of these sections.

■ Shōmyō and Buddhist Services

- **Shōmyō is chanted in:**
  - Hōe (the gatherings for Buddhist services at a temple) and,
  - Hōyō (the specific Buddhist ceremonies such as praying for someone's safety or soul).

  Program of a *hōyō* ceremony: Shōmyō → Prayer → Chanting sutras

- The *shōmyō* chanted for the *hōe* varies depending on its type.

● Types of *hōe*

- **Mitsudate-hōe**
  - *Kyōdate*: *Kyō* (sutras) is mainly chanted.
  - *Kōshikidate*: *Kōshiki* (written Chinese, read in Japanese) is mainly chanted.
  - *Shudate*: *Shingon* (written Chinese, read in Chinese) is mainly chanted.

  (Exclusively for esoteric Buddhism)

- **Kendate-hōe**
  - *Kyōdate*: *Kyō* (sutras) is mainly chanted.
  - *Kōshikidate*: *Kōshiki* (written Chinese, read in Japanese) is mainly chanted.

  (For non-esoteric Buddhism)

● Program of *hōe*

Section	Purpose and Procedure	Types of *shōmyō* chanted
1. Introduction	Entrance of priests, bowing to Buddha, praying a deity to descend from heaven	sōrai (sōrai-kada), sanrai, kuyōbun, san, saimon, kanjō
2. Adoring	Praising Buddha and Bodhisattva, adoring the hall to cleanse the place	bai, sange, bon'non, shakujō (the *hōe* with these four is called '*shikahōyō*')
3. Main part	Executing the *hōyō* ceremony, the purpose of the *hōe*	hyōbyaku, jinbun, butsumyō, kyō, kōshiki rongi, ge, shingon, kassatsu, hōgō
4. Ending	Blessing the attendance and extending the blessing to other people	ekō, sanrai

Scenes from *hōe*

(Courtesy of Hanae Maeda)
(Courtesy of Nishidaiji)

Structure of Shōmyō—Hakase passed down its 1200-year history

The music theory of *shōmyō*, based on the theory introduced from the continent, is very simple and rational. When *gagaku* adapted the Chinese music theory, *shōmyō* were also influenced by it and shared the almost all musical terms and interpretation with *gagaku*. For example, five scale degrees '*kyū, shō, kaku, chi* and *u*', five keys '*ichikotsuchō, hyōjō, sojō, ōshikichō* and *banshikichō*', and two modes '*ryo* and *ritsu*' are used in *gagaku* and *shōmyō*.

There are some differences between the two, however. For instance, *gagaku* uses a key called '*taishikichō*' in addition to the 5 keys and *shōmyō* uses a mode called '*chūkyoku*' in addition to the two modes. Moreover, in *shōmyō*, each note is named after a Buddhist deity such as *Dainichi-nyorai*.

Shōmyō had a great influence on Japanese music, especially vocal music, afterwards. For example, the *yonanuki* scale, which is a typical Japanese pentatonic scale without 4th and 7th degrees in a Western major or minor scale, and the concept of *shojū* (an octave), *nijū* (two octaves) and *sanjū* (three octaves) were originated from *shōmyō*. *Shōmyō* are characterized by a unique 'endeca-scale' and a scale constructed by a conceptual 'note' which humans can hardly produce.

Based on the music theory mentioned above, a unique musical notation system, called *hakase*, is used in *shōmyō*. There are two types of *hakase*: *goin-hakase* (or *bokufu*) which shows pitches of the five notes and *meyasu-hakase* (or *karifu*) which visually shows contours of melodic lines. Interestingly, *meyasu-hakase* is similar to the neumatic notation, used for Gregorian chants, for instance, which graphically indicates melodic lines.

At present, only the Shingon Sect uses *goin-hakase* and the rest use exclusively *meyasu-hakase*. Each sect has altered and simplified *meyasu-hakase* into its own unique system. These notation systems of *shōmyō* also have greatly influenced the musical notations of Japanese music afterwards such as *heikyoku*, *yōkyoku* (*Noh* chants) and *jōruri*.

The 1200 year history of *shōmyō* are preserved by these musical notation systems which have gradually changed with time, resulting in different versions of even the same chant of the same sect.

Traditional Japanese Music at a Glance

■Structure of *Shōmyō*

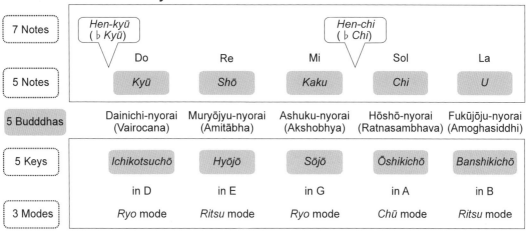

●11-note scale in 3 octaves

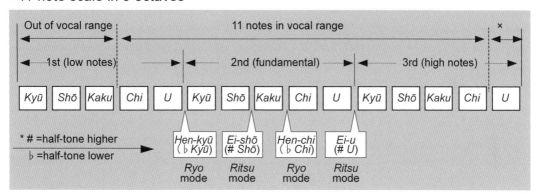

●*Hakase* (Music notation system)

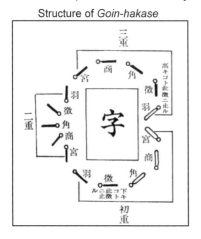
Structure of *Goin-hakase*

Goin-hakase (or *bokufu*)

Meyasu-hakase

30-Year Ascetic Practice for the Full Initiation

Today, it is not rare to see a single Buddhist priest perform all procedures of a Buddhist memorial service by himself. For *shōmyō*, however, a group of priests chant. There is a leader called *dōshi* (a master) who begins with a solo of the *shōmyō* followed by the chorus who chant in unison. *Shōmyō* are monophony consisting of only a single melody, based on no concept of harmony or chords.

Although they use scores called *hakase*, they cannot chant *shōmyō* only by looking at them. *Hakase* is just manuals or memoranda and the oral instruction, a man-to-man system, is indispensable to learn *shōmyō*. Every priest is required to learn *shōmyō* but it is very difficult for him to master it.

The chart on the right page shows the steps for a newcomer to follow to learn *shōmyō* of the Nanzan-shinryū, one of the Shingon sects. After finishing the basic vocal training by chanting the sutra, and then reciting *saimon* (paean to gods) in front of an assembly, a trainee finally begins to learn the quintessence, "Gyozan-shū (Gyozan Collection)". Only six items of "Gyozan-shū" are listed on the right page, *san* among which, for instance, has more than ten items which are further divided into Sanskrit and Chinese versions. In addition to merely memorizing melodies and texts, he must understand the profound contents. After finishing this step, he carries on to the next step.

Kada (*gaathaa* in Sanskrit) and *kōshiki* are chanted in Chinese and Japanese, and a trainee must learn both versions even if identically titled. He must also learn how to handle his fan and rosary as well as a series of etiquettes of the manners while chanting *shōmyō*. How long does it take a trainee to master *shōmyō*? Depending on the difference among individuals, it may take at least five or six years. Mastering *kōshiki* alone, for example, is said to take three years at least. It takes roughly thirty years for a priest to satisfy everyone, including himself, and fulfill his goal with the achievement after mastering *Sanka hiin*, three kinds of the secret *shōmyō* which only excellent elites are inducted into. Learning *shōmyō* is indeed an ascetic practice.

The disciplinant must not have an obnoxious voice, four types of which are described on the right page. Even if he has a good voice, there are three commandments, also described on the right page. The owner of a good voice will fail to learn the profound beauty of *shōmyō* if he indulges himself in his talent or is too proud of his voice.

■Singing Style of *Shōmyō*

●Chanting form in monophony

1. Master's solo ---------------------------- *sanrai*
2. A member's solo ---------------------- *bai*
3. Taken over by the group --------------- *san*
4. Alternation of the solo and group --------- *ekō*
5. Juxtaposition of different *shōmyō* -------- *kōshikikada* (for example, for Jōrakue Hōyō Ceremony)

> • Always a soloist starts.
> • The solo section is called '*tō no ku* (head part)' and the soloist is called '*tōnin* (head person)'.

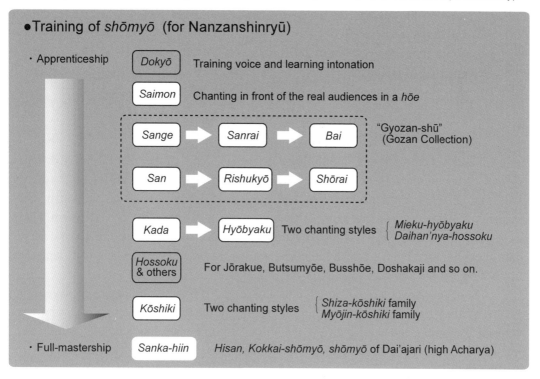

●Things to keep in mind on *shōmyō* training:

· Four types of obnoxious voice:

1. Mournful voice — Singing with sorrow and grief
2. Tone-deaf voice — Singing out of tune
3. Weak voice — Singing weakly like a sick infant
4. Hoarse voice — Singing loudly and screaming

· Three types of weakness:
  1. Owners of beautiful voice; 2. Owners of a rhythmic sense; 3. Those who jump to conclusions.

Chapter 3: Shōmyō

From Paean to Funeral Hymns

Shōmyō are a part of Buddhism, the history of which goes back before Christ. The origin of *shōmyō* were born at Yushan (Fish Mountain) in China in the 3rd century. When Buddhism was introduced into Japan from Baekje of Korea, *shōmyō* were also, probably, introduced along with Buddhist images and sutras though there is no conclusive evidence. In Japan *shōmyō* appeared for the first time in literature "Tengyōshōrei" (the methods of chanting sutras) and the Inaugural Ceremony of Great Buddha at Tōdai-ji in the Nara period. Most importantly in *shōmyō* history, Shingon *shōmyō* were established by a Buddhist priest Kūkai and Tendai *shōmyō* were established by another priest En'nin in the Heian period. At that time, the chants of the two sects seemed not so different. According to a record, the priests from the Shingon Sect, including Kūkai, attended the ceremony of the Tendai sect and chanted the same repertoire. These important *shōmyō* of the two sects were later completed by the hierarchs such as Kanchō of the Shingon Sect in the 10th century and Ryōnin of the Tendai Sect in the 12th century. They established Japanese-style *shōmyō*, from which other styles, unique to each sect, would be derived.

With time, differences in the interpretation of tenets and in management in both the Shingon and Tendai sects resulted in many offshoots. This further caused many different *shōmyō* styles unique to each sect. In the Kamakura period (1185–1333), people endured wars, famine, and natural disasters which affected the tenet and beliefs of Buddhism. New religious movements were welcomed, causing more new offshoots of Buddhism. New sects of the Pure Land, especially, were enthusiastically supported by the general public since they employed prayers with melodies and *wasan* (newly created chants in Japanese) which were simple and easy to sing for the propagation of the sects.

Soon, each sect gained power, crossing religious boundaries, and even developing its own military against the lords and the authorities at the time. Those in power who were stumped by these trends and the riots which occurred in many parts of the country suppressed and emasculated the sects of Buddhism. Imposed with restrictions such as the *danka* system, a system of voluntary and long-term affiliation between Buddhist temples and households, each sect did not need propagation anymore and Buddhism gradually turned into religion for funerals. The Buddhist ceremonies such as the burial and memorial services became the places of gathering of the general public and Buddhist priests. As a result, *shōmyō* turned into the vocal music sung for the ceremonial funerals.

Traditional Japanese Music at a Glance

■History of *Shōmyō*

Ancient Times	• Buddhism born in 5 BC. • Buddhism introduced to China in ca. 1 BC and 1 AD. • Buddhism introduced to Korea (372). • Caozhi creates *shōmyō* inspired at Fish Mountain in 3 AD.
Asuka (538-710)	• **Buddhism introduced to Japan** (538); Statue of Buddha and sutras given by Seong of Baekje. • Prince Shōtoku writes "Sangyō Gisho" (600?). • Chinese monk Xuanzang returns home from India (645).
Nara (710-794)	• "Tengyōshōrei" established by Tang priest Dōei (720). • **Six sects in Nara** established (718). • **Shika-hōyō** performed for Inaugural Ceremony of Great Buddha at Todai-ji Temple (752). • Jianzhen (Ganjin in Japanese) came to Japan (754).
Heian (794-1185)	• Kūkai and Saichō visit China (804) and introduce **shōmyō** to Japan. • Saichō founds **Tendai** sect at Mt. Hie'i (806); Kūkai founds **Shingon** sect at Mt. Kōya (816). • En'nin visits China (838) and establishes Tendai *shōmyō*. *Biwa-hōshi* emerge (late 9C). • Genshin (Eshin Sōzu) writes "Ōjōyōshū", the possible prototype of *wasan* (982). • Kanchō composes "Rishukyō Chūkyoku". • Shingon *shōmyō* completes (late 10C). • **Gagaku** established (894). • Nanzanshinryū moves to Mt. Kōya (late 11C). • Ryōnin leaves Mt. Hiei and establishes Ōhara *shōmyō* at Raikō-in Temple (1109). • Kakuban leaves Mt. Hiei and founds Shingi Shingon-shū at Negoro-ji Temple (1140).
Kamakura (1185-1333)	• New Buddhism leaders appear one after another from Tendai Sect at Mt. Hie'i (late 12C-13C). • Hōnen founds **Jōdo-shū** (1198). • Shinran propagates in the east region (1214). • **Heikyoku** appears (early 13C). • Eisai founds **Rinazai-shū** (1202). **Wasan** prospers (Kamakura peiod). • Dōgen founds **Sōdō-shū** (1244). • Nara Buddhism evolves (13C). • Ippen begins propagating (1267). • Nichiren founds **Nichiren-shū** (1253). • **Sarugaku-noh** appears (mid Kamakura peiod).
Nanbokucho (1336-1392)	**Mugen-noh** completed (1380).
Muromachi (1336-1573)	• **Ji-shū** sect organized (1460?). • Ren'nyo founds **Jōdoshin-shū** (1473). • Shinran writes "Shōshinge" • Ikkō-shū Uprising (1466-1570).
Momoyama (1573-1603)	• Buddhism suppression. • Buzan-ha and Chizan-ha factions derived from Shingi Shingon-shū sect (1601).
Edo (1603-1868)	• Ingen founds **Ōbaku-shū** (1661). **Danka** system • Buddhist funeral standardized.
Meiji-Taisho-Showa-Heisei (1868-)	**Meiji Restoration** (1868). • '*Haibutsu kishaku*' (anti Buddhism) and Nationalization of Shinto.

Shōmyō and Buddhist Music as the Roots of Japanese Music

Buddhist music is mainly represented by *shōmyō*. But it also consists of other music such as *hōe gagaku* which is played during a *hōe* (a mass) and *en'nen* which is performed as the entertainment after the ceremony. Buddhist music contains a wide range of genres from instrumental music performed by priests to the newly composed modern works based on Buddhist subjects. However, it is not widely known that Buddha avoided music and songs as obstruction to the religious austerities. Music was integrated into Buddhism probably after rituals had been established and formalized as the religious essentials.

Later, storytelling *biwa* (lute) music by the *biwa-hōshi* (lute priests) was derived from *biwa* music of *hōe gagaku* of Buddhist music. Mixed with this storytelling *biwa* music and the elements and subjects of *kōshiki* (*shōmyō* written in Chinese and read in Japanese) and *rongi* (discussion) of *zatsu-shōmyō*, *heikyoku*, which is the origin of the narrative music, was born. Based on the musical and narrative style of *heikyoku*, *jōruri* was established which further helped the development of the theatrical music such as *kabuki*. In addition, *tsukushi-goto* was derived from the *koto* music of *hōe gagaku*, from which the singing style called *kumiuta* was derived. Finally, a stringed instrument called *shamisen* entered the stage which would help the establishment of *utaimono*, or melodic songs, seeding the gorgeous Japanese music during the Edo period. On the other hand, influenced by other music such as *rongi* of *zatsu-shōmyō*, *jushi-sarugaku*, one of the various public entertainment incorporated in *en'nen* which was performed after a *hōe* ceremony, became *sarugaku-noh*.

Wasan and *goeika*, both vocal music of Buddhism, interacting with *imayō*, another popular vocal music at the time, became the origin of folk and popular songs deep-rooted in people's lives. Even non-musical sermons began adopting musical elements because the serious, and boring, discourse was difficult for the public to follow. They developed into *fushidan-sekkyō*, a form of giving sermons in a storytelling style still observed today. It became public entertainment such as *sekkyō-bushi* and *sekkyō-jōruri*.

It is no exaggeration to say that without Buddhist music, especially *shōmyō*, Japanese music and public entertainment would not exist as observed today. Buddhism is the root of the Japanese culture.

Shōmyō and Buddhist Music

- **Buddhist music includes:**
  - *Shōmyō*, *hōe-gagaku* and *en'nen* used for Buddhist ceremonies,
  - *Kada*, *ge*, and *goeika* to express faith,
  - *Shakuhachi* and *biwa* music played by Buddhist monks, and
  - Songs composed or performed based on the themes related to Buddhism.

  - **Budda and music:** Budda did not get involved with any musical activity during his lifetime. He rather prohibited his apprentices from playing musical instruments, singing, dancing or appreciating music in order to not be swayed by passion. *Bonbai* (chants in praise of Buddhas virtues) were created after his death and the Buddhist Community was organized.

- **Influences of Buddhist music on Japanese traditional music:**

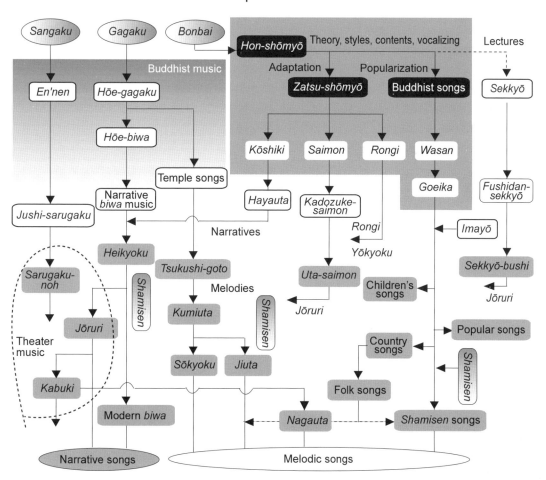

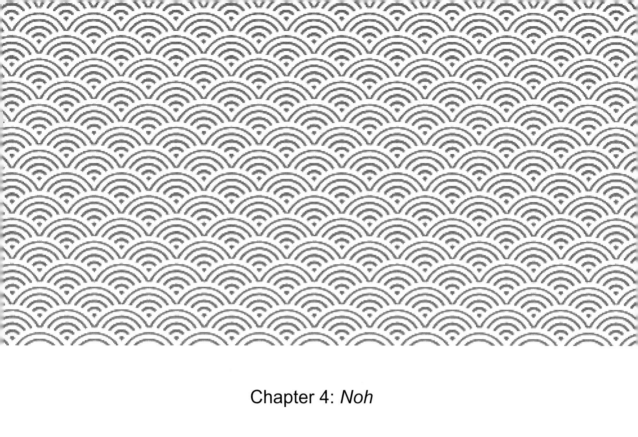

Chapter 4: *Noh*

Inseparable Noh and Kyōgen

Noh and *kyōgen* are collectively called '*nohgaku*'. It was fixed during the Meiji period but until then they were called *sarugaku* ('*saru*' can be written with two different kanji characters but both mean a monkey). *Noh* and *kyōgen* originated from *sangaku* and there are several theories why they were called *sarugaku*. The most common theory is that it was simply a mispronunciation of *sangaku*. Another common theory is that they originated from a public entertainment by monkeys. Another is that the kanji character for 'saru' came from that of *kagura*, a masked dance, established by Prince Shōtoku (573-621) to reproduce the event of the myth Amano Iwato. A less common theory is that the kanji characters for '*saru*' and '*hatano*' of Hatano Kawakatsu, who was regarded as the father of *sarugaku* among *noh* performers, have a common Chinese pronunciation. There is no established theory.

It may sound strange why *noh*, a solemn and philosophical performing art, and *kyōgen*, a comical, dialogue play, are paired as *nohgaku*. That is because they shared the same origin and kept close relationship during their development process. Unlike some other traditional performing arts which took separate paths although they originated from the same source, *noh* and *kyōgen* were two sides of the same coin while independently developing.

In a full-scale presentation, *noh* and *kyōgen* are alternately performed. When performed as an independent work, a *kyōgen* play is called '*hon-kyōgen* (real *kyōgen*)'. If *kyōgen* actors appear in a *noh* play, their scenes or their characters are called '*ai-kyōgen*'. For a grandeur *noh* work with two acts, *kyōgen* actors appear on the stage during the intermission. Sometimes *kyōgen* actors play important roles within a *noh* play. Occasionally the *noh* instrumental musicians appear and accompany *kyōgen*. In other words, though *noh* and *kyōgen* seem independent, they are integral and inseparable parts of *nohgaku*. When studying *noh* and *kyōgen* closely, we find that they have dualism—commonality and heterogeneous-ness.

Noh and Kyōgen

● Nohgaku:

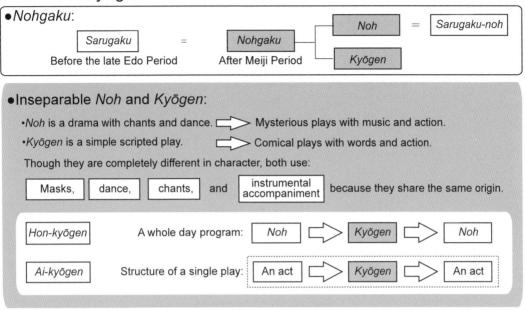

● Inseparable Noh and Kyōgen:

- Noh is a drama with chants and dance. ⇒ Mysterious plays with music and action.
- Kyōgen is a simple scripted play. ⇒ Comical plays with words and action.

Though they are completely different in character, both use:

Masks, dance, chants, and instrumental accompaniment because they share the same origin.

| Hon-kyōgen | A whole day program: | Noh ⇒ Kyōgen ⇒ Noh |
| Ai-kyōgen | Structure of a single play: | An act ⇒ Kyōgen ⇒ An act |

● Commonality and Heterogeneity of Noh and Kyōgen:

		Kyōgen	Noh
Commonality	Space	Noh stage	
	Performer	Mainly male actors	
	Style	Simplicity, abbreviation and exaggeration; Bold and flexible space and time management	
	Plot	Story lines that fire our imagination	
	Action	Stable performance by lowering the center of gravity of the body and sliding feet	
	Voice	Voice reaching far by abdominal breathing	
	Stage effects	Masks, costumes, props, dancing, chanting, instrumental accompaniment	
	Music	Vocalizing styles, nori (rhythm) styles, utai (chanting), instrumental accompaniment, dancing, acting	
Heterogeneity	Structure	Realistic, openhearted, straightforward	Solemn, intensive, elegant
	Acting	Narration, dialogue, miming	Chanting, dancing
	Expression	Frank and outspoken attitude	Emotionless, controled, and patterned choreography
	Character	Humorous and realistic	Serious and symbolical
	Leading role	The weak and the satirized power	Spirits, warriors, the beauty, the noble

Development Process of *Noh* and *Kyōgen*

It is a generally accepted opinion that *nohgaku* originated from *sangaku*, the aggregate of the miscellaneous entertainments from the acrobatics to the music and dancing, which was introduced from China to Japan in the Nara period. *Sangaku* was first used as the music and dancing for rituals at the Nara Imperial Court when introduced.

The acrobatics were separated from *sangaku* in the Heian period and the rest of *sangaku* became public entertainment called '*sarugaku*'. It was mainly composed of comical mimes and farces from which the professional *sarugaku* performers emerged. At the time, the doctrine of esoteric Buddhism was preached at temples by means of gestures of shamans, not by the speeches of the priests. *Sarugaku* performers began to act for the shamans. For the Bean Throwing Night at the holiday at the end of winter, derived from Chinese *nuoxi* (masked dramas), the *sarugaku* performers wearing masks played ogres. These performances became public entertainment from which *jushi-sarugaku* (or *shushi-sarugaku*) was derived. Also, *okina-sarugaku* was developed based on the Japanese traditional religion, Shinto. This is how the groundwork of the nature of *sarugaku* was laid.

In the Kamakura period, '*za*', a troupe of *sarugaku* performers, was established in various parts of Japan such as Yamato (today's Nara), Ōmi (Shiga), Kawachi (Osaka) and Tanba (Kyoto), and backed by local temples and shrines where they actively performed for religious rituals and *hōe* gatherings. Consequently, the troupes became competitive and developed the newer accomplishment while inspiring each other. As a result, they expanded their repertoires from the comical mimes and farces to new plays with story-line, called '*noh*', accompanied by music and dancing.

In the meantime, there was a public entertainment called '*dengaku*', or rice-planting dance, derived from the Shinto rituals to pray for a good crop of rice. By the end of the Heian period, the professional *dengaku* groups called '*dengaku* priests' appeared. Influenced by the prosperity of *sarugaku-noh*, they began playing dramas and added '*noh*' plays to their repertoire. The intense competition between *sarugaku-noh* and *dengaku-noh* led to the accomplishment of *noh*.

Noh was established in its present-day form during the Muromachi period (ca. 1333 to 1573). It was accomplished with the fusion of various public entertainment from *sangaku*, *nuoxi* and *gigaku* introduced from China to public entertainment by Buddhist and Shinto shamans and rice planting rituals.

Traditional Japanese Music at a Glance

■Development Process of *Noh* and *Kyōgen*

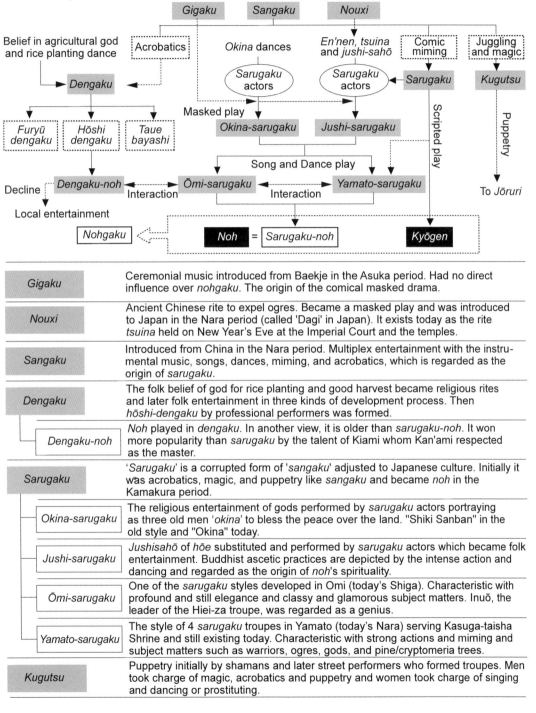

Gigaku	Ceremonial music introduced from Baekje in the Asuka period. Had no direct influence over *nohgaku*. The origin of the comical masked drama.
Nouxi	Ancient Chinese rite to expel ogres. Became a masked play and was introduced to Japan in the Nara period (called 'Dagi' in Japan). It exists today as the rite *tsuina* held on New Year's Eve at the Imperial Court and the temples.
Sangaku	Introduced from China in the Nara period. Multiplex entertainment with the instrumental music, songs, dances, miming, and acrobatics, which is regarded as the origin of *sarugaku*.
Dengaku	The folk belief of god for rice planting and good harvest became religious rites and later folk entertainment in three kinds of development process. Then *hōshi-dengaku* by professional performers was formed.
Dengaku-noh	Noh played in *dengaku*. In another view, it is older than *sarugaku-noh*. It won more popularity than *sarugaku* by the talent of Kiami whom Kan'ami respected as the master.
Sarugaku	'Sarugaku' is a corrupted form of 'sangaku' adjusted to Japanese culture. Initially it was acrobatics, magic, and puppetry like *sangaku* and became *noh* in the Kamakura period.
Okina-sarugaku	The religious entertainment of gods performed by *sarugaku* actors portraying as three old men '*okina*' to bless the peace over the land. "Shiki Sanban" in the old style and "Okina" today.
Jushi-sarugaku	*Jushisahō* of *hōe* substituted and performed by *sarugaku* actors which became folk entertainment. Buddhist ascetic practices are depicted by the intense action and dancing and regarded as the origin of *noh*'s spirituality.
Ōmi-sarugaku	One of the *sarugaku* styles developed in Omi (today's Shiga). Characteristic with profound and still elegance and classy and glamorous subject matters. Inuō, the leader of the Hiei-za troupe, was regarded as a genius.
Yamato-sarugaku	The style of 4 *sarugaku* troupes in Yamato (today's Nara) serving Kasuga-taisha Shrine and still existing today. Characteristic with strong actions and miming and subject matters such as warriors, ogres, gods, and pine/cryptomeria trees.
Kugutsu	Puppetry initially by shamans and later street performers who formed troupes. Men took charge of magic, acrobatics and puppetry and women took charge of singing and dancing or prostituting.

Like Father and Son: Kan'ami and Zeami

While *sarugaku* and *dengaku-noh* (or simply *dengaku*) were in rivalry, *dengaku* won the popularity due to two extremely popular master performers: Icchū at Hon-za and Kiami of Shin-za. Icchū was such a popular actor that when he held *kanjin-dengaku*, a fundraising performance for temples and shrines, in 1349, the house was packed to capacity and the box seats collapsed claiming many lives.

On the other hand, the troupes of *sarugaku* including Yūzaki-za, to which Kan'ami, the father of *noh*, belonged, mainly performed plays with dialogues of the uncouth characters like ogres or mimes. Kan'ami who respected Icchū of *dengaku* as "my teacher of my style" introduced a wide range of innovations to *sarugaku* while studying the style of *dengaku* and boldly improved *sarugaku*.

To create new music and dramas, he deviated from traditional *sarugaku* at Yamato, by crossing the popular songs at the time, such as *kouta* and *sōga*, with the stylish music and dance of *dengaku* as well as with the graceful and elegant taste of *sarugaku* at Ōmi, and by laying *noh* chants over the rhythm of *kusemai*, a form of chants and dances with a strong irregular beat. This new style became more popular than *dengaku*.

Yoshimitsu Ashikaga (1358-14080, the third shogun of the Ashikaga shogunate), was fascinated by *sarugaku-noh* performed at Imakumano Shrine by Kan'ami and his son Zeami, a twelve-year-old handsome and talented boy, and became the patron of the Kan'ami family. Backed by the shogunate, their Yamato *sarugaku* surpassed other schools in their social status and popularity.

When Zeami was twenty-one years old, his father Kan'ami died in Suruga Province, the central part of Japan, while touring there and Zeami became the second leader of his troupe Yūzaki-za (present Kanze School). Though Yoshimitsu continued to back the family after Kan'ami's death, he and the public preferred the style of *ōmi-sarugaku* characterized by its mysterious elegance and tender emotion brought about by the great actor Inuō (or Dōami) of Hie-za to Yamato *sarugaku*. Thereupon, Zeami abandoned the mimes called '*genzai-noh*' which depicted normal and realistic events and was the main and traditional repertoire of Yamato *sarugaku* at the Kan'ami era, and changed the course to establish *noh* of fantasy called '*mugen-noh*' which deals with supernatural worlds by *shite*, a lead character.

The word 'mime' may be associated with mimicking something or someone but the mime of *noh* means the realistic acting.

Traditional Japanese Music at a Glance

■Process to Completion

(1) Kan'ami's Invention:
- Reforming the style
- Emphasizing chants and dance
- Introducing rhythmic aspect
- Creating new chants and dramas

(2) Zeami's Invention:
- Standardizing *noh* with chanting and dancing
- Emphasizing principal characters
- Systematizing *noh* theory
- Establishing *mugen-noh*

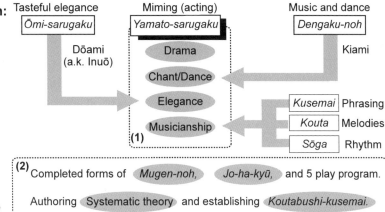

Kusemai	Simple dance with a fan over the rhythmical chants popular in the late Kamakura to Muromachi periods. Initially it was a narrative song. Later Kan'ami made it more sophisticated into *koutabushi-kusemai* in the elegant *noh* style.
Kouta	*Kouta* (ballad) exists in any period. *Kouta* in this period was called '*muromachi-kouta*' and liked by the intellectuals such as court nobles, warriors and priests. The poems for *kouta* were collected in "Kanginshū". The melodies were assumed to be sophisticated.
Sōga	Rhythmical songs in unison and slow tempo over the grand and rhetorical verses in seven-and-five syllable meter, popular among the noble and the samurai class from the Nanboku-cho to the middle of Muromachi periods. Also called '*enkyoku*', it was used for the banquets or the ceremonies in the temples and shrines.
Kōwakamai	Probably derived from *kusemai* in the Nanboku-cho period, it was mainly narrative on the subjects such as the war chronicle and rarely accompanied by dances. Several performers chant like *noh* but they are not in costume. Unlike narrative *heikyoku*, the narration is accompanied by actions. There is no direct influence to *noh*.
Kan'ami	Founder of the Kanze-za troupe. He was a *shite* actor and the leader of Yūzaki-za of *yamato-sarugaku*. Lord Yoshimitsu was so impressed by the performance by him and his son Zeami at Ima-kumano Shrine that he became their patron. Kan'ami reformed *yamato-sarugaku* by adopting *kusemai* to create narrative *noh* chanting.
Zeami	The son of Kan'ami, taking over Kan'ami's reform. He adapted music and dancing to establish *mugen-noh* dealing with supernatural worlds. In Yoshinori's regime, he lost Yoshimitsu's patronage and was exiled to Sado Island where he died without returning to Kyoto.
Dōami	*Noh* actor, a.k.a. Inuō, of the Hie'i-za troupe of *ōmi-sarugaku*. He changed his name to Dōami after the Buddhist name of Yoshimitsu who seemed to love him more than Zeami. His style was elegant with rich emotions and he was the leading figure in the *noh* world after Kan'ami's death.
Kiami	Master-hand of Shin-za of *dengaku-noh* which was, along with Icchu's Hon-za, more popular than early *sarugaku-noh*. His style, different from the *sarugaku* style, was musically excellent, and Zeami was said to highly praise it after watching his performance.

Mugen-noh and Jo-ha-kyū

After the Kan'ami's death, his son Zeami became a young leader, burdened with the heavy responsibility to lead the troupe.

His rival Inuō's repertoire with the subtle and profound elegance won the popularity among the intellectual nobles who patronized performing arts at the time. Zeami realized that he had no choice but to pursue subtle and profound beauty favored by the noble class and finally established the new styles: *mugen-noh* (fantasy *noh*) and *monogurui-noh* (*noh* of madness).

In general, *mugen-noh* has two acts: the first act, in which the main character in the past appears as a spirit at this moment in time; and the second act, in which the character re-appears in its true form. This means the play has a double structure in time and dimensions. The highlight of the act one is *noh* chanting, or *utai*, and the highlight of the act two *noh* dance, or *mai*. *Mugen-noh* was complete as a chanting and dancing play with subtle and profound beauty.

On the other hand, *monogurui-noh* is a type of *genzai-noh* (realistic *noh*) in which a realistic story unfolds in real time. The word '*monogurui*' stands for madness. *Shite* (lead character) expresses the state or process of going mad due to parting from his/her child or spouse by emotionally chanting and dancing. The enthusiastic performance of the mad scene highlights *monogurui-noh*.

Zeami aimed to establish *noh* with the profound and quiet elegance in which each word makes a beautiful chant and each action makes an attractive dance that highlights the climax. Stylized by this concept, Zeami's *noh* became immortal in Japanese theatrical arts.

Zeami's accomplishments are the invention of new styles such as *mugen-noh* and authoring many books in which he systematized and theorized his aesthetics. Among a score of his books, "Fūshi-kaden" is the most well known that contains the famous remark "a flower (beauty) exists in silence" which means that the secrecy provokes our interest or when concealed, things look more interesting. His remarks reflecting his artistic ideas are still useful for modern people.

In his writing, Zeami developed the *jo-ha-kyū* concept. *Jo-ha-kyū* was originally the term to describe the sections of *gagaku* (or *bugaku*) works. Zeami adopted it to theorize everything of *noh* production, from the formation of a play to the program of a whole day, and from the script structure to the musical changes. His *jo-ha-kyū* concept had a broad influence on all traditional Japanese performing arts in addition to *noh*.

■Types of *Noh*

Types	Characters	Programs and Structure	Description
Mugen-noh (Dream *noh*)	Spirits — Such as gods, Buddhas, ghosts, the incarnation, or spirits	1st and/or 5th play in a whole day program. Basically in two acts	Artistic *noh* established by Zeami. A human (*waki*) of the real world meets the incarnation (*shite*). The incarnation talks about the tale related to the place, hints what he really is, and disappears. [Intermission] *Shite* reappears as a spirit and performs *shikatabanashi* (talking with gestures) and a dance.
Genzai-noh (Real world *noh*)	Real people — Human in the real world	3rd and/or 4th play. Mostly in a single act	It depicts the living human in the real world in real time. Unlike *mugen-noh*, there is no fixed patterns except the actor's entrance, the story lines and the dance.
Dream-like *genzai-noh*	Semispirits — Spirits with flesh such as ogres or long-nosed goblin	4th and/or 5th play	The leading characters (*shite*) are ogres (demon) or long-nosed goblins from another world. It has an atmosphere like *mugen-noh* but the expression is realistic. It is in between *mugen-noh* and *genzai-noh*.

● Zeami theorized *Jo-ha-kyū*. The concept of the three sections (movements) in the Japanese music and folk entertainment. It originated from the typical structure of the *bugaku* works in *gagaku*.

Four-section structure	Three-section structure		Structure of a single work	A whole day program	Divisions of a *utai* chant	Beats of *yatsu-byōshi* (8 meter)
Ki	Jo	Introduction	Section of *jo*: *Waki*'s entrance	1st play	Section before *uchikiri* (instrumental ensemble part at the end)	1st beat 2nd beat
Shō Ten	Ha	Development	1st section of *ha*: *Shite*'s entrance 2nd section of *ha*: Dialog of *waki* and *shite* 3rd section of *ha*: *Shite*'s tale [Intermission]	2nd play 3rd play 4th play	Section before *ageha* (the beginning of *shite*'s climax)	3rd beat 4th beat 5th beat 6th beat
Ketsu	Kyū	Ending	Section of *kyū*: *Shite*'s re-entrance [Ending]	5th play	Section after *ageha*	7th beat 8th beat

Patronage from Shogun

Noh has a 600 or 700 year history depending on how we define its starting time. If we put the origin of *noh* on the introduction of *sangaku* or on the first performance of *sarugaku*, the history of *noh* could be over 1,000 years, not just 700 years. However, it is a general opinion that *noh* began in the Nanbokucho period (1185–1392, the beginning of the Muromachi period) when Kan'ami and Zeami, the genius father and son, established the present form of *noh*, including *mugen-noh*, regarded as an art.

As shown in the chronological table on the right page, *noh* evolved, always patronized by shogun, the power at the time, starting with Ashikaga Yoshimitsu (1358-1408) followed by Oda Nobunaga, Toyotomi Hideyoshi, Tokugawa Ieyasu until the end of the shogunate. It is possible to say that *noh* was a performing art which had been supported and made sophisticated by the warrior class. During the warring states times, warriors, who faced their death every day, must have felt that *noh* was more than an entertainment and its subtle '*ma* (space or timing)' with tension and their swordman ship had a lot in common. Therefore, when a male actor plays a woman, as usual in performing arts at the time, his voice and gestures do not mimic women unlike what *kabuki* actors do, holding in a manly atmosphere as if it were a male role.

Obligated to adhere to traditional rules as Tokugawa shogunate's ritual music, *noh* preserved its invariable style during the Tokugawa period. However, when the Tokugawa shogunate suddenly lapsed due to the Meiji Restoration, *noh* lost its only patron and actors and musicians of various *noh* schools were out in the cold. But soon, the new nobles and the new rich became the patrons in the Meiji period. In short, *noh* was an art continuously patronized by high classes in Japan.

For other traditional performing arts such as *kabuki* and *bunraku*, the educational services, for example, an earphone guide, are provided to the audience today, but, no assistant except a program brochure is provided for at a *noh* performance. In other words, the audience is supposed to have prerequisite knowledge of *noh* and understands what is happening on the stage. That distinguishes *noh* from other performing arts.

Traditional Japanese Music at a Glance

■History of *Noh*

Asuka (538-710)
- Gigaku introduced by Mimashi (612).

Nara (710-794)
- Sangaku introduced. *Sangaku* Department was established in *Gagaku-ryō* (701).

Heian (794-1185)
- Tōdai-ji Inaugural Ceremony of Great Buddha (752). Shōmyō introduced by Kūkai (806).
- Sarugaku appears (947). Gagaku established (894). Imayō appears (1008).
- *Dengaku* becomes popular in Kyoto (1096). • Jushi performs at Hōjō-ji (1025).
- *Dengaku* and *sarugaku* performed at Kasuga Wakamiya Festival (1136).

Kamakura (1185-1333)
- Sarugaku-noh begins (mid-Kamakura period).
- Outdoor *sarugaku* under torches performed at Kasuga Wakamiya Kōfuku-ji Temple (1255).
- *Sarugaku*, *kusemai* and *sōga* become popular (1310). Heikyoku appears (early 13C).
- Kan'ami is born (1333). • Priests perform "Okashi (Humor)" at Tango Kokubun-ji (1334).

Nanbokucho (1336-1392)
- Zeami is born (1363?). Kyōgen appears.
- Ashikaga Yoshimitsu sees the *noh* play by the Kanzes in Imkumano (1375).
- Kan'ami dies (1384); Zeami takes over his troupe.
- Mugen-noh is completed under the patronage of Yoshimitsu.

Muromachi (1336-1573)
- "Fūshi-kaden" is written by Zeami (1400).
- On'ami and Konparu-zenchiku become popular.
- Zeami exiled to Sado (1434). Kōwakamai begins (1442).
- *Sarugaku* suffered from civil wars (1470). Kanshō Famine (1460).

Momoyama (1573-1603)
- Nishi Hongan-ji North Stage is built (1561). Ōnin War (1467).
- Nobunaga entertains Ieyasu with *noh* (1582). Shamisen introduced (ca.1560).
- Hideyoshi learns *noh* in Nagoya and plays *shite* in the Kinchūnoh performance (1593).

Edo (1603-1868)
- Kabuki dance and Jōruri puppetry begin (early 17C).
- *Noh* performed to celebrate Ieyasu's appointment to Shogun at Nijo-jo Castle (1603).
- *Noh performed* by the four schools (troupes), open to public, at Edo-jo Castle (1607).
- Tokugawa Government appoints *noh* as its official ritual music (1610). *Noh* performed to celebrate the inauguration of Shogun and entertain honored guests.
- *Kanjin-noh* for fundraising held outside Onari Gate of Edo-jo Castle (1620).
- Government issues laws for common people to live frugally (1647).
- *Noh* schools (Kanze, Konparu, Hōjō、Kongō and Kita) lose their Government patronage (1868).

Meiji (1868-1912)
- Meiji Restoration (1868).
- Organization Nohgakusha and its theater Nohgakudō established in Shiba Park (1881). The name 'nohgaku' established.
- *Noh* performed to entertain foreign guests and higher class.
- *Noh* performed with the Emperor in attendance at Tomomi Iwakura's residence (1876).
- The four schools appointed as official performers in Imperial Court (1878).
- Edward S. Morse and Ernest F. Fenollosa study *noh* with Minoru Umewaka (1883).

Taisho-Showa-Heisei (1912-)
- Kanze Troupe visits USA and was broadcast (1927).
- *Noh* Department established in Tokyo Music School (1931).
- "Ōharagokō" banned for lese majesty by Metropolitan Police Department (1939).
- Most *noh* theaters burned down by Great Tokyo Air Raid (1945). End of WWII (1945).
- Strife between Kanze and Umewaka schools intervened by GHQ.
- Female *noh* performers allowed (1948).
- *Noh* designated as a world intangible cultural heritage (2001).

Noh Performance All Day Long

In the Edo period, a *noh* performance as ritual music was *gobandate*, or a five-play program, in which five *noh* plays and four *kyōgen* plays were performed. The *kyōgen* plays of this program, called *hon-kyōgen*, are independent, not explanatory or subordinate to the *noh* plays. Until the Momoyama period, there was a seven-play or a twelve-play program. A *noh* performance called *kanjin-noh*, which collect fees to fundraise for building or repairing of the temples and shrines, occasionally had a seventeen-play program in a single day. It was a big job for the audience, too.

The five *noh* plays of *gobandate* are chosen from five different categories: a god appears in the first play called '*waki-noh*'; a warrior appears in the second play called '*shura-noh*'; a woman appears in the third *noh* called '*kazura-noh*'; the fourth play is one of the miscellaneous titles called '*zatsu-noh*' or '*monogurui-noh*' because many Zeami's *monogurui-noh* belong to this category; and a demon appears in the last play called '*kiri-noh*'.

There are approximately two hundred and fifty *noh* titles preserved today. They are categorized and further subcategorized based on the lead character, the story and the structure. The plays dealing with a woman are not necessarily categorized as *kazura-noh*. If she becomes mad, the play belongs to the fourth group '*monogurui-noh*'.

The title "Okina (Old Man)" is specially treated, considered as the ancient and sacred. It is often performed to pray for the peace over the land in the specific rituals such as the New Year's *noh* performance and Shinto ceremonies. The actor who was going to play Okina used to comply with strict rules; for example, he had to purify himself for seven days and had to take meals cooked by fire exclusively for him, separated from his family's. A performance of "Okina" and five *noh* plays, called '*gobandate* with Okina', was the standard program as formal ritual music in the Edo period. Today in general, a performance of *noh* contains two *noh* plays with one *kyōgen* play. In the modern society, everything goes at a quicker pace and the program of *noh* is not an exception.

Traditional Japanese Music at a Glance

■Noh Performance of *Gobandate* (Five-play Program)

■ = Mugen-noh   □ = Genzai-noh   ▨ = Dream-like Genzai-noh   □ = Kyōgen

Lead roles	Programs	Description and Major titles					
Okina (old men)	*Shikisanban*	The ancient rites for festive occasions such as New Year's Day. Three old men solemnly pray and dance for the bumper crops and long lives.					
Gods	1st play	The incarnation of god appears and dances to celebrate for the peace and safety over the land. Auspicious *noh* mostly in the *mugen-noh* style.					
	Waki-noh	God "Takasago"	Old man god "Rōmatsu"	Goddes "Seiōbo"	Red wig "Chikubushima"	Evil mask "Dōmyō-ji"	
	1st *kyōgen*	*Waki-kyōgen*	Good fortune *kyōgen*	Farmer *kyōgen*	Marchant *kyōgen*	Lucky fellow *kyōgen*	
Samurai warriors	2nd play	A warrior or a young nobleman, who died in a battle and could not rest in peace, gets lost in the spiritual world and beseeches for the repose of his soul. Mostly in the *mugen-noh* style.					
	Shura-noh	Hero "Hachijō"	Nobleman "Kiyotsune"	Young warrior "Atsumori"	Old warrior "Sanemori"		
	2nd *kyōgen*	Master *kyōgen*	Servant *kyōgen*				
The beauty	3rd play	In general, a young, beautiful woman is the lead role. The core plays in the delicate *noh* genre with elegant chants and dance. Many are in the *mugen-noh* style.					
	Kazura-noh	The beauty "Izutsu"	Old woman "Ubasute"	Spirit "Kakitsubata"	Hansome man "Oshio"	Old tree "Saigyōzakura"	The beauty "Yuya"
	3rd *kyōgen*	Groom *kyōgen*	Woman *kyōgen*	Priest *kyōgen*	Blind man *kyōgen*		
Miscellaneous	4th play	Mainly 'mad *noh*' and 'devotion *noh*' and various other types.					
	Zatsu-noh	Goddes "Hagoromo"	Eldery "Ugetsu"	Devoting woman "Kinuta"	Devoted man "Kayoikomachi"		
		Mad woman "Hanjo"	Unmasked "Ataka"	Chinese play "Kantan"	Artistic play "Jinenkoji"	Prayer "Dōjō-ji"	
	4th *kyōgen*	Demon *kyōgen*	Mountain monk *kyōgen*	Dance *kyōgen*	Misc. *kyōgen*		
Demons	Final play	A visitor from another world is the lead role. Lively, bold and fast.					
		Woman "Ama"	Nobles "Tōru"	Warriors "Kumasaka"	Ogres "Nomori"	Dragons "Kasuga-ryūjin"	Animals "Nue"
	Kiri-noh	Special "Yamauba"	Celebration "Shakkyō"	Semi-prayer "Funa-benkei"	Goblins "Kurama-tengu"	Wiping-out-ogres "Ōeyama"	Miracles "Matsuyama-kagami"

Abbreviated Performances of Noh

In today's *noh* performance, the stage, costume and stories are often simplified in addition to reducing the programming from a five-play program to a double feature. The performance by all actors in full costume with a mask is called '*shōzoku-noh*' while the one by actors in no costume and masks but plain traditional clothes is called '*hakama-noh*'. Also, though actors wear full costume and a mask, staging only the second act, the climax of a two-act play, is called '*han-noh* (half *noh*)'.

Furthermore, the components of *noh* such as dances, chants, gestures and instrumental parts are disassembled and then each component can be freely combined and performed. The chart on the right page summarizes those components. This kind of variation is also common in Western operas and ballets. For example, operas can be staged in a concert style without any stage setting and/or costume. The ballet music can be performed without dancers, as well.

However, *noh*'s components can be fragmented into pieces. For example, the fragment of the instrumental parts '*icchō*' and '*ikkan*' listed in the chart on the right page can be performed by a fife or a *tsuzumi* drum. The whole, the main section, or the climax of a dance or a chant can be performed independently. *Noh* components are thoroughly disassembled: each component in the chart in the next page can be freely combined and the all resulting form is specifically named. This fragmentation and reconstruction is possible probably because *noh* is a highly accomplished art form, each element of which is also complete and independent.

There is an anecdote that a farmer chanted a *noh* chant while planting rice in Sado Island during the Edo period. People at the time learned *noh* chants, dancing, and playing instruments. In Japanese historical dramas or movies, we often see a warrior chant a *noh* chant and dance holding a commander's fan. These scenes show how people adopted and loved *noh* without costume and instrumental accompaniments.

In today's double-feature program shorter than the bygone five-play program, '*shimai* (*noh* dancing in plain traditional clothes)' and '*su-utai* (unaccompanied *noh* chanting)' are occasionally performed. It is not rare to see an audience, holding a chant book, softly chant along with the actor on the stage.

Abbreviated *Noh* Programs

Legend
- ○: Yes
- ▲: Yes and No
- ●: Yes to the second half of a play
- △: Yes for the lead chanter

	Performer				Prop	Element			Part			Description
	Shite	Other roles	*Noh* chorus	Wind	Percussion	Mask/Costume	Prop/Stage setting	*Utai* (chanting)	*Hayashi* (instruments)	*Shosa* (acting)	Whole work	Highlights	Small sections	Instrumental part	
Noh	○	○	○	○	○	○	○	○	○	○	○				Fundamental form to perform a complete play with masks, costume and accompaniment.
Hakama-noh	○	○	○	○	○			○	○	○	○				Whole play (or a half) by performers in crested garments without masks and costume.
Han-noh	○	○	○	○	○	○	○	○	○	○		●			Second act only from a two-act play in masks and costume.
Banbayashi	○	○	○	○	○			○	○		○				Whole play by performers in crested garments sitting without *shosa* (acting).
Ibayashi	○	▲	○	○	○			○	○			○			Highlights (or the second half) by performers in crested garments sitting without *shosa* (acting).
Maibayashi	○	▲	○	○	○			○	○	○		○			The same as *ibayashi* but with *shite*'s dancing.
Su-bayashi				○	○				○				○	○	Instrumental performance by accompanists without actors.
Su-utai	○	○	○					○			○		○		Whole *utai* part by a chanter sitting and chanting without chorus and accompaniment.
Dokugin	△							○				○			*Utai*'s highlights by a chanter sitting and chanting.
Ko-utai	△	▲						○					○		A short phrase by a chanter for an auspicious or mourning occasion.
Shimai	○		○					○		○		○			Highlight of dances without accompaniment.
Ikkan				○					○					○	Variations based on a *hayashi* part by a single wind.
Icchō	△				○			○				○			Highlights of a play performed by a chanter and a drummer.
Icchō-issei	△				○			○				○			Variant of *icchō*. *Issei* (*shite*'s entrance chant) is inserted.
Icchō-ikkan	△			○	○			○				○			Another variant of *icchō* with added wind. Variations based on a *hayashi* part is performed.

Noh Actors: Shite and Waki

Noh performers are divided into two groups: *hayashikata* who play the musical instruments and *tachikata* who take charge of everything, including acting, other than playing the instruments. In *noh*, there are no backstage staff such as a director, a stage manager, a sceneshifter, a property master, and a wardrobe master who commonly work for theatrical arts. In other words, the *noh* actors not only act on the stage but also take care of all jobs of the backstage. *Tachikata* are divided into groups named uniquely to *noh*: *shite*, which is used for *kyōgen* as well, and *waki*.

All characters of *shite* and *waki* are fixed. Supported by the *iemoto* (the head master of a school,) system, both were exclusively specialized and preserved "as is" and traditionally kept out each other out. Their pedigree has many-hundreds-of-years history.

Shitekata (*shite* actors) are the core of *noh*: they play *shite* and *shite-tsure*, the leading and sub-lead characters respectively; take charge of *jiutai* (back chorus) for *shite*'s chanting and assist *shite*'s acting on the stage and dressing in the backstage as *kōken*. *Kōken* stands for an understudy and a substitute for a *shite* actor. He performs if the *shite* actor is impossible to appear in a *noh* play due to a sudden illness, for example. In addition, *shitekata* make properties used on the stage. The child actors must be *shitekata*'s family members. As a result, the number of the *shitekata* members tops among *noh* performers: about 1000 out of approximately 1500.

Waki play supporting characters who are contrastive to the lead characters. In other words, they support and emphasize the character of *shite*. A Japanese word 'wakiyaku', meaning a supporting role in modern movies and dramas, derived from *waki* of *noh*. Since *waki* are the supporting actors to *shite*, their costume is subdued compared with that of *shite* and they wear no mask, which is called *hitamen*.

In short, *noh* dramas after Zeami are produced and staged centering thoroughly around *shite*. The *kyōgen* actor appears on the stage as an actor of *hon-kyōgen* (an independent *kyōgen* play) as well as *ai-kyōgen* (comic interlude) performed during the intermission of a *noh* play. They also play an important role to explain to the audience about the story and background of the *noh* play during the interlude.

Instrumental musicians called *hayashikata* appear on the *noh* stage and play music except the vocal parts. Each performer of the fifes and the *tsuzumi* drums belongs to a specific school with a long history.

Shite schools are proud of their six or seven century long history, second only to *gagaku*. For example, Sakado Magotarō-Ujikatsu I of Kongō School of *shite* was born in 1280 and Kiyotsugu Kan'ami, the founder of Kanze School, was born in 1333. The four major schools, Kanze, Hōshō, Konparu, and Kongō, belongs to Yamato *sarugaku* and Kita School was derived from Kongō School, backed by Tokugawa shoguns Ieyasu and Hidetada in the Edo period.

Similarly, it is possible to ascend to the 15th century, the early Muromachi period, to trace the origin of the schools of the *waki* and *kyōgen* actors and the *hayashi* musicians. It is natural that *noh* is highly esteemed internationally since the art, tradition and genealogy of the families have been preserved to the modern society.

■Tasks

	Parts	Tasks	Schools	
Actor	Shite	• Plays *shite* (lead role) or *tsure* (or *shitetsure*, companion of *shite*) of *noh* • Chants *jiutai* (chorus) and acts as *kōken* (gardian) of *noh* • Crafts props and stage settings	Kanze School Konparu School Kita School	Hōshō School Kongō School
Actor	Waki	• Plays *waki* (supporting role) or *wakitsure* (companion of *waki*) of *noh*	Takayasu School Shimogakari-hōshō School	Fukuō School
Actor	Kyōgen	• Performs "Sanbasō" of "Okina" • Plays *ai* (a story teller role) of *noh* • Plays various roles of *kyōgen* and chants *jiutai*	Ōkura School	Izumi School
Accompanist	Wind	• Performs the accompaniment part of *noh* and *kyōgen*	Morita School Fujita School	Issō School
Accompanist	*Kotsuzumi* (shoulder drum)		Kanze School Kōsei School	Kō School Ōkura School
Accompanist	*Ōtsuzumi* (hip drum)		Takayasu School Ōkura School Kanze School	Kadono School Ishii School
Accompanist	*Taiko* drum		Kanze School	Konparu School

A Stage without Curtains

A *noh* stage set indoors today has a roof and four columns. This is traced to the time when *noh* originally staged in the open. The *sumo* wrestling ring also has a roof hung from the ceiling but the columns were eliminated in order to avoid injuries of *sumo* wrestlers.

The columns of the *noh* stage is important not only to support the roof but also for the actors to act on the stage. *Shite* can see only a part of the stage through the small eye holes of his *noh* mask. As named *metsuke-bashira* (signpost), columns are necessary for actors to know their position on the stage. Their relation is like that of a vessel and a lighthouse. That is why a simplified stage in a modern hall or for *takigi noh* (outdoor *noh* illuminated by bonfire) needs columns, not a roof.

The stage is approximately six meters (twenty ft.) square and apparently looks narrow. Because *suriashi* (sliding feet) is the fundamental technique of *noh* dancing, the stage floor must be sparklingly polished. With *kagami-ita* (backdrop) on which a big old pine tree is painted and *hashigakari* (gangway bridge) which is the path to the stage and also occasionally means the other world, the stage itself is a stylized and perfect beauty. The combination of a cathedral ceiling of the roof and a pot installed under the floor creates the sounds like timpani as *shite* dances on the stage. This structure has not changed at all for hundreds of years. Generally, a theatrical stage has a proscenium arch and is confined with walls and curtains and all seats are set in front of the stage. On the other hand, a *noh* stage has no curtain and is surrounded by the seats in the L shaped area. Instead of raising a curtain, the music called *oshirabe* announces the start of a *noh* play.

■Noh Stage

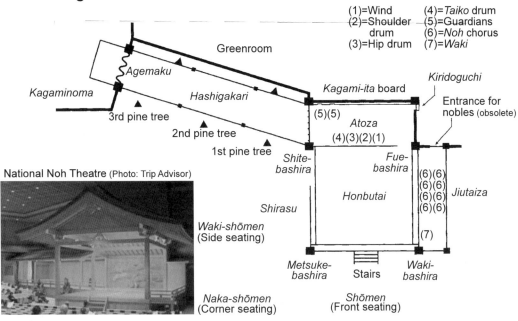

(1)=Wind
(2)=Shoulder drum
(3)=Hip drum
(4)=*Taiko* drum
(5)=Guardians
(6)=*Noh* chorus
(7)=*Waki*

National Noh Theatre (Photo: Trip Advisor)

Honbutai	The main stage for actors to perform. Open to three directions. The floor is polished for sliding feet.
Hashigakari	The aisle for actors to enter the stage. Also used to represent another world distinguished from the stage, the real world. *Kabuki*'s *hanamichi* was derived from it.
Kagaminoma	The mirror room. The important space, different from the greenroom, for a *shite* actor to prepare himself mentally. *Agemaku* (curtain) shields it from audience's view.
Atoza	*Noh* instrumentalists seating area, also called '*yokoita*', locating to the rearward of the stage. Guardians' seating area is behind it in front of the *kagami-ita* board.
Jiutaiza	*Noh* chorus seating area on the right side from the audience view of the stage. All chorus members line up in two rows facing the stage.
Kiridoguchi	Small wooden, side door at the rear of a *noh* stage through which the chorus members and guardians enter or exit. Actors who were killed also exit through it.
Kagami-ita	A backdrop of a *noh* stage on which an old pine tree, the symbol of power, is painted. When *kabuki* theater performs a *noh* related program, a *kagami-ita* backdrop is used.
Agemaku	Curtain, also called '*honmaku*', for screening the entrance to *hashigakari*. When *shite* or *waki* appears, the curtain is raised inside with two bamboo sticks.
Metsuke-bashira	One of the four named pillars. Downstage right pillar (front, left pillar from the audience view) used as a positioning guidepost for a narrow-sited *shite* actor wearing a mask.
Shōmen	Stage front seats where only the higher class used to be seated. Seating areas surrounding the stage are named based on the angle to *kagami-ita*.
Shirasu	White gravel separating a *noh* stage from the audience, retaining the traces of the seats for common people when the *noh* play was performed outdoors in the past.

Delicate and Mysterious *Noh* Masks

The most well known *noh* mask (*omote*) is the one of the young woman called '*ko-omote*'. We often use a phrase "like a *noh* mask" to describe an expressionless face. However, a close look at the eyes and the mouth of a *ko-omote* mask changes our impression about the *noh* mask completely. It has a mysterious, delicate and subtle expression, like a smile of Da'Vinci's Mona Lisa, that looks to be reproachful or joyful, reflecting the viewer's feelings. Mona Lisa's portrait does not move but the look of the *noh* mask changes significantly due to a subtle movement of the actor who wears it. In many traditional Japanese performing arts, cultural activities such as tea ceremony, and martial arts, there are detailed choreographed patterns of movements, called '*kata*'. In *noh*, there is *kata* called '*shiori*', for example. The actor bends his head, covering his face diagonally with stretched fingers. With this posture, the *noh* mask declines a little and gives the appearance of sobbing.

Noh masks are called '*omote*'. There are probably more than two hundred types of *noh* masks, which are roughly grouped into three: old men, women, and demons called *oni*. However, it will be appropriate to classify them into seven categories from *okina* masks to special masks, as shown on the right page, which can be subdivided further. Especially, the masks of women varying from young to old women to accommodate many characters. The character of a specific person like a historical figure has a specified mask. All characters, except for real people who exist at present, wear a mask. The unmasked faces of the real people who exist at present are also regarded as masks called '*hitamen*'. Therefore, the actors of those characters must keep a stony look without emotions. Interestingly, masks are more expressive than human faces in *noh*.

Masks are not merely properties but express a spiritual existence. It is customary practice for *shite* to bow to his mask praying for a successful performance and then let a *kōken*, a *shite* actor who assists him, put it on him in the *kagamino-ma*, the mirror room adjacent to the bridge, right before appearing on the stage.

There is no stage set but limited types of properties like fans which *shitekata* make with bamboo and cloths in advance of the *noh* performance. *Noh* is the ultimate art of simplicity.

■Masks, Fans and Props of *Noh*

●*Noh* Masks:

Okina   Koushijō   Han'nya   Ko-omote   Kobeshimi
(Courtesy of Seiun Kawai)   (Owned by Kiyoshi Yoshida)
(Photo by Kōji Murakami)

Groups	Characters	Name of masks
Okina	A sacred old man. Regarded as a divine mask. The jaw is separate.	Haku-shikijō, Koku-shikijō (for "Sanbasō"), Chichinojō, Enmeikaja
Jō	'Jō' reffers to an old man. Always with a beard.	Koushijō, Koakujō, Shiwajō, Ōakujō, Beshimi-akujō
Otoko	All men but old men. Warriors, nobles, priests and boys. Some have unique look.	Chūjō, Imawaka, Heita, Jūroku, Dōji, Kasshiki, Kantan-otoko
On'na	All kinds of women, from girls to old women, with vague emotion.	Ko-omote, Waka-onna, Zō-onna, Nakizō, Shakumi, Rōjo, Uba, Komachi
Onryō	Vengeful ghosts bearing a grudge. The lead role of *mugen-noh*.	Yase-otoko, Ayakashi, Chigusa-otoko, Kawazu, Han'nya, Deigan, Ja, Ryūjo
Kishin	Demon gods with a fierce expression. No horns.	Ōtobide, Ōbeshimi, Kumasaka, Kurohige, Shishiguchi, Tenjin, Shikami
Tokushu	Special masks for specific human characters.	Kagekiyo, Shunkan, Semimaru, Yorimasa, Shaka, Fudō, Shōjō, Yamanba
Hitamen	A face without a mask. Since an actor's face is regarded as a mask, he must be emotionless.	

●*Noh* Fans:

Called '*chūkei*' in *noh* and used in almost all plays. It is a prop for showing dignity, not for fanning. Masks, costume and fans are the three necessary props. There are numerous patterns and marks on fans designated to specific plays and characters.

●*Noh* Props and Settings:

There are no realistic backdrops or stage settings in *noh*. The settings are simple and made by *shite* actors each time a *noh* play is performed. They are limited and simple enough to fire our imagination. So are the props though there are some splendid props.

▶Pine tree stand, one of the common props

▼*Okina* fan   ▼*Kami* (god) fan   ▼*Kazura* (female role) fan

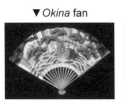 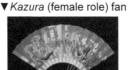 

(Courtesy of Tomatsuya, Karasuma Sanjō, Kyoto)   (Photo: Yoshirō Kuramoto)

Noh Costume and Fashion

The *noh* costume is based on the full Japanese court dress and sticks to formalities. With the advanced dyeing and weaving skill, with expensive materials such as the gold thread and silk, and luxurious woven patterns and design, the *noh* costume is an artwork, more than the stage costume.

The design of early *noh* costumes is unclear in many aspects. Until the time of Zeami who valued the inner character and the performance of actors more than the superficial attraction, the *noh* costume was probably not much different from the everyday clothes at the time. Then, during the Azuchi Momoyama period (approx. 1573-1603), patronized by Lord Hideyoshi (1536-1598) who loved flashy things and built a gilded teahouse, the *noh* costume became dazzlingly gorgeous and showy with a novel design. Gold brocade and damask were introduced from the Ming Dynasty of China, which were called "Chinese fabrics" and manufactured at Nishijin, a city famous for its textile industry. Only important people, such as the Generalissimo, were permitted to wear the Chinese fabrics. However, they were also given to the *sarugaku* actors, which means that *noh* was exceptionally well treated and protected. Today, the Chinese fabrics and *surihaku* (gilded fabrics) can be seen only on the *noh* stage.

Noh is a play without realism, which requires the audience to have a good imagination. It does not reflect daily lives at the time. It is the world of "subtle and profound beauty" so completely stylized and abstracted that there is no feeling out of place even if the actor plays the role of a farmer or a fisherman but wears a silk costume. In addition to wearing a splendid costume, the actor wears it on stage very stylishly. Those styles are named, for instance, *nugikake* in which the right sleeve of the robe is not worn, but hung. For *tsubo-ori* the bottom of the robe is pulled up to the knees, and both sides of the collar are loosened to the chest in a more curvy style. For *koshimaki* the costume is wrapped around the waist, while for *mogidō* only a short-sleeved robe is worn. The beautiful fashion show unfolds on the *noh* stage, depicting the sentiment of the character as well.

There are about 200 *noh* titles performed at present but the types of costume are limited to only 30-40. However, there are many woven patterns, designs and colors of fabrics used in a combination for various characters, except for the fixed designs for particular people.

■Noh Costume

Kitsuke: Outer garments worn under the upper garment, but not as underwear.	
Surihaku	*Kosode* (short-sleeved *kitsuke*) for women made of plain-woven silk gilded with gold or silver. Worn under *karaori*.
Shiroaya	*Kosode* made of pure-white woven silk. White is the most prominent color in *noh* and used for "Okina" and so on.
Nuihaku	*Kosode* made of gilded and embroidered shiny silk. Used for nobles, women, children and so on.
Noshime	Worn under *mizugoromo* or *suō* as outer garments. Patternless one is used for priests or servants and horizontally striped one for warriors.
Atsuita	*Kosode* made of the thick textile in various colors and drawing patterns, mainly used as men's outer garments.

Uwagi: Upper garments worn over *kitsuke*.	
Karaori	Gold-brocaded satin damask introduced from China. The most gorgeous and representative in the *noh* costume.
Chōken	Long upper garments with wide sleeves made of thin silk gauze. Used for female dancers as well as male characters.
Mizu-goromo	Unlined with wide sleeves. Widely used for priests, *jō* (old men), old women, men, women, children and so on.
Suō	Type of *hitatare* made of hemp. Plain clothes for warriors and general male characters. Used as a formal dress with *naga-hakama*.
Kariginu	Formal silken clothes of the noble, originated from hunting clothes. Round neck, wide sleeves, up-rolled front with a waist-cord.
Happi	Upper coats with wide sleeves without chest strings, made of the same textiles as *kariginu*'s. Patterns woven with gold threads.
Sobatsugi	Lined *happi*-style upper garments with no sleeves to depict armors. Worn by warriors or Chinese characters.

Hakama: Man's formal divided skirts.	
Ōguchi	Typical *noh hakama* wide-legged and pleated. Color shows the character and his social position.
Hangire	*Hakama* for male characters wearing lined *kariginu* and *happi*. In the same shape as *ōguchi* with woven, golden patterns.
Sashinuki	Ballooned *hakame* with the hems tied, worn along with *kariginu* by characters of the highest status.

Obi: Practical or decorative *noh* belts.	
Katsura-obi	A decorative wig belt put on a female mask and hung down over the back. Absolutely essential accessory for a female character.
Koshi-obi	A belt put on over *kariginu*, *happi*, or *mizugoromo*, knotted and hung in front. It varies in patterns and color.

Nuihaku

Noshime

Karaori

Chōken

Kariginu

Ōguchi

(Courtesy of Sasaki Noh-robes)

Kakegoe (Yells): the Essence of Noh Music

The music of *noh* is roughly divided into two: *utai* (vocal part) and *hayashi* (instrumental part).

Noh is a chanting and dancing drama which progresses along with a story. There are speeches and melodic chants to describe the story, scenes, and mental states uttered by the characters. The speeches, called *kotoba*, of the character have peculiar accents and intonation. *Fushi*, the melodic lines, are chanted by *jiutai*, a chorus, generally composed of eight members in addition to *shite*, *tsure* and *waki*.

Hayashi, the instrumental part of *noh*, accompanies the *noh* chants and dances. It is composed of four instruments: three types of drums, *kotsuzumi* (shoulder drum), *ōtsuzumi* (hip drum) and *taiko* (stick drum), and a flute, *fue*, the only pitched instrument in *noh*. This structure is called *shibyōshi* meaning four instruments. In a set of dolls for the Girls' Festival, there is a group of five musicians, which is composed of *shibyōshi* and an *utai* chanter.

The instrumental part of *noh* contains no string instruments, which contributes to determine the characteristic of the structure and quality of *noh* music. *Noh* is composed of small module-like units called *kata*, meaning patterns, which is fundamental to Japanese arts. The acting, dancing and music of *noh* are constructed from a series of freely combined basic patterns. These basic patterns of *noh* are called *shōdan*. There are some types of *shōdan* such as *kuse*, *kuri*, *sashi*, and *kudoki* in the vocal parts, and *deha*, *sagariha*, *iroe*, *jo-no-mai* and *chū-no-mai* in the instrumental parts.

Noh music is characteristic with its peculiar *kakegoe*, or yells. Those who see a *noh* play for the first time should be surprised by the powerful yells of musicians. The yells are so intensely piercing that we feel as if we were watching a swordplay match. There is no conductor for the instrumental musicians and their yells are used to time the performance. In other words, the yells are cues for performers to synchronize. In addition, the yells are also cues for the whole stage, not only instrumental performers but also *shite* and *jiutai*, to time. Without *kakegoe*, *noh* music would be chaos.

Traditional Japanese Music at a Glance

■Musical Structure

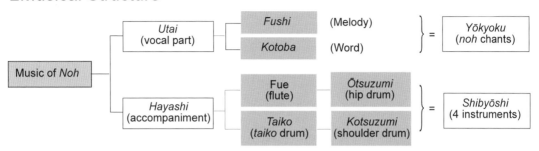

■*Shōdan* (small unit) = a basic, melodical unit of *noh*:

- *Utai, hayashi* and *shosa* (acting) are categorized by the *shōdan*.
- Each *shōdan* is integrated into a *noh* play like a piece of a mosaic work.
- *Shōdan* is independent and can be freely omitted, added and replaced.

Tegumi (rhythm unit)	A rhythm unit in which specific *tsubu* (grains) and *kakegoe* (yells) are arranged in a specific order.
Tsubu (grains)	A single note of strikes of percussion instruments.
Kakegoe (yells)	The means to cue the counts of beats and important moments, and indicate the rhythmic sense by changing intonations, durations, and pace.

	Number of *tsubu*	Playing method	Variants of *tegumi*
Kotsuzumi	1 for each beat	The tension of the string that tightens the drum skin is changed.	170 variants
Ōtsuzumi	1 for each beat	Dynamics as well as the pressure of the skin is changed.	200 variants
Taiko	2 for each beat	Dynamics as well as the pressure of the skin is changed.	100 variants

Basic 4 types of *kakegoe*	Ya*	Before the first and fifth beats.	* 'Ya' can be heard as 'yo' on stage. ** 'Ha' can be heard as 'ho' on stage.
	Ha**	Before the second, third, fourth, sixth, seventh and eighth beats.	
	Iya	Before the odd numbered beats.	
	Yoi	Mainly before the third beats.	

Yōkyoku: Restrained and Monotonous Melodies

Since *noh* is a chanting and dancing play, it is often compared with Western operas and musicals. However, the melody of *yōkyoku*, a collective name of *utai* (*noh* chants), is based on only three—high, middle, and low—sounds, and is not melodic like opera arias. Those who hear it for the first time may think if it is a melody.

Utai is chanted by the *shite* actor and the *jiutai* chorus, seated in two rows to the right of the stage. There is a chief of the chorus, called *jigashira*, but he does not conduct like a Western conductor.

There are two types of vocalization in *noh* chanting: *yowagin*, the gentle voice, and *tsuyogin*, the strong voice with lots of vibratos. Those names are different for different schools, for example, *jyūgin* and *gōgin* respectively.

In addition, there is a peculiar rhythmic type called *norigata*. The basic meter of *norigata* is octuple (eight-fold) time on which they allocate a verse when chanting. There are following patterns of the allocation:

The most common *hiranori* places twelve syllables of the seven-and-five syllable meter, the traditional pattern in Japan, over eight beats. *Chūnori* places sixteen syllables of the eight-and-eight syllable meter over eight beats, that is, two syllables for each. *Ōnori* places eight syllables of the four-and-four syllable meter over eight beats, that is, one syllable for each. Since the five-and-seven syllable meter suits the Japanese sense, *hiranori* sounds stable and comfortable. On the other hand, we feel like getting chased with *chūnori* and easy and drowsy with *ōnori*.

Those three allocations are called *hyōshi-ai*, meaning 'synchronized', because beating is clear. When the verse is chanted freely and elastically against beatings, it is called *hyōshi-awazu*, meaning 'un-synchronized'. Speeches, or *kotoba*, are uttered without melodic elements. They are a sort of *hyōshi-awazu* and have patterned intonations characteristic of *noh*. '*Sōrō*', the obsolete word 'be' or 'do' used by the *samurai* class, appears frequently. Modern people, feel somewhat out of place with them.

■Utai

●Jiutai

A chorus to chant the vocal part on the stage to tell the story and background or read the lines of actors. Composed of eight members sitting in two rows. '*Jigashira*', the leader who behaves as a concert master, sits in the back row.

Jiutai (Courtesy of Kyoto Kanze-kai)

●Scales

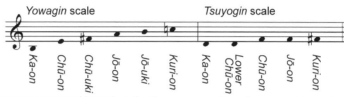

Scale notes are named based on the three ranges: *jō-on* (upper register notes), *chū-on* (middle register notes), and *ka-on* (lower register notes). Melodies are composed of notes in the three registers in a certain, systematic order.

Chanting methods

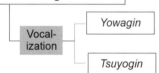

Yowagin: Noh's stardard vocalization. It is technically accomplished with the gentle breath control on a complicated scale, and used for elegant, gentle, and melancholic scenes.

Tsuyogin: Vocalization with vigorous breath control emphasizing muscularity in a narrow and flexible register. It is used for heroic, exciting and solemn scenes.

●Rhythmic structure

Periodic eight beats make one basic unit called *yatsu-byōshi* (eight meter) on which syllables of a verse are allocated and chanted. There are also *futa-byōshi* (two meter), *mutsu-byōshi* (six meter) and *yotsu-byōshi* (four meter) though they are not common.

●Nori (metered rhythm) with a sample text:
Naniga nanishite nantoyara (This is this and that is that...).

Beats:	1	2	3	4	5	6	7	8
Hiranori:	Na-	niga	na-	nishi	te-	nan'	to-	yara.
Chūnori:	Nani	gana	nishi	tena	n'to	yara,	hoi	hoi.
Ōnori:	Na- n-	ni- to-	ga- ya-	na- ra-,	ni- ho-	shi- i-	te- ho-	na- i-.

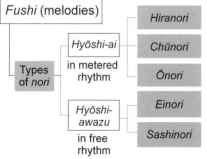

Hiranori: The most common. The verse in seven-and-five syllable meter is allocated to 12 notes in 8 beats. Also called '*shōnori*'.

Chūnori: Eight-and-eight syllable meter of 16 notes. Fast *utai* by 2 notes per beat. Also called '*shuranori*'.

Ōnori: Four-and-four syllable meter of 8 notes. Monotonous feeling. Called '*taikoji*' with a drum accompaniment.

Einori: Chanting melodic *rōei* of Japanese *waka* or Chinese poem.

Sashinori: Simply chanting less-melodic verse in seven-and-five syllable meter focusing on the meaning of the poem.

Kotoba (words): Since it is the speech part, there is no specific vocalization styles but some patterns of intonation in free rhythm.

Hayashi, Instrumental Ensemble in the Middle Ages

The instrumental ensemble of *noh*, usually a quartet, is called *shibyōshi* which may or may not include *taiko* (stick drum) and does not always play all together. The wind, the only pitched instrument in the ensemble, is *nohkan*. Though it looks similar to *ryūteki* of *gagaku*, *nohkan* has a built-in special device called *nodo* (throat) to emit the unique and peculiar high-pitched sound called *hishigi*. It is a pitched instrument but does not play melodies like the Western songs since *noh* chants are monotonous.

Tsuzumi drum is constructed from a hollow body and two skin frames that are tightened with linen strings to both sides of the body. Based on the size of the frame, there are two types: *kotsuzumi* (small *tsuzumi*) and *ōtsuzumi* (large *tsuzumi*). The way to play them is different according to the type. The performer shoulders *kotsuzumi* on his right shoulder with the left hand and strikes it with the right hand. The *ōtsuzumi* is held under the left armpit and is struck with the right hand. In general, if the structure of the musical instrument is the same, the bigger body the lower sound. However, *tsuzumi* is not the case: smaller *kotsuzumi* sounds lower than larger *ōtsuzumi*. The reason is that the tension and the moisture of the skins are not the same. The strings are tightened up for *ōtsuzumi* while they are somewhat loose for *kotsuzumi*. Besides, the skin of *ōtsuzumi* is dried with heat such as charcoal fire while that of *kotsuzumi* is always moist. As a result, *ōtsuzumi* creates more metallic and high pitched sounds than *kotsuzumi*. Because the performer could injure his fingers if he strikes the firm skin of *ōtsuzumi* with the bare hand, he wears fingerstalls called *yubikawa* or *ate* to protect his fingers. Probably originated from a hip drum of the rice dance, *taiko* has a similar structure as *tsuzumi* but it is flat and wider. The *taiko* performer beats simple and clear rhythm with drumsticks, and brings about a joyful mood and to a climax at the finale.

The instrumental part for "Okina (Old Man)", one of the older shaman type *noh* repertoires, consists of a flute and three *kotsuzumi* drums, which probably proves that a flute and *tsuzumi* first accompanied *noh* plays. *Taiko* is considered to have joined later when newer *noh* plays were created.

Method of drum performance consists of patterns related to three types of tempos: *nami-byōshi* (standard), *nori-byōshi* (rhythmic) and *sashi-byōshi* (non-rhythmic). Striking drums in *nami-byōshi* is called *awase-uchi* (matching strikes) since the drummer matches the rhythm with the *noh* chanting. Striking in *sashi-byōshi* is called *ashirai-uchi* (arbitrary strikes) since he strikes arbitrarily. *Nori-byōshi* could be either of the above. The performance of the fife consists of two types of patterns similar to the drums. In the same way as the *noh* masks, hundreds of years old musical instruments are still used.

■Hayashi: Instrumental Ensemble

Type of noh plays (* 'Mono' stands for 'types'.)		Fue (flute)	Kotsuzumi (shoulder drum)	Ōtsuzumi (hip drum)	Taiko (taiko drum)	Jiutai (chorus)
Shikisanban	"Okina"	O	O × 3			O
	"Sanbasō"	O	O × 3	O		
Daishōmono* (without taiko)	Shuramono Kyōjomono	O	O	O		O
Taikomono (with taiko)	Waki-noh Kichikumono	O	O	O	O	O

Nori of hayashi (rhythm and tempo)

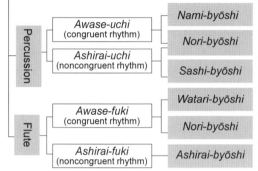

Percussion
- Awase-uchi (congruent rhythm)
  - Nami-byōshi — Highly flexible, congruent rhythm type. Responsive to other's breathing and pace.
  - Nori-byōshi — Constant and metered rhythm type. Used for utai of ōnori or hyōshi-awazu (noncongruent rhythm).
- Ashirai-uchi (noncongruent rhythm)
  - Sashi-byōshi — A type of the unclear rhythm with unclear kakegoe (yells) and unclear tsubu (grains).

Flute
- Awase-fuki (congruent rhythm)
  - Watari-byōshi — Rhythmical instrumental accompaniment for actor(s) to enter the stage while dancing.
  - Nori-byōshi — Common metered type for hayashi only. Used for various dances or shite's entrance.
- Ashirai-fuki (noncongruent rhythm)
  - Ashirai-byōshi — Independent from the rhythm or melodies of utai. Used for utai accompaniment or hayashi.

●Instruments of hayashi

(Instruments: Courtesy of Kyoto Kanze-kai)

Fue: Distinguished from other transverse flutes, it is called 'nohkan', made from bamboo with one blowing hole and seven finger holes. Similar to gagaku's ryūteki and nagauta's shinobue but structurally very different from them due to the thin bamboo piece, called 'nodo (throat)', inserted inside the pipe.

Kotsuzumi: Also called 'tsuzumi'. Two, front and back, iron rings skinned with horsehide and a hollowed body of cherry wood are assembled with the hemp cords called 'shirabeo'. A player grabs the cords and holds the drum over the right shoulder with his left hand and strikes it with his right hand. The skin location to hit and the cord tension affect the timbre. The skin needs moderate moisture.

Ōtsuzumi: Also called 'ōkawa'. Structurally it is similar to kotsuzumi and a little larger than that. A player holds it with his left hand on the left knee and strikes with the right hand. The skin must be dry unlike kotsuzumi and warmed up over the charcoal fire before a performance. The player braces the cord with all of his strength to create metallic, high-pitched sounds.

Taiko: A doubleheaded drum. Skinned with cowhide and the body is flat and big. There is a patch called 'bachikawa' made of deerskin on the front head and the player strikes on it with two sticks called bachi with his both hands. Hand techniques to strike with bachi and hold them affect the timbre.

Kyōgen: Sophisticated Humor

We tend to think that *kyōgen* is subordinate to *noh*, but, it is the legitimate heir of *sarugaku* which is essentially a comical entertainment. It is even recorded in writing that in 1339, ten years before *sarugaku* was performed by shrine maidens at Kasuga Wakamiya Shrine Festival, an entertainment, called "*okashi* (fun)", similar to *kyōgen* was performed by Buddhist monks at Kokubun-ji Temple in Tanba Province, present central Kyoto and parts of Hyogo and Osaka.

The word *kyōgen* was derived from a Buddhist term '*kyōgen-kigo*' which stands for 'nonsense' or 'falsehood' and was applied to the mimicking and comical programs of *sarugaku*. Today the word *kyōgen* is often used as a 'faked', 'joked', or 'staged' something which is not complimentary. In order to distinguish the drama and the dance in *kabuki*, the former is called *kabuki-kyōgen*, and the latter *kabuki* dance. We use *noh-kyōgen* or simply *kyōgen*.

Unlike *noh*, the characters of *kyōgen* are not the nobles or historic figures but ordinary and companionable people. *Kyōgen* is a play based on dialogue in which the lives of ordinary people in the Middle Ages are vividly depicted. The language used in *kyōgen* is ancient and contains a lot of obsolete words and the dialogue is also uttered and vocalized in the way peculiar to *kyōgen*. However, we, modern people, can follow the story from the context and nuance.

Kyōgen finally became Shogunate's ritual music and its humor was not vulgar but always sophisticated, smart, polished and refined. We wonder how the *samurai* warriors, whose code of chivalry forbid them to laugh or grin in front of others, reacted to funny *kyōgen*.

Many of the *kyōgen* repertoires ridicule the ignorance, greed, or tricks of the pompous people. In these repertoires the common peole satirize socially powerful people at the time such as the lords, the Buddhist priests, and the itinerant Buddhist monks. The lead character of such comical plays, generically named Tarō-kaja, is an extremely cheerful guy. Though it is a problem in a modern society, the socially disadvantaged are also ridiculed in *kyōgen*.

As mentioned before, a *kyōgen* play independently performed is called *hon-kyōgen*. When a *kyōgen* actor plays a character in a *noh* play, it is called *ai-kyōgen*. These roles vary from *katari-ai* to *ashirai-ai* as shown in the chart on the right page. In the special *noh* "Okina", *kyōgen* actors dance "Sanbasō" as a farmer. *Kyōgen* is an integral part of *noh*.

Similar to *gobandate* (five-play program) of *noh*, a *kyōgen* performance is roughly composed of four parts from the first *waki-kyōgen* to the fourth. These titles are categorized based on the lead characters: lords, son-in-laws, women, demons, Buddhist priests, and itinerant Buddhist monks.

The lead character is called *shite*, the same as *noh*, but, the supporting character is called *ado*, not *waki*.

■What the Word *'Kyōgen'* Refers to:

The word *'kyōgen'* was derived from a Buddhist term which stands for 'nonsense' or 'falsehood'.

Kabuki drama was called *kabuki-kyōgen* or simply *kyōgen*.

Noh-kyōgen = *Kyōgen* of (and) *Noh* = *Kyōgen*

●*Kyōgen* types and actors

Hon-kyōgen		An independent *kyōgen* of *nohgaku* performed as an interlude between *noh* plays. The word 'hon-kyōgen' is not used in general but only used to distinguish it from 'ai-kyōgen'.
Ai-kyōgen		Refers to a *kyōgen* actor who appears as a character in a *noh* play, or refers to a *noh* play or scene in which a *kyōgen* actor appears. Often abbreviated as 'ai'.
	Katari-ai	*Ai* (actor) tells stories that connects the first and second half of a *noh* play.
	Igatari	*Ai* tells stories of *shite* to *waki* while sitting in the center of the stage.
	Tachishaberi	*Ai* tells sories to audience while standing alone.
	Ashirai-ai	A *kyōgen* actor appears as a character in a *noh* play.
	Kuchiake-ai	'*Kyōgen* opener' to create the setting at the beginning of a *noh* play.
	Oshie-ai	*Ai* tells *shite* or *waki* the episodes or things related to the plot.
"Okina"		A special *noh* play. *Shite* performs the old man in "Okina" while *kyōgen* actors perform in the "Sanbasō" section. In some schools, the pre-dance is performed by *kyōgen* actors.

Music of *Kyōgen*

Though it is mainly based on dialogue, sixty percent of the *kyōgen* titles contain chants and dances. Also, the peculiar intonation and clearly uttered speeches were developed by *utai* or *noh* chanting.

The music of *kyōgen* consists of *kyōgen-utai*, the vocal part, and *kyōgen-ashirai*, the instrumental part.

There are two types of *kyōgen-utai*: "a play within a play" type and a "certain pattern" type. In *kyōgen* there is a unique dance called *komai*, which is accompanied by chanting called *komai-utai*. They are kinds of incidental dances and music used to depict a scene, such as a banquet, talked about in the dialogue, as it were a play within a play. *Komai* and *komai-utai* are the highlight in a *kyōgen* play.

The "certain pattern" type is performed in certain titles only. For this type, some parts of the speeches related to the plot are chanted like a Western musical or most of the play is chanted. Also, the style of *mugen-noh* (fantasy *noh*) is copied and called *noh-kyōgen*.

Kyōgen followed the trend of the times. For example, popular songs of periods such as *kouta*, *heike-bushi* and *jōruri-bushi* became a part of *kyōgen* and their names have remained as *kyōgen* terms.

Shite and *ado* chant. There is also *jiutai*, a chorus, chants in *kyōgen* but it does not accompany the whole play unlike *noh*. *Kyōgen-utai* is more complex than *noh* and there are many types and patterns based on its rhythm and scenes it accompanies.

As shown in the chart on the right page, the music of *kyōgen-ashirai* is sectioned and named, like *noh*, based on the scenes. In addition, each musician in *shibyōshi* is clearly assigned for his responsibility.

Prefixed with '*kyōgen*', for example, *kyōgen-shidai* and *kyōgen-issei*, the section names from *shidai* (*shite*'s entrance music) to *kakko* (dance music) are distinguished with their counterparts of *noh*. From this, it is understood that *noh* and *kyōgen* are inseparable like the two sides of a coin.

Traditional Japanese Music at a Glance

■Music of *Kyōgen*

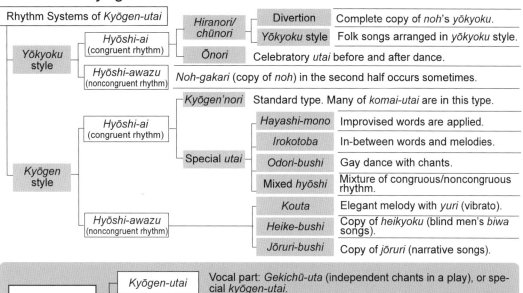

Rhythm Systems of *Kyōgen-utai*		
***Yōkyoku* style** — *Hyōshi-ai* (congruent rhythm)	*Hiranori/chūnori* — Divertion	Complete copy of *noh*'s *yōkyoku*.
	Yōkyoku style	Folk songs arranged in *yōkyoku* style.
	Ōnori	Celebratory *utai* before and after dance.
Hyōshi-awazu (noncongruent rhythm)		*Noh-gakari* (copy of *noh*) in the second half occurs sometimes.
***Kyōgen* style** — *Hyōshi-ai* (congruent rhythm)	*Kyōgen'nori*	Standard type. Many of *komai-utai* are in this type.
	Special *utai* — *Hayashi-mono*	Improvised words are applied.
	Irokotoba	In-between words and melodies.
	Odori-bushi	Gay dance with chants.
	Mixed *hyōshi*	Mixture of congruous/noncongruous rhythm.
Hyōshi-awazu (noncongruent rhythm)	*Kouta*	Elegant melody with *yuri* (vibrato).
	Heike-bushi	Copy of *heikyoku* (blind men's *biwa* songs).
	Jōruri-bushi	Copy of *jōruri* (narrative songs).

Music of *kyōgen*	
Kyōgen-utai	Vocal part: *Gekichū-uta* (independent chants in a play), or special *kyōgen-utai*.
Kyōgen-ashirai	Instrumental part: Entrance music, dance music, music unique to *kyōgen*.

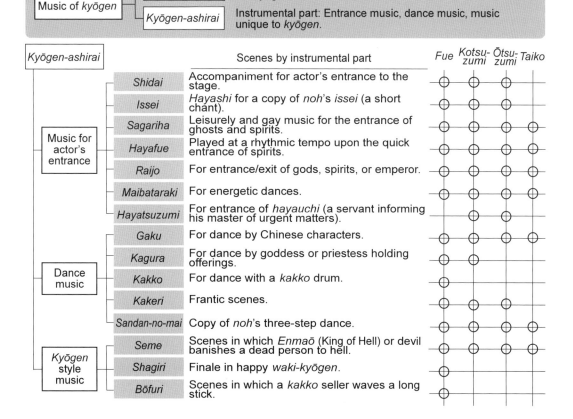

Kyōgen-ashirai		Scenes by instrumental part	Fue	Kotsu-zumi	Ōtsu-zumi	Taiko
Music for actor's entrance	*Shidai*	Accompaniment for actor's entrance to the stage.	⊕	⊕	⊕	
	Issei	*Hayashi* for a copy of *noh*'s *issei* (a short chant).	⊕	⊕	⊕	
	Sagariha	Leisurely and gay music for the entrance of ghosts and spirits.	⊕	⊕	⊕	
	Hayafue	Played at a rhythmic tempo upon the quick entrance of spirits.	⊕	⊕	⊕	⊕
	Raijo	For entrance/exit of gods, spirits, or emperor.	⊕	⊕	⊕	⊕
	Maibataraki	For energetic dances.	⊕	⊕	⊕	⊕
	Hayatsuzumi	For entrance of *hayauchi* (a servant informing his master of urgent matters).		⊕	⊕	
Dance music	*Gaku*	For dance by Chinese characters.	⊕	⊕	⊕	⊕
	Kagura	For dance by goddess or priestess holding offerings.	⊕	⊕	⊕	⊕
	Kakko	For dance with a *kakko* drum.	⊕			
	Kakeri	Frantic scenes.	⊕	⊕	⊕	
	Sandan-no-mai	Copy of *noh*'s three-step dance.	⊕	⊕	⊕	⊕
***Kyōgen* style music**	*Seme*	Scenes in which *Enmaō* (King of Hell) or devil banishes a dead person to hell.	⊕	⊕	⊕	⊕
	Shagiri	Finale in happy *waki-kyōgen*.	⊕			
	Bōfuri	Scenes in which a *kakko* seller waves a long stick.	⊕			

Masks, Costume and Props of *Kyōgen*

Because most of the characters of *kyōgen* are living human beings unlike *noh*, they are generally played by actors without a mask. 20 % (or 30 %) of the entire titles are probably performed by actors with a mask.

The masks of *kyōgen* look expressive in contrast to ambiguous and static *noh* masks. Masks such as *usobuki* and *kentoku* are very humorous and even vicious demons such as *buaku* look funny and friendly. It is amazing that these playful masks were made several hundred years ago.

The masked characters are mostly limited to something other than human, such as gods, demons, and spirits, as illustrated on the right page. However, masks are used for old men and certain types of human women.

All female characters in *noh* always wear a mask while ordinary women in *kyōgen* don't. Instead, they appear in a special manner called *binan-kazura* in which the actor who plays a female role wraps his head with the white linen cloth and grabs both of the hanging braids of the cloth at his waist. He wears costume for female characters such as *nuihaku* but appears without a mask, showing his unpainted, male face.

For kyōgen costume, *nuihaku*, *noshime* (supple silk robe), and *mizugoromo* (knee-length robe) of *noh* are also used. Chinese fabric is rarely used in *kyōgen* but *nuihaku* for female characters are more frequently used than *noh*. Those are common costume for *noh* and *kyōgen*.

There are costumes unique to *kyōgen*. *Kataginu* (sleeveless jacket) and *kyōgen-bakama* (trousers), both standard costume of the lead character Tarō-kaja, *naga-kamishimo* (long trousers) of his master, and *suō* (formal dress of *samurai* class) of the lord are all made of linen in contrast to the luxurious silk costume of *noh*.

The stage setting of *kyōgen* is more abstract and simpler than that of *noh*. However, various properties are used in *kyōgen*. Especially *kazuraoke* (bucket) plays an important role in many scenes, used as a chair, a prow of the ship, barrels or a tea pot. Even its lid is used as a wine cup or wine bottle.

■Masks, Costume and Props of *Kyōgen*

● **Masks:** These masks are exclusively for *kyōgen* and used in 20% of *kyōgen* plays.

Groups	Name of masks	Characters
Kami	*Kuro-shikijō, Fuku-no-kami, Ebisu, Daikoku*	Various gods and deities
Oni	*Buaku, Kaminari*	Demons or *Enma*
Rei	*Tsūen, Heiroku, Nushi*	Ghosts
Kemono	*Kosaru* (small monkey), *Kitsune* (fox), *Tanuki* (racoon dog), *Tonbi* (kite)	Animals or spirits of animals/plants
Zatsu	*Kentoku, Usobuki*	Spirits of houses, cows, dogs, crabs and mosquioes, scarecrows, goblins
Otoko	*Ōji, Hakuzōsu*	Ordinary old men, human
On'na	*Oto, Otogoze*	Young or old women

Buaku

Kentoku

Oto

(Masks: Courtesy of Kyogen Yamatoza)

● **Costume:**

Various *noh* costume such as *nuihaku*, *noshime*, or *mizugoromo* are used in *kyōgen* but costumes mentioned below are unique to *kyōgen*:

Name	Description
Kataginu	Men's sleeveless jacket made of hemp. Lead character *Tarō-kaja* wears it with *kyōgen-bakama*, striped *noshime* (jacket) and crested *koshiobi* (waist-cord).
Kyōgen-bakama	Typical *kyōgen-bakama* (divided skirt) worn with *kataginu*. Big crests are printed.
Suō	Warrior's ceremonial dress used for feudal lords and so on. A set of top and bottom in the same color and patterns with wide sleeves and long *hakama*.
Naga-kamishimo	Simplified *suō*, the suit in the same color and patterns. The sleeves are shorter than *suō* for easier movements.

Kyōgen-bakama

Suō
(Costumes: Courtesy of Sasaki Noh-robes)

● **Fans, settings and props:** Stage settings are limited but various props are very commonly used.

Name	Description
Fans	*Chūkei* fan for *noh* is rare while *shizume-ōgi* in three background colors and various design is frequently used.
Settings/props	Only simple settings such as tree stands are used. There are many hand-held props.
Kazura-oke	The lacquered tub substitutes as a seat, a sake bottle or a vase, and the lid is used as a wine cup, for instance.

Kazura-oke
(Courtesy of Kyogen Yamatoza)

Chapter 4: Noh

Noh and Kyōgen Preserved in Local Regions

Generally, we associate the phrase, "a *noh* performance", with a play at a *noh* theater or *takigi noh* held on a special stage built outdoor by five main *shite* schools established in the Muromachi period, Kanze, Hōshō, Konparu, Kongō and Kita. However, other *noh* groups with a longer history than the five schools exist in various parts of Japan. The table on the right page only lists major ones among them. Most of *noh* groups preserved in the local regions, including the ones listed, are specified as the national or local important intangible folk-cultural property.

Noh was completed by Kan'ami and his son Zeami in the Muromachi period, but there are many other *noh* groups which began before the two. These older *noh*, for example, "Okina (Old Man)", are ritual *noh* performed by shamans at Shinto shrines or Buddhist temples. They have been preserved and maintained in part by the shrines and temples but mostly by the local people such as the shrine parishioners. Some groups are proud of their long—several hundreds to more than a thousand year—history. Whether or not those numbers are true, one of the most famous such local *noh* groups is the one at Kasuga Wakamiya Shrine Festival in Nara that keeps the oldest *sarugaku-noh* performance ever recorded in writing. Held in December annually, the Festival is open to the public so that anyone can watch "Okina" and *dengaku* as the ancient rites.

Descended from *noh* at the time of Zeami, Kurokawa-noh, the famous Shinto ritual *noh* at Dewa Kasuga Shrine, has kept its style independent from other schools though it is closely related to the five major *shite* schools. Amazingly, 540 *noh* and 50 *kyōgen* repertoires have been preserved for more than 500 years only by 240 shrine parishioner families and 160 actors and instrumental musicians from the young to the elder. This group has preserved unique styles in addition to the *noh* performance at the shrine: *Rōsoku* (candle) *Noh*—a *noh* play illuminated by candles and staged in a room of a residential house; and Water-Fire *Noh*—a *noh* play performed on the stage built waterside and illuminated by bonfire. Kurokawa *Noh* is so popular that only the lucky lottery winners can attend the performance.

As for the other local *kyōgen*, Mibu-kyōgen in Kyoto is well known. This *kyōgen* originated from the exaggerated gestures of the Buddhist monks, who preach to large gatherings of worshippers without speakers or megaphones at that time. Many historical figures probably watched Mibu-kyōgen.

Traditional Japanese Music at a Glance

■*Noh* and *Kyōgen* Preserved in Local Regions

Name	Location	Affilation	Description	History (Birth year)
Kasuga Wakamiya Shrine Festival	Nara, Nara Prefecture	Kasuga Wakamiya Shrine	Ancient festive style	850 years (1136)
Kurokawa-noh	Tsuruoka, Yamagata Prefecture	Kasuga Shrine	Not lineage of five major *shite* shools	500 years (mid-Muromachi period)
Sarugaku of Nōgō	Motosu, Gifu Prefecture	Hakusan Shrine	*Sarugaku* in ancient style	500 years (Muromachi period)
Matsubayashi of Kikuchi	Kikuchi, Kumamoto Prefecture	Kikuchi Shrine	Ancient style	650 years (1350?)
Mizumi-noh	Ikeda, Fukui Prefecture	Ukan Shrine	Ancient style (*Dengaku* and dance)	750 years (early Kamakura period)
Dengaku of Nishiure	Hamatasu, Shizuoka Prefecture	Nishiure Kannon-do	Ancient style	1250 years (719)
Okina-mai	Narasaka, Nara Prefecture	Nara Zuhiko Shrine	Shinto dance	1200 years (8th C)
Shinji-mai	Katō, Hyogo Prefecture	Sumiyoshi Shrine	Shinto dance	700 years (late Kamakura period)
Isshiki-noh	Ise, Mie Prefecture	Isshiki Shrine	"Waya-za" troupe at Ise	450 years (mid-Muromachi period)
Okina-mai of Kuruma	Kobe, Hyogo Prefecture	Kuruma Ōtoshi Shrine	Ancient style (5-dancer "Okina")	300 years (mid-Edo period)
Noh of Sado	Sado, Niigata Prefecture	Kasuga Shrine	Honma Family of Hōshō School	400 years (1604)
Matsuyama-noh	Sakata, Yamagata Prefecture	Shinmei Shrine	Lineage of Kanze School	300 years (mid-Edo period)
Yamato-noh	Tsuoka, Yamagata Prefecture	Kawauchi Shrine	Shinto *noh*	500 years (mid-Muromachi period)
Noh of Shinshiro	Shinshiro, Aichi Prefecture	Tominaga Shrine	Folklore	270 years (mid-Edo period)
Snow Festival of Niino	Anan, Nagano Prefecture	Izu Shrine	*Kagura, dengaku, sarugaku*	650 years (Muromachi period?)
Noh Dance of Higashidōri	Higashidōri, Aomori Prefecture	Menafudōin Temple	*Shugen-noh* (by mountain priests)	500 years (mid-Muromachi period)
Toyoma-noh	Tome, Miyagi Prefecture	Hachiman Shrine	Ritual music of Date Domain	230 years (late Edo period)
Mibu-kyōgen	Chukyo Ward, Kyoto	Mibudera Temple	Pantomine *kyōgen*	700 years (late Kamakura period)
Saga-dainenbutsu-kyōgen	Ukyo Ward, Kyoto	Seiryō-ji Temple	Pantomine *kyōgen*	700 years (late Kamakura period)
En'nen of Mōtsu-ji Temple	Hiraizumi, Iwate Prefecture	Mōtsu-ji Temple	*En'nen* and *dengaku* dances	800 years (late Heian period)
En'nen of Obasama	Kurihara, Miyagi Prefecture	Hakusan Shrine	*En'nen* and *dengaku* dances	800 years (late Heian period)

Chapter 5: *Biwa* and *Shigin*

Origin of *Biwa* and Family of Plucked String Instruments

It is the generally accepted theory that a Japanese *biwa* originated from an Arabic *oud* (fretless lute) and was introduced from China via the silk road in the 8th century. It is unknown if the Arabic *oud* was derived from an ancient Persian *barbat*, a pear-shaped plucked string instrument, or if the Persian *barbat* was derived from the Arabic *oud*. According to another theory, the Japanese *biwa* originated from an Indian *veena*. Though we do not know which theory is correct, there is one thing for certain: the crusade brought the *oud* back to Europe where it was improved and became a lute which has a similar pair-shape body and the bent neck. The guitar and the mandolin were developed from the lute, which means many plucked stringed instruments were derived from the *oud*.

There are also some theories about the origin of the Japanese name '*biwa*'. A theory says that two Chinese characters '*pipa*' to describe how to pluck strings became '*biwa*' in Japan. Another, based on the *veena*-origin theory, says that when the Indian *veena* was introduced to China, it was written and pronounced as '*biba*' in Chinese. By the way, the loquat, a fruit, was named '*biwa*' in Japan because the shape of the fruit resembles the musical instrument. It is incorrect to think the other way around.

There are also various theories when the instrument was introduced into Japan. A theory says that it was the 8th century when the origin of *gagaku* along with the Persian style *gakubiwa* was introduced from China. Another says that when Buddhism originated in India was introduced into Kyushu, the southern part of Japan, via China in the 6th century, the prototype of *mōsō-biwa*, a blind monk's *biwa*, was also introduced. In regard to these various theories, many scholars are still trying to find the answer. The five-stringed *biwa*, crafted with mother-of-pearl, stored in the national treasures in the Shōsōin Repository, was brought from the Tang Dynasty during the Nara period and has a straight neck, which means it did not originate from the *oud*. This particular *biwa* probably came from India.

A modern Chinese *pipa* has 30 frets and is plucked by finger picks while Japanese *biwa* generally has five frets and is plucked by a big plectrum. The instrument in the Tang Dynasty, the one introduced to Japan, was improved into today's modern *pipa* in China in the 1950's.

In Japan, the original structure of *biwa* was basically kept and the unique *biwa* music was established.

Traditional Japanese Music at a Glance

●Roots of *Biwa*

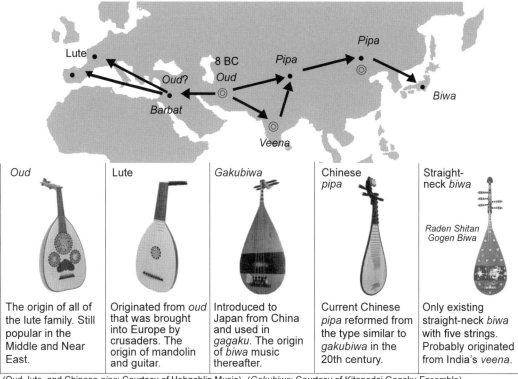

(Oud, lute, and Chinese *pipa*: Courtesy of Hobgoblin Music) (*Gakubiwa*: Courtesy of Kitanodai Gagaku Ensemble)
(*Raden Shitan Gogen Biwa*: Courtesy of Shōsōin)

●Introduction to Japan via multiple routes

- *Gakubiwa* (*gagaku biwa*): Introduced to Japan in the 7-8th century.
  Persia origin→Silk road→China→Japan

- *Mōsō-biwa* (blind monk's *biwa*): Introduced to Japan in the 6th century.
  India origin→China (during the Three Kingdoms period)→Southern Japan.

●'*Biwa*' (Note: the fruit '*biwa*' was named after the instrument.)

Pi (bi)	= Plucking a string outward.
Pa (wa)	= Plucking a string inward.

• Veena (Sanskrit) in India

⬇ Translated into Chinese

It was pronounced as '*biba*'.

⬇ More frets added.

Modern Chinese pipa

• The origin of lute:
Definite article + ud =

al'ud ➡ { lute (English)
luth (French)
laute (German)
liuto (Italic)
laud (Spanish)

Modern *satsuma-biwa*
owned by late Kinshi Tsuruta
(Photo: Kakujo Nakamura)

Biwa-hōshi: The Earliest Minstrel of Narrative Music

The *biwa* introduced into Japan along with *gagaku* was used as a rhythmic instrument to punctuate the ensemble and was not used to play melodies. Combined with *shōmyō*'s vocalization, this feature resulted in the unique Japanese narrative music.

The famous poet, Semimaru, whose poem was included in the "*Ogura Hyakunin Isshu* (Ogura Anthology of One Hundred Tanka by One Hundred Poets)", was a blind *biwa-hōshi*, which means that they had already existed in the Heian period (794-1185). The *biwa-hōshi* was a traveling minstrel in a Buddhist priest robe though he was not a monk. He made a living by performing narrative music with *biwa* at the request of wealthy people in the region where he traveled. According to the episode of Semimaru included in "Konjaku Monogatari (The Tales of the Past and Present)", the subjects of the narrative music performed by the *biwa-hōshi* at the time seem to be the Chinese historical figures such as emperors and heroes in the tales introduced from the Tang Dynasty.

A couple of centuries later, in the middle of the 13th century, the prototype of "The Tale of the Heike" was formed and spread along with the music called '*heike-biwa*' to all over the country by the *biwa-hōshi*. The *biwa-hōshi* then organized schools under each head master. They passed down the style or expressions unique to each school through an oral tradition. These organizations evolved into *tōdōza*, a guild for blind men backed by the government nationwide in Edo period, and lasted until the Meiji Restoration.

In the meantime, apart from the *biwa-hōshi*, there was a different group of blind *biwa* performers who wore a Buddhist robe and performed narrative music called '*mōsō-biwa* (blind priests *biwa*)' in the Kyushu area. They were truly Buddhist monks belonging to Mōsō Temple exclusively organized for blind priests in the 8th century. It was recorded in writing that they took charge of a ground-breaking ceremony for the main hall of Enryaku-ji Temple at Mt. Hiei. Originally, the blind monks performed *hōyō-biwa* as the part of the Buddhist ritual to pray for gods of the cooking stove or the house. They then began to recite narrative music as a side show like the *biwa-hōshi,* at the request of the temple parishioners.

In the Edo period, the *mōsō-biwa,* originated in the Chikuzen and Satsuma (today's Fukuoka and Kagoshima respectively) regions, spread over all of Kyushu and began to have contention over the right to perform narrative *biwa* music with the *tōdōza* of the *biwa-hōshi*. Although they lost, the *mōsō-biwa* in Chikuzen and Satsuma became the basics of modern *biwa* music.

Traditional Japanese Music at a Glance

■*Biwa* Music and Blind Buddhist Priests

Biwa music = Narrative songs.

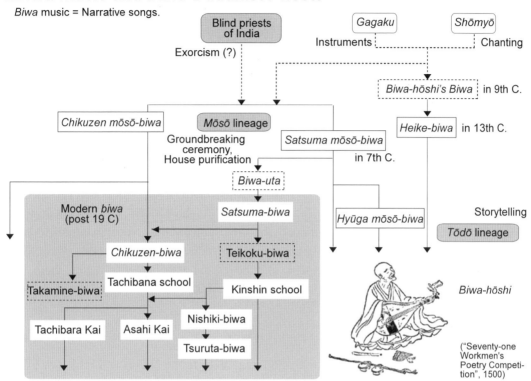

●*Biwa-hōshi* and *mōsō-biwa*

	Biwa-hōshi	*Mōsō-biwa*
Emergence time	Heian period (9th C.)	Edo period (17th C.)
Appearance	Blind laymen	Blind priests
Social rank	Entertainers	Clergy
Attire	In Buddhist priest's robes	In Buddhist priest's robes
Instrument	*Biwa*	*Biwa*
Performance style	Storytelling	Suitra reciting (& storytelling)
Purpose	Daily income	Part of Buddist services
Performance location	Streets, house frontage	Temples, parishioners' houses

⬇

Heike-biwa (*tōdō za*)

●Example of *mōsō-biwa*
(*Chikuzen-biwa*, Gensei School of Tendai Sect)

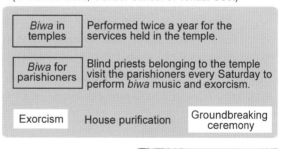

Semimaru, the first *biwa-hōshi*

("Seki" from "53 Stations by Two Brushes" by Hiroshige and Toyokuni III, 1854)

Heikyoku and "The Tale of the Heike"

Heikyoku is narrative music of an epic saga of the struggle between the Taira (or the Heike) and Minamoto clans (or the Genji) recited by *biwa-hōshi* to the accompaniment of *biwa*. The episodes recited by the *biwa-hōshi* were later compiled in a book called "Heike Monogatari (The Tale of the Heike)". As indicated by Lafcadio Hearn's "Hōichi the Earless", the *biwa-hōshi* performed *heikyoku* at the request of the warrior class in addition to the commoners. The *heikyoku* used to be called '*heike*' by *tōdōza*, the blind men's guild, but recently it is called '*heikyoku*' in general.

Shinanono Zenji Yukinaga compiled the tales of the Heike, popular among people, and had Shōbutsu, a blind monk, recite them, which later spread among other *biwa-hōshi*. Yukinaga knew *gagaku* and *biwa* very well, and his financial supporter, Jien (a Japanese poet, historian, and Buddhist priest), was a master of Tendai *shōmyō*, and Shōbutsu was a *biwa-hōshi*. That is, four elements of *heikyoku*—the subject, *biwa*, vocalization of *shōmyō* and *biwa-hōshi*—met here. After Yukinaga, new episodes and interpretations were added to the tales of the Heike by the *biwa-hōshi* and the temple preachers who recited them, and then newly established schools created their own versions. Among them, "Kakuichi Version", which had "Kanjō no Maki (Epilogue)" appended by the excellent master Akashi Kakuichi of Ichikata School, became the standard of "The Tale of the Heike".

It was the times when there were not much information and amusements. The stories of the past, but not far from their time regarding to the battles and tragedies of the noblemen of the Heike, recited by the *biwa-hōshi*, struck a chord in the hearts of the illiterate people and became extremely popular. As illustrated on the right page, *heikyoku* had a great influence on a wide range of consequent literature, music and public entertainment.

As the tales of the Heike spread wider, other performing arts such as *noh*, *jōruri*, and *kabuki* created many easy-to-understand and visually attractive productions based on them. Ironically, it caused the decline of the originating *heikyoku*. As a result, the *biwa-hōshi* of the *tōdōza* were forced to abandon *heikyoku* as their primary art and to turn to *jiuta* and *jōruri* of newly popular *shamisen* or *koto* music.

Traditional Japanese Music at a Glance

■What is *Heikyoku*?

Style: Narrative music to recite the tales of the Heike to the accompaniment of *biwa*.
Name: '*Heikyoku*' in general, but formally '*heike*'. Also called '*heike-biwa*' or '*heigo*'.
Birth: Established around the 13th century. When Shinanono Zenji Yukinaga, the *gagaku* musician and a hermit, lived off Jichin, the Buddhist priest of Tendai Sect, he had a blind Buddhist priest named Shōbutsu recite the tales to the accompaniment of *biwa*, according to the 226th section from "Tsurezuregusa (Essays in Idleness)" by Yoshida Kenkō.

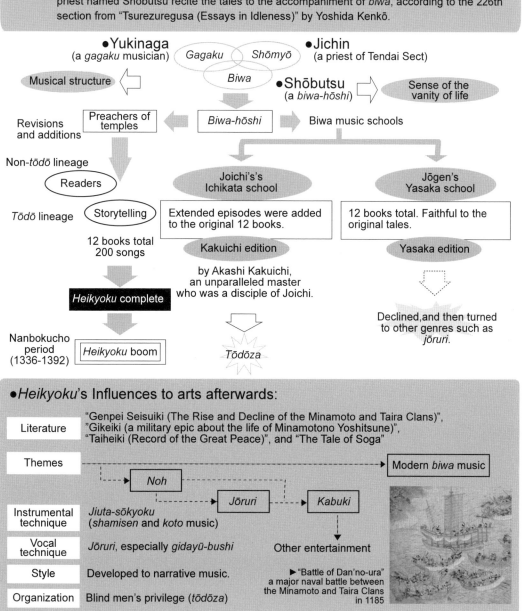

▶ "Battle of Dan'no-ura" a major naval battle between the Minamoto and Taira Clans in 1185

Structure of *Heikyoku*

Many movies and TV shows based on "Heike Monogatari (The Tale of the Heike)" have been produced. The book narrates an epic saga of the struggle between the Taira (or the Heike) and Minamoto (or the Genji) clans for control of Japan at the end of the 12th century, during the fateful five years after 1180. The rapid decline and tragic downfall of the Taira clan struck a chord in the heart of Japanese. However, famous episodes such as the first encounter of Minamotono Yoshitsune and Benkei at Gojō Bridge or the story of "Kanjinchō" in *kabuki* (or "Ataka" in *noh*) is not included in the original "The Tale of the Heike". Those well known episodes are actually based on a wide range of literary works, such as "Gikeiki" and "The Genpei Seisuiki", written after "The Tale of the Heike". Those subsequent books were written because "The Tale of the Heike" was extremely popular. "The Tale of the Heike" had a big influence on the literature, art, music and public entertainment.

"The Tale of the Heike" is composed of twelve volumes with more than 200 episodes. Surprisingly the blind *biwa-hōshi* memorized and passed down all of them by oral tradition. The *heikyoku* pieces based on the tale are divided into three categories: *hiramono* which are basic pieces, *naraimono* which are special pieces for people who have mastered 50-100 pieces, and *hiji* which are secret pieces which only specially qualified people can study. To master all, a long time and hard practice are needed. Because the tale is so long that we cannot finish it in a single day, the digest version, "Heike-mabushi (or Heike-shōsetsu)", was often used to substitute for the full version.

The melodic elements of the narrative music are called '*kyokusetsu*' which are roughly divided into seven categories. Originated from *shōmyō*'s vocalization, they were used for not only *heikyoku* but also subsequent *shamisen* music such as *jōruri*.

There are, of course, unique musical characteristics of *heikyoku*. In general, in traditional Japanese music, the key of a song changes relatively to the vocal range of a singer except *gagaku* which has absolute pitches, like the middle A of Western music. Because the *biwa* of *heikyoku* was derived from a *gagaku* instrument, *heikyoku* is recited to the accompaniment of *biwa* with the same absolute pitches as *gagaku*. It is conceivable that *biwa* is not merely an accompaniment but gives the pitches to the person who recites.

Structure of *Heikyoku*

●Outline of "The Tale of The Heike" (200 episodes in 12 books total)

Book 1	Arrogant Tairano Kiyomori of the Heike takes over power from his father Tadamori. A plot to assassinate him is uncovered.
Book 2-6	Shunkan, one of the rebels, is banished. Minamotono Yorimasa of the Genji rebels and loses against Kiyomori. Kiyomori dies of illness.
Book 7-9	The Heike starts declining. Yoshitsune defeats Yoshinaka (both of the Genji). Young Tairano Atsumori dies in the battle.
Book 10-12	Tairano Koremori and Emperor Antoku drown themseves at Dan'noura. Tairano Rokudai, the last descendant, dies and the Heike falls.
Book "Kanjō"	Tokuko, the mother of Emperor Antoku, becomes a nun. She is visited by Emperor Goshirakawa and talks about "Rokudō (6 desire realms)". The tale ends with her death.

Heike-mabushi = The digest version for *heikyoku*.

Since it is almost impossible to run through all 12 books, reciting excerpts from each book is regarded as a complete performance. The two volumes compiled by Ogino Kengyō of Maeda School in 1776 are used. They are composed of the following episodes from each book:

Volume 1
- "Suzuki"
- "Sotoba-nagashi"
- "Mumon-no-sata"
- "Itsukushima-kangyo"
- "Tsukimi"
- "Kōyō"

Volume 2
- "Chikubushima-mōde"
- "Usa-gyōkō"
- "Ikezuki"
- "Kaidōkudari"
- "Nasuno Yoishi"
- "Tosanobō-kirare"

●Types of *heikyoku*

Hiramono	Refers to standard songs. Can be learned and played without any licenses or fees.
Fushimono	Melancholic and lyrical songs in slow tempo.
Hiroimono	Heroic and typical narrative songs in variable tempo.
Naraimono	Songs that must be taught by teachers. Mastering 50-100 *hiramono* is pre-required.
Yomimono	Rhythmical Chinese poems. Mastering more than 50 songs is pre-required.
Enjōmono	
Gokumono	Mastering more than 50 songs is pre-required.
Soroimono	
Kanjō-no-maki	Beautiful melodies. Purifying oneself for three days is required.
Hiji	Secret music. Only limited people are allowed to learn through protocols and commitment.

●Major components of *heikyoku*:

Shirakoe	Narrative parts with chest voice commonly used in folk entertainment in Japan.
Kudoki	Basic, simple melodic phrases of syllabic, spoken language in the fourth interval.
Sage	Short phrases in *sanjū* (high register), *chūon* (middle register), and *origoe* (portamento) to conclude *kudoki* and connect it to the following melodious phrase.
Hiroi	Syllabic phrases to depict the battle or warrior in variable tempo.
Fushi	The melody parts in *fushimono* used for the sections in the ornate style where vibrato in three registers (*sanjū*, *chūon* and *shojū*) is effective.
Origoe	Sorrow and pathetic scenes. The name derives from downward portamento ornating every note.
Uta	Melodious music such as *ageuta*, *sageuta*, or *kuseuta* that accompanies narrative *waka*.

Genealogy of Modern *Biwa*

In the late 16th century, the lord Shimazu Tadayoshi of the Satsuma Domain ordered Fuchiwaki Ryōkō, the blind monk at Jōrakuin Temple in Satsuma, to compose "*biwa* songs", the instructive songs with a *biwa* accompaniment, in order to reanimate the morale of the warriors. The songs became popular as '*shifū-biwa* (*biwa* in the warrior class style)' among the warrior class, and then spread as '*machifū-biwa* (*biwa* in the townsman class style)' to the merchant class as well.

In the late 17th century, the blind monks who did not belong to the *tōdōza* rose up in judgment against *tōdōza*'s exclusive right for performing '*kuzure*', popular side shows to entertain the attendees after rituals, but they lost. The blind monks were not allowed to perform any public entertainment other than chants of *jishinkyō*, the sutras for praying for gods. Despite their public position, people were not satisfied if they did not play even a single popular song. At the time, the *shamisen* music began to become popular and the blind monks improved *biwa* to create similar effects to *shamisen*. They made the *biwa*'s body smaller and held it more vertically so that the left hand could move more freely. Also, they made bridges higher so that they could change the pitches by pressing a string down between bridges. As a result, more elaborate melodies became possible.

Combined with the simple and sturdy warrior class style *biwa* and the elegant and more sophisticated townsman style *biwa*, both derived from *biwa* songs, this instrumental improvement resulted in *satsuma-biwa* developed at the end of the Edo period and more lyric and melodious *chikuzen-biwa* developed in the Meiji period. When the new government was established, the Satsuma Domain warriors in great numbers came to Tokyo and they brought *satsuma-biwa* with them, which became popular in Tokyo. It was the beginning of the modern *biwa* music.

Though modern *biwa*, originated from blind monks' *biwa*, had already lost religious taste, it was still narrative music. The subjects of the songs were varied from the tales of the Heike, of course, to historical epics, revenge tales, and recent wars such as the Satsuma Rebellion and the Russo-Japanese War. But, the verses were mostly recited syllabically, and therefore, we, modern people, can easily follow the content. *Chikuzen-biwa*, which had undergone influence by *satsuma-biwa* and the *shamisen* music, influenced back to *satsuma-biwa*, and as a result, Nishiki-biwa School was derived from Kinshin School in the 1920's. This is how modern *biwa* music was formed and how the *biwa* turned into a melodious instrument from a rhythmic one.

■Genealogy of Modern *Biwa*

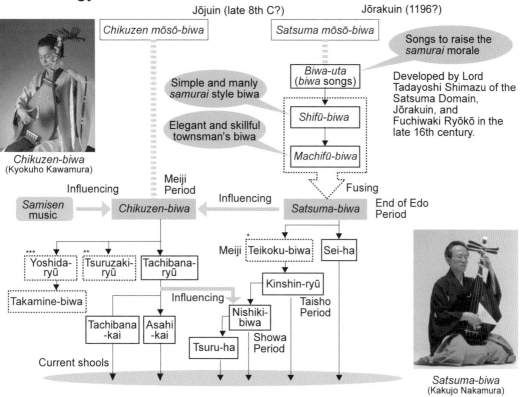

School	Founder	Description
Satsuma-biwa	Jinbei Ikeda	Integrated strong points of *shifū-biwa* and *machifū-biwa*.
Sei-ha	Myōju	In Satsuma (today's Kagoshima), he established *shifū-biwa* by observing the authentic heroic style of Shimazu Tadayoshi.
Kinshin-ryū	Kinshin Nagata	He established elegant and sophisticated style for town's people in Tokyo from simple and manly *satsuma-biwa*.
Nishiki-biwa	Kinjō Suitō	She established a new *satsuma* style with new skills, for instance, narrating to the accompaniment of *biwa*, by adopting *chikuzen-biwa*.
Tsuru-ha	Kinshi Tsuruta	She reformed the instrument and established a new style based on the technique of *nishiki-biwa*.
Chikuzen-biwa	Chijō Tachibana (a.k.a. Kyokuō I)	He established a new style by adapting *satsuma biwa-uta* (*biwa* songs) and *shamisen* songs into *chikuzen mōsō-biwa*.
Asahi-kai	Kyokuō III	Founded one of the three Tachibana-ryū schools established by Kyokuō I.
Tachibana-kai	Chijō Tachibana (a.k.a. Kyokusō I)	Son-in-law of Kyokuō I. Regarded as a *biwa* master. He developed 5-string *biwa* and founded the offshoot Asahi-kai.

*Satsuma's Teikoku-biwa was absorbed into Kinshin-ryū school.   **Chikuzen's Tsuruzaki-ryū school disappeared.   ***Yoshida-ryū school resolved into Takamine-biwa.

Biwa Music in Transition

As the *biwa* preserved in the Shōsōin Repository proves, *biwa* was certainly introduced along with *gagaku* in the 8th century. However, it is recorded in writing that the prototype of *mōsō-biwa*, the *biwa* of blind monks, had already been brought into Kyushu from China at the time of Emperor Kinmei (550 AD). Also that a blind monk in Kyushu had been summoned to the capital to pray for the god and perform the *biwa* for Emperor Genmei's accession to the throne at the Imperial Palace in 707. This event seems to lead to the ground-breaking ceremony for Enryaku-ji Temple's main hall by blind monks, which means that the *biwa-hōshi* had probably existed before the *gakubiwa* was introduced. If this record is correct, the *biwa* music, introduced before *gagaku*, could be the oldest after the ancient songs in Japan.

Heikyoku was complete with four factors: the subjects, that is, the tales of the Heike; vocalization of *shōmyō*; an instrument called *biwa*, and a chanter called *biwa-hōshi*. The *biwa-hōshi* were originally traveling minstrels but finally organized their powerful guild, *tōdōza*, and led *heike-biwa* to the peak. However, later, other performing arts such as *noh* and *kabuki*, adopting the essence of "The Tale of the Heike", became more popular than *heikyoku*. As a result, the blind performers of the *tōdōza* turned to the *shamisen* music such as *jōruri* but faced a crisis that the *biwa* schools barely survived in the Edo period.

After the Meiji Restoration, the techniques, the role, the style, and the subjects of the *biwa* music significantly transformed, adjusting itself to the changing society. New schools were established one after another. The *biwa* music has revived.

The shape of the history of the *biwa* music in the 2D chart is like a calabash with the narrow middle. During the end of the Edo period, which lies on the narrow middle, the tales of the Heike provided a lot of subjects to the literature as well as performing arts such as *noh*, *jōruri*, and *kabuki*. Also, the vocalization of *heikyoku* and the rendering style and the technique of *biwa* was succeeded by *shamisen* and developed into *shamisen*'s narrative music.

In recent years, "November Steps" for *shakuhachi* and *biwa* composed by late Japanese composer Toru Takemitsu introduced the sound of *biwa*, exotic to Western music, to the whole world.

One of the phrases recited by the *biwa-hōshi* is "the prosperous must decay" and *biwa* music witnessed the rise and fall of itself.

■History of *Biwa*

Asuka (538-710)
Mōsō-biwa introduced to Kyushu, the south region of Japan (550).

Nara (710-794)
- *Biwa* introduced to Japan (8C?). • Tōdai-ji Inaugural Ceremony of Great Buddha (752).
- Ground-breaking ceremony of the main hall of Enryaku-ji Temple performed by blind priests.
- Straight-necked, 5-string *biwa* offered to Shōsōin Repository. • Jōjuin Temple built in Chikuzen.

Heian (794-1185)
- *Shōmyō* introduced by Kūkai (806). *Gagaku* established (894). Semimaru portrayed in literature (late 9C).
- *Biwa-hōshi* appears (late 9C). The Heike falls (1185).
- Jōrakuin Temple moves to Satsuma (present Kagoshima prefecture). (1196)

Kamakura (1185-1333)
- *Heikyoku* appears (early 13C?). • Yukinaga and Shōbutsu probably collaborate (1221).
- "Jishō Monogatari" (regarded as the origin of the tales of the Heike) written (1240).
- War chronicles "The Tale of the Hogen War" and "The Tale of Heiji" written (late 13C). *Sarugaku-noh* began (mid-Kamakura).
- 2 *heikyoku* schools founded: Ichikata-ryū of Joichi and Yasaka-ryū of Jōgen (mid-13C).
- Yoshida Kenkō writes "Tsurezuregusa (Essays in Idleness)" (1331).
- "Genpei Seisuiki (The Rise and Fall of the Minamoto and Taira Clans)" written (late Kamakura).

Nanbokucho (1336-1392)
- Kakuichi completes the addendum "The Book of Kanjō" (early 14C).
- Chronicle "Azuma-kagami" compiled (late 13-14C). *Mugen-noh* completes (1380).
- Kakuichi becomes a *kengyō* (a grand master). Tōdōza established.

Muromachi (1336-1573)
- *Heikyoku* booming (15C)
- "Gikeiki" (a military epic about the life of Yoshitsune) written (early Muromachi).
- 6 books of "Enkyō-bon" on the Heike written. • 20 books of "Nagato-bon" transcribed (early 15C).
- "Illustrated Handscrolls of the Tale of the Heike" complete (mid-Muromachi).
- After Ōnin War, *heikyoku* loses popularity (1470). Kanshō Famine (1460).

Momoyama (1573-1603)
Ōnin War (1467).
Shamisen introduced (ca.1560).

Edo (1603-1868)
- *Heikyoku* players turn to *jōruri* (mid-16C). • Noh becomes official music for Government (1610).
- Tōdōza monopolizes *koto* and *shamisen* music (16C). *Jiuta* for *shamisen* established (1650).
- *Koto-kumikyoku* composed by Yatsuhashi Kengyō (1630).
- *Biwa-uta* established at request of Shimazu Tadayoshi (late 16C).
- *Kabuki* dance and *Jōruri* puppetry begin (early 17C).
- Takemoto Gidayū founds the puppet theater Takamoto-za (1684).
- 2 Offshoots from Shidō-ha of Ichikata-ryū: Hata-ryū and Maeda-ryū (17C).
- Dispute between Tōdōza and Mōsōza and the music activity of blind priests is banned (1674).
- *Heikyoku* music published. *Heikyoku* booming among intellectuals (mid-17C).
- 'Heike-mabushi' completes (1776).

Meiji Restoration (1868).

Meiji (1868-1912)
- *Satsuma-biwa* booming in Tokyo (ca, 1870). • Tōdōza abolished (1868).
- *Chikuzan-biwa* established (1887).

Taisho-Showa-Heisei (1912-)
- *Kinshin-ryū* founded (early 20C). Asahi-kai founded (1909).
- *Nishiki-biwa* founded (Showa). Tachibana-kai founded (1920).
- Toru Takemitsu's "November Steps" premiered in NY (1967). End of WWII (1945).

Shigin and *Gin'ei*: Recitation of Poems

Recitation of a poem is called '*shigin*' or '*gin'ei*'. Strictly speaking, *shigin* means recitation of a Chinese poem and *gin'ei* means recitation of any poems including Japanese *waka*. *Gin'ei* was derived from *biwa* songs chanted to the accompaniment of *satsuma-biwa* or *chikuzen-biwa*. A Chinese poem was quoted as the climax in a *biwa* song. The part became so popular that it became independent as *gin'ei*.

Chinese poetry is called '*kanshi*' in Japan. Actually it means Han poetry and poems written during the Tang Dynasty were especially well accepted. Chinese poetry was introduced into Japan in the Nara period. It became so popular that collections of the Chinese poems were compiled by the Japanese. In *gagaku*, recitation of Chinese poems became the vocal music, *rōei*.

According to the generally accepted theory, the present *shigin* style was established by the students of Rai Sanyō (1780-1832), historian, *kanshi* poet, and literary scholar. Though this theory is actually not proven, it is true that in their time, the end of the Edo period, the patriots sympathized with the indignant lamentation over the evils of the times expressed by Chinese poems and recitation of them became very popular among patriotic warriors. When they recited a Chinese poem during a banquet, for instance, they often danced with a drawn sword, which was the origin of the sword dance called '*kenbu*'.

During the Taisho period, those heroic poems were unpopular but got promoted during the imminent war of the early Showa period for morale encouragement for the youth since their patriotic nature matched the Japanese national spirit. After the Second World War, *shigin* was avoided for a while on the rebound of patriotism but is gradually gaining back in popularity. Current *gin'ei* has a tendency of becoming public entertainment and all kinds of poems, in addition to Chinese and Japanese poems, are recited. It is also common to combine it with a popular song or a folk song, and to recite a poem to the accompaniment of a musical instrument.

The recitation of a Chinese poem and the sword dance used to be a pair. But today, *gin'ei* is occasionally paired, as a show, with flower arrangement, calligraphy, tea ceremonies and so on.

Traditional Japanese Music at a Glance

■*Shigin*

Shigin is a performance of reciting poems with unique intonation.
It is often called *gin'ei* but they are not necessarily the same.

→ Differences between *shigin* and *gin'ei*:

Shigin recites Chinese poems read in Japanese.

Gin'ei was derived from *biwa-uta* (*biwa* songs) which recite Japanese *waka* or Chinese poems read in Japanese.

●Chinese poetry:

It flourished in the Tang Dynasty period. Many famous poets emerged such as Li Po, Du Fu, Wang Wei and Bai Juyi. It was introduced to Japan in the Nara period.

- Chinese poetry became popular in Japan in the Heian Period. New poems were written by the Japanese and collections and anthologies were compiled.

- "Kaifūsō": The earliest anthology of Chinese poems written by the Japanese, containing 124 poems by 67 poets.

Vocal music in the Palace	Poetry reading	Only for *waka*
	Rōei	Reciting Chinese poems and *waka*

Influences

Formalized in the Meiji period.

●Birth of *shigin*:

In the late Edo period, the Tokugawa government built Shōhei School. The students of the school recited Chinese poems written by Rai Sanyō, the Japanese scholar, with melodies.

The patriot danced with a sword to *shigin* reciting at a drinking party, which became a "sword dance".
(Byakko Festival, Fukushima)

Indignant *shigin* became popular among patriots.

Schools
- Kangien-ryū (Oita)
- Jishūkan-ryū (Kumamoto)
- Kusaka-ryū (Yamaguchi)
- Seidō-ryū (Tokyo)

In the Meiji period. Influencing to: *Satsuma-biwa* and *Chikuzen-biwa*

 Biwa-uta

A boom — Reciting became independent.

In the Taisho period, Japan was democratized. *Shigin* schools declined.

In early Showa period, *shigin* reciters, Kimura Gakufū and Yamada Katsuyoshi, emerged.

Gin'ei — The number of female *shigin* chanters was increased (turned from *biwa* musicians).

During WWII, *shigin* was used to encourage young student soldiers.

Popular entertainment

After WWII, due to the relation to militarism, *shigin* declined.

●Collaboration:
(*Gin'ei* and other arts)

- Poetry dance
- Flower arrangement
- Tea ceremony
- Calligraphy
- Storytelling

Pop songs / Folksongs / Accompaniment + *Gin'ei* + Chinese poem / *Waka* / Haiku / Modern poetry / Western poetry / Prose poetry
Crossover music

Shigin as performing art is gradually reviving today.

The Nature of *Kanshi*

Kanshi, Chinese poems, have strict norms for the number of the characters and phrases unlike the prose style lyrics of today's popular songs.

The example on the right page is "Spring Dawn" by the Tang Dynasty poet, Meng Haoran, a poem well known in Japan. The form of the poem is called '*jueju* (*zekku* in Japanese)' and consists of quadripartite structure: introduction, development, turn and conclusion. Each line consists of five or seven syllables: the five-syllable-long form is called '*wujue*', and the seven- syllable-long form '*qijue*' in Chinese. If there are eight lines, four couplets are in the quadripartite structure.

Because the structure of Japanese is different from that of Chinese, if the poem is read as is, it is not well understood even if each Chinese character still conveys its meaning. As a result, punctuation and guiding marks are used for rendering Chinese into Japanese. The example on the right page shows the comparison between the unpunctuated Chinese texts and their renderings in Japanese. Reciting the Japanese renderings is *shigin*.

The system of the *shigin* music, shown on the right page, is completely different for each school. For example, there are the staff notation without notes, the lines to show ups and downs of pitches, and the nine-line staff notation. What is common among those systems is that the music shows no absolute pitches but the relative ones of high, middle, and low.

Some systems precisely indicate ups and downs of the pitches. However, as long as the chanter keeps "the principle" of the breath locations, the emphasized vowels, and the expressions, it is believed to be better for him/her to chant more freely without focusing on exact melody lines.

Recently, it is a common practice that an instrument accompanies the chanter as a foil to the vocal part. It also determines the pitches and leads the melody lines for the chanter. The melody of *shigin* is in a minor scale in Western terms. *Shigin* is characteristic of the pathetic and melancholic feeling. This pathetic sense is the essence of *shigin* and strikes a chord in the heart of Japanese.

■Chinese Poetry and Recitation

●**Structure:**

Jueju	Poem in four lines (quatrain)	
Lushi	Poem in eight lines	
Pailu	Long poem in *lushi* form	

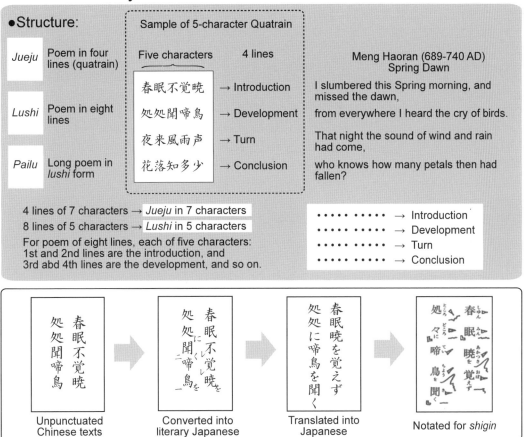

Sample of 5-character Quatrain

Five characters — 4 lines

春眠不覚暁 → Introduction
処処聞啼鳥 → Development
夜来風雨声 → Turn
花落知多少 → Conclusion

Meng Haoran (689-740 AD)
Spring Dawn

I slumbered this Spring morning, and missed the dawn,
from everywhere I heard the cry of birds.

That night the sound of wind and rain had come,
who knows how many petals then had fallen?

4 lines of 7 characters → *Jueju* in 7 characters
8 lines of 5 characters → *Lushi* in 5 characters
For poem of eight lines, each of five characters:
1st and 2nd lines are the introduction, and
3rd abd 4th lines are the development, and so on.

•••••••••• → Introduction
•••••••••• → Development
•••••••••• → Turn
•••••••••• → Conclusion

| Unpunctuated Chinese texts | Converted into literary Japanese | Translated into Japanese | Notated for *shigin* |

●**Method for reciting *shigin*:**

- The pitches depend on the chanter (basically, male in D minor and female in G minor).
- In many cases, the song or phrase ends with the tonic (Mi).
- Pausing on the tonic or auxilary tonic at the ∟ mark in the notation and takes a breath (see the notated version above).
- Breathing three times in two lines.
- Melismatically elaborating the last vowel of a verse.
- Reciting with a clear voice and correct pronunciation.
- Expressing the meaning and feeling of the poem.

●**Basic eight notes** (in a pentatonic scale)

Lower register	Middle register	Upper register
△	▷	▽
La Ti Do	Mi Fa	La Ti Do

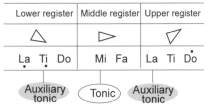

* There are passing tones between the core notes mentioned above. The notation system varies for each school.

●**Accompaniment:**

Modern *shigin* recites to an accompaniment. Since *shigin* is not a rhythmic music, the accompaniment should be improvised by following or leading the chanter and placing a counter melody between verses. Both Japanese and Western instruments are used, for instance, *shakuhachi*, *koto*, *shamisen*, *taiko* drums, winds, piano, guitar, accordion, harp, violin, cello.

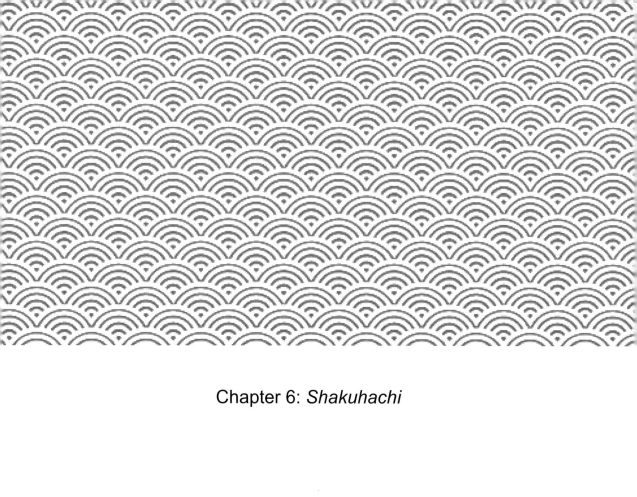

Chapter 6: *Shakuhachi*

The Roots of *Shakuhachi*

According to one established theory, *shakuhachi* descended from a Chinese bamboo flute, *dongxiao*, the origin of which goes back to the end-blown reed flute, *sebi*, seen on the murals in Egypt around 2000 B.C., or *nay* in West Asia. They were introduced to China during the Han Dynasty via the Silk Road or India and the reed body was replaced with bamboo in China. According to another theory, it could be derived from the ancient, native Chinese vertical bamboo flute, called *yue* or *xiao*. The "Book of Tang", the first classic work about the Tang Dynasty, states that a musician named Lucun improved end-blown flutes known as *chiba* (or *shakuhachi* in Japanese) which means "one foot and eight tenths (about 30cm plus 24.5cm)" (see the right page). This episode is generally accepted to be true.

This end-blown bamboo flute was introduced along with the Tang music to Japan during the Nara period (710-794). However, it was recorded in writing that Prince Shōtoku (573-621) played a flute, which was the tribute from Korea during the Asuka period (538-710, or 592-645). Eight original flutes introduced in the Nara period are preserved in the Shōsōin Repository of Tōdai-ji Temple and another in Hōryū-ji Temple. They are called '*shōsōin shakuhachi*' or '*kodai* (ancient) *shakuhachi*'. Some of the *kodai shakuhachi* in the Shōsōin Repository are not made of bamboo, but of stone, jade or ivory and are engraved with imitations of bamboo nodes.

In comparison to ancient *shakuhachi*, modern *shakuhachi*, the number and shapes of the finger holes, the angle of the blowing hole, the number of the nodes, and which part of bamboo is used are different. Interestingly, *kodai shakuhachi* are generally shorter than modern *shakuhachi*. This is because the unit of measurement of the Tang Dynasty when the *kodai shakuhachi* was created is different from that of present Japan. A Chinese foot at the time was 24.5 centimeters, equivalent to 0.81 of a Japanese foot (30.3 centimeters).

In China, the *chiba* lineage created by Lucun did not survive and no successor uses the name. It survived and evolved as *shakuhachi* in Japan and became an important part of the Japanese culture.

The Roots of *Shakuhachi*

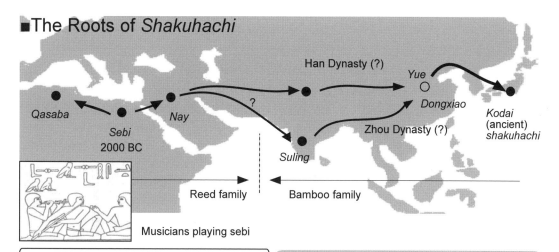

Musicians playing sebi

●Lucun's *Shakuhachi*

According to "The Book of Tang", vol. 29 "Life of Lucun", a Chinese musician named Lucun created end-blown flutes in twelve sizes based on the twelve pitches of the Chinese chromatic scale in the Jougan period (627-649) of the Tang Dynasty. The longest one for the first note of the scale, *huangzhong* (*ōshiki* in Japanese), was 1 foot (*shaku*) and 8 (*hachi*) tenths in length of Chinese measurements from which the name *shakuhachi* was derived.

●*Shakuhachi* introduced to Japan

Three theories how eight *shakuhachi* in the Shōsōin Repository came to Japan:
1) Four *shakuhachi* were presented by King Uija of Baekje (641-662) of Korea,
2) They came to Japan along with *sankangaku* (music from three Korean kingdoms) and *tōgaku* (music from Tang) in the 7-8th century,
3) Musicians and musical instruments, including *shakuhachi*, from various Asian countries came for the Tōdai-ji Temple Inaugural Ceremony of Great Buddha (752).

●*Kodai shakuhachi* preserved in the Shōsōin Repository

	Material	Size (cm)	Characteristic
1)	Chinese bamboo	43.7	Carved exterior
2)	White jade	34.35	Imitation of bamboo with three joints
3)	Chinese bamboo	38.25	
4)	Chinese bamboo	38.5	Crafted with cherry bark
5)	Agalmatolite	36.1	Carved three joints
6)	Ivory	35.2	Carved three joints
7)	Chinese bamboo	39.3	Inscribed "Todaiji"
8)	Chinese bamboo	40.9	Slightly thicker than others

An old Chinese foot was 24.5 cm, equivalent to a 0.81 Japanese foot (30.3 cm).

Comparison of *kodai* and modern *shakuhachi*

	Kodai Shakuhachi	Modern *Shakuhachi* (in D)
Holes	6 (5 in front, 1 in the back)	5 (4 in front, 1 in the back)
Hole shape	Oval	Circular
Length (cm)	34.4 - 43.7	54.5
Diameter (cm)	Average 2.3	Approx. 3.5
Material	Bamboo, stone, tusk	Japanese timber bamboo only
Nodes	3	7
Mouth shape	Rounded	Diagonally sharp
Reinforcement	None	Reinforced with ivory, etc.
Tube end	Between joints	Uncrafted root

Legends of Japanese *Shakuhachi*

There are five types of *shakuhachi*: *kodai shakuhachi*, *tenpuku* and *hitoyogiri* (which are no longer used), *fuke shakuhachi* which is still used, and modern *shakuhachi* with extra holes, the current standard. *Fuke shakuhachi* and modern *shakuhachi* look almost the same but they have different timbre and volume due to the different internal structures of the pipe. *Fuke shakuhachi* is often called *kokan* (old pipe) to be distinguished from the modern one.

Kodai shakuhachi was originally a member of the ensemble in playing Tang music, the music imported from China to Japan. It was played by the nobles, as part of their culture between the Nara and the Heian periods, but became obsolete during the process of the *gagaku* reform at the end of the Heian period. The reason for its decline was probably due to reducing the number of players and similar musical instruments in the *gagaku* ensemble. At any rate, *kodai shakuhachi* disappeared from center stage.

By the Kamakura period (1185–1333), street performers, such as *dengaku* performers who appeared as monks but often were not real priests, began to blow an end-blown flute. It was similar to *shakuhachi* and gradually popularized. Among those performers were mendicant monks. This flute was called *hitoyogiri*, the ancestor of today's *shakuhachi*. *Hitoyogiri* means a piece of bamboo 'cut from a single node'. It has five holes, rather than six of *kodai shakuhachi*. There is an unconfirmed legend that a Chinese Zen monk named Roan introduced *hitoyogiri* to Japan from China. *Hitoyogiri* was very popular until the middle of the Edo period (1603-1868). Soon, connected with the Fuke sect, a branch of Zen Buddhism, the mendicant monks and *rōnin* (wandering lordless *samurai* warriors) became the mendicant Zen priests called *komusō*. They played a flute larger than *hitoyogiri*, which was called *fuke shakuhachi*. As *fuke shakuhachi* was in its golden age, *hitoyogiri*, in contrast declined and almost disappeared by the end of the Edo period.

As the *komusō* became more socially influential, they claimed *shakuhachi* to be a sacred religious device. As a result, it was forbidden for the general public to play and was also excluded from instrumental ensembles. This restriction lasted until the Fuke sect was abolished in the Meiji Restoration in 1866.

However, despite the restriction and the official stance that it was sacred, in reality common people played *fuke shakuhachi* in the Kyoto-Osaka region where it was very popular. When the Fuke sect was abolished and the ban on *fuke shakuhachi* was lifted, the general public openly enjoyed *shakuhachi* as a musical instrument. It became popular both in art music and at home in the Meiji period.

■ *Shakuhachi* adapted to Japanese Culture

Old *shakuhachi*				Modern *shakuhachi*	
Kodai shakuhachi	*Tenpuku*	*Hitoyogiri*	Holes Joints	*Fuke shakuhachi*	*Shakuhachi* w/ 7 or more holes
6 holes, 3 joints	5 holes, 3 joints	5 holes, 1 joint	Holes Joints	5 holes, 7 joints	7 - 9 holes, 7 joints
1.8 foot (Chinese foot, 43.7 cm)	Little less than 1 *shaku* (30.3 cm)	1.11 *shaku* (33.6 cm)	Size	1.8 *shaku* (54.5 cm)	1.8 *shaku* (54.5 cm)
Chinese bamboo (stone, tusk)	Fishpole bamboo	Japanese timber bamboo stalk	Material	Japanese timber bamboo root end	Japanese timber bamboo root end
Asuka (538-710)	Muromachi (1336-1573)	Kamakura (1185-1333)	Emergence	Edo (1603-1868)	Taisho (1912-1926)
Gagaku but discarded in the Heian period	Solo and accompaniment for folk songs	Solo and accompaniment for *noh* songs	Usage	*Suizen*, mendicant, *sankyoku*	Wide range from *sankyoku* to modern works
• Kept in Shōsōin Repository. • Came to Japan along with *tōgaku* or as the present from China.	• Became popular only in the Satsuma region. • Volume is soft. • Origin is unknown.	• Widely used for the music in those days. • Introduced to Japan by Roan.	History	• Was a religious device of the mendicant Fuke priest. • Similar to modern *shakuhachi*.	• With additional holes, a choromatic scale now possible. • Stable pitches, easier fingerings.

● Modern *shakuhachi* developed from *fuke shakuhachi*:

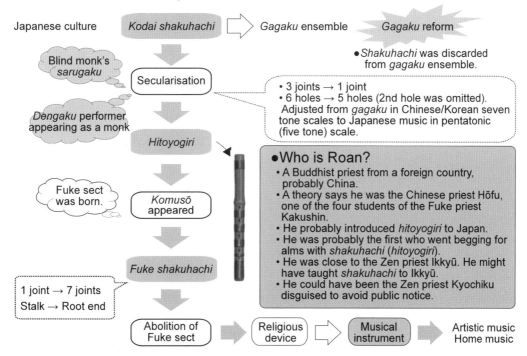

131

Mysterious Cult: Fuke Sect and *Komusō*

The Fuke sect belonged to the Rinzai sect, a branch of Zen Buddhism. Abolished during the Meiji Restoration, it is now defunct. The method of the practice of the Fuke sect was not usual Zen meditation but blowing *shakuhachi*, which was called *suizen*. In other words, blowing *shakuhachi* was the Zen training and replaced sutra chanting.

A legend says that the Chinese Zen monk Roan brought *hitoyogiri*, the predecessor of *shakuhachi*, with him when he came to Japan. An unconfirmed story is that Ikkyū, a famous Japanese Zen monk, suggested Roan to blow *shakuhachi* as a sign of a monk's begging since Roan could not speak Japanese. At its prime, there were more than seventy Fuke temples mostly in the Kantō region, the middle part of Japan. Ichigatsu-ji Temple in present Chiba, Reihō-ji Temple in present Tokyo, and Myōan-ji Temple in Kyoto in the later period, became the head temples of the Fuke sect, functioning as government-sect liaison temples. Those temples belonged to the Rinzai sect.

The mendicant Zen priests of the Fuke sect were called '*komusō*'. They wore a sedge basket-like hat, *tengai*, to hide their unshaved head, and carried an alms box marked with characters of '*myō-an* (light and darkness)' hung on the chest, blowing *shakuhachi* for meditation, while wandering in all parts of the country. Before connection with the Fuke sect, they were called *komosō*, ordinary beggars who played *shakuhachi* to beg. The figure 1 on the right page shows the beggar who wandered carrying *komo*, the bedclothes made of straw, described as "a beggar in rags" in "Tsurezuregusa (Essays in Idleness)" written by the monk Yoshida Kenkō between 1330 and 1332.

Most, if not all, *komusō* were often described as a good guy or a spy of the Tokugawa government in movies and novels, but were hooligans in reality. In the Edo period, there were a lot of wandering lordless *samurai* warriors nationwide who often faked themselves as *komusō* and made trouble when their excessive demands were not met in the village where they did monk's begging. As a result, the villagers offered rice and money to the local Fuke temples to avoid such trouble with them. The above-mentioned legendary monk Ikkyū, regarded as the father of *komusō*, was in fact a free-spirited depraved monk, not a ready-witted, cute novice described in children's stories.

■Fuke Sect and *Komusō*

Ikkyū Sōjun, the Zen priest
(portrayed in 15th C)

Fuke Sect: One of the schools of the Rinzai sect, Zen Buddhism.
Suizen: The practice of Zen by blowing *shakuhachi*.

Zen → Fuke Sect, Shakuhachi, Komusō

Usage of *fuke shakuhachi*

- Services: *Shakuhachi* was played with recited sutra for services.
- Mendicancy: *Shakuhachi* was played for mendicancy and offerings are regarded as good deeds.
- Zen training: *Suizen* is as important as Zen meditation.

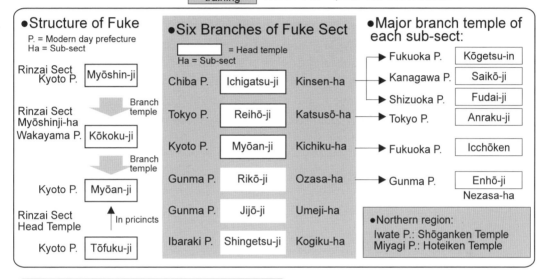

●**Structure of Fuke**
P. = Modern day prefecture
Ha = Sub-sect

- Rinzai Sect, Kyoto P. — Myōshin-ji
  ↓ Branch temple
- Rinzai Sect Myōshinji-ha, Wakayama P. — Kōkoku-ji
  ↓ Branch temple
- Kyoto P. — Myōan-ji
  ↑ In pricincts
- Rinzai Sect Head Temple, Kyoto P. — Tōfuku-ji

●**Six Branches of Fuke Sect**
☐ = Head temple
Ha = Sub-sect

Prefecture	Temple	Sub-sect
Chiba P.	Ichigatsu-ji	Kinsen-ha
Tokyo P.	Reihō-ji	Katsusō-ha
Kyoto P.	Myōan-ji	Kichiku-ha
Gunma P.	Rikō-ji	Ozasa-ha
Gunma P.	Jijō-ji	Umeji-ha
Ibaraki P.	Shingetsu-ji	Kogiku-ha

●**Major branch temple of each sub-sect:**

- ▶ Fukuoka P. — Kōgetsu-in
- ▶ Kanagawa P. — Saikō-ji
- ▶ Shizuoka P. — Fudai-ji
- ▶ Tokyo P. — Anraku-ji
- ▶ Fukuoka P. — Icchōken
- ▶ Gunma P. — Enhō-ji

Nezasa-ha

●Northern region:
Iwate P.: Shōganken Temple
Miyagi P.: Hoteiken Temple

●***Komusō*:**

- Buddhist priests of the Fuke sect, Zen Buddhism. Their training includes *suizen* and mendicancy. Their instrument, *fuke shakuhachi*, was regarded as a religious device, and was not allowed for ordinary people to play.
- In 1614, the Tokugawa government issued "Keichō no Okitegaki (Ordinance of Keichō Era)" regarding the rights and duties of the Fuke sect and its members. The special privileges granted to the *komusō* included freedom of travel, a monopoly on the use of *shakuhachi*, and the right to bear arms, hide a face with a basket hat, and protect the *samurai* who killed someone and sought refugee at a Fuke temple.
- They kept these expedient privileges during the Edo period but actually they were not so different from a gang of rowdies.

●**Changes of *komusō*'s attire**

1. *Komosō*, a beggar with *komo* (a straw mat).
2. *Komusō* of the mid-Edo period by Katsushika Hokusai (1760-1849).
3. *Komusō* of the Showa period.

Legends of Fuke Sect

The Fuke Zen in Japan is attributed to the monk Kakushin (1207-1298), posthumously known as Hottō Kokushi, who studied Zen Buddhism in China. He was initiated into the playing of *shakuhachi* as a form of meditation from Chōsan, the 16th generation disciple of the founder of the Zen Buddhism in China, Zhenzhou Puhua. Kakushin founded Saihō-ji temple (later renamed Kōkoku-ji) in Kii of Wakayama Prefecture when he returned to Japan. He is noted for bringing the *shakuhachi* from China, and also for introducing the process of *miso*, fermented soybean paste. Kii is famous for manufacturing *miso* today.

According to the legend of Myōan-ji temple, which has a lineage of Kōkoku-ji, the Zen monk Kichiku Zenshi, one of the disciples of Kakushin, was inspired by the exquisite music he heard in a dream, and composed *shakuhachi* pieces "Mukaiji" and "Kokū" at Mount Asama in Ise, and founded Myōan-ji temple in Kyoto. Another legend says that the monks Kinsen and Katsusō, the disciples of the monk Hōfu, one of the four Chinese Buddhist laymen who came to Japan accompanying Kakushin, founded Ichigatsu-ji temple and Reihō-ji temple respectively in the Kantō region. In addition, there is a strange story that Kichiku and Hōfu, both mentioned above, were actually Roan who came from China and lived in Kyoto. Those legends with regard to the Fuke sect are not so convincing although interesting. The Fuke sect was probably established in the Kan'ei era, about 400 years after Kakushin's return home. The Myōan-ji temple was supposed to be built in the same era. It does not make sense that the sect was established in the time when Kichiku, who was Kakushin's pupil, lived. In his "Historical Views of Kinko School Shakuhachi" (1939), a scholar Chikuzen Nakatsuka, who studied about these legends at the beginning of the Showa period, concludes that most of those anecdotes were fictitious, made up for adding to the authority of the Fuke sect.

The reasons why those legends are not believable are: a Zen monk called Puhua (Fuke in Japanese) did exist in China, but the persuasion called Fuke did not; it is unknown whether or not a monk called Kichiku existed; there was no evidence that Kakushin played *shakuhachi*, and so on. Those legends are simply fictions. They were made up to authorize *komusō*, who were actually a bunch of rogue *samurai* warriors, and to cover up the fact that they were beggars. Such legends were inevitable to religions or cults and those fictitious anecdotes of the Fuke sect were believed until the late Edo period.

■Legends of Fuke Sect

> **True or False?**
>
> There are many legends regarding the origin of the Fuke sect. But they were probably made up later to lend authority to the sect.
>
> ● "Kyotaku Denki Kokujikai"
> (History of Kyotaku Japanese Translation)
> Compiled by Yamamoto Morihide (1795)

Zhenzhou Puhua, the Chinese Chán (Zen) master, begged for alms with bells (circa 9 C, Tang Dynasty).
↓
His disciple Chang Po followed him with a bamboo flute (*kyotaku*).
↓
Chôsan, the 16th head priest of the Chinese Chán, taught Zen to Japanese student priest Kakushin.
↓
After finishing his study in China, Kakushin came back home in 1254.
↓
He then founded Kōkoku-ji and established Fuke Zen.

Two legends after Kakushin's home-coming

● "Kyoreizan Engi" (1735)
(Origin of Myōan-ji Temple)

- Master Kakushin taught *kyotaku*.
  ↓
- His disciple Kichiku (later Master Kyochiku) composed "Mukaiji" and "Kokū" inspired by a divine dream at Kokūdō Temple.

  Myōan-ji was built in Kyoto.

● "Shakuhachi Hikki" (1813)
(Notes on Shakuhachi) by Miyaji Ikkan

- Kakushin returns home from China with four Buddhist laymen.

  Hōfu, Kokusa, Risei, and Sōjo

  Hōfu's disciples — Kinsen founded Ichigatsu-ji in Chiba.

  — Katsusō founded Reihō-ji in Tokyo.

●Chikuzen Nakatsuka's research on Fuke and *shakuhachi*:

Chikuzen Nakatsuka, the scholar and performer, researched the historical record on *shakuhachi* thoroughly and wrote numerous articles in 1936-39. They were compiled in the 1979 publication "Kinko-ryū Shakuhachi Shikan (Historical Views of Kinko School Shakuhachi)". According to him:

- Kōkoku-ji Temple in Wakayama preserves Kakushin's letters and diaries. There is no writing about *shakuhachi*.
- The existence of Kichiku (later Master Kyochiku) is unknown.
- Hōfu and other Buddhist laymen were merely house servants and should not have played *shakuhachi* well.
- Myōan-ji Temple was built in the Edo period (1603-1868), not in the Kamakura period (1185-1333).
- Until the early Edo period, Myōan-ji Temple was merely accommodation for *komosō*.
- There was no Chinese counterpart of Japanese Fuke Sect.
- The music "Kyorei" that Kakushin was supposedly taught does not exist in China.
- Chinese Chang Po and Chôsan were Buddhist laymen and not priests.
- "Keichō no Okitegaki" supposedly written by Tokugawa Ieyasu himself does not exist.
- There are many copies of "Okitegaki" which are discrepant in content.
- "Kyotaku Denki Kokujikai" was a translation of a Chinese book but the original book does not exist (later the original book was found in the Tozan School archive but its authenticity is questionable).

Kurosawa Kinko, Father of *Shakuhachi* Music, and Other Schools

(Note: In this page all names are written with the family name followed by the given name.) Though the reliability about the legends of the origin of the Fuke sect and the behavior of *komusō* are questionable, some *komusō* were earnest and seriously tried to explore the world of *shakuhachi*. They improved the musical quality of *fuke shakuhachi*.

The two main Fuke temples in the Kantō region were so far from Edo (present Tokyo) that training centers were established inside Edo by the middle of the 18th century. Kurosawa Kinko was installed as the instructor in the centers. While teaching, he collected the pieces handed down by *komusō* all over the nation and established thirty-six pieces as *honkyoku*, which stands for original pieces (the rest are called *gaikyoku*). Then, he manufactured instruments and organized the rendering style, the notation system, and the order of the training works, and later founded the Kinko School.

In the Kyoto-Osaka region, Ozaki Shinryū maintained the authentic Myōan-ji style based on *honkyoku* while his pupil Kondō Sōetsu established his own Sōetsu School centering on *gaikyoku*, but it ceased without any immediate successor. The Shōchō School of Sōetsu's pupil also ceased without a successor but the Chikuho School by another pupil survived succeeding Sōetsu's style. Finally, Nakao Tozan who studied with Ryūkichi Komori, the pupil of Sōetsu, emerged and contributed to significantly develop *shakuhachi* music by creating new pieces, inventing a new notation system, and developing an ornamental accompaniment style called *kaete* (or *kaede*).

Nakao Tozan was not *komusō*. Common people other than *komusō* were not allowed to play *shakuhachi*, a religious device, but actually they learned *shakuhachi* and played it with other musical instruments at the end of the Edo period. The training center at Asakusa in Edo, where Kurosawa Kinko was teaching, even issued a license called '*honsoku*', which means that the official stance that *shakuhachi* was a religious device had been in effect already at the time.

At the Meiji Restoration, the Fuke sect, as well as *komusō*, was abolished. However, seventeen years after the abolition order, the lineage of the Myōan School in Kyoto revived as the Myōan Society focusing on traditional *honkyoku* against all odds by the efforts of Higuchi Taizan who learned the Seien School's *shakuhachi* at Fudai-ji temple in Shizuoka. During the Meiji period, the new *shakuhachi* schools, such as Kinko, Tozan, Ueda, and Chikuho, were at the height of prosperity. However, Myōan Taizan School, the most prominent sect in the Myōan Society, maintained the strictly conventional style.

■Fuke Temples and *Shakuhachi* Schools

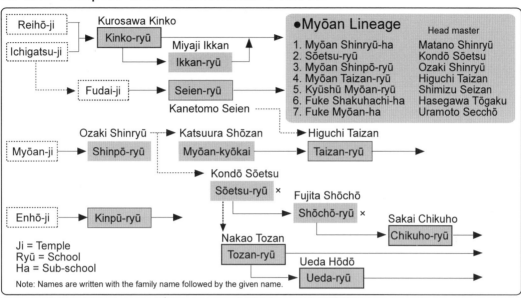

Ji = Temple
Ryū = School
Ha = Sub-school

Note: Names are written with the family name followed by the given name.

School	Founder	Description
Kinko-ryū	Kurosawa Kinko (1710-71)	After the Fuke sect abolished, the school focused on *sankyoku* with *koto* and *shamisen*. His *honkyoku* deviated from Buddhism and became more artistic. His *gaikyoku* tends to cohere with *shamisen* and *koto* music.
Seien-ryū	Kanetomo Seien (1818-95)	They were based at the cultural city Nagoya, prospering in *gaikyoku* with unique soft and mellow sounds. Descendant from Fudai-ji and the ancestor of Taizan-ryū.
Taizan-ryū	Higuchi Taizan (1856-1915)	Taizan of Myōan-kyōkai became the master of Seien-ryū and then took over Myōan-ryū in place of Shinpō-ryū. Focused on *honkyoku* with straight and bright sounds. Formal name is Myōan Taizan-ryū.
Chikuho-ryū	Sakai Chikuho (1892-1984)	Chikuho started a new school with *gaikyoku* from Shōchō-ryū and *honkyoku* from Sōetsu and Shinpō-ryū after a quarrel with his master Fujita. Using of the staff notation, he has both modern and traditional sides.
Tozan-ryū	Nakao Tozan (1876-1956)	Although Tozan studied with Komori Ryūkichi of Sōetsu-ryū, he mostly learned by himself and founded a new school. He developed a notation system and wrote new works and arrangements with virtuosity.
Ueda-ryū	Ueda Hōdō (1892-1974)	Hōdō took the top post of Tozan-ryū at 19 but was expelled due to his new work without master's permission. He started a new school with his disciples. He composed a hundred *honkyoku* as well as *gaikyoku*.
Kinpū-ryū	Yoshizaki Hachiya (1798-1835)	Hachiya learned Nezasa-ha *shakuhachi* by the order of his lord. His Kinpū-ryū with a unique performing style was popular in Tsugaru (the northern region) as the taste of warriors independent from Fuke Sect.
Shinpō-ryū	Ozaki Shinryū (1820-88)	Was the successor of Myōan-ryū faithful to classical *honkyoku* and the religious nature. Myōan-kyōkai was established by the effort of the disciple Shōzan, but the school was taken over by Taizan-ryū.
Sōetsu-ryū	Kondō Sōetsu (1821-67)	Sōetsu studied with Ozaki Shinryū of Shinpō-ryū. He started his own school with his *gaikyoku* and younger Katsuura Shōzan's *honkyoku*. There was no direct successor and Chikuho-ryū was its descendant.
Shōchō-ryū	Fujita Shōchō (1710-71)	Shōchō of Sōetsu-ryū founded his own school focusing on *gaikyoku* but did not have a direct successor. He quarreled with his disciple Sakai Chikuho who composed new works without his permission.

Splendid Transformation and New World of *Shakuhachi*

The *fuke shakuhachi* in its golden age, replacing the predecessor *hitoyogiri*, was on the verge of a crisis due to the order to abolition the Fuke sect under the Meiji Restoration in 1866. It is generally thought that the new Meiji government tried to get rid of *komusō* who were subordinates as spies for the Shogunate, the previous ruler of Japan, but it might be inevitable to abolish them since many of *komusō* were nuisances. Use of *shakuhachi* as only a religious device was also abolished.

It was the Kinko School masters such as Kodō Araki and Icchō Yoshida who rescued the *shakuhachi* from the crisis and reinstated it as a pure musical instrument in the society, independent from the Fuke sect. In addition to the efforts of these two, despite the fact that it was an official stance that *shakuhachi* was a religious device with only priests were allowed to play, it was already spread among common people. The drawing on the right page shows how common people enjoyed instrumental trio music called *sankyoku* at the time. *Sankyoku* is an ensemble of the most typical three Japanese instruments, *shamisen*, *koto* and *shakuhachi*.

After the verge of extinction following the abolition of the Fuke sect, *shakuhachi* prospered at once like a blooming flower. As if it were a rebellion to the suppression in the past, new schools were established one after another exploring the new boundary of *shakuhachi* music. It was the modernization of *shakuhachi*. Each school developed its own style by improving the instrument and the musical notation system, analyzing and studying established works and theories, and creating new works.

The schools in Kyoto-Osaka region, especially, Tozan School, a novel school established by Tozan Nakao who was unrelated to the Fuke sect, were keener to the new trends than others. Tozan Nakao actively joined the *sankyoku* performances and befriended Michio Miyagi, one of the most novel *koto* players and composers in history, expanding the possibility of *shakuhachi* music. He is credited with sowing the seeds of *shin nihon ongaku* (new Japanese music in 1920's), *shin hōgaku* (new traditional style Japanese music in 1930's), and *gendai hōgaku* (contemporary traditional Japanese music after 1950's) of later generations. At present, many *shakuhachi* schools established after the abolition of Fuke sect are taking an active role in a wide range of music from the traditional style to the Western style. On the other hand, the lineage of Myōan School and Kinpū School has obstinately handed down the *fuke shakuhachi* style and has performed only the original works called *honkyoku*. In addition, there is a genre called "folk *shakuhachi*" in which *shakuhachi* is used for the accompaniment of folk songs and *gin'ei* which further expands the boundary of *shakuhachi* music.

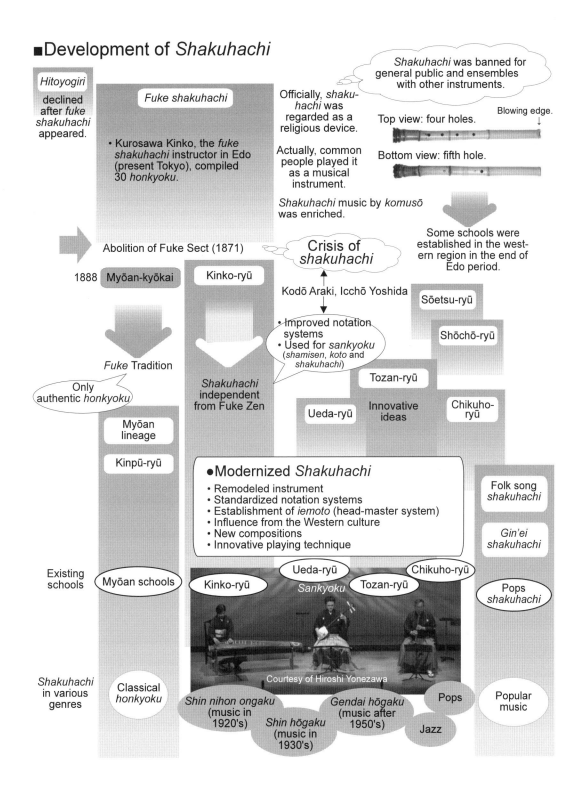

Shakuhachi World Reflecting Times: Honkyoku and Gaikyoku

The word 'honkyoku' is a shakuhachi term which stands for "the original shakuhachi works", that is, the music only for shakuhachi. And 'gaikyoku' refers to "all kinds of music with shakuhachi other than honkyoku", that is, instrumental or vocal music accompanied by or arranged for shakuhachi. Among honkyoku, the collection handed down in the Fuke sect is specifically called the 'orthodox honkyoku'. Moreover, three orthodox honkyoku works, "Kyorei (Empty Bells)", "Mukaiji (Flute on Misty Sea)" and "Kokū (Empty Space)" receive special treatment and "Shika no Tōne (Distant Call of Deer)" and "Tsuru no Sugomori (Nesting of the Cranes)" are regarded as the perfection of beauty. Honkyoku is not necessarily a solo work. Some are duets.

However, the concept of honkyoku changed after new schools were established in modern times and the works which met the dogma of a school or the works exclusively created for a school also became defined as honkyoku, although new. For instance, schools such as Tozan, Ueda, and Chikuho, have their own honkyoku. As a result, honkyoku with the same title in different schools can be a homonym or a namesake.

This is not applied to the schools that adhere to the doctrine from the Fuke sect and observe the rigid definition of honkyoku. The most conservative Myōan Taizan School, for example, does not allow any works other than the three mentioned above to be called honkyoku.

Gaikyoku was mostly works for the instrumental trio sankyoku but various styles were established along with the times of the "Shin Nihon Ongaku (new Japanese music)" movement from the early stages of Showa to current works. After the Meiji period, shakuhachi became more important for accompaniment of folk songs. For example, one cannot sing the folk song "Esashi Oiwake" without a shakuhachi accompaniment. Shakuhachi has a so unique timbre that it is impossible for other musical instruments to mimic, and allows it to interact with other genres such as the innovative jazz and pop music.

As shown on the right page, shakuhachi music can be categorized by the musical characters of works other than the traditional concept of honkyoku and gaikyoku.

Honkyoku and Gaikyoku

● Original definition

Honkyoku: Music originally or exclusively made for *shakuhachi*.

Gaikyoku: All music other than *honkyoku*, such as ensemble with other instruments or voice, or arrangements from other type.

● As new schools emerged:

However, '*honkyoku*' refers to works unique or significant to the school.

● Fuke Sect schools that value tradition, such as Myōan Taizan-ryū, only regards three classical works, collectively called '*Sankyorei*', as *honkyoku* and all other works as *gaikyoku*.

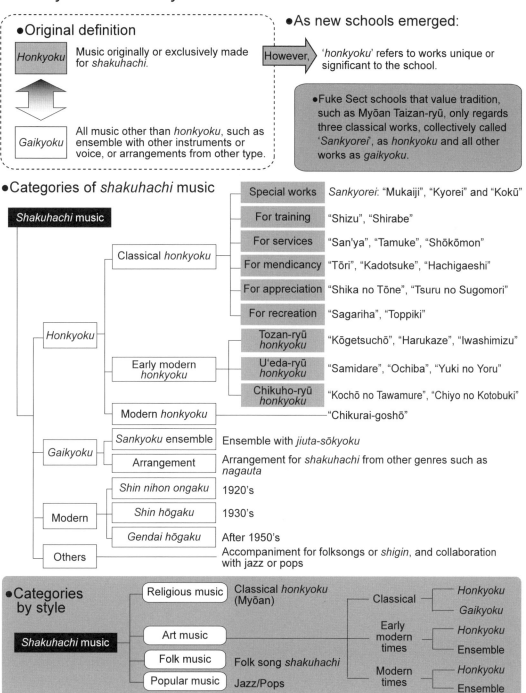

● Categories of *shakuhachi* music

- **Honkyoku**
  - **Classical *honkyoku***
    - Special works — *Sankyorei*: "Mukaiji", "Kyorei" and "Kokū"
    - For training — "Shizu", "Shirabe"
    - For services — "San'ya", "Tamuke", "Shōkōmon"
    - For mendicancy — "Tōri", "Kadotsuke", "Hachigaeshi"
    - For appreciation — "Shika no Tōne", "Tsuru no Sugomori"
    - For recreation — "Sagariha", "Toppiki"
  - **Early modern *honkyoku***
    - Tozan-ryū *honkyoku* — "Kōgetsuchō", "Harukaze", "Iwashimizu"
    - U'eda-ryū *honkyoku* — "Samidare", "Ochiba", "Yuki no Yoru"
    - Chikuho-ryū *honkyoku* — "Kochō no Tawamure", "Chiyo no Kotobuki"
  - **Modern *honkyoku*** — "Chikurai-goshō"
- **Gaikyoku**
  - *Sankyoku* ensemble — Ensemble with *jiuta-sōkyoku*
  - Arrangement — Arrangement for *shakuhachi* from other genres such as *nagauta*
- **Modern**
  - *Shin nihon ongaku* — 1920's
  - *Shin hōgaku* — 1930's
  - *Gendai hōgaku* — After 1950's
- **Others** — Accompaniment for folksongs or *shigin*, and collaboration with jazz or pops

● Categories by style — *Shakuhachi* music
- Religious music — Classical *honkyoku* (Myōan) — Classical — Honkyoku / Gaikyoku
- Art music — Early modern times — Honkyoku / Ensemble
- Folk music — Folk song *shakuhachi* — Modern times — Honkyoku / Ensemble
- Popular music — Jazz/Pops

Shakuhachi Notation Systems: From Timbres to Methods

What attracts us the most to *shakuhachi* is its unique timbre. It is one of the most difficult instruments to play. Probably, a beginner cannot make even a single note. That is because the structure of *shakuhachi* is so simple that the technique of a player directly affects the sound-production and timbre. Its body is made of a bamboo stalk with all nodes removed and with simple five finger holes.

Like other pipes, opening and closing the holes changes pitches. The finger holes are manipulated with full, half, and quarter opening or closing. There are also variations of fingerings and combinations of holes which alter the timbre. In addition to the fingering, the player must learn two other techniques: blowing and changing the angle of the jaw. These three techniques must be integrated and managed well.

Quantitative, dynamical and temporal changes of wind also affect the timbre. The angle of the jaw against the blowing hole is another important factor to subtly change pitches and tone colors. The distance between the lips and the blowing hole also affects the pitches. The technique to bend the pitches without changing finger positions is called *meri* to lower a note by pulling the jaw away from the blowing hole and *kari* to raise a note by pushing the jaw toward it. By combining this technique with finger positions and the blowing technique, the player can produce infinite timbre changes and pitch bends like portamento. These factors create the unique *shakuhachi* world which may be the other extreme to the mechanical and rational Western musical instruments to produce and sustain stable pitches and timbre. Uncertainty of the instrument results in infinite possibilities. It is said, in general, that a *shakuhachi* learner takes three years for shaking his head and eight years for fingering, which plainly expresses how difficult it is to play, and how profound the *shakuhachi* world is, as well.

Oral tradition is basically used for *shakuhachi* instruction but musical notations are also used. Although the notation systems vary for each school, katakana characters are commonly used. The difference of the system of each school shows how it notates the ornaments unique to *shakuhachi* music. Because they all employ the one-character-per-note system, *shakuhachi* scores can also be used to practice singing.

■Performing Technique of *Shakuhachi*

The attraction of *shakuhachi* is found in its subtleties of pitches.

"Bobbing and waggling head"
Extremely unique and difficult *shakuhachi* technique

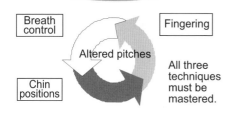

Breath control
Fingering
Chin positions
Altered pitches
All three techniques must be mastered.

●Natural notes and fingering
for the standard D *shakuhachi* (1.8 *shaku*)

Holes: ○=opened ●=closed

	Ichi-kotsu	Shō-zetsu	Sōjō	Ōshiki	Shin-sen	Ichi-kotsu
5	●	●	●	●	●	○
4	●	●	●	●	○	○
3	●	●	●	○	○	○
2	●	●	●	○	○	●
1	●	●	○	○	○	●

Fingering
Fully opened/closed
Half opened/closed (*kazashi*)
Hitting (*uchi*)
Momentary opening and closing (*okuri*)
Sliding (*suri*)

Breath control
Vehement blowing (*muraiki*)
Tongue fluttering/throat vibration (*tamane*)
Pulsating breath technique (*komibuki*)
Breathing out naturally (*kyosui*)
Gradual fading out (*kusabibuki*)

Chin positions
Raising the pitch by a chin movement upwards (*kari*)
Lowering the pitch by a chin drop (*meri*)
Rapid or slow pitch modulations by head movement (*yuri*)
A modulation upwards from *meri* to *kari* (*nayashi*)
Trills of the lowest 2 notes (*koro*)

●*Shakuhachi* notation systems

Letters for natural notes:
ロ = Ro   ツ = Tsu   レ = Re   チ = Chi
リ = Ri   ヒ = Hi   イ = I

- Two basic systems:
  Finger names written by letters
  Relative pitches written by letters

- Auxiliary marks:
  Registers:
  呂 (1st, lowest, octave)
  甲 (2nd octave)
  Or, other letters/marks

Raised/lowered notes:
メ (= *meri*)
中 (= half-*meri*), etc.
Other letters/marks for special notes such as *koro-koro*

Note values and rhythm:
Visual or intuitive methods, for example, changing letter sizes or using lines and dots, etc.
A box as a measure (Tozan-ryū)
Side lines for each letter

* Each school employs its own notation system though the basic ideas are common.

	All	1	2	3	4	5
Kinko-ryū	ロ	ツ	レ	チ	リ	ヒ
Tozan-ryū	ロ	ツ	レ	チ	ハ	ヒ
Taizan-ryū	ロ	ツ	レ	チ	ハ	イ

Examples of different notation systems depending on the school

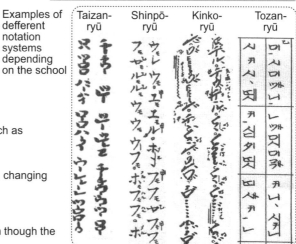

Taizan-ryū   Shinpō-ryū   Kinko-ryū   Tozan-ryū

Shakuhachi: Oldest and Newest Instrument

There are two peaks in the history of *shakuhachi* whose origin can be traced back to an Egyptian fife in 2000 B.C. It was introduced into Japan as early as the Asuka period (538-710 or 592-645 AD) and used as one of the *gagaku* instruments in the imperial court. However, when excluded from *gagaku* ensembles during the *gagaku* reform, *shakuhachi* almost instantly disappeared from the musical front. This *shakuhachi*'s dormant state stretched over a period of about 500 years from the end of the ninth century to the middle of the Muromachi period (approximately 1336-1573) until a bamboo flute called *hitoyogiri* emerged.

During this period, *shakuhachi* is only remembered because of a few written records, for example, "the *shōmyō* of the priest En'nin was accompanied by *shakuhachi*...", "the *dengaku* performers or blind priests played an end-blown flute...", and so on. We don't see any *shakuhachi* activity other than those recorded ones.

As if in order to fill this long void, *fuke shakuhachi* legends were created in the later period, and still exist, having been handed down as the authentic history by certain factions. When *hitoyogiri* emerged, it was the time of frequent wars and a period of natural disasters. Towns were exuberant with street performers and itinerant entertainers and this end-blown flute, plainly structured and easily made by anyone, at once became popular as the instrument for a means of a livelihood.

Later, *hitoyogiri* virtuosi such as Ōmori Sōkun (1570-1625) of Kyoto and Takasabu Ryūtatsu (1527-1611) of Osaka emerged. It is said that the Zen monk Ikkyū connected *hitoyogiri* with monk's 'begging'. Then, *fuke shakuhachi* and *komusō* of the Fuke sect were born, and *shakuhachi* as a legitimate religious device prevailed. Setting their rowdy acts aside, *komusō* developed *shakuhachi* music as stated in the history of *fuke shakuhachi* in the previous sections. After *shakuhachi* was emancipated in society by the abolition of the Fuke sect during the Meiji Restoration, new leaders emerged, new schools were established, and new works were created.

Recognized internationally, *shakuhachi* has broken the walls between Western classical, pop, and jazz and Japanese music. The sounds produced by this simply structured musical instrument are as profound and mysterious as Zen concepts and fascinate foreigners. Now, foreign players worldwide are as active as the Japanese players and grand masters.

Traditional Japanese Music at a Glance

■History of *Shakuhachi*

Ancient Times	• End-blown reed flutes: *sebi* in Egypt and *nay* in West Asia (2000 BC). • The word '*dongxiao*' is recorded in Han Dynasty, China (2 BC).
Asuka (538-710)	• A legend says Lucun created *shakuhachi* during Tang Dynasty, China (ca. 630). • **Sankangaku** of Korea introduced (683). • *Kodai-shakuhachi* came to Japan with musicians from the continent.
Nara (710-794)	• *Shakuhachi* is played at Tōdai-ji Inaugural Ceremony of Great Buddha (752). • *Dongxiao* (origin of shakuhachi) spreads in China. • 8 *kodai-shakuhachi* with 6 holes stored in Shōsōin Repository.
Heian (794-1185)	• **Gagaku** established (894). • *Shakuhachi* excluded from *gagaku* ensembles. • En'nin of Tendai Sect uses *shakuhachi* instead of *shōmyō* chanting. • "Kyōkunshō" (1233) states "A blind priest plays this [*shakuhachi*] in *sarugaku*."
Kamakura (1185-1333)	• Priest Kakushin came home from China with four Buddhist laymen (1254). • Kakushin (a.k.a. Hottō) founds Kōkoku-ji Temple (1258).
Nanbokucho (1336-1392)	• *Dengaku* performers in monk clothing play *shakuhachi*.
Muromachi (1336-1573)	• *Hitoyogiri* appears (by Zen priest Ikkyū). • *Komosō* play *hitoyogiri* for begging. • Music book "Taigenshō" states about *shakuhachi* (1512). • "Shichiku Shoshin-shū" compiled by Ōmori Sōkun (1570-1625) who revived *hitoyogiri*.
Momoyama (1573-1603)	**Shamisen** introduced (ca.1560). • Reihō-ji Temple moves to Ōme, Tokyo (1613).
Edo (1603-1868)	• Decree "Keichō no Okitegaki" regulates the duty and privileges of *komusō* (1614). *Shakuhachi* is regarded as a religious device. • *Fuke shakuhachi* drives out *hitoyogiri* (17 C). • The number of Fuke temples exceeds 70 nationwide. • Myōan-ji becomes the branch temple of Kōkoku-ji (1703). • Offices of Ichigatsu-ji and Reihō-ji temples are founded in Asakusa, Tokyo (mid-18 C). • *Shakuhachi* instructor Kurosawa Kinko I institutes 30 *honkyoku* (ca. 1750). • Various schools centering *gaikyoku* established in the Kyoto-Osaka region. Unofficially *sankyoku* is performed. • Kurosawa Kinko II establishes **Kinko-ryū** (later 18 C).
Meiji-Taisho (1868-1926)	**Meiji Restoration** (1868). • Fuke Sect abolished by "Decree by the Grand Council of State" (1871). • **Myōan-kyōkai** re-established (1888). **Tozan-ryū** established (1896). • "Shin Nihon Ongaku (new Japanese music)" movement (1920's).
Showa-Heisei (1926-)	• Chikuzen Nakatsuka examines the truth of legends of *shakuhachi* in his "Kinko-ryū Shakuhachi Shikan" (1939). • "Shin Hōgaku (new traditional style Japanese music)" movement. • "Gendai Hōgaku (contemporary traditional Japanese music)" movement. • Group "Shakuhachi Sanbon-kai" founded. • Katsuya Yokoyama premieres Takemitsu's "Novenber Steps" in NY (1967). • Hōzan Yamamoto appeared in Newport Jazz Festival. • Various *shakuhachi* festivals held internationally.

Chapter 7: *Koto*

Koto with or without Bridges

Koto is a stringed instrument belonging to the zither family. Two kanji (Chinese) characters are used for *koto*, but strictly speaking, their meanings are slightly different and should be used more carefully. The character 琴, also read as *kin* (*qin* in Chinese) or *gon*, means *koto* without bridges. The other character 箏, also read as *sō*, means *koto* with bridges. Since Japanese *koto* has bridges, the *koto* music is called *sōkyoku*. The two characters are often and widely mixed up. For example, the Japanese native *gagaku koto* is called *wagon* with the character 琴 though it has bridges. The character 琴 originally stood for 'strings' but was used for 'musical instruments', for example organ, during the Meiji period after the introduction of Western music. Due to the confusion, the Japanese *koto* is generally written in two ways without clear distinction.

We know, based on some instances like the wooden fragment of an ancient *koto* or the ancient clay figurine of a man playing *koto* excavated in the historic ruins, that *koto* existed in Japan from the old times. Musical instruments introduced from the continent mostly seem to have originated in West Asia such as Persia but the *koto* family probably originated in various parts of East Asia, particularly China.

The bridgeless types, some of which are a kind of vertical harp, were introduced from Korea around the Asuka period (538-710 or 592-645). The types with bridges were introduced from China along with the court music, *gagaku*, in the Nara period (710-794). The aristocracy of the Heian period (794-1185), for instance, Hikaru Genji, the hero of "The Tale of Genji", loved the bridgeless type, *shichigen-kin* (7-stringed Chinese *guqin*). However, the bridgeless types were superseded by the types with bridges and died out for unknown reasons in Japan.

The tuning of *koto* without bridges is fixed while *koto* with bridges can be tuned freely because the bridges are movable. The movable *koto* bridge is called *kotoji* (or simply *ji*). The type of *koto* is categorized by whether it has them or not. As mentioned already, we cannot distinguish between the two types simply by looking at the kanji characters used for the instrument.

Traditional Japanese Music at a Glance

■Various Zithers in East Asia

●Two kanji (Chinese) characters to refer to *koto*:

At present, two Chinese characters 琴 (*kin* or *koto*) and 箏 (*sō* or *koto*) are used for *koto*. The character 琴 (*kin*) appeared as early as in the Heian period. At the time, it referred to strings. However, during the Meiji period, the character was also used for the translations of musical instruments introduced from the Western world, for instance, *teikin* (violin), *fūkin* (organ), *tefūkin* (accordion) and *mokkin* (xylophone).

●Three types of zither from East Asia (mainly China)

	琴 *Qin* (Japanese *kin*)	箏 *Zheng* (Japanese *sō*)	瑟 *Se* (Japanese *shitsu*)
Origin	It is stated that Emperor Shun of China (23-22 BC), Kings Wen-wang and Wu-wang (12-11 BC) of Zhou Dynasty, and Confucius (ca. 500 BC) played the koto.	A legend says that General Meng Tien (3 BC) of the Qin Dynasty invented *zheng*. According to another legend of the Qin Dynasty, a master of 25-string *se*, who had two children, split his instrument into two for them: one with 12 strings and one with 13 strings. That was the origin of *zheng*.	*Se* appeared in Chinese literature such as "Shi-jing (Book of Odes)" (10-7 BC).
Structure	*Qin* has 7 strings on the 125 cm long fretless board, inlaid with 13 dots (*hui*) of ivory, jade, or mother-of-pearl, without	The early *zheng* (or *guzhen*) in the Han Dynasty had 12 strings, and 13 strings in the Tang Dynasty. At present, it has 18-23 or more strings and movable bridges.	Today's *se* has 25 strings and 25 movable bridges. Chinese found the 12-note chromatic scale and octave relations.
History in Japan	*Kin* was introduced in the Nara period and favored by the noble until the mid-Heian period but gradually replaced by *koto*.	The 13-string *zheng* of the Tang Dynasty was introduced in the Nara period. *Gakusō* (*koto* in the *gagaku* ensemble) was developed into *Tsukushi-goto* and *koto* in the early Modern Times.	*Shitsu* was introduced in the Nara period to Japan but the detail is unknown.
Types	*Shichigen-kin* (7-string *qin*), **Gayageum*, **Wagon* (6-string Japanese *koto*), *Suma-goto* (1-string Japanese koto). *Has movable bridges.	*Gakusō*, *Tsukushi-goto*, *koto* (with 13 or 17 strings)	●*Konghou* (Japanese *kugo*) Ancient Chinese harp. It was introduced to Japan via Korea in the Nara period and called *kudara-goto* or *kugo*. A *kudara-goto* brought from China has been preserved in the Shōsōin Repository. There were three types of *konghou*, one vertical and two horizontal types.

●Generally 琴 refers to *koto* without bridges and 箏 refers to *koto* with movable bridges but they are not clealy defined.

Kotoji (movable bridges)

Does the zither have movable bridges?

No → 琴
Yes → 箏

Kugo (Shōsōin Repository)

What is *Sōkyoku*?

The *koto* music is called *sōkyoku*. You might think *sōkyoku* is instrumental music, represented by masterpieces like "Rokudan no Shirabe (Six Steps)" and "Haru no Umi (The Sea in Spring)" and so on, but it is actually vocal music. A player sings to one's own accompaniment of *koto*. *Shamisen* also joins in *sōkyoku* in general. Famous *koto* solo pieces such as "Rokudan no Shirabe (or simply Rokudan)" and some modern *koto* works are instrumental but they are rather exceptions in *sōkyoku*.

Normally, the *sōkyoku* players play the *koto* and *shamisen*: a *koto* player is concurrently a *shamisen* player. They are also singers and sing the vocal part. In some works, players switch their parts, from *koto* to *shamisen* and vice versa. As described in detail in the *jiuta* section of this book, the *koto* music, *sōkyoku*, and *shamisen* music, *jiuta*, were developed closely to each other. They interacted with each other in terms of the style and technique and as a result it became normal for a player to play both instruments. The musical term '*jiuta-sōkyoku*' was even invented in order to describe their musical fusion.

Behind this fusing was *tōdō* (or *tōdōza*), a guild of the blind male musicians who played both *koto* and *shamisen*. *Jiuta* and *sōkyoku* were developed by the members of the *tōdō*. In order to be an excellent *koto* player, one was required to be an excellent *shamisen* player as well. The world of *sōkyoku* and *jiuta* was created by multi-talented musicians.

This trend accelerated the development of the instrumental trio, called *sankyoku*, of *koto*, *shamisen* and *shakuhachi* (or *kokyū*). The trend also caused the repulsion against the fusion of the two, originally different, instruments and stimulated the idea of reviving the pure and independent *koto* music.

Traditional Japanese Music at a Glance

What is *Sōkyoku*?

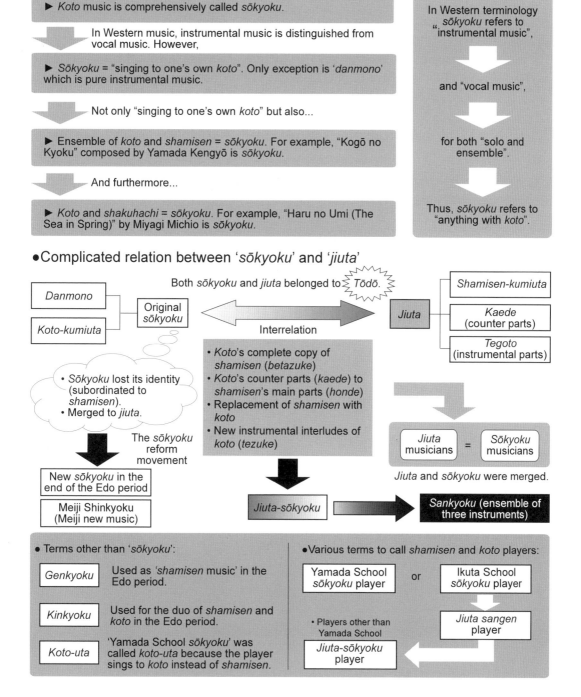

Transformation of *Tsukushi-goto* and Genius Yatsuhashi Kengyō

Once *koto* was exclusively used for *kangen*, the instrumental ensembles without dances in *gagaku* music. The various picture scrolls of the Heian period depict that *koto* was loved by the nobles as part of their culture of poetry and musical performances.

At first, the melody from the *gagaku* "Etenraku" was hummed without words to the accompaniment of the mostly arpeggiated chords of *koto*, and then, the words of a popular song at the time, generally called *imayō*, were fit in on the melody. The songs, called '*Etenraku* songs', became extremely popular. When *gagaku* became the "temple *gagaku*" connected with the Buddhist rituals, '*Etenraku* songs' began to play an important role as "temple chants" in the rituals.

After the '*Etenraku* songs' style had become firmly established, the priest Kenjun (1547-1536) of Zendō-ji temple in Kyushu, the southern part of Japan and archaically called Tsukushi, devised a new style. He did this by combining the temple music and the 7-stringed *kin* (Chinese *guqin*) music and arranging the melodies or parts of songs accompanied by *koto* into instrumental music. This innovative music and its instrument were called Tsukushi School *sōkyoku* and *tsukushi-goto* respectively.

Young Yatsuhashi Kengyō (an honorary title given to blind masters) studied Tsukushi School *sōkyoku* with Hōsui, the pupil of Kenjun. He later improved *tsukushi-goto* and composed thirteen *kumiuta*, suites for voice and *koto*, and three *danmono*, purely instrumental solo pieces. They are regarded as historical achievements. As a result, the music of *koto* became to belong exclusively to *tōdō*, the guild of blind musicians. The *koto* of Yatsuhashi *sōkyoku* was called *zokusō*, secular *koto* distinguished from the *koto* of the noble and Buddhist priests. It means that his *koto* music was widely propagated among common people.

His merits include: composing innovative works, setting up new tunings, training many excellent pupils, spreading his music all over the nation, and improving *koto* music into an art form. The music Yatsuhashi established survives today. According to recent research, Yatsuhashi's famous masterpieces "Rokudan (Six Steps)" and "Hachidan (Eight Steps)" may not be his but the works of his pupils, Kitajima Kengyō and Kurahashi Kengyō. Even if it is true, the accomplishment of Yatsuhashi would not be tarnished. He was an absolutely great artist.

Traditional Japanese Music at a Glance

■Birth of Early Modern *Sōkyoku*

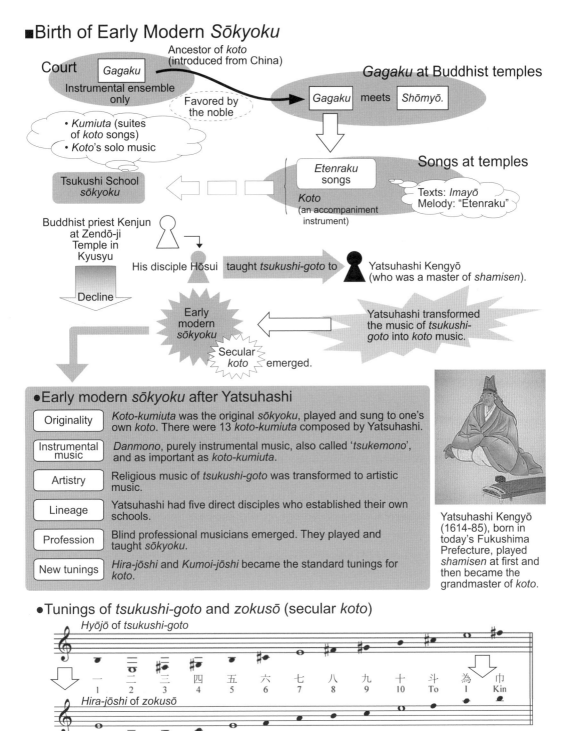

- **Early modern *sōkyoku* after Yatsuhashi**

Originality	*Koto-kumiuta* was the original *sōkyoku*, played and sung to one's own *koto*. There were 13 *koto-kumiuta* composed by Yatsuhashi.
Instrumental music	*Danmono*, purely instrumental music, also called '*tsukemono*', and as important as *koto-kumiuta*.
Artistry	Religious music of *tsukushi-goto* was transformed to artistic music.
Lineage	Yatsuhashi had five direct disciples who established their own schools.
Profession	Blind professional musicians emerged. They played and taught *sōkyoku*.
New tunings	*Hira-jōshi* and *Kumoi-jōshi* became the standard tunings for *koto*.

Yatsuhashi Kengyō (1614-85), born in today's Fukushima Prefecture, played *shamisen* at first and then became the grandmaster of *koto*.

- **Tunings of *tsukushi-goto* and *zokusō* (secular *koto*)**

Transformation of Yatsuhashi Kengyō's *Sōkyoku*

Yatsuhashi Kengyō's *sōkyoku* was succeeded to his pupil Kitajima Kengyō. Kitajima exercised his ingenuity on what he learned from Yatsuhashi and passed it to Ikuta Kengyō. Ikuta established Ikuta School based on it, further adopting *jiuta* songs of *shamisen*.

During the times of Yatsuhashi, popular songs were occasionally played by ensembles of *koto, shamisen*, and *hitoyogiri*. But even Yatsuhashi, who was also a *shamisen* virtuoso, seems to have distinguished those arrangements from *koto* music. Ikuta Kengyō treated *sōkyoku* and *jiuta*, which had been regarded as belonging to different worlds, as the same kind and improved *koto*'s techniques and tuning systems in order to play the two instruments in concert. The reason why this revolutionary fusion was possible in the vertically segmented and closed world of the Japanese culture was that both *sōkyoku* and *jiuta* were played by members of *tōdō*, the male blind musicians' guild. As a result, the Ikuta School musicians had to be *koto* as well as *shamisen* players. Ikuta's *sōkyoku*, started in the Kyoto-Osaka region, spread nationwide by the instrumentality of his pupils and settled and developed in various places.

However, it did not become popular readily in Edo (present Tokyo) probably because the Kyoto-Osaka style *jiuta* was not the taste of people in the eastern region. Yamada Kengyō, a *koto* player of Ikuta School in Edo, contrived new songs with *koto* accompaniments, a sort of narrative music, adopting then popular *jōruri* songs like *icchū-bushi* and *katō-bushi*. This Yamada *sōkyoku* became very popular. This is how Ikuta and Yamada, two major schools in the *koto* music history, were established. Later, Ikuta School further leaned toward *jiuta*, actively adopting *jiuta* songs, and even prohibited composing new *koto-kumiuta*. As a result of such inclinations, Ikuta School lost the originality of their *sōkyoku*.

Against this trend at the end of the Edo period, Mitsuzaki Kengyō and Yoshizawa Kengyō established the new *sōkyoku* in order to revive the pure *koto* music, the music at the time of Yatsuhashi. Their music was later called *bakumatsu shinsōkyoku*, meaning new *sōkyoku* at the end of the Edo period. In the Meiji period, the blind men's guild, *tōdō*, was abolished, and their monopolistic *sōkyoku* was allowed for the public to play and became popular as the home music. In the meantime in the Meiji period, Western music was introduced and stimulated new, prolific trends: for example, new *sōkyoku* called '*meiji shinkyoku*', and '*shin nihon ongaku* (new Japanese music)'.

Traditional Japanese Music at a Glance

■Development of *Sōkyoku*

Early modern *sōkyoku*
- Professional performers

• Emergence of *sōkyoku* by secular *koto* (*zokusō*)
  - Birth of *koto-kumiuta* and *danmono*
  - Invention of new tunings

Yatsuhashi Kengyō (1614-85) composed 13 *kumiuta* and 3 *danmono*.

Ikuta School *sōkyoku*
- Development of *jiuta*
  • Intrumental parts: *kaede* and *tegoto*
  • Vocal parts: *chōka* (long songs) and *sakumono* (comical songs)

• Interaction with *jiuta*
• Offshoots spreading as schools
  - A new addition to *jiuta*
  - Insertion of *koto*'s *kaede* in *jiuta*
  - *Tegotomono* for *jiuta*
  - *Koto*'s complete copies of *jiuta* works

Kitajima Kengyō (?-1690).
Ikuta Kengyō (1656-1715).
Ichiura Kengyō developed *kaede* of *koto*.
3 kengyōs, Kawarazaki, Urasaki and Yaezaki, developed Kyoto-style *tegotomono*, and arranged *jiuta* for *koto*.

Yamada School *sōkyoku*
- Edo-style

• Emergence of new style songs
  - Adaptaiton of Edo-style *jōruri* songs
  - The main section of *jōruri* music played by *koto*
  - Highlights alloted to performers
  - Trio of 2 *koto* and 1 *shamisen*

Yamada Kengyō (1757-1817) established Yamada School *sōkyoku*.

New *sōkyoku* at the end of Edo period
- Tenpō and Kyōhō Reforms (emphasis on frugality)

• *Sōkyoku* Reform
  - Casting off restraint of *shamisen* music
  - Renaissance of pure *sōkyoku* (*kumiuta* & *danmono*)
  - New works in *kumiuta* style
  - Tunings adapted from *gagaku* scales

Mitsuzaki Kengyō "Akikaze no Kyoku".
Yoshizawa Kengyō "Chidori no Kyoku".
Suzuki Koson's Kyōgoku School *sōkyoku*.

Meiji shinkyoku (Meiji new music)
- Tōdō abolished
- Introduction of Western music

• Song Reform and New style *sōkyoku*
  - Transformation from risque music to moral music
  - Duo of high and low parts and improved songs
  - New tunings without half tones
  - Abolished *tōdō* and emergence of independent musicians

Kikutaka Kengyō "Mikuni no Homare".
Kikumatsu Kengyō "Saga no Aki".
Tateyama Noboru "Hototogisu no Kyoku".
Kikuzuka Yoichi "Meiji Shōchikubai".

Shin nihon ongaku (New Japanese music)

• Modernized traditional Japanese music for citizens
  - New works based on Western music theory
  - Improvement of instruments and musical forms
  - Significant development of performing techniques
  - Ensemble with Western instruments

Michio Miyagi "Haru no Umi".

Gendai hōgaku (Contemporary traditional Japanese music)

• New creation of Japanese music
  - Globalized Japanese traditional music
  - Development of instrumental music and ensembles
  - Interest by Western style composers

Kin'ichi Nakanoshima "Three Fragments".
Enshō Yamakawa "Fantaisie Impromptu".
Shūretsu Miyashita "Sōjō no Kyoku".

Varieties of Early Modern *Sōkyoku*

Early modern *sōkyoku*, which developed and changed during the transition from the times of Yatsuhashi Kengyō to the early years of Meiji period, can be roughly categorized into six groups, as shown on the right page. *Koto-kumiuta* and *danmono* established in the times of Yatsuhashi Kengyō was the origin of *zokusō*, secular *koto*, of early modern *sōkyoku*. *Kumiuta* is vocal music and *danmono* purely instrumental music. Both centered on *koto*, which is the reason why they are called *sōkyoku*. *Kinutamono*, derived from *noh* play, was treated as the same kind as *danmono* since both are instrumental and were required for learners to master in order to get their license to teach.

Shamisen's *jiuta* songs were transcribed or arranged for the duos of *koto* and *shamisen*, and, this new music became the characteristic genre to Ikuta School. Begun by Ikuta Kengyō, it was the mainstream of early modern *sōkyoku*. The musical ideas and techniques developed for *jiuta shamisen*, for example, *kaede* and *tegoto*, were adapted to *koto* music. *Kaede* is the counter melody added to the original melody in later years, both melodies of which are played independently as a solo or played in concert as a duo. *Tegoto* is a long instrumental section placed between two vocal sections. Later the *tegoto* section became independent and became purely instrumental music. As a result of these cross-breeding with *shamisen* music, *sōkyoku* significantly evolved. However, as the proverb "too much of a good thing" says, *sōkyoku* became subordinate to *jiuta* and the originality of *koto* music was lost. Even *koto-kumiuta* was banned from being composed.

In the end of the Edo period, concerned about such trends, Mitsuzaki Kengyō and Yoshizawa Kengyō tried to revive the originality of *koto* music. They composed works based on new scales such as the '*yō*' mode, an anhemitonic pentatonic scale (a pentatonic scale containing no semitones) primarily used in *gagaku*. Their innovative music, called '*bakumatsu shinsōkyoku*' in later years, was like the Renaissance of *sōkyoku*.

Independently of the development of Ikuta School, Yamada Kengyō, the founder of Yamada School, arranged *jōruri* songs such as *icchū-bushi* and *katō-bushi*, representative music of the Edo culture in those days, into *koto* works. His *sōkyoku* became very popular in the eastern region. In this *sōkyoku* based on the narrative music, *koto* was the primary instrument though it was performed with *shamisen*, and established its unique music world different from the other schools of Ikuta.

During the Meiji period, new *koto* techniques and new ensembles with other instruments were developed under the influence of Western music. Also, reflecting the modernized society, the once degenerate texts of vocal music were improved in their moral and educational content. *Sōkyoku* created under this trend is called the *meiji shinkyoku* (Meiji new music). When Western music was introduced, it was koto players that immediately adapted themselves to new circumstances.

■Types of Early Modern *Sōkyoku*

Types	Description	Major work titles
Tsukushi-ryū *sōkyoku*	Tsukushi-ryū *sōkyoku* is a song suite performed by a single performer who sings to his own *koto*. It was established as the 'temple song', derived from 'temple *gagaku*', by the priest Kenjun at Zendo-ji Temple in Kyushu.	Rinzetsu, Fuki, Shiki, Hana no En
Early modern *sōkyoku*	The general term for *koto* and its music after Yatsuhashi. The *koto* after Yatsuhashi is also called *zokusō* (secular *koto*) distinguished from *gakusō* (*gagaku koto*) and *tsukushi-goto*.	
Koto-kumiuta	Classical song suites composed of independent, short songs performed by a single performer who sings to his own *koto*. The texts are basically 4 verses in seven-and-five syllable meter in 64 time (128 beats). There are fixed patterns in the beginning and ending.	Fuki, Umegae, Tenkataihei, Suma, Kiritsubo, Shiki no Fuji, Usugoromo, Setsugetsuka
Danmono/ Kinutamono	*Danmono* is solo instrumental music for *koto*, also called '*shirabemono*'. Composed of some steps which are basically in 52 time (104 beats). *Kinutamono* is a generic term for music themed on '*kinuta* (the sound of beating cloth)' which is composed of steps, similar to *danmono*.	Rokudan no Shirabe, Hachidan no Shirabe, Midare, Godan Kinuta
Integration with *jiuta*	*Koto* music integrated and fused with *jiuta*, established by Ikuta Kengyō. Typical Ikuta-ryū *sōkyoku*. In the early stage, *koto* was a complete copy (*betazuke*) of *shamisen*. Later *koto*'s counter parts (*kaede*) and solo parts (*tegoto*) were developed, becoming the standard of *sōkyoku*.	Ujimeguri, Yūgao, Shiki no Nagame, Torioi, Yaegoromo, Nanakomachi, Miyamagi, Chaondo
Bakumatsu shinsōkyoku	*Sōkyoku* Reform flourished in the end of Edo period. Rebound from the *koto*'s tendency to subordinate to *shamisen*, a new movement arose to return to the origin of *koto* music, that is, purely instrumental music, *kumiuta* and *danmono*, by Yatsuhashi.	Akikaze no Kyoku, Yamazakura, Chidori no Kyoku, Kara-goromo, Shin-setsugetsuka, Hatsuse-gawa, Haru no Kyoku
Meiji shinkyoku	New type of *sōkyoku* in the Meiji period, somewhat influenced by then popular '*Minshin-gaku* (Music from China)'. It is characterized by a new pentatonic scale without semitones ('*yō*' scale), the moral texts avoiding indecent expressions following the Song Reform movement, the instrumental section (*tegoto*) by a duo of high and low parts as an interlude.	Aioi no Kyoku, Unohana, Aki no Kotonoha, Gaika no Kyoku, Kongōseki, Saga no Aki, Ōuchiyama
Yamada-ryū *sōkyoku*	Based on popular *uta-jōruri* of Edo (Tokyo) such as *katō-bushi* and *icchū-bushi*, new style songs were created against unpopular *kumiuta*. The accompaniment was composed of two or more *koto* with auxiliary *shamisen* and each highlight of the songs was sung by different performers.	Hatsune no Kyoku, Yuya, Chōkonka no Kyoku, Aoi no Ue, Kasugamōde, Kotobuki Kurabe, Matsu no Sakae
Modern *sōkyoku*	→ *Shin nihon ongaku* (New Japanese music), *Shin hōgaku* (New traditional Japanese music), *Gendai hōgaku* (Modern traditional Japanese music)......*Sankyoku* (music of 3 instruments)	

Differences between Ikuta and Yamada

The general answers to the question "what is the difference between Ikuta School and Yamada School" are summarized on the right page. There are other *sōkyoku* schools besides these two, of course, but, why do Ikuta and Yamada generally represent *koto* music schools.

There are eight schools belonging to Ikuta, including Edo Ikuta and Tsugaru Ikuta (for the detail about the *sōkyoku* schools, see the next section). The musical basics were mostly the same among the Ikuta's offshoots, and the only difference among them is the selection of the esoteric or secret works and the method or mechanisms to hand them down. On the other hand, the schools founded by the immediate pupils of Yatsuhashi Kengyō in various places, before Ikuta School was established locally survived and developed their own unique style though they were minorities. For example, Tsugaru Ikuta School, originally one of Ikuta lineage but independently developed with different kanji characters for the name "Ikuta", has carried through to the present. Tsuguyama School and Shin-Yatsuhashi School directly descended from the Yatsuhashi School and had a strong tie and influences with Ikuta. They were closely related to *jiuta* songs and belonged to the same *tōdō* as old and new Ikuta School in Osaka.

Yamada School put the accent on the narrative music, different kinds from Ikuta music, while all Ikuta schools, essentially homogeneous, strongly attached to *jiuta*. Though Yamada School was derived from Ikuta lineage, Ikuta School and Yamada School are regarded as two major schools in a broad sense. Strictly speaking, the name 'Ikuta School' refers to a group, not a single school.

Koto players of any Ikuta schools do not play works of Yamada School but Yamada School's players sometimes play *kumiuta* and *danmono*. Lately, performers of both schools often appear together at a contemporary music concert and the conservative division between the two has been gradually disappearing. Simply put, *koto* players of both schools primarily aim at creating better music overall. Today, since handing down *kumiuta* is not so important, it can be said that all schools other than Yamada and venerable ones descended from Yatsuhashi in Okinawa (southern Japan), Tsugaru (northern Japan) and Matsushiro (central Japan), are the schools or the genealogy of Ikuta.

■Two Major Koto Schools: Ikuta and Yamada

*Ryū = school

	Ikuta-ryū*	Yamada-ryū
Birth location/ Endemic area	Kansai region (Kyoto and Osaka)	Edo (Tokyo)
Formation process	Integration with *jiuta* (*shamisen* music)	Adaptation of *uta-jōruri* (*jōruri* songs accompanied by *shamisen*)
Main factor	Instrumental techniques such as *kaede* and *tegoto*	Singing
Instrumentation	2 *shamisen* (*honde*+*kaede*) + 1 *koto*	1 *shamisen* + 2 or more *koto*
Koto's role	*Shamisen* is primary and *koto* secondary.	*Koto* is primary and *shamisen* is auxiliary.
Singing	Highlights of songs are not allotted to performers.	Highlights of songs are alloted to different performers.
Plectrum/ Sitting position	Square plectra/sitting diagonally to the instrument	Rounded plectra/sitting at a right angle to the instrument
Instruments	Derived from ornamental *gakusō* (*gagaku koto*), 1.91 m (6' 32") in length	Improved *koto*, 1.81 m (6') in length
Shamisen	*Jiuta shamisen* (medium-neck), *jiuta* bridge (flat-based), *Tsuyama* style plectrum	*Nagauta shamisen* (thin-neck), *nagauta* bridge, *nagauta* plectrum

Although they have differences as listed above, Ikuta and Yamada schools are not opposed to each other.

●Relation between Ikuta and Yamada

Incorrect view: They are just two schools.　　　Correct view: Completely different types of *koto* music.

Sōkyoku (Ikuta, Yamada)　　　　　　　　　　Ikuta-ryū sōkyoku　　Yamada-ryū sōkyoku

Since Yamada-ryū was derived from Edo Ikuta-ryū, Yamada performers play *koto-kumiuta* and Ikuta-ryū *sōkyoku*. However, the performers of Ikuta-ryū lineages never play Yamada-ryū *sōkyoku* in general.

●Interaction

No. Do they play their counterpart? Yes. (Ikuta-ryū ↔ Yamada-ryū)

	Kumiuta	Singing to own's koto
Ikuta-ryū	Danmono	Instrumental music
	Tegotomono	*Shamisen* music played together with *koto*
Yamada-ryū	Yamada-ryū *sōkyoku*	Ensemble of *koto* and *shamisen*

●Ikuta-ryū as a collective name

Ikuta-ryū is composed of many direct or indirect lineages.

- Okinawa *sōkyoku*
- Matsushiro Yatsuhashi-ryū
- Yamada-ryū
- Tsugaru Ikuta-ryū

●Ikuta lineages:

- Osaka Shin-ikuta-ryū
- Kyushu Ikuta-ryū
- Chūgoku Ikuta-ryū
- Osaka Ko-ikuta-ryū
- Kyoto Ikuta-ryū
- Nagoya Ikuta-ryū

As well as...
- Osaka Yatsuhashi-ryū
- Tsuguyama-ryū

Pedigree of Early Modern *Sōkyoku*

The *sōkyoku* schools of the early modern era, or pre-Meiji period, are summarized in the list on the right page. Only the name of the person who represents the school is listed for each school since it is impossible, of course, to list all the names of important people in this book.

In the beginning of *sōkyoku*, Yatsuhashi Kengyō and Kitajima Kengyō did not give their schools a name, and Ko-Yatsuhashi School (Old Yatsuhashi), for instance, was named so by the future generations. The school names of Sumiyama, Satsuma-Yatsuhashi, Yasumura, and Fujiike Schools ceased to exist after the founder's death but their styles were handed down by the pupils. Tsugaru Ikuta School changed the kanji characters for the name of Ikuta at the end of the Edo period. Though it is not confirmed, some advocate that Soroichi, the founder of Tsugaru Ikuta, was the pupil of Yatsuhashi Kengyō, not Ikuta Kengyō.

There are so many school names but they are roughly classified into three groups. The first is the group of the direct descents of Yatsuhashi, which settled down in the various regions such as Tsugaru, Matsushiro, and Okinawa. The second is the group of Ikuta. The pupils and the lineage of Ikuta Kengyō spread, settled down, and developed in the various regions. There are two prefixes for school names: *shin* (new) and *ko* (old). The older one with the same name is called with the prefix '*ko*'. Shin-Yatsuhashi School and Tsuguyama School in Osaka were the lineage of Yatsuhashi but since they had a strong tie with Ikuta School in Osaka, it is regarded as one of the Ikuta schools. The last is Yamada School. As stated in the previous section, derived from Edo Ikuta School, Yamada School established a new style *sōkyoku* different from Ikuta *sōkyoku* and is regarded as an independent school. These early modern *sōkyoku* schools have been succeeded to the present.

In reality, however, the offshoots from these original schools often form bigger organizations in size than the head houses. The offshoots are called *kai* (society) or *ha* (sect), and so on, and their individual names are actually used instead of their head house names. For example, Miyagi-kai and Seiha Hōgaku-kai, that belong to Ikuta School, are huge organizations with more than 10,000 members each, well surpassing their head family of the schools.

Yamada School has four offshoots founded by the immediate pupils of Yamada Kengyō. At present, similarly to Ikuta School, new sects with a new name have been founded by players who became independent from the head house. Moreover, these offshoots actively co-perform with others, which further accelerate subdivisions of the school.

■Genealogy of Early Modern *Sōkyoku*

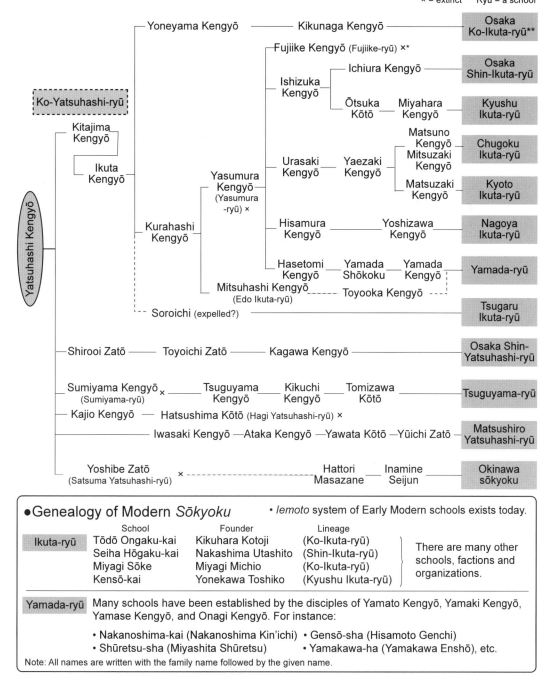

Note: This genealogical chart does not reflect the periodization.
*× = extinct ** Ryū = a school

- **Genealogy of Modern *Sōkyoku***
- *Iemoto* system of Early Modern schools exists today.

School	Founder	Lineage	
Ikuta-ryū	Tōdō Ongaku-kai	Kikuhara Kotoji	(Ko-Ikuta-ryū)
	Seiha Hōgaku-kai	Nakashima Utashito	(Shin-Ikuta-ryū)
	Miyagi Sōke	Miyagi Michio	(Ko-Ikuta-ryū)
	Kensō-kai	Yonekawa Toshiko	(Kyushu Ikuta-ryū)

There are many other schools, factions and organizations.

Yamada-ryū: Many schools have been established by the disciples of Yamato Kengyō, Yamaki Kengyō, Yamase Kengyō, and Onagi Kengyō. For instance:

- Nakanoshima-kai (Nakanoshima Kin'ichi)
- Gensō-sha (Hisamoto Genchi)
- Shūretsu-sha (Miyashita Shūretsu)
- Yamakawa-ha (Yamakawa Enshō), etc.

Note: All names are written with the family name followed by the given name.

Sōkyoku of Modern Times

The system reform by the Meiji government had great influence on arts and music. The *tōdō* guild and the Fuke sect were abolished, and *sōkyoku* (and *jiuta*) and *shakuhachi*, which were in security with a privilege until then, received a big blow. *Noh* lost patronage from the *samurai* class and faced a crisis on the verge of extinction. *Kabuki* and *bunraku* theaters were self-supported on their income from public performances and did not undergo influence as much as *Noh*.

During this chaotic time, the *koto* prodigy Michio Miyagi (1894-1956) debuted. He composed his first major work "Mizu no Hentai (Metamorphosis of Water)" at the age of fourteen and became the *koto* grand master at the age of twenty. In 1919, he held a recital and performed his original works in the traditional style and a new style influenced by Western music. The Western music performers and the people in the literary world were favorable to his works but Japanese music performers harshly criticized his music as "an odd and disgusting imitation".

In the meantime, the *nagauta* musician Sakichi Kineya IV held a recital and performed his purely instrumental works for *shamisen*, called *sangen shusōgaku*. It was around 1919 and 1920 that Japanese were interested in foreign culture due to the Russian Revolution and the First World War, and many famous foreign players visited Japan to hold a Western music concert. Though *koto* and *shamisen* was trying to regain the popularity as the home music by targeting the middle class women after barely recovered from the blow by the Meiji Restoration, they were placed in a tight spot again by this Western music boom. With a sense of impending crisis, Miyagi and Kineya were exploring for a solution for the new Japanese music.

Miyagi then held a joint recital with the composer Nagayo Motoori who tried to approach Japanese music from the point of view of Western music in contrast to him. Moreover, he invented new instruments for the lower registers and composed new works adopting Western methods. The music in the similar style as his was called the '*shin nihon ongaku* (new Japanese music)' and many Japanese traditional musicians sympathized with this concept. Miyagi was followed by Kin'ichi Nakanoshima, an excellent musician, who created innovative *sōkyoku* differing from Miyagi, and later led with epoch-making *koto* music.

These changes stimulated the Western style composers and the Japanese music, once called 'unrefined', was able to greet the new era of *gendai hōgaku*, the contemporary traditional Japanese music.

Traditional Japanese Music at a Glance

■Road to Modern *Sōkyoku*

●Michio Miyagi (1894-1956): Pioneer of New Music

His achievement in his first 'Recital of New Works' (1919) includes:
- Adaptation of Western music theory (musical forms, motifs, harmony, rhythm, etc.)
- Adaptation of Western instrumental technique (staccato, glissando, tremolo, arpeggio, pizzicato, etc.)
- Effective, multiple parts (independent instrumental parts in a composition)
- Orchestral ensemble (large ensemble with Western and Japanese instruments)
- Invention of new instruments (17-string koto, 80-strings koto, short koto, etc.)

●Collaboration with Western music

'Joint Recital of New Works' (1920) by Miyagi and Nagayo Motoori (1885-1945)

Received mixed reviews.
Positive reaction from Western style musicians: "New activity against laziness".
Negative reaction from traditional musicians: "Destruction of tradition to get attention...".

Shin nihon ongaku (New Japanese music) named by Seifū Yoshida (1891-1950)
New compositions for traditional instruments to break stereotypes.

●Modernization in *shamisen* music

Sakichi Kineya IV (1884-1945) established '*sangen shusōgaku*', instrumental works for *shamisen*.

- *Shamisen* is no longer an accompaniment instrument to songs.
- Adaptation of Western music theory.
- Big ensemble with additional bass parts.
- Invention of new instruments.

Some traditional Japanese musicians sympathized with the new movement:
Shakuhachi: Tozan Nakao, Randō Fukuda
Sōkyoku: Utashito Nakashima
Scholars: Hisao Tanabe, Kashō Machida

●Sense of impending crisis for traditional Japanese music

With visiting foreign musicians and sales of records, Western music was extremely popular in the Taisho period. *Koto* and *shamisen* were regarded unpolished while violin and piano were stylish. This sense of impending crisis for traditional Japanese music triggered the new movement.

●Kin'ichi Nakanoshima: Another Pioneer

Shin hōgaku (New traditional Japanese music)

↓

Gendai hōgaku (Modern traditional Japanese music)

↓

Gendai sōkyoku (Modern sōkyoku)

Kin'ichi Nakanoshima (Yamada School, 1904-84) sympathized with the "Shin Nihon Ongaku" movement in the early Showa period and became the father of modern traditional Japanese music. His achievement includes:
- Melodies and harmony on major/minor scales
- New tuning based on the *Okinawa* scale, and renovative rhythm
- New *koto* technique such as hitting the strings left side of the bridges with a stick

- Miyagi's music: 'European, classical and romantic, melodical, passionate, intelligible'

- Nakanoshima's music: 'Asian, modern, rhythmic, intelectual, cultivated'

●Names to remember:

- Modern *sōkyoku* performers:
  Shin'ichi Yuize, Enshō Yamakawa, Genchi Hisamoto, Shūretsu Miyashita, Akiko Nosaka, etc.
- Modern composers who wrote works for traditional instruments:
  Yoshiro Irino, Minoru Miki, Mareo Ishiketa, Michio Mamiya, Toru Takemitsu, etc.
- Educational institutes:
  NHK School for Young Professionals, Department of Traditional Music at Tokyo University of Arts and other schools

Sōkyoku Blooming in the Edo Period: Summary of *Koto* Music History

The origin of *koto* can be tracked down to ancient myth but *sōkyoku*, *koto* music as we generally hear today, began in the Edo period.

The earliest *koto* was introduced in the Nara period when other *gagaku* instruments were introduced from the continent. At the end of the Heian period, *koto* was used as a rhythmic instrument for *kangen* and *saibara*. But it is more important in the history of *koto* music that the nobles loved it as the musical instrument for poetry and music. However, *koto* was inactive during the long period after *gagaku* had been connected with the Buddhist ceremonies and until the monk Kenjun fathered Tsukushi School *sōkyoku* based on 'Etenraku songs' in the Momoyama period. *Koto* music changed sparked by the time the blind musician Yatsuhashi Kengyō met *tsukushi-goto*. Undoubtedly the accomplishment by Yatsuhashi Kengyō is immeasurable: for example, the establishment of *kumiuta* and *danmono* and the new tuning systems, and so on. Yatsuhashi owed a lot for his achievement to the blind men's guild called *tōdō* (or *tōdōza*), to which he belonged.

Without *tōdō*, the vertically structured organization founded in the various places nationwide, it is impossible to talk about the development of *sōkyoku*. Banding together and working as one for a common cause, *tōdō* developed and handed down their music, based on the music theory cultivated with *heikyoku*, the narrative songs accompanied by *gagaku biwa*, and later replaced *biwa* with *shamisen* and *koto*. The guild produced star musicians, gifted with the art of composition and performance, one after another, including Ikuta Kengyō.

Thanks to the musical talents of *tōdō*, *shamisen*'s *jiuta* and *koto*'s *sōkyoku* were closely related and fused, and then pure *sōkyoku* was revived against such fusion, and finally new Yamada School *sōkyoku* emerged, reflecting well-cultivated tastes of Edo. In the Meiji period, the *tōdō* system was abolished. *Koto* players and *koto* music, unconnected with public performances, were on the verge of extinction. As if being the savior, Michio Miyagi, the gifted *koto* player, emerged and established new *sōkyoku*, reflecting the modern society and enduring criticism from the conservative people. His music became the foundation of modern *sōkyoku* today.

Inspired by the activity of Miyagi, who was regarded as the father of the restoration of *sōkyoku*, the *koto* music as well as the whole Japanese traditional music world was animated, leading to contemporary music of today. *Koto* and *shamisen*, born in the beginning of Edo period or the beginning of early modern times, are the fruit of the early modern culture and are the root of today's Japanese music.

Traditional Japanese Music at a Glance

■History of *Koto*

Ancient Times	• Musical instruments such as pipe, *koto*, and drums existed in ancient times. A clay figurine of a man playing the *koto* was excavated.
Asuka (538-710)	• *Gayageum* probably came with the musicians from Silla (453). • *Konghou* (*kugo* in Japanese) probably came with the musicians from Baekje (554). • *Sankangaku* introduced and played (683). • Gagakuryō established in the Ministry of Ceremonies (701). • *Koto* introduced (ca. 8C).
Nara (710-794)	• Kibino Makibi returned from China with the book "Gakusho Yōroku" and musical instruments, including Tang's 13-string *koto* (735). • Tōdai-ji Temple Inaugural Ceremony of Great Buddha (752). • Tang's 13-string *koto* is preserved in the Shōsōin Repository.
Heian (794-1185)	• Ōutadokoro (Folk Music Office), a training school for *kuniburi no utamai*, was established (816). *Wagon* was used. • 'Music System Reform' began in Emperor Ninmyō's reign (833-850). • *Gagaku* established (894). Sending *Envoys to Tang* ends (894). • *Gakusō* (*gagaku koto*) joined the ensemble for *kangen* and *saibara*. • *Gyoyū* begins (908). • 'Poetry and music' and *koto* are favored by the noble. • Temple *gagaku* established (late 10C).
Kamakura (1185-1333)	• *Heikyoku* appears (early 13C?). • Temple songs '*Etenraku* song' began (13C).
Nanbokucho (1336-1392)	• Kakuichi became a *kengyō*. Tōdōza established. • *Mugen-noh* established (1380).
Muromachi (1336-1573)	• *Heikyoku* flourished (15C).
Momoyama (1573-1603)	• *Shamisen* introduced (ca.1560). • Kenju established *Tsukushi-goto* (end of 16C).
Edo (1603-1868)	• *Heikyoku* performers turned to *jōruri* (mid-16C). • Tokugawa Government appoints *noh* as its official ritual music (1610). • Yatsuhashi Kengyō composed 13 *koto-kumiuta* (1630). • '*Hondegumi* (old)' and '*hadegumi* (new)' of *jiuta shamisen-kumiuta* composed (1650?). • Tōdōza monopolized *koto* & *shamisen* (17C). *Jōruri* & *Kabuki* established (early 17C). • Ikuta Kengyō founded *Ikuta-ryū* (1695). • *Sōkyoku* & *jiuta* fused together (17C). • Urasaki Kengyō and Yaezaki Kengyō remodeled old *koto* melodies into *hadegumi* (18C). • *Shamisen* and *koto* completely fused to *jiuta-sōkyoku* : Yasumura Kengyō banned new *koto-kumiuta* and developed an instrumental style, *Kyoto tegotomono* (1755). • Yamada Kengyō wrote "Enoshima no Kyoku". *Yamada-ryū sōkyoku* began (1777). • Mitsuzaki Kengyō's "Godan Kinuta" to revive original *sōkyoku* (early 19C). • "Bakumatsu Shin Sōkyoku" movement (mid-19C). • Yoshizawa Kengyō's "Chidori no Kyoku" to revive original *koto-kumiuta*. Meiji Restoration (1868).
Meiji (1868-1912)	• Tōdōza and *Fuke* Sect abolished (1871). • '*Jiuta* Guild' → Tōdō Ongaku-kai (1875). • *Sōkyoku* & *shakuhachi* allowed for general public. • Shakuhach joined *sankyoku* (early 20C). • '*Meiji shinkyoku*' began (ca. 1910). • Koson Suzuki began Kyōgoku-ryū *sōkyoku* (1907). • Michio Miyagi began "Shin Nihon Ongaku" movement (1920).
Taisho (1912-1926)	• Sakichi Kineya established '*sangen shusōgaku*' (1920). • Michio Miyagi invented 17-string *koto* (1921), and composed "Haru no Umi" (1929).
Showa-Heisei (1925-)	• Kin'ichi Nakanoshima's "Three Fragments" performed (1942). • Department of Japanese Music is established at Tokyo University of Arts with instructors, Miyagi and Nakanoshima. • Western style composers began writing modern *sōkyoku*. • Fragmented wooden *koto* of the Yayoi period discovered at Toro, Shizuoka (1945). • Takemitsu's "November Steps" premiered in New York (1967).

Other Members of *Koto* Family

Ichigen-kin (1-string *koto*) is a plucked string instrument with a simple structure made of a flat long board with a single string and no fret or bridge. It is said that it is called *suma-goto* because Ariwara no Yukihira, the Heian period courtier and bureaucrat, made it at Suma where he was banished in the 9th century. However, according to the general theory, *ichigen-kin* was used for the popular music in China during the Sui Dynasty and introduced into Japan around the 17th century.

Nigen-kin (2-string *koto*) is basically the same as *ichigen-kin* but it has two strings. When two strings tuned on the same pitch are plucked at the same time, they create more delicate sound than does one string. *Nigen-kin* is also called *izumo-goto* since it was offered as the musical instrument to Izumo-taisha Shrine at the end of the Edo period, or *yakumo-goto* after the famous work "Yakumo" for the instrument. It was popular from the end of the Edo period to the Meiji period but declined after that. In the early Meiji period, *Azuma-ryū nigen-kin*, a variant of *nigen-kin*, became popular as an accompaniment instrument for *hauta* and other popular songs. This instrument was significantly improved into *taishō-koto* (also called *taishō-goto*) in the Taisho period. The improvement includes the steel strings instead of silk strings, the typewriter keys placed at the finger positions, and the numbered musical notation to be used. As a result, *taishō-koto* with easiness to play and read music was extremely popular from the Taisho to Showa periods, but declined because it was only used to accompany the popular songs and its own music was not developed.

Taishō-koto was "the new musical instrument which the Japanese invented". For a period of time, it was exported to the foreign countries, such as the South East Asia and Africa, where it was adapted to their cultures. There is an episode that a Japanese traveler was surprised when the local person showed it to him as their traditional musical instrument. It has gradually revived by older women, recently, because it is easy to play, and by school children due to the curriculum in the elementary schools that adopted it.

Other than those listed on the right page, there are many variants of *koto*: 15-string *koto*, 17-string *koto* (bass *koto*), 21-string *koto*, 25-string *koto*, 30-string *koto* and so on. There was even an impractical 80-string *koto* invented by Michio Miyagi.

Fifteen hundreds of years have passed since *koto* was introduced into Japan and numerous kinds of *koto* exist. However, although there are some minor changes, for instance, the shapes and materials of *kotoji* (bridges), plectra, and strings, the finish of the surface, and the way to string, the basic structure remains unchanged.

Traditional Japanese Music at a Glance

■Other Members of *Koto* Family

| *Ichigen-kin* (1-string koto) | Also called *han-kin* or *suma-goto*. This simple stringed instrument are widely found in the world. |

(Courtesy of Kochi City, Kochi Pref.)

Structure: Simple structure with a board strung with a single string.
Size: 111 cm long × 11 cm (at head) and 8 cm (at tail) wide
Performance: Pressing the string with a tubular device to change the pitches and plucking with a tubular plectrum.

How to play *ichigen-kin* (or *nigen-kin*)

- Press the string(s) at one of the marked finger positions with the tubular device (*rokan*) put on the middle finger of the left hand.
- Pluck the string(s) with the tubular plectrum (*ryūsō*) put on the index finger of the right hand.

(Courtesy of Yokosuka City, Kanagawa)

| *Nigen-kin* (2-string koto) | Also called *izumo-goto* or *yakumo-goto*. Invented based on *ichigen-kin* by Nakayama Kotonushi in 1820. |

(Photo: Kindenryū School)

Structure: Simple structure with a board strung with two strings tuned on the same pitch. In the early stage the body was made of bamboo, and later ceder or paulownia wood.
Size: Basically the same as *ichigen-kin* but slightly wider.
Performance: Similar to *ichigen-kin*, pressing the strings with a tubular device called *rokan* to change the pitches and plucking with a tubular plectrum called *ryūsō*.

| *Taishō-koto* | Also called *taiishō-goto*. A key board similar to the typewriter have been added to *nigen-kin*. Keys are placed at the finger positions. Invented by Gorō Morita in 1912. |

Improvement:
- Steel strings
- Keys placed at the finger positions
- Numbered musical notation
- Portability
- Easy accompaniment for pop songs

▲ One of the earliest *taishō-koto* (1914)
(Photo: Kindenryū School)

▶ Modern *taishō-koto*
(Photo: Kindenryū School)

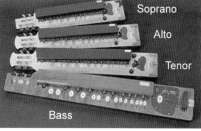
Soprano
Alto
Tenor
Bass

Chapter 8: *Shamisen* (1) *Jiuta*

Tōdōza: Blind Men's Guild

In the popular movie "Zatōichi, The Blind Swordsman", a blind masseur and swordsman, named Zatōichi, plays the title role. Ichi is his name and '*zatō*' his title, or class, in the hierarchy of the blind men's guild called *tōdōza* (or simply *tōdō*). In the Muromachi period (the 14th century), *tōdōza* was authorized by the Shogunate government as a benefit society for blind men, but not for women. *Biwa-hōshi*, the blind minstrels who play the *heike-biwa* while in monk's costume, organized the guild independently from any religious organization. It was the *heikyoku* master Kakuichi Akashi who completed the system of the guild. According to legends, the founder of *tōdō* was Imperial Prince Saneyasu, the son of Emperor Ninmyō, or maybe Imperial Prince Semimaru, the son of Emperor Daigo, but the stories are thought to be fabrications made up to bring the guild additional prestige.

The members of *tōdōza*, initially *heikyoku* players, improved *shamisen*, and then established and handed down *jiuta* (*shamisen* music), *sōkyoku* (*koto* music), and *kokyū* (a bowed string instrument) music as specialties of the guild. This nationwide guild had four classes in its hierarchy, from the lowest *zatō* to the highest *kengyō*, which were divided into sixteen subclasses which were further divided into seventy three orders. Because a member had to pay money to the guild every time he climbed one rank, it is said that most members could hardly afford to become higher than *zatō*. However, even the lowest-ranked *zatō* wore the esteemed purple and white garment made of silk and received monetary gifts of congratulation from people. That image is very different from Zatōichi in the films, in worker's happi and pants.

In the Edo period, administered by the Tokugawa Shogunate magistrate of temples and shrines, the guild was authorized to perform music; practice three medical therapies: acupuncture, moxibustion, and massage; and engage in moneylending. Their loan money was called *zatō* money, which imposed considerable interest. They were given top priority to collect money from debtors and on some occasions acted like a loan shark and made people suffer.

In addition to *jiuta* the new genre *jōruri* was established adapting the narrative *heikyoku* recited to the accompaniment of *biwa*. Sawazumi Kengyō, who belonged to *tōdō*, began this style and the members of *tōdō* were exclusively authorized to teach it, at first. Soon, the *jōruri* schools were formed and spread out with styles that deviated from the territory of *tōdō*.

Because *tōdō* received the most favorable treatment among organizations for blind men by the Shogunate government, the abolition of *tōdō* at the Meiji Restoration was a big blow to its members.

Traditional Japanese Music at a Glance

■ Tōdōza

● Tōdōza (or simply tōdō)
- The *biwa-hōshi* (minstrels in monk's robe) belonged to the religious organization, mainly the Tendai Sect.
- Among them, *mōsō* (blind monks) performing *heikyoku* formed an irreligious group 'za'.
- Under the patronage of the Shogunate, Akashi Kakuichi systematized the organization with the rank system and facilities.
- Blind men's professions were performing music, three medical treatments (acupuncture, moxibustion and massage) and moneylending.
- In 1871, the new government disbanded the *tōdōza* and stripped the members of their privilege.

● Music of tōdō

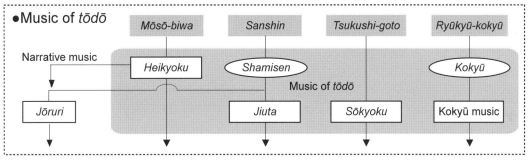

● Ranks of tōdō

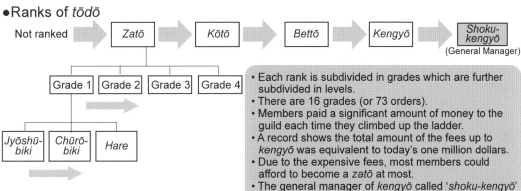

- Each rank is subdivided in grades which are further subdivided in levels.
- There are 16 grades (or 73 orders).
- Members paid a significant amount of money to the guild each time they climbed up the ladder.
- A record shows the total amount of the fees up to *kengyō* was equivalent to today's one million dollars.
- Due to the expensive fees, most members could afford to become a *zatō* at most.
- The general manager of *kengyō* called '*shoku-kengyō*' was worth more than the value of a territorial lord of a population of 100,000.

● Who founded tōdō?
- A theory says it was Imperial Prince Saneyasu (Emperor Ninmyo's 4th son), a.k. Amayo no Mikoto.
- Or, Semimaru, Emperor Daigo's 4th son and the *biwa-hoshi*, famous for his *waka* included in "The Hundred Poems by One Hundred Poets".

● Origin of the name tōdō
- A blind man who loved poetry and music said "this is my *tōdō* (the right way)". The name *tōdō* was derived from his words.

● Other guilds for the blind performers

Mōsōza — This is the guild for the *biwa-hōshi* who performed religious rituals such as chanting the sutra for the god of the earth or purifying the hearth of houses. Mainly they belonged to the Tendai Sects in various places in Kyusyu. Those who performed *heikyoku* left this guild and founded *tōdōza*.

Gozeza — This is the guild for the female blind entertainers who sang or narrated a tale to her own *shamisen*. They got their living by strolling the various local areas. In some areas, especially northern parts of Japan, where there were accommodations for them.

Shamisen: Flower of Edo Culture

Shamisen is used for various kinds of Japanese music, which is roughly classified into four groups: *jiuta*, *jōruri*, *nagauta*, and Edo short songs. The typical folk entertainments with which *shamisen* is involved are, for example, *gidayū-bushi*, *tokiwazu-bushi*, *kouta*, and *hauta*. They are subdivisions in the groups *jōruri* and Edo short songs. Folk songs are often sung to the accompaniment of *shamisen* but are not regarded as *shamisen* music. *Tsugaru shamisen*, originating in the northern parts of Japan and increasingly winning popularity in the Western countries, can be classified in *shamisen* music but it is rather regarded as a type of folk song.

The four groups mentioned above is just one of the many classification systems. *Shamisen* music is complexly diversified that it can be categorized into different groups, based on the musical styles, the purpose of the music, or the location where it is played. For example, *utaimono* (melodic songs) or the *katarimono* (narrative songs) based on the texts of the song, or *kabuki* music or *zashiki* songs based on whether it is sung in a *kabuki* theater or *zashiki* (a private parlor). Or, it is possible to classify based on the structure of music or the properties of players: for example, vocal or instrumental music, singing to one's own accompaniment or singing with a separate accompanist, or whether the player belongs to *tōdō* or not. Classification of *shamisen* is not simple.

During the Edo period, the public entertainment became closely connected with the lives of the townspeople of the merchant class and new forms were established. *Shamisen* was so versatile that it corresponded to those new public entertainment. That is why *shamisen* music became diversified.

Many musical instruments were introduced to Japan from foreign countries. They were little changed structurally and their music generally kept the original form. On the other hand, *shamisen* music substantially changed its structure because of the reasons mentioned above. The transformed *shamisen* became the foundation of the new music culture in the Edo period. During times of national isolation, the ensemble styles of *shamisen* such as *jiuta-sōkyoku* and *sankyoku gassō* (the instrumental trio) were closely related to the theatrical arts such as *kabuki* and *bunraku* puppetry. Music, literature, and dances were fused, creating the rich Edo culture.

Traditional Japanese Music at a Glance

■Classification of *Shamisen* Music

Unlike the music of *biwa* or *shakuhachi*, there are several classifications of *shamisen* music depending on what element it is based on.

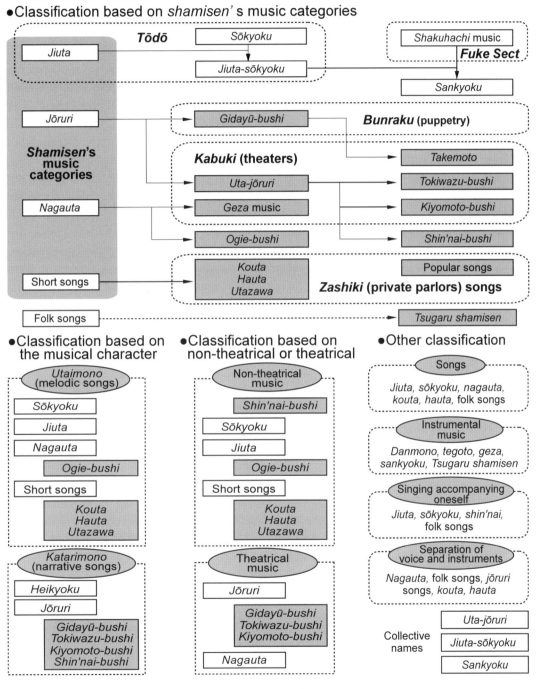

Guns, *Shamisen* and Xavier

The ancestor of *shamisen* is thought to be Chinese *sanxian* (literally "three strings"). Some advocate that *sanxian* originated from ancient Egyptian *nefer* (3-stringed lute), but this is not established. In any case, the ancestral form of *sanxian* existed in the Qin Dynasty (2nd century B.C.) before the East and West trade had begun. Southern *sanxian*, also called *quxian*, smaller than northern *sanxian* in size, was introduced to Okinawa, the southern island of Japan, around the 14th century and later became Japanese *sanshin*. *Sanxian* and *sanshin* are slightly different in length, but their similarity, for example the round sound box skinned with snake skin, shows their close relationship.

In the middle of the 16th century, about ten years after the introduction of guns from Europe (1543), Okinawan *sanshin* was brought to the Sakai harbor in the mainland Osaka, the port for foreign trade in those days. According to the most widely believed theory, the *biwa-hōshi* Ishimura Kengyō, regarded as the father of *shamisen-kumiuta*, obtained *sanshin* first and adapted it to the Japanese climate. He was a *biwa* player, so was influenced to introduce a plectrum similar to that of *biwa* instead of using finger picks for Chinese *sanxian*. In addition, some put forward a theory that since it was difficult to obtain big snakes in the mainland, dog or cat skin was used instead of snake skin. However, there is another convincing theory that the snake skin, less durable than dog or cat skin, could not endure the impacts from the plectrum banging against the skin in the *biwa*'s performing style. The body shape was also modified: the straight neck of *sanshin* was changed to the angled neck of *biwa*. Moreover, the concept and term of *sawari* (buzz sounds) was inherited from *biwa* (for *sawari*, see the *biwa* sections).

It is noted that there is a musical instrument similar to *shamisen*, called *gottan*, with a sound box made of wooden boards without animal skin in Kagoshima (southern Japan). Because *gottan* exists in Kagoshima which had a trading history with Okinawa, some put forward a theory that the location in the mainland where the origin of *shamisen* had been introduced was Kagoshima, not the Sakai port of Osaka.

Furthermore, there are other theories regarding how *shamisen* was introduced and altered. For example, *shamisen* was derived from 2-stringed instruments; it was directly introduced from China; the *tōdō* member Nakashō-ji in Sakai remodeled it; and so on.

During the short period between the introduction of guns and *shamisen*, the Roman Catholic missionary Francisco Xavier (1506-1552), who brought Christianity to Japan, arrived at Kagoshima (1549). Interestingly, these three introductions completely changed Japan's society, manner of war, and music culture.

■Roots of *Shamisen*

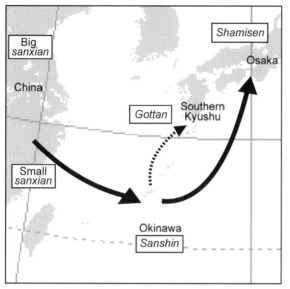

China	Sanxian	Also called *xianzi*.	
Northern China	Big *sanxian*	Also called *shuxian*. × Not introduced to Japan.	
Southern China	Small *sanxian*	Also called *quxian*.	
	↓ 14th century (?)		
Okinawa	Sanshin	Also called *jabisen* (snake skin *sanshin*).	
	↓ 1558-1570		
Osaka	Sanshin		
	Transformed ↓		
Kyoto-Osaka	Shamisen	Also called *sangen* (3 strings).	

Cradle	Name	Another name	Skin type	Length	Related music
Northern China	Big *sanxian*	Shuxian	Snake skin	119.8 cm	*Dagu* (drum) music, *bajiaogu* (octagonal tambourine) music
Southern China	Small *sanxian*	Quxian	Snake skin	107.0 cm	*Kunqu* (musical drama), *Tanci* (narrative music), *nan'yin*
Okinawa	Sanshin	Jabisen	Snake skin	75-80 cm	*Kumiodori* (musical drama), songs, folk songs
Kyushu	Gottan	Ita-shamisen	Cedar boards	90.8 cm	Buddhist songs
Kyoto-Osaka area	Shamisen	Sangen	Cat/dog skin	99.0 cm	Vocal and instrumental music, dance, folk songs

●How *shamisen* was transformed?

- Since *biwa-hōshi* played *sanshin* first, they used a plectrum like *biwa*.

1) The drum body became bigger and the frame was made of four pieces of wood.
2) Smooth cat or dog skin replaced snake skin.
3) The straight neck was angled like *biwa*.
4) The lowest string created buzz sounds called '*sawari*'.
5) The bridge was changed in shape, size and weight.
6) The inside of the drum frame was curved for better sonority.

●Who transformed *shamisen*?

Ishimura Kengyo, who was probably the same person called Nakashōji, the *biwa* performer.

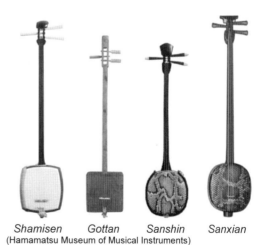

Shamisen   Gottan   Sanshin   Sanxian
(Hamamatsu Museum of Musical Instruments)

Birth of *Jiuta* and Schools of *Shamisen* Music

In its early stages, *shamisen* was used only with open strings and a few finger positions on the finger board to accompany the popular ditties. The ditties in those days were, for example, *ryūtatsu-bushi* first chanted by the priest Ryūtatsu in Sakai, and *rōsai-bushi* first chanted by the funny monk Rōsai. Soon, counter melodies (*kaede*) against the original melodies (*honde*) and virtuosic styles (*hade*) were developed, and *shamisen-kumiuta*, a song suite composed of all sorts of kinds of songs, was born. Ishimura Kengyō, who had transformed *sanxian* to *shamisen*, allegedly established the *shamisen-kumiuta*, regarded as the oldest *shamisen* music. The members of *tōdō* began to perform 'nagauta', the long songs with entirely consistent texts and the short songs '*hauta*'. The *nagauta* and *hauta* mentioned here were developed in the western district, mainly Kyoto and Osaka, and are different from the songs with the same names: '*edo nagauta*' of *kabuki* and Edo short songs '*hauta*', discussed later in this book.

    The Kyoto-Osaka *nagauta* and *hauta* developed into an important *shamisen* genre, *jiuta*, which would be the future ensemble forms and home music. The name, *jiuta*, was used and became firmly established in the Meiji period, after a surprisingly long time. As the right page illustrates, *jiuta* was called in a wide range of names due to its diversified characters in the Edo period.

    At the same time *jiuta* was established, some *biwa-hōshi*, members of *tōdō*, replaced their specialty *biwa* with *shamisen*. The one who began using *shamisen* first was allegedly Sawazumi Kengyō. Because he was afraid of what others might think if he performed "The Tale of the Heike" with *shamisen*, he chose other subjects such as "Jōruri Hime Monogatari (The Tale of Princess Jōruri)" from "Otogi-sōshi", a collection of ancient Japanese fables. His "The Tale of Princess Jōruri" was extremely well reputed and soon accepted as a new genre, *jōruri*, narrative music accompanied by *shamisen*. With many similar cases like this, *shamisen* music was swiftly diversified in a very short period of time after the ancestor of *shamisen* had been introduced and adapted to the Japanese climate.

    Connected with puppet shows, the *jōruri* became *ningyō-jōruri*, the puppet theater, accompanied by a narrative chants and *shamisen*. In the meantime, a female entertainer named Izumo no Okuni began *kabuki odori* (dance) which would also be connected with *shamisen*. The birth of *shamisen* led to the birth of the most typical music and public entertainment of early modern Japan.

Traditional Japanese Music at a Glance

■Emergence of *Shamisen* Music

During the early Modern Times, blind musicians developed *shamisen* music called *jiuta* in Kamigata (the Kyoto-Osaka area). It was non-theatrical music at the private parlors and home, and could contain *koto*.

Jiuta stands for 'regional songs'.

Jiuta was also called:

- *Kamigata-uta* (songs of Kamigata)
- *Hōshi-uta* (songs of blind monks)
- *Genkyoku* (string music)
- *Uta or kakyoku* (songs)

- Originally *jiuta* referred to the songs in the local area, in this case, Kamigata.
- It was named so to distinguish it from songs of Edo when they were introduced to Kamigata.
- The songs of Edo, mainly *jōruri* songs (*nagauta* and *bungo-bushi*), were called '*edo-uta*'.
- The name '*jiuta*' became standard in the Meiji period.

■Development of *Shamisen* Music

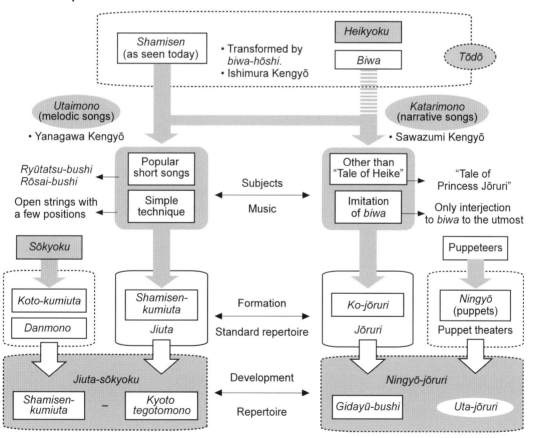

Versatility of *Jiuta*

Jiuta is a collective name for *shamisen* music consisting of nine groups, as illustrated on the right page. While it is classified into nine groups in this book, some scholars or *shamisen* schools classify it more minutely.

The first group is *shamisen-kumiuta* (song suites). It is named after *koto-kumiuta*. Thirty two *shamisen-kumiuta* exist at present, composed by Ishimura Kengyō and other *shamisen* musicians. Yanagawa Kengyō, one of them, devised the *hade* (virtuosic) style. The modern word '*hade* (showiness or flashiness)' originated from this *shamisen* term.

Initially, the texts of *shamisen-kumiuta* were composed of unrelated poems. With time, consistent texts of one topic were used with the same title and these long songs were called *nagauta*. In addition, short and independent songs, *hauta*, were composed. *Hauta* was also used as the accompaniment music for dancing. The texts of *kumiuta* and *nagauta* were derived from the songbooks such as the collections of the popular songs or the folk songs in those days, as well as the selections from "Kokinshū (A Collection of Ancient and Modern Poetry)". Various public entertainment became popular among the townsman of the merchant class in a big city, from which a wide range of subjects and music styles were adapted to *shamisen* music. The popular shows and songs of *noh*, *kabuki*, and *jōruri* gradually formed new *shamisen* genres as the *noh* songs, the theater songs, and the *jōruri* songs, expanding the boundary of *jiuta*. *Sakumono*, comical songs sung ad lib in the parlors in the gay quarters also became a new kind of *jiuta*. These songs prove that *jiuta* widely pervaded the lives of the merchant class.

Furthermore, the new performance techniques such as *kaede* (counter parts) and *hade* developed from *honde*, the original *jiuta* songs, changed *jiuta* itself. A new music genre was established from the close relationship with *sōkyoku* as well; especially, the instrumental section as a merely short interlude inserted between vocal sections developed into *tegotomono*, an independent instrumental music. In addition, the effective polyphony of '*kaede* style *sōkyoku*', a duet of *shamisen* and *koto*, became Kyoto style *tegotomono*, a purified art form leading to today's musical art. As a result, *jiuta* became firmly fixed as the home music in the society in those days. *Tōdō* members were exclusively authorized to teach it but when their guild was abolished at the Meiji Restoration, they lost their privilege and were left out in the cold.

■Category of *Jiuta*

Types	Birth year	Founder and Successor	Description	Major works
Shamisen-kumiuta	1600	Ishimura Kengyō, Torazawa Kengyō, Yanagawa Kengyō	The oldest classics of *shamisen* music. Formal name is '*shamisen-honde*'. A suite of popular short songs with unrelated texts centering on *shamisen*.	Ryūkyūgumi, Hindagumi, Nanatsugo
Nagautamono	1661	Sayama Kengyō, Yanagawa Kōto	The texts of songs, based on the *nagauta* (long songs) from "The Kokinshū", are consistent, focusing more on vocal parts. This *nagauta* is different from *kabuki*'s *nagauta*.	Sakurazukushi, Kiyari, Kumoirōsai, Fuyukusa
Hautamono	1703	Tsuguhashi Kengyō, Utagi Kengyō, Minezaki Kōto	A newly created type against classics, composed of *shibaiuta* and popular songs in the gay quarters. This type only refers to short songs to distinguish it from *shibaiutamono*.	Tsuru no Koe, Yuki, Aoba, Kuchikiri, Kakurenbo
Sakumono	1751	N/A	Narrative songs improvised for fun with humorous contents in the *jōruri* style, also called '*odokemono*'. Since they were improvised, it is not known who composed them.	Arenezumi, Kawazu, Shirizukushi, Egao, Tanuki, Tanishi
Shibaiutamono	17-18C	Kishino Jirōza	The songs for *kabuki* in the Kyoto-Osaka area was taken into *jiuta*. In its early stage, it was part of *hauta*. The *kabuki*'s Edo songs became independent as *nagauta*.	Aoba, Kigisu, Toribayama, Hōkasō
Utaimono	1800(?)	Fujio Kōto	The subjects or texts of *utai* (noh chants) were diverted into *shamisen* songs. In its early stage, it was part of *hauta* and later *shibaiutamono*.	Aoi no Ue, Shakkyō, Kantan, Takasago, Ko-dōjōji
Jōrurimono	17-18C	Tsuruyama Kōto	Non-theatrical Edo *jōruri* popular in the Kyoto-Osaka area, such as *handayu-bushi*, *eikan-bushi* and *shigetayū-bushi*, were taken into *jiuta*. The songs and players are scarce	Ikensoga, Nureōgi, Usuyuki, Konkyō-ji
Tegotomono	1790	Mitsuhashi Kōto, Ichiura Kengyō	The instrumental short interludes between songs developed to *tegoto*. The music focusing on *tegoto* was called *tegotomono* which was gradually sophisticated and the duo of *honde* (main melodies) and *kaede* (counter melodies) emerged.	Echigo-jishi, Shōchikubai, Sarashi, Nebiki no Matsu
Kyōfū Tegotomono	1830	Urasaki Kengyō, Matsuura Kengyō, Yaezaki Kengyō	A.k.a *kyōmono*. Koto joined *shamisen* and many *kaede*, the variants of the melodies, were composed in Kyoto. Koto and *shamisen* were played in concert or independently.	Uji-meguri, Shiki no Nagame, Iso-chidori

● *Tegotomono*

Maeuta → Tegoto → Atouta

Interlude — Regarded as important as vocal parts. Highlights of instrumental technique.

Structure of *tegotomono*

Maebiki → Maeuta → Tegoto → Atouta → Atobiki

Maebiki → Maeuta → Tegoto → Nakauta → Tegoto → Atouta → Tegoto

Two Wheeled Vehicle: *Jiuta* and *Sōkyoku*

Jiuta evolved by crossbreeding and reciprocal influence with *koto* music, *sōkyoku* (for detail, see the *sōkyoku* section). Such interaction sprouted before the establishment of both *jiuta* and *sōkyoku* since *shamisen*, *koto* and *hitoyogiri* (the ancestor of *shakuhachi*) had already been played in concert. However, the main reason why the two different instruments had a very close relationship was that they shared common factors: firstly, they were vocal music recited to player's own accompaniment; and secondly, the players of the two instruments were the same members of *tōdōza*, the blind men's guild. The right page illustrates the flow of the development of *jiuta* and *sōkyoku*. Continuously and jointly devising innovative techniques and creating new works, they were fused into a new music world. The synergy effect of invention and implementation expedited their evolution. In other words, there were many creative, knowledgeable, and well-trained musicians in *tōdōza*.

As *shamisen* and *koto* music evolved from simple songs to complicated and structural *tegotomono*, a term, *jiuta-sōkyoku*, referring to the highly artistic music, was finally born. The music was a complete fusion of *jiuta* and *sōkyoku*, not just their simple coordination. This fusion applied to not only music but also musicians. Many multi-talented players emerged, who completely mastered *koto* and *shamisen* as well as *kokyū*, a unique Japanese bowed string instrument which appeared at the same time as *shamisen* and also became the specialty of *tōdōza*. They contributed to establish a new ensemble style, *sankyoku gassō*, a trio of *shamisen*, *koto* and *kokyū*.

On the other hand, some *koto* players repelled the loss of musical originality of *koto* music and began a movement to abandon *jiuta* and revive pure *sōkyoku*. We should think that this movement was not a deviation from the *tōdō* music but rather a new creative activity.

At the Meiji Restoration, the Fuke sect and the *tōdō* system were simultaneously abolished. *Shakuhachi*, which used to be limited to Buddhist monks as a religious device, was liberated as an ordinary musical instrument and joined the *sankyoku gassō*, replacing *kokyū*. As a result, three worlds of *jiuta*, *sōkyoku*, and *shakuhachi* music, further developed and the boundary of *shamisen* music expanded.

Traditional Japanese Music at a Glance

■Lineage of *Jiuta-sōkyoku*

```
                    ← Within tōdōza →
    ┌─────┐                              ┌─────────┐
    │Jiuta│ ──→   Interaction   ←──      │ Sōkyoku │
    └─────┘                              └─────────┘
```

Ishimura Kengyō (*Shamisen-kumiuta*) ── *Hitoyogiri+Shamisen+Koto* ── Yatsuhashi Kengyō (*Koto-kumiuta* & *danmono*)

Torazaki Kengyō

This combination extisted before Yatsuhashi.

Sawazumi Kengyō (*Jōruri*) — Yanagawa Kengyō (*Hadegumi*) ··· | Honde | Hade |

| Shamisen | Koto | — Kitajima Kengyō

— Ikuta Kengyō (*Ikuta-ryū*)

Sayama Kengyō (*Nagauta*)

| Shamisen | Koto |
| Honde | Kaede | — Ichiura Kengyō

Utagi Kengyō (*Hauta*)

Mitsuhashi Kōtō (*Shamisen*'s *tegoto*) ··· | Honde | Kaede | Inovation ⇒ ✕*Jiuta* ○*Jōruri*
                                                                   Yamada-ryū sōkyoku

Minezaki Kōtō | Tegotomono |

💭 A multi-talented performer = *shamisen* and *koto* player and singer

| *Sōkyoku* transcribed from *jiuta* | — Urazaki Kengyō

| *Jiuta* | *Koto*'s *kaede* | — Yaezaki Kengyō (*Koto*'s *kaede* added to *jiuta*)

↓ Integration

Tegotomono of *koto*'s *kaede*   Kikuoka Kengyō | **Kyōfū Tegotomono** | Matsuura Kengyō
                                   Ishikawa Kōtō   Mitsuzaki Kengyō

Jiuta? *Sōkyoku*?

💥 *Tōdōza* abolished

| *Jiuta-sōkyoku* | Deviation ⇒ ✕*Jiuta* ○Pure *koto* music
                                    Bakumatsu shin aōkyoku

• Another *tōdō*'s instrument: | *Kokyū* |

| *Shakuhachi* | as religious device → a musical instrument

💥 Fuke Sect abolished

↓

Sankyoku

Tracing the History of *Jiuta*

The history of schools of early modern *sōkyoku* can easily be traced, from the times when Yatsuhashi Kengyō, the father of *sōkyoku*, was active to the end of the Edo period. However, it is very difficult to trace the history of *jiuta* and its schools.

Ishimura Kengyō and Torazawa Kengyō, regarded as the fathers of *jiuta*, established *shamisen-kumiuta* and the norms for their schools called *omotegumi*. Yanagawa Kengyō, the pupil of Torazawa's pupil, founded the Yanagawa School and established *hadegumi*, the new norms. Hayasaki Kengyō, the pupil of Yanagawa's pupil, succeeded his style and founded Hayasaki School in Kyoto. Nogawa Kengyō, Hayasaki's fellow pupil, revised the Yanagawa style of *shamisen-kumiuta* to his own and founded the Nogawa School in Osaka. The difference between the Yanagawa and Nogawa schools is not so much as that of Ikuta and Yamada Schools of *sōkyoku*. The only differences between the two are: the unique Yanagawa *shamisen* was used for Yanagawa School; and each had slightly different works required for the acquisition of licenses and slightly different esoteric works.

Yanagawa and Nogawa Schools further differentiated through offshoots, but it is only possible to trace them in the early stages of *jiuta*. That is because *jiuta* had fused indivisibly with *sōkyoku* and its succession system and offshoots were deeply and complicatedly connected with the *sōkyoku* schools. As illustrated on the right page, the founder of each *jiuta* school also belonged to another *sōkyoku* school. By the end of the Edo period, the schools of *jiuta* and *sōkyoku* were jumbled together. Today, *koto* and *shamisen* music schools always show both names of *koto* and *shamisen* schools in their advertisements.

Nogawa School handed down thirty-two normal works and Yanagawa School six normal works, at present. It is alleged that initially Yanagawa School had thirty-six works. We find many similarly titled works among the repertories of these schools for works derived from the same source, but actually they are very different when we listen to them.

When *jiuta* became commonly played in the gay quarters of Kyoto and Osaka, the popular songs or comical songs such as *sakumono*, and virtuosic instrumental music such as *tegotomono* were lionized, rather than classical *nagauta* and *hauta*.

Traditional Japanese Music at a Glance

■Genealogy of *Jiuta*

▶ Schools are differentiated by their normal *shamisen-kumiuta* titles, not by the style.
▶ Schools are called '*ryū*' and sub-schools are called '*ha*' or '*suji*'.

Shamisen improved by Ishimura Kengyō
  └─ Torazawa Kengyō — established norms called '*omotegumi*'.

Jōruri begun by Sawazumi Kengyō ─── To *jōruri*
  └─ Yamanoi Kengyō ─── Yanagawa-ryū
         Yanagawa Kengyō — established new norms called '*hadegumi*'.
              ├─ Asari Kengyō ─── Hayazaki Kengyō — Hayazaki-ryū
              └─ Asazauma Kengyō ─── Nogawa Kengyō — Nogawa-ryū

• Kyoto schools
• Osaka schools

●Relationship between *jiuta* and *sōkyoku* schools

▶ Kyoto schools (Yanagawa lineage)

Factions	Founder	Sōkyoku schools
• Kami-ha	Furukawa Rōsai	Kyō Ikuta-ryū
• Shimo-ha	Matsuzaki Kengyō	Kyō Ikuta-ryū
• Fushimi-ha	Ihara Kengyō	Kyō Ikuta-ryū

▶ Osaka schools (Nogawa lineage)

Factions	Founder	Sōkyoku schools
• Kiku-suji	Kikunaga Kengyō	Ko Ikuta-ryū
• Tomi-suji	Tomisawa Kōtō	Tsuguyama-ryū
• Naka-suji	Nakagawa Kengyō	Shin Ikuta-ryū
• Take-suji	Tatei Kengyō	Shin Ikuta-ryū

●Other local schools: Nagoya schools, Kyushu schools, and Chugoku schools.

●Today's *jiuta* schools:
• Tōdō Ongaku-kai in Osaka: Developed from 'Jiuta Society' after the abolition of *tōdō* (Kikuhara Hatsuko).
• Kyoto Tōdō-kai in Kyoto: The society was established after the abolision of *tōdō* (Hagiwara Seigin).
• Local performers who proceeded to Tokyo: Satoko Kawase (the Kyushu school), Seikin Tomiyama (the Osaka school), Fumiko Yonekawa (the Chugoku school), and so on.

●Norms and *shamisen-kumiuta* titles required for the professional license

Nogawa-ryū

Norms:	Work titles
Omotegumi:	Ryūkyūgumi, Torigumi, Koshigumi, Fushōgumi, Hindagumi, Shinobigumi, Ukiyogumi
Hadegumi:	Matsunigozare, Nagasaki, Hirayakomatsu, Kyōganoko, Shimōsa, Kurenai, Katabachi
Uragumi:	Shizu, Nishikigi, Aoyagi
Nakamoto:	Hayafune, Yawata, Rangoya, Misu, Yurikan, Nayoshi, Rōsai
Ōmoto:	Nanatsugo, Asagi, Chawan, Matsumushi, Seiran, Sakai, Nakashima, Hosori

Yanagawa-ryū

Norms:	Work titles
Omotegumi:	Ryūkyūgumi, Hindagumi
Hadegumi:	Matsunigozarita, Kuzu no Ha, Shimōsa Hosori
Nakamoto:	Hayafune

●*Kumiuta*: Song suites composed of unrelated short songs

	Source of texts	Verse style	Poems	Musical form	Character
Koto-kumiuta	Waka or imayō	Literary	Noble literature	Stereotyped/fixed	Elegant/simple
Shamisen-kumiuta	Popular songs	Colloquial	Popular songs	Free	Diversified

Originally, family music for young and eldery women   *Shamisen-kumiuta* fixed and normalized.

Later, ⇩ Character   ⇩ Clientele   ⇩ Diversity

Non-theatrical music   Gay quarters, entertainers, dilettantes   Nagauta, hauta, utaimono, sakumono
                                                                 New & popular songs

Kokyū, Bowed String Instrument

Though it seems to be irrelevant to *jiuta*, *kokyū*, a bowed string instrument, is discussed here because it had a close relationship with *jiuta*. *Kokyū* is the only bowed string instrument among Japanese instruments.

There are three theories about *kokyū*'s origin though not verified: it originated from *shamisen*, Okinawan *kūchō*, or European rebec. The Chinese bowed string instrument, *erhu*, looks similar but is different from *kokyū*. The family of Chinese bowed string instruments is called *huqin*. The bow of *erhu* is inserted between two strings and rubs both strings at the same time. On the other hand, the bow of *kokyū* rubs the top of a string as with the violin. The violin player changes the bow angle to select the string but the *kokyū* player vertically holds and rotates the instrument to select the string.

Kokyū music was established by *tōdōza* as an independent genre in addition to *jiuta* and *sōkyoku*. The schools of *kokyū* were also formed within *tōdōza*, and, like *shakuhachi* music, *honkyoku*, or original works for *kokyū*, and *gaikyoku*, or works were created for ensembles of *kokyū* with other instruments. However, during the process of the birth and development of the ensemble forms of *jiuta* and *sōkyoku*, *kokyū* music, which also belonged to *tōdō*, was absorbed in *sankyoku gassō*, an instrumental trio, and lost its originality. Finally, it was replaced by *shakuhachi*, another melodic instrument, in the trio. At present, *kokyū* is rarely joined in *sankyoku gassō* except as the accompaniment for the Kamigata (Kyoto-Osaka region) dances, called *kamigatamai*.

There are old drawings depicting street entertainers playing *kokyū* in its early stages. Today, *kokyū* is occasionally and only locally used to accompany folk songs. For example, "Ecchū Owarabushi" in Toyama, famous for the summer festival and *bon* dances, is well-known because the melancholy tone of *kokyū* arouses our feeling of sympathy. One of the most famous theatrical works for *kokyū* is "Akoya no Kotozeme", a scene from the *kabuki* or *jōruri* play. Other than *sankyoku gassō*, *kokyū* is used in the *geza* (offstage) music of *kabuki*. The sorrowful tone of *kokyū* is indispensable for the tragic scenes. Its melancholy tone seems to echo its own ill fate.

■Music of *Kokyū*

Only bowed traditional string instrument in Japan.

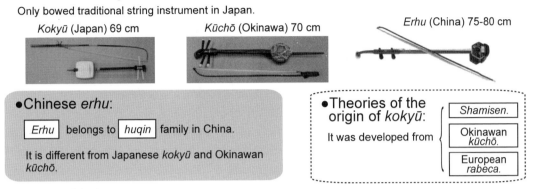

Kokyū (Japan) 69 cm   *Kūchō* (Okinawa) 70 cm   *Erhu* (China) 75-80 cm

●Chinese *erhu*:

| Erhu | belongs to | huqin | family in China.

It is different from Japanese *kokyū* and Okinawan *kūchō*.

●Theories of the origin of *kokyū*:

It was developed from { Shamisen. / Okinawan *kūchō*. / European *rabeca*. }

●History of *kokyū*

- In the Edo period...
- Strolling musicians played *kokyū*. ("Illustrated Sino-Japanese Encyclopedia" published in 1712)

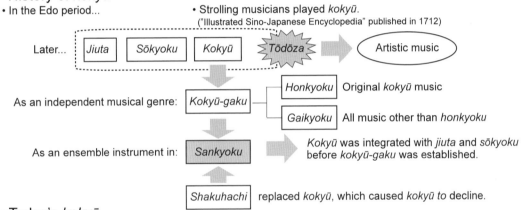

Later... Jiuta, Sōkyoku, Kokyū → Tōdōza → Artistic music

As an independent musical genre: Kokyū-gaku
- Honkyoku — Original *kokyū* music
- Gaikyoku — All music other than *honkyoku*

As an ensemble instrument in: Sankyoku → *Kokyū* was integrated with *jiuta* and *sōkyoku* before *kokyū-gaku* was established.

Shakuhachi replaced *kokyū*, which caused *kokyū* to decline.

●Today's *kokyū*

Jōruri	The scene 'Akoya no kotozeme' from "The War Chronicles at Dannoura".
Kabuki	The same scene from a *kabuki* version and *geza* music (Instrumental accompaniment) for the sorrowful scene.
Folk songs	Folksong "Ecchū Owarabushi" of Kaze no Bon Festival in the northern part of Japan, and so on.
Sankyoku	Accompaniment for the Kamigata (Kyoto-Osaka) dance, and so on.
Others	Door-to-door entertainments by *goze* (blind female strolling musicians), and religious rites of Tenriism (Tenri-kyō).

Kokyū player circa 1900

●Schools

Cradle	School name	Founder	Description
Tokyo	Fujie-ryū	Fujie Kengyō	Created 4-string *kokyū*. Accompaniment for Yamada-ryū songs.
Osaka	Masajima-ryū	Masajima Kengyō	Established artistic solo works.
Kyoto	Udesaki-ryū	Udesaki Kengyō	Udesaki was regarded as a virtuoso but he had no successor.
Nagoya	Yoshizawa-ha	Yoshizawa Kengyō	Original *kokyū* melodies in ensemble, e.g. "Chidori no Kyoku".

Sankyoku

Though they are used indiscriminately at present, the terms '*sankyoku*' and '*sankyoku gassō*' had different meanings. Initially, '*sankyoku*' meant three music genres of *shamisen*, *koto* and *shakuhachi*, and '*sankyoku gassō*' meant a trio of the three instruments. *Sankyoku* also means three major works, like three great symphonies or three famous violin concertos. Today, *sankyoku* refers to an ensemble of Japanese instruments in general.

As discussed previously in this book, there had already been an ensemble form of three instruments, *sangen* (another name of *shamisen*), *koto* and *hitoyogiri* in the early Edo period before *jiuta* and *sōkyoku* were established. This is according to "Shichiku Shoshin-shū (A Collection of Pieces for Beginners of Strings and Bamboo)" (1664) and "Shichiku Taizen (The Complete Works for Strings and Bamboo)" (1699).

Hitoyogiri was generally a solo instrument at that time. However, the existing musical score shows that the popular songs or dance songs in those days were accompanied by instrumental ensemble including *hitoyogiri*. These songs were called *rangyoku*. Among the songs in that style were seemingly original melodies of famous *koto* works "Rokudan no Shirabe (Six Steps)" and "Midare (Chaos)" by Yatsuhashi Kengyō. This ensemble form existed in the time of Yatsuhashi (1614–1685), but he seemed not to be interested. *Koto* and *sangen* were actively played in concert during the life of Ikuta Kengyō (1656-1715). Then, the instrumental techniques of *sangen* and *koto* developed, as *tegotomono* shows, and *kokyū*, a melodic bowed string instrument which also belonged to *tōdō*, joined the duo of these plucked string instruments, and expanded a new musical possibility of the trio.

In the Meiji period, *shakuhachi* replaced *kokyū* in the trio. Influenced by Western music, *sankyoku gassō* became the new ensemble form different from the traditional ensemble, which led to the Japanese music of the new age. As for the modern *sankyoku gassō*, the musical elements which did not exist in the Japanese traditional music before, such as the ideas of harmony and complicated rhythm, were introduced by the Western style composers. As a result, the new ensemble style containing Japanese instruments was established, and is often large in size.

Traditional Japanese Music at a Glance

■*Sankyoku*

There are two terms: '*sankyoku*' and '*sankyoku gassō*'.
Strictly speaking they are slightly different.

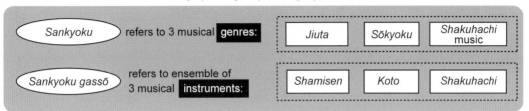

- *Sankyoku* refers to 3 musical **genres:** Jiuta | Sōkyoku | Shakuhachi music
- *Sankyoku gassō* refers to ensemble of 3 musical **instruments:** Shamisen | Koto | Shakuhachi

●History of *sankyoku*

- Early 17C — Shamisen | Koto | Hitoyogiri — This combination was recorded in "Shichiku Taizen"(1687 or before) and so on.
- Late 17C — Jiuta | Sōkyoku — The two were fused into *jiuta-sōkyoku* in Ikuta School.
- During 17C — Shamisen | Koto | Kokyū — They were played together by *tōdō* members.
- Lete 19C — Shamisen | Koto | Shakuhachi — *Shakuhachi* replaced *kokyū* in the Meiji period.

●Relation of *jiuta-sōkyoku* and *shakuhachi*

After the abolition of *tōdōza* and Fuke Sect, *shakuhachi* was closely related with *jiuta-sōkyoku*.

Shin nihon ongaku: The new traditional Japanese music movement by Michio Miyagi and Tozan Nakao.
New *sōkyoku* broadened the boundary.

Today *sankyoku* is regarded as:

A chamber music of traditional musical instruments.

A painting of *sankyoku* with *kokyū*. Already family music in the Edo period.

(Courtesy of Seikin Tomiyama)

●Another meaning of '*sankyoku*'

The word '*sankyoku*' also refers to 'three masterpieces' similar to the idea of '3 big...'

- *Biwa*: "Ryūsen", "Takuboku", and "Yōshinsō"
- *Heikyoku*: "Tsurugi no Maki", "Shūron", and "Kagami no Sata"
- *Noh*: "Hatsuserokudai", "Tōgokukudari", and "Saikokukudari"
- *Sōkyoku*: "Shiki no Kyoku", "Ōgi no Kyoku", and "Kumoi no Kyoku"
- *Shakuhachi*: "Kyorei", "Kokū", and "Mukaiji"

In Western music, three big violin concertos, for instance, are composed by Beethoven, Tchaikovsky and Mendelssohn.

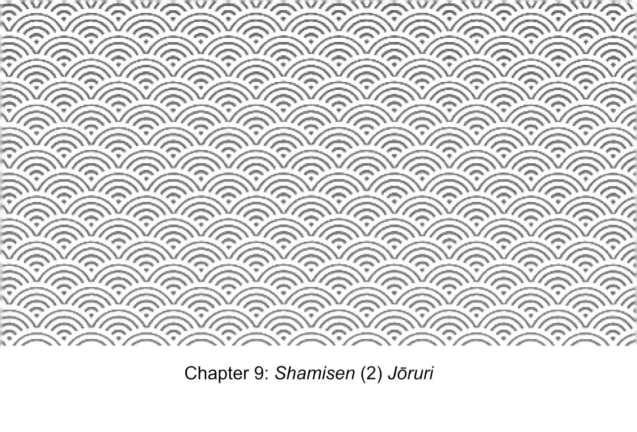

Chapter 9: *Shamisen* (2) *Jōruri*

What is *Jōruri*?

The Japanese puppet theater, widely known as *bunraku* which was the new name first used in the Meiji period, is formally called *ningyō-jōruri*. *Ningyō-jōruri* is a composite art of a puppet show and music called *jōruri* with *shamisen* that accompanies narration or songs. The name '*jōruri*' was derived from the title of the first such work "Jōruri Hime Monogatari (The Tale of Princess Jōruri)".

Jōruri is classified into two groups: *ningyō-jōruri* (puppet *jōruri*) and *uta-jōruri* (lyric *jōruri*). *Uta-jōruri* is lyric narrative music used for *kabuki* dancing and so on and has nothing to do with puppet shows. *Ningyō-jōruri* gained immensely in popularity when the *jōruri* master, Takemoto Gidayū, substantially improved the stage of the puppet shows. He called his music, *gidayū-bushi*, as the "new style" and, as a result, *jōruri* before his *gidayū-bushi* was called the "old style" or *ko-jōruri*.

Uta-jōruri was used first for *kabuki* and then in the parlors (*zashiki* in Japanese) of the gay quarters. Thus, *uta-jōruri* is classified into two groups according to where the songs are sung: *kabuki-jōruri* primarily for theatrical stages, and *zashiki-jōruri* for parlors and banquets.

The term, *jōruri*, means a musical genre of *katarimono* (narrative songs) recited to the accompaniment of *shamisen*. However, the name, *ningyō-jōruri*, is often shortened to '*jōruri*' without '*ningyō*'. That is, *jōruri* means '*bunraku*' as well. In addition, in *bunraku*, a *jōruri* narrator and his narration are often called *jōruri*, distinguished from *shamisen* accompaniments. In Osaka, the term, *jōruri*, means *gidayū-bushi* or the puppet show accompanied by *jōruri*.

The term, *bunraku*, was derived from the name of the puppet theater, Bunraku-za, established by the impresario Uemura Bunrakuken in Osaka at the end of the Edo period. It is said that *ningyō-jōruri* became called *bunraku* after this name. However, until the name, *bunraku*, was widely accepted, the puppet theater was called by various names. *Jōruri* refers to many things making it complicated and confusing.

■Jōruri

Originated from "The Tale of Princess Jōruri", '*joruri*' refers to *katarimono* (narrative songs) sung to *shamisen* accompaniment or the entertainments containing it in the Early Modern Age.

• *Ningyō-jōruri* a.k.a. *bunraku* (puppet theater) is one of the public entertainments. It was begun in the Early Modern Age combining music, literature and drama. It is one of the three big Japanese theatrical arts: *noh*, *kabuki*, and *bunraku*.

●Categories of *jōruri*

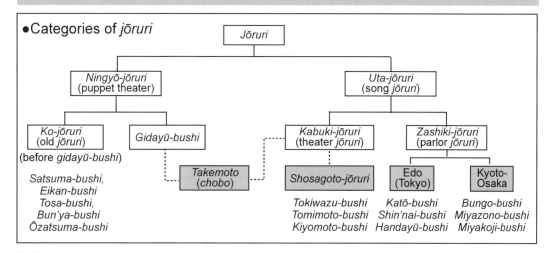

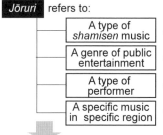 refers to:

A type of *shamisen* music	• *Katarimono* of *shamisen* music such as *gidayū-bushi* or *tokiwazu-bushi*.
A genre of public entertainment	• *Bunraku*, theatrical art, by puppeteers and *jōruri* performers.
A type of performer	• *Jōruri* chanters other than *shamisen* performers or accompanists.
A specific music in specific region	• *Gidayū-bushi* used only in Osaka.

●Variations of the name '*ningyō-jōruri*'

- In the Edo period, as narrative songs were focused on, *ningyō-jōruri* was called:

    ayatsuri, *ayatsuri-jōruri*, or *jōruri-ayatsuri*.

- In the Meiji periods, as puppets and stages were focused on, *ningyō-jōruri* was called:

    jōruri with puppets, or *jōruri* drama with puppets.

- In the Taisho and Showa periods, as the story and dramaturgy were focused on, *ningyō-jōruri* was called: *ningyō-jōruri*.

- Today, as traditional music has been recognized as an art, *ningyō-jōruri* is called: *bunraku*. It was named after the Bunraku-za theater by Uemura Bunrakuken.

●Jōruri Hime Monogatari
(The Tale of Princess Jōruri)

- A love story popular in Aichi during the early Muromachi period (1392-1573), also called "Jūnidan-zōshi" or "Jōruri-jūnidan".

- It came from a tale of miracles narrated by a temple maiden at Hōrai-ji temple in Aichi.

- Story: The young prince Yoshitsune of the Genji Clan who fell in love with the beautiful princess Jōruri died once but was miraculously resuscitated by her devotion. The elegant lyrics of the songs and the devotion of the lovely princess achieved universal popularity.

Birth of Ningyō-jōruri

Ningyō-jōruri (present *bunraku*) combines *shamisen* music and puppet shows but was not initially played by *shamisen* players and puppet operators.

Before *jōruri*, there were other narrative songs such as *heikyoku* recited to the performer's own accompaniment of *biwa*, *kōwakamai* chanted to the performer's own dancing, and *sekkyō-bushi* recited by door-to-door performers. *Heikyoku* and *sekkyō-bushi* dealt with tragic tales of the Heike family, the bloody war chronicles, and the serious miraculous virtue stories. On the other hand, "The Tale of Princess Jōruri", the first music recited to *shamisen*, from which the name, *jōruri*, originated, was a romantic love story about a young hero and a beautiful heroine, and was enthusiastically received by the public. Even the members of *tōdō*, whose specialty was *heikyoku*, favored the delightful *jōruri*. In the early stages, *jōruri* was recited to the accompaniment of *biwa* or rhythmic beats of fans but when *shamisen* improved by *tōdō* was used for the accompaniment, it became a more flowery entertainment. The original story of "Princess Jōruri" was dramatically revised. The narration became more melodic and musical, and then, the puppet show was added in order to provoke visual interests. As it became more popular, the number of *jōruri* narrators increased. Their characteristic narrative styles and melodies were called 'so-and-so *bushi*' after the name of the master-narrator. And then *shamisen* players that specialized in *jōruri* emerged, parting from *jiuta shamisen* of *tōdō*. Theaters exclusively for puppet shows were built in Osaka, Kyoto, and Edo (present Tokyo) where *ningyō-jōruri* was continually staged. As a result, the puppet theaters could not stage the same "The Tale of Princess Jōruri" over and over again so the *jōruri* narrators had to seek new programs which would be well-received by the audience.

Among the new programs, the stories of heroes called '*kinpira-jōruri*' won big popularity. They are fantastic tales of the hero Sakata Kinpira. These tales of heroes spread nationwide and had an influence on both *kabuki* and *jōruri*.

It was the time of *ko-jōruri* and the division of labor system by puppet operators and musicians was not yet established, as it is in present *bunraku*,. The old *ningyō-jōruri* was simple: there was only one dedicated puppet operator, and the *jōruri* narrator occasionally seemed to play two roles of a puppet operator and a narrator. Though the storytelling was simple and the performance was plain, undoubtedly it was the most favorite pastime of the public in those days.

Traditional Japanese Music at a Glance

■Initial *Jōruri*

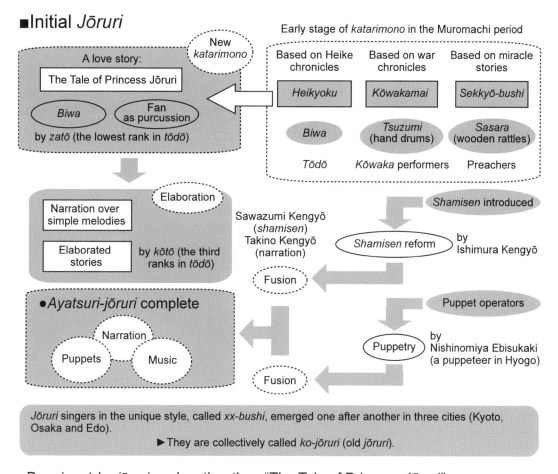

Jōruri singers in the unique style, called *xx-bushi*, emerged one after another in three cities (Kyoto, Osaka and Edo).
▶ They are collectively called *ko-jōruri* (old *jōruri*).

●Prominent *ko-jōruri* works other than "The Tale of Princess Jōruri"

- The Middle Ages subjects: "Amida-munewari", "Gō no Hime"
- Miracle tales of high priests: "Shinran-ki"
- Tales of Yoshitsune (prince of the Genji Clan) or Soga: "Takadachi", "Yashima", "Kosode-soga"
- Tragedies or quarrels of clans: "Hanaya", "Muramatsu", "Aguchi no Hangan"
- *Kōwakamai* works: "Kamata", "Atsumori"

▶ Drastic changes in 1655-73: The new storylines with dramatic technique gained popularity.

Kinpira-jōruri established. The spectacular adventure tales of Kinpira, one of four big heroes.

●Narration, texts and puppets of *ko-jōruri*

- Basically a play contained six acts and the stage unfolded along with the storyline.
- The texts were the simple verse in seven-and-five syllable meter.
- In its early stage *shamisen* was played by *tōdō* members (*jiuta* performers).
- A single puppeteer. In its early stage the narrator also manipulated a puppet in some cases.

Ko-jōruri in Transition

The flowchart on the right page illustrates the simplified genealogy of various *ko-jōruri* styles, called 'so-and-so *bushi*'. Superfluous details are eliminated to avoid the complexity. Many minor styles are omitted and only those representing the style are listed in the flowchart. What we know from this genealogical chart is that a style established as 'so-and-so *bushi*' ceased to exist after the death of the originator because his pupil founded a newly named style. In the feudal *iemoto* (head of a school) system of the Japanese traditional music, it may sound strange that the direct pupil founded a new style. Each pupil began a new style by devising a unique idea based on the style established by his master, and in some cases, the pupil's style absorbed the master's. For example, *handayū-bushi* ceased to exist but its style was handed down to *katō-bushi*. There were many similar cases to that in the history of *jōruri*.

In a way, this phenomenon was not uncommon probably because *jōruri* was in transition, not because the performers and the teacher-pupil relationship of *jōruri* were unprincipled. The puppet show and *shamisen* joined in the middle of its development and *jōruri* narrators also had to continuously alter the programs. In addition, the styles were not succeeded as *jōruri* but the style or melodies might have, partly or entirely, absorbed to other genres of public entertainment. For example, *shigetayū-bushi*, *handayū-bushi*, and *eikan-bushi* were integrated into *jiuta*; *ōzatsuma-bushi*, *geki-bushi*, and *kinpira-bushi* into *nagauta*; *hizen-bushi* and *katō-bushi* into *kabuki geza* (offstage) music; and *kakudayū-bushi* and *bun'ya-bushi* into *gidayū-bushi*. These cases also show that *ko-jōruri* was a developing and changing folk art at that time.

In the flowchart, the names, Kyoto, Osaka, and Edo, refer to the main locations where the style prospered. For example, *bungo-bushi* was founded in Kyoto but it is marked as Edo in the chart because it prospered in Edo. As this case shows, there were a lot of comings and goings and cultural exchanges among the three cities in those days. One of the most famous musicians, Takemoto Gidayū, is marked with Osaka but he originally came from Kyushu and was patronized by the lord of the region.

Traditional Japanese Music at a Glance

■Genealogy of *Ko-jōruri*

- This chart shows the relations of prominent *ko-jōruri* styles. Only major styles are listed and sorted out and all other minor ones are omitted.
- Thus the placement of each style does not reflect the exact timeline.
- The time of *ko-jōruri* spans seventy years from 1615.

  References: "Hōgaku no Sekai" by Naoharu Yamakawa (Kodan-sha, 1991).

Legends:
- XX-*bushi* Existing today.
- XX-*bushi* Fused into *jiuta* or *kabuki* music.
- XX-*bushi* x Extinct styles.

The cradle of each "-*bush*" is shown as:
Ⓚ = Kyoto, Ⓞ = Osaka, Ⓔ = Edo (Tokyo).

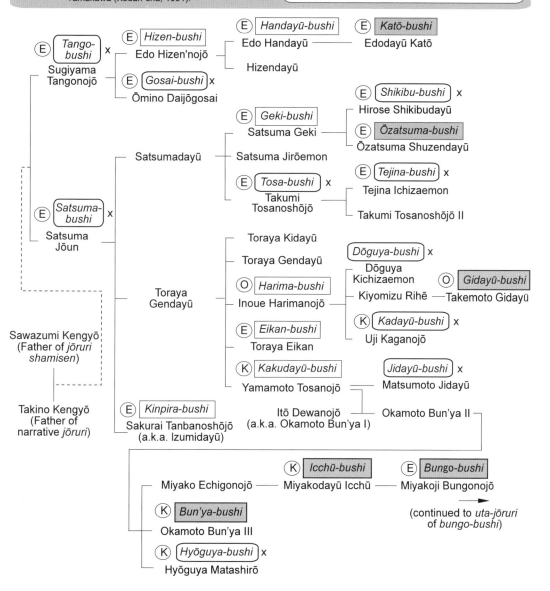

Takemoto Gidayū, an Epoch-making *Jōruri* Chanter

Since Takemoto Gidayū called his *gidayū-bushi* as the "new style" to mark its novelty, *jōruri* before *gidayū-bushi* is called the "old style" (or *ko-jōruri*) in the *jōruri* history. This innovative *gidayū-bushi* became the standard of *ningyō-jōruri* and ousted all other styles called 'so-and-so *bushi*' from the puppet shows.

Gidayū-bushi is characterized with an innovative way of reciting. The speeches were realistically uttered and the narration was meticulously set to melodies, word by word. As a result *gidayū-bushi* became significantly dramatic.

One of the reasons why it became so dramatic is that Chikamatsu Monzaemon, the dramatist exclusively belonging to the Takemoto-za theater owned by Takemoto Gidayū, wrote many new popular scripts for him. His new style, called *sewamono*, the drama dealing with common people's life, was so influential that it determined the future of *ningyō-jōruri*. Thick neck *shamisen*, which was a good match for the powerful *giayū* narration, was used as the accompaniment instrument. The *shamisen* player did not simply accompany the narrative melodies but also employed various techniques, for example, the short interlude and sound effects, in order to more effectively dramatize the show. In addition, the puppets acted so realistically that *ningyō-jōruri* was not merely narrative music with a puppet show but became an artistic drama.

Soon, Toyotake Wakadayū, the pupil of Takemoto Gidayū, established his own theater, Toyotake-za, in Osaka where Takemoto-za had been built. The competition between the two theaters increased the popularity of *ningyō-jōruri*. The development of *ningyō-jōruri* continued. Three puppet operators took charge of part of a single puppet which allegedly expressed human nature better than the human being, and then the operators, who usually hid, showed themselves on the stage. The scripts were written with the collaboration of multiple dramatists, such as Namiki Sōsuke, after the death of Chikamatsu. Many programs, including the three most popular and famous repertoire such as "Yoshitsune Senbon Zakura", were staged one after another. *Ningyō-jōruri* became so popular that *kabuki* as well as other *jōruri* barely existed, as people said.

With ever continuous innovation and the concentration on duty by everyone in the division of labor system, *ningyō-jōruri* with *gidayū-bushi* was completed as a composite art of the early modern Japan. Naturally, the new *jōruri* improved from the old *jōruri* and gained popularity of the public, and the name, *gidayū*, became a synonym of *ningyō-jōruri*. In the long history of Japanese music, only Gidayū, the name of an individual, became the name of a genre.

■Emergence of the New *Jōruri*, *Gidayū-bushi*

In 1684, (Puppet troupe Takemoto-za opened in Osaka.) Their innovative productions caused → Decline of *ko-jōruri* (old *jōruri*).

●What's new in *gidayū-bushi*?

Production	Composite art composed of purely narrative songs and theatrical elements.
Jōruri style	Realistic depiction; meticulously made melodies; elegant, mournful and heroic feelings
Playwright	Chikamatsu Monzaeon, attached to Takemoto-za, invented a new genre called 'sewamono', a play dealing with the lives of ordinary people.
Instrument	Dynamic *futozao* (thick-neck) *shamisen* for accompaniment, short interludes, and sound effects.
Team work	Dramatic collaboration of three parties of narration, *shamisen*, and puppets.

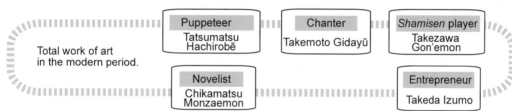

Total work of art in the modern period.
- Puppeteer: Tatsumatsu Hachirobē
- Chanter: Takemoto Gidayū
- *Shamisen* player: Takezawa Gon'emon
- Novelist: Chikamatsu Monzaemon
- Entrepreneur: Takeda Izumo

●Synergistic effect of two rival troupes in Osaka

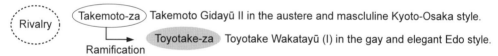

Rivalry: Takemoto-za — Takemoto Gidayū II in the austere and mascluline Kyoto-Osaka style.
Ramification → Toyotake-za — Toyotake Wakatayū (I) in the gay and elegant Edo style.

●New development of the puppet theaters

Three-man puppet manipulation	More realistic and smoother puppet actions.
Musicians' on-stage appearance	The chanter and puppet players appear onstage.
Work gang	New productions by a group.

●Three big works

"Sugawara Denju Tenarai Kagami", "Yoshitsune Senbon Zakura", and "Kanadehon Chūshingura".

The puppet theaters were so popular that people said that *kabuki* was no match for it.

▶Takemoto Gidayū (?-1714)

- Born as a farmer named Gorobē in Tennō-ji Village, Osaka.
- He loved *jōruri* so much that he became a student of Kiyomizu Rihē, the disciple of Inoue Harimanojō.
- He changed his name Gorobē to Kiyomizu Ridayū and then Takemoto Gidayū.
- He became a supporting chanter for Uji Kadayū (a.k.a. Kaganojō) of Kyoto.
- He established his style combining *harima-bushi* and *kaga-bushi* styles.
- He collaborated with the master playwright Chikamatsu and established the modern *jōruri*.

▶Takemoto Gidayū (Featured on a Japanese postage stamp)

Chikamatsu Monzaemon

An integrated team of a *jōruri* narrator, a *shamisen* player and puppet operators unfold the *ningyō-jōruri* story. The system is called *sangyō*, three divisions of work.

The puppet is manipulated by three operators in cooperation: the main operator takes charge of the movement of the neck and the body; the left-hand operator takes charge of the movement of the left hand; and the foot operator takes charge of the movement of the bottom of the puppet. The party of five, two musicians and three puppet operators, must synchronize with each other naturally and effortlessly, without too much strain, to create the wonderful world of the puppet theater. In other words, the timing is the key to the mental and physical harmony of five people engaging in the activity. Three puppet operators on the stage would seem to be too many and annoying to the audience, but actually, and strangely, they disappear from our sight and don't bother us at all.

Among the joint works by Takemoto Gidayū and Chikamatsu Monzaemon, the plays called *sewamono* were the most popular at that time. The word '*sewa*' means rumors or gossip. The stories were based on the actual love suicides and the adultery cases which attracted people's interest in those days. They were similar to today's "behind the scene" gossip shows and it is no wonder that people loved them. After *sewamono* was born, the plays that featured historical events were called *jidaimono* (period plays). Both types were staged on a day-long performance. *Jidaimono* is composed of five sections and *sewamono* one section.

The story and development of *sewamono* and *jidaimono* were skillfully crafted by the gifted dramatist Chikamatsu. He is often, and naturally compared with his European counterpart, Shakespeare. In those days, the set of *ningyō-jōruri* programs were staged for spending nearly a whole day. If the programs were only composed of dramatic and serious plays, the audience would be tired. In order to ease their tension and refresh the mood of the audience, a short dance drama in one act, called *keigoto* or *michiyuki*, was placed in the program. The scene of this dance drama was usually a place of scenic beauty, and the dancing accompanied by vocal and instrumental music was cheerful. Chikamatsu developed this *michiyuki* significantly. He set the *michiyuki* scene in the *sewamono* "Sonezaki Shinjū (The Love Suicides at Sonezaki)" as a "*michiyuki* of the death" of the desperate lovers who fell in forbidden love and were seeking a place to die. The audience was drawn into the dramatic world in this *michiyuki* by the choreographic movements of the puppets, the exaggerated lament by the *jōruri* narrator, and the effective *shamisen* performance. Even we, modern people, are so mesmerized by the dramatic stage that we understand how enthusiastically the audience reacted in those days.

■Types and Structure of *Ningyō-jōruri*

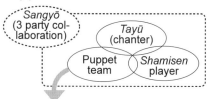

It is not easy for three puppeteers to work in harmony.

Jidaimono play "Yoshitsune Senbon Zakura"

Sewamono play "Date Musume Koi No Higanoko"
(Photos: Yoshirō Kuramoto)

Jidaimono — Period setting plays based on the story before the Edo period. It was standard until *sewamono* emerged.

- **Theme:** Historical events of the nobles or *samurai* class. This type includes *sogamono* (revenges), *hanganmono* (Yoshitsune's stories), and *oiesōdōmono* (noble family disputes).

- **Five-act structure**
    - Act I: Begging
    - Act II: Development
    - Act III: Climax
    - Act IV: New development with *keigoto*
    - Act V: Finale (a happy end or catastrophe)

Sewamono — Contemporary setting plays in the Edo period, dealing with daily lives of ordinary people.

- **Theme:** Story of ordinary people, especially merchants or people in gay quarters. This type includes *shinjūmono* (love suicides), *shobatsumono* (punishment), and *kantsūmono* (adultery).

- **Three-scene structure (in a single act)**
    - Scene I: Beginning, e.g., a money trouble.
    - Scene II: Development (temporary solution and new development)
    - Scene III: Tragic finale, e.g., double suicide or punishment.

Keigoto — Also called '*michiyuki*', *keigoto* is a lyric scene with musical and dancing elements.

- This lyric scene has the effect of changing the mood of the audience during the long piece in contrast to dramatic and epic scenes. It is part of Act IV.
- Scenery of traveling. The costume of puppets is spectacular and so is music suitable for dancing.
- *Michiyuki* in *sewamono* was the path to the grave which gained enormous popularity.

Musicians onstage (*degatari*)
(Photo: Yoshiro Kuramoto)

►Chikamatsu Monzaemon (1653-1725)

- Born Sugimori Nobumori, as the second son of the clansman in today's Fukui.
- He abandoned his *samurai* status and became a disciple of the *jōruri* master Uji Kadayū.
- Wrote his first play "Yotsugi Soga" and then "Shusse Kagekiyo" in collaboration with Takemoto Gidayū.
- He began writing *kabuki*'s *keiseimono* (plays of harlots) for the actor Sakata Tōjūrō.
- He returned to Takemoto-za and wrote "Sonezaki Shinjū (Love Suicides at Sonezaki)" for which he won a reputation.
- After Gidayū's death, he continuously wrote master pieces such as "Kokusen'ya Kassen".

Bold *Gidayū-bushi*

In order to rival narrative *gidayū-bushi*, *ko-jōruri* focused on the melodic elements, and as a result, it became more like lyric songs. Though *gidayū-bushi* initially succeeded the *ko-jōruri* style, it added the dramatic element and became *katarimono* (narrative songs) partly because of Chikamatsu's style.

In *gidayū-bushi*, for example, the narrative style is used to depict the actions and state of mind of the character or the circumstance, and the colloquial style is used for the speeches of the characters. The melodic and narrative phrases of *gidayū-bushi* are composed of three elements: *ji* (melodious body), *kotoba* (words and the realistic speeches), and *iro*, somewhat in between. The plot unfolds with more detailed and specific melodic phrases based on the circumstance or the scene. Reciting varies the speed and style according to circumstances: syllabic (one note per syllable) melodies, which are easily and clearly followed, are used for speeches and narration, and melismatic (multiple notes per syllable) melodies are used for lyric scenes. The reciting of *gidayū-bushi* is characterized with bipolarity, very realistic expression and extreme exaggeration, which are skillfully mixed and harmonized.

Whether *jidaimono* (drama that features historical events) or *sewamono* (drama dealing with common people's life), most of the themes were tragic, focusing on the conflict between the human nature and the social system or the feudalistic morality in those days. The audience was carried away by the drama, empathizing with the characters. *Ningyō-jōruri* held sway over the minds of the people at that time.

Gidayū shamisen is a good match to the *jōruri* narrator, and establishes a unique musical world. The sound of *gidayū shamisen* is powerful. The player corresponds to *jōruri* narrator's reciting, sometimes delicately and sometimes boldly by hitting the drum skin with his plectrum, producing intense sounds. Therefore, the *jōruri* narrator and the *shamisen* player of *gidayū-bushi* must be a perfect pair, harmonizing mentally and physically.

■Characteristics and Terminology of *Gidayū-bushi*

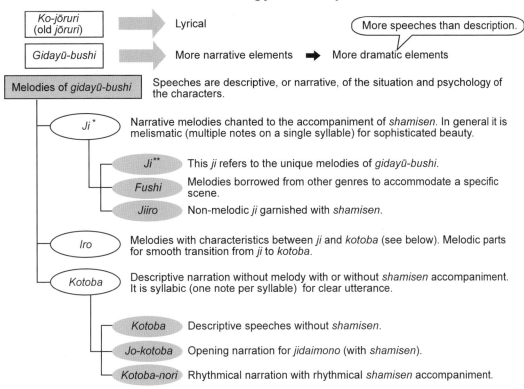

Ko-jōruri (old *jōruri*)	→	Lyrical
Gidayū-bushi	→	More narrative elements → More dramatic elements (More speeches than description.)

Melodies of *gidayū-bushi* — Speeches are descriptive, or narrative, of the situation and psychology of the characters.

- **Ji*** — Narrative melodies chanted to the accompaniment of *shamisen*. In general it is melismatic (multiple notes on a single syllable) for sophisticated beauty.
  - **Ji**** — This *ji* refers to the unique melodies of *gidayū-bushi*.
  - **Fushi** — Melodies borrowed from other genres to accommodate a specific scene.
  - **Jiiro** — Non-melodic *ji* garnished with *shamisen*.
- **Iro** — Melodies with characteristics between *ji* and *kotoba* (see below). Melodic parts for smooth transition from *ji* to *kotoba*.
- **Kotoba** — Descriptive narration without melody with or without *shamisen* accompaniment. It is syllabic (one note per syllable) for clear utterance.
  - **Kotoba** — Descriptive speeches without *shamisen*.
  - **Jo-kotoba** — Opening narration for *jidaimono* (with *shamisen*).
  - **Kotoba-nori** — Rhythmical narration with rhythmical *shamisen* accompaniment.

* = *Ji* in the broad sense.
** = *Ji* in the narrow sense. The definitions vary based on theories.

The vocal style of *gidayū-bushi* — Vocalization by abdominal respiration with intelligible and deeply emotional pronunciation.

- **Vocal mimicry** — *Tayū* (the chanter) mimics all characters, men and women of all ages.
- **On-zukai (differentiation)** — Proper chanting of both syllabic and melismatic phrases.
- **Realism/Exaggeration** — Realistic narration vs. exaggerated cries and laughter.
- **Osaka accent** — Based on Osaka accent though characters' birthplaces are considered.
- **Voice quality/volume** — Voice range and volume are more important than voice quality.

Gidayū-bushi shamisen — Strings/skin/bridges /*bachi* (plectrum) of *futozao* (thick neck) are used.

Accompaniment	Supports narrator's chanting.	Various, from delicate to impulsive, sounds with strings and drum skin.
Short interlude	A short part between narrations.	
Background music	Creates an atmosphere for long narration.	
Sound effect	Contributes puppets' actions such as scuffles.	

Birth of *Uta-jōruri*

Overwhelmed by *gidayū-bushi* that struck out in new directions, one after another, other *jōruri* could not rival *gidayū-bushi* unless they changed. Inevitably, they began focusing on melodies or lyric songs in contrast to the narrative character of *gidayū-bushi*. In *heikyoku*, the narrative songs, the *biwa-hōshi* only complementarily plucked *biwa* between the breaks of the narrative phrases. In case of *jōruri* other than *gidayū-bushi*, influenced by or rivaling *gidayū-bushi*, the *shamisen* part became more decorative and played in parallel with the vocal part, and the *jōruri* narrator began reciting more melodiously. Developed in this way, the lineage of *jōruri* other than *gidayū-bushi* soon found a way out to the *kabuki* theater rather than the puppet show.

Since *kabuki* was artistically still immature and *nagauta* was not completed either in the Genroku period (1688-1704), *jōruri* found a niche for itself as the background music of the various scenes such as *deha* (coming out), *michiyuki* (road-going), and *aragoto* (robust style of acting). Originally, *jōruri* was narrative music with the story composition and development. Especially, the story-nature *jidaimono*, historical drama, of *uta-jōruri* became indispensable for the dancing of the similarly story-nature *kabuki* in five sections: *oki* (introduction), *michiyuki* (road-going), *kudoki* (lament), *odoriji* (dance music), and *dangiri* (finale).

Thus, *jōruri* gradually separated into two types: *ningyō-jōruri* as the traditional narrative songs and *uta-jōruri* as melodic songs. Most *ningyō-jōruri* shows, except the one with *gidayū-bushi*, suffered and fell into decline. Some of them were barely handed down as local public entertainment.

All of *uta-jōruri* was not suitable for *kabuki* dance. The repertoire which did not meet the essential condition of dancing, such as timing, was excluded from the stages. However, they found a means of escape in other places such as the parlor, called *zashiki* in Japanese, of the gay quarters. As a result, *uta-jōruri* also separated into two types: *kabuki-jōruri* (theatrical *jōruri*) and *zashiki-jōruri* (parlor *jōruri*). *Jiuta shamisen*, which crossed over with *jōruri* in the early stages, continuously interacted with it and absorbed some of *jōruri*.

Traditional Japanese Music at a Glance

■Birth of *Uta-jōruri*

● Narrative *jōruri* and lyric *jōruri*

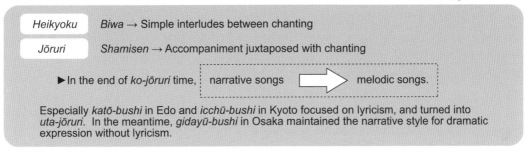

* 'Bungo's Big 3' refers to *tokiwazu-bushi*, *tomimoto-bushi*, and *kiyomoto-bushi*.

● *Jōruri*'s transformation into *shamisen* songs: **Uta-jōruri**

| Heikyoku | Biwa → Simple interludes between chanting |
| Jōruri | Shamisen → Accompaniment juxtaposed with chanting |

▶ In the end of *ko-jōruri* time, narrative songs ⇒ melodic songs.

Especially *katō-bushi* in Edo and *icchū-bushi* in Kyoto focused on lyricism, and turned into *uta-jōruri*. In the meantime, *gidayū-bushi* in Osaka maintained the narrative style for dramatic expression without lyricism.

● New music demanded in the *kabuki* world   **Kabuki-jōruri**

▶ Accompaniment for dancing

Basic five section structure:

Oki	Introduction to create an atmosphere.
Michiyuki	Entrance of the main characters.
Kudoki	The main part, or the climax, of the music.
Odoriji	Rhythmical music for rhythmical dances.
Dangire	Ending of the music, or exit of the main character.

▶ Incidental music (*yosogoto-jōruri*)

● Transformation from theatrical music to non-theatrical music   **Zashiki-jōruri**

- Popular *kabuki* songs were played in the private parlors.
- Songs unsuitable for *kabuki* dances were brought into the gay quarter.
- The extracts from party music or the climax of puppetry music were welcomed in the private parlors.

Also called:
nagusami-jōruri, *sakana-jōruri*
yatsushi-jōruri, *hitokuchi-jōruri*
mitori-jōruri

Lineage of *Bungo-bushi*

Until Takemoto Gidayū emerged, the *jōruri* world was flooded with the 'so-and-so *bushi*' styles. They mixed with the new and old, but it was narrowed down to the three major styles in the three big cities by the beginning of the 18th century: *gidayū-bushi* in Osaka, *icchū-bushi* in Kyoto, and *katō-bushi* in Edo. Among them, *katō-bushi*, also called *edo-bushi*, that absorbed its parents, *handayū-bushi* and *hizen-bushi*, targeted private parlors in the end, although once performed on the *kabuki* stage. It was popular among the common people, at first, but because it was supported by the prosperous class, it declined except among wealthy patrons at the gay quarters. *Katō-bushi* had an influence on Yamada School *sōkyoku* (for detail, refer to the section of *koto*).

Established by Miyakodayū Icchū, *icchū-bushi* was grace and lyric rather than narrative. It was also the lineage of '*naki-bushi* (crying songs)' of Okamoto Bun'ya. Thus, it was *zashiki-jōruri* from the beginning. Though criticized to be monotonous, *icchū-bushi* marked an epoch as it was said, "none but *icchū-bushi* can create such an elegant atmosphere". Miyakoji Bungonojō (1660-1740), the pupil of Miyakodayū Icchū, became independent and established *bungo-bushi* (initially called *hanchū-bushi*, *kunidayū-bushi* or *miyakoji-bushi*). He won the popularity for "Mutsumajiki Renri no Tamatsubaki" based on the case of an actual double suicide. He was so popular that his hairstyle and garments became extremely fashionable in those days. However, since his *bungo-bushi* was blamed for double suicides and elopements that frequently occurred in Edo, it was banned from public performance. He then left Edo and died in the depths of despair. After his tragic death, his style was handed down through his pupils. The three successors of Bungonojō established their own styles and became popular, called the "Bungo's Big Three": *tokiwazu-bushi* by Tokiwazu Mojidayū, *tomimoto-bushi* by Tomimoto Buzendayū, and *kiyomoto-bushi* by the Tomimoto's pupil Kiyomoto Enjudayū. They ushered in a new phase in the *kabuki* dance, surviving until today. *Shin'nai-bushi* was the lineage of *zashiki-jōruri* and the successor of Bungonojō's immediate pupils, Fujimatsu Satsuma and Tsuruga Shin'nai, and established a new "strolling player" style. In addition, Miyakoji Sonohachi, the pupil of Bungonojō in Kyoto established *sonohachi-bushi* (or *miyazono-bushi*). The greater part of *uta-jōruri* was the lineage of *bungo-bushi*.

Traditional Japanese Music at a Glance

■Genealogy after *Ko-jōruri*

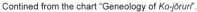
Contined from the chart "Geneology of *Ko-jōruri*".

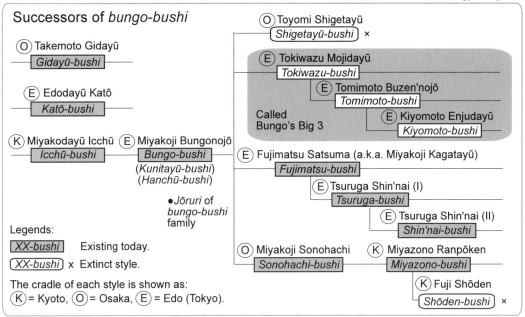

Name	History and Characteristics
Katō-bushi	Also called '*edo-bushi*', assimilating its parents *handayū-bushi* and *hizen-bushi*. Overcome by *bungo-bushi*, it turned to the gay quarters from its ground *kabuki* theater. Elegant short songs.
Icchū-bushi	Succeeding *naki-bushi* of his master Okamoto Bun'ya, it is more lyric than narrative. Exclusively non-theatrical songs though there were early dance songs. Moved to Edo from its cradle Kyoto.
Bungo-bushi	Popular with its sad love suicide themes but later banned due to actual love suicides caused by it. Though the school was extinct, Bungonojō's disciples dominated *kabuki* music.
Tokiwazu-bushi	Number one of Bungo's Big 3. After Bungonojō's banishment, his disciple Tokiwazu remained in Edo and established *kabuki*'s dance music with the taste of *bungo-bushi*.
Tomimoto-bushi	One of Bungo's Big 3. Tomimoto, once Tokiwazu Mojidayū's assistant, established his own school with sophisticated and amorous melodies of *bungo-bushi*. Overcome by *kiyomoto-bushi* and declined.
Kiyomoto-bushi	One of Bungo's Big 3. Derived from *tomimoto-bushi*, it dominated *kabuki* dance music. Contemporary, and bright and witty style, accompanying *kabuki* dance with *nagauta*.
Fujimatsu-bushi	Fujimatsu Satsuma (a.k.a. Miyakoji Kagatayū) established his own school against his colleague Mojitayū after Bungonojō's death. Mainly parlor songs.
Shin'nai-bushi	Established by Tsuruga Shin'nai (II), after Tsuruga Shin'nai (I) of *fujimatsu-bushi* established *tsuruga-bushi*. Its melancholic and sad style gained popularity. The pioneer of strolling *shamisen* performers.
Miyazono-bushi	After *sonohachi-bushi* was established by Miyakoji Sonohachi of *bungo-bushi*, Miyazono (II) changed his name to Ranpōken and established *miyazono-bushi*. Maintaining the Kyoto-Osaka style of *bungo-bushi*, it is used for *michiyuki* (*keigoto*).

Jōruri vs. Kabuki

Even after the death of Takemoto Gidayū I, *gidayū-bushi* of the next generation continuously dominated *ningyō-jōruri*. After Chikamatsu died, Namiki Sōsuke, Takeda Izumo II, and Miyoshi Shōraku authored the scripts in collaboration. *Ningyō-jōruri* reached its peak when they staged their big three shows in succession: "Sugawara Denju Tenarai Kagami", "Yoshitsune Senbon Zakura", and "Kanadehon Chūshingura". *Kabuki* suffered from the repercussions and went downhill so much that people said "*kabuki* barely exists".

However, *kabuki* soon revived by taking an astonishing method: they entirely adapted the successful shows of *ningyō-jōruri* into *kabuki* plays. When the big three shows of *ningyō-jōruri* were staged, for instance, they transformed them into *kabuki-kyōgen* in no time. They copied everything from the storyline and the dramaturgy to the *shamisen* music and costume, and replaced puppets and the *jōruri* narrator with actors for acting and speech. It is the plagiarism in the modern society, but since there was no concept about the copyright at that time, they did not suffer from a guilty conscience. This resulted in the complete revival of *kabuki* and the gradual decline of *ningyō-jōruri*. The songs of *uta-jōruri* brought the dance of *kabuki* into prominence, and the scripts of *ningyō-jōruri* were adapted into *kabuki* plays. In short, *ningyō-jōruri* helped its enemy and was defeated by its enemy, as the proverb says, "Give him an inch, he'll take a mile". Those *kabuki-kyōgen* adapted from *ningyō-jōruri* were called '*maruhon-kabuki*' or '*gidayū-kyōgen*' and the *gidayū* music was called '*takemoto*' or '*chobo*'. They were the disparaging terms named by the *gidayū-bushi* side, the originator.

Afterwards, *ningyō-jōruri* continuously played second fiddle to *kabuki* and both once-flourishing Takemoto-za and Toyotake-za closed. After a while, Uemura Bunrakuken, the puppet operator of Awaji, established the Bunraku-za theater in Osaka and finally, '*bunraku*' became the popular name of *ningyō-jōruri*. At present, *bunrakus* is named as the intangible important cultural asset and the puppet theater is administered by the nonprofit organization Bunraku Association. The puppet shows, other than *bunraku* were handed down in various places, some of which began in the times of *ko-jōruri*. Famous Awaji Ningyō-jōruri in the Awaji Island allegedly existed before *ko-jōruri*.

■Drastic Events of *Ningyō-jōruri* History

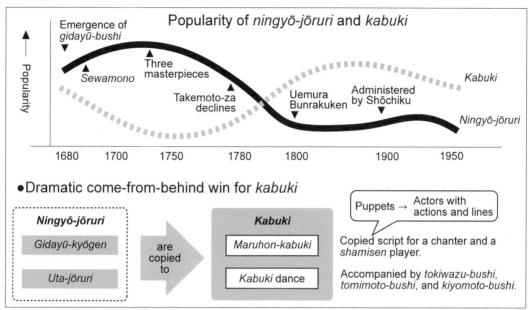

- **Dramatic come-from-behind win for *kabuki***

  Ningyō-jōruri (Gidayū-kyōgen, Uta-jōruri) are copied to *Kabuki* (Maruhon-kabuki, Kabuki dance).

  Puppets → Actors with actions and lines. Copied script for a chanter and a *shamisen* player. Accompanied by *tokiwazu-bushi*, *tomimoto-bushi*, and *kiyomoto-bushi*.

- **Ups and down of *ningyō-jōruri***
  - In late 18C, Takemoto-za and Toyotake-za declined.
  - In early 19C, Uemura Bunrakuken opened a puppet theater → Bunraku's play → Bunraku
  - In late 19C, the promoter Shōchiku took over the troupe. Hikoroku-za theater opened in Osaka and gained popularity.
  - In early 20C, *bunraku* declined due to motion pictures and other public entertainment.
  - After WWII, *bunraku* was designated as an Important Intangible Cultural Asset. Non-profit organization Bunraku Kyokai to support *bunraku* was established.

- **Ningyō-jōruri handed down in the local areas**

  - **Awaji Ningyō-jōruri**
    Designated as Important Intangible Folk Culture Asset.
    Structure: *Gidayū-bushi* and the 3-men puppet manipulation system.
    Puppets: Larger than today's *bunraku* puppets.
    Repertoire: Awaji's original plays have been lost. Now the same as Bunraku Kyokai's repertoir:
    "Keisei Awa no Naruto", "Tōkaidōchū Hizakurige" "Hidakagawa Iriaizakura", "Tsubosaka Reigenki" "Kiichihōgen Sanryaku no Maki", etc.
    History: It was established in Awaji Island 500 years ago during Toyotomi Hideyoshi's prime time. Some say it is older than *ko-jōruri*. It is unknown when *gidayū-bushi* and the 3-men puppet manipulation system were employed. Uemura Bunrakuken was a *ningyō-jōruri* puppeteer in Awaji Island.

  - **Awa Ningyō-jōruri**
    Designated as Important Intangible Folk Culture Asset.
    It has been preserved in today's Tokushima same as Awaji Ningyō-jōruri.
    In 1804-1829, there were 48 troupes which were on road in various regions and left traces nationwide.

    Other puppetry in Japan:
    - Kaga Bun'ya Ningyō (Toyama)
    - Satsuma Bun'ya Ningyō (Kagoshima)
    - Hyūga Bun'ya Ningyō (Miyazaki)
    - Noroma Ningyō (Sado, Niigata)
    - Shiroku Kushi Ningyō (Saitama)
    - Nanbu Karuishi Ningyō (Iwate)
    - Imada Ningyō (Inaya, Nagano)

Buddhist Sermons: *Sekkyō-bushi*

In the same age as *ningyō-jōruri*, there was a popular public entertainment called *sekkyō-bushi*, similar to *jōruri*. '*Sekkyō*' means a 'sermon' or 'preaching' of Buddhism.

In the Kamakura period (1185-1333), Buddhist monks vigorously preached sermons to commoners, who often did not follow the daunting talks. As a result, the professional preacher emerged, and with his clear and beautiful voice (as well as beautiful face), he delivered a sermon using a simple metaphor. In order to make plain talks more dramatic, he chanted sutras with melodies borrowed from *shōmyō* and *heikyoku*, and used *sasara* (percussion made of a piece of a bamboo stalk with the tip split) to punctuate his sermons. This was the origin of *sekkyō-bushi* and soon spread outside the temple and became a public entertainment. At first, it was a door-to-door entertainment accompanied by *sasara* and then became a street performance accompanied by the musical instruments such as a small gong, *kokyū*, or *shamisen*. Then, it connected with a puppet show and developed into a public entertainment, called a sermon puppet show, preceding *ningyō-jōruri*.

Allegedly, *sekkyō-bushi* grew and once became more popular than *ningyō-jōruri* and even established the Sekkyō-za theater in Kyoto, Osaka and Edo. The original purpose of the show was to praise Buddhas' merit and virtue. The performers livened up the followers by chanting the mythology of temples and shrines, the tales of miracles of the gods and Buddha, and the tales of destiny and so on, so skillfully that this fascinating and dramatic show grabbed the audience in those days.

There were five masterpieces of *sekkyō-bushi*, one of which was the original story of "Sanshō the Bailiff (the tale of two aristocratic children sold into slavery)", later novelized by Ōgai Mori and filmed by Kenji Mizoguchi. *Sekkyō-bushi* was the most suitable to depict the hellish world of slaves and praise the miraculous efficacy of the gods and Buddha to the public. However, though it was at the height of its popularity, *sekkyō-bushi* was defeated by popular *ningyō-jōruri* and declined because its subject was no better than moral stories and the public got tired.

Among the various styles of *sekkyō-bushi*, there was a show only composed of the narration without using puppets or accompaniment instruments. This art of storytelling with skillful melodies and narration is believed to be the origin of some folk entertainments such as *naniwabushi* or *rōkyoku*, *rakugo* and *kōdan*.

■ *Sekkyō-bushi*, the Origin of Japanese Puppetry

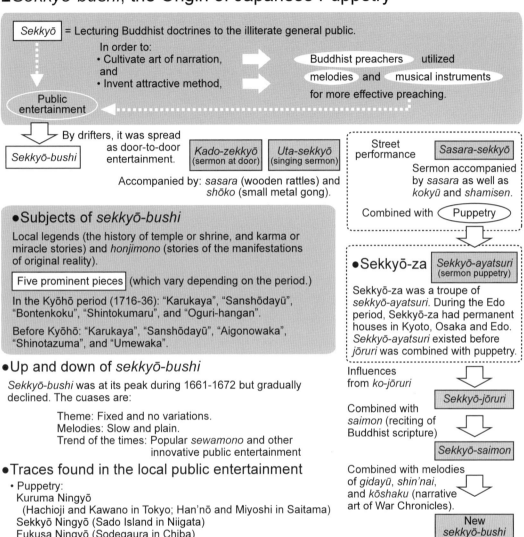

- **Subjects of *sekkyō-bushi***

  Local legends (the history of temple or shrine, and karma or miracle stories) and *honjimono* (stories of the manifestations of original reality).

  Five prominent pieces (which vary depending on the period.)

  In the Kyōhō period (1716-36): "Karukaya", "Sanshōdayū", "Bontenkoku", "Shintokumaru", and "Oguri-hangan".

  Before Kyōhō: "Karukaya", "Sanshōdayū", "Aigonowaka", "Shinotazuma", and "Umewaka".

- **Up and down of *sekkyō-bushi***

  Sekkyō-bushi was at its peak during 1661-1672 but gradually declined. The cuases are:

  Theme: Fixed and no variations.
  Melodies: Slow and plain.
  Trend of the times: Popular *sewamono* and other innovative public entertainment

- **Traces found in the local public entertainment**
  - Puppetry:
    Kuruma Ningyō
     (Hachioji and Kawano in Tokyo; Han'nō and Miyoshi in Saitama)
    Sekkyō Ningyō (Sado Island in Niigata)
    Fukusa Ningyō (Sodegaura in Chiba)
  - Narrative arts:
    Itako medium (Northern regions),
    Goze songs (Niigaka),
    Shrine maiden's "Yuriwaka-sekkyō" (Iki Island in Nagasaki)

- ***Fushidan-sekkyō***

  Fushidan-sekkyō originated from the chants established by the father and son priests Chōken (?-1203) and Seikaku (1167-1235) of Tendai Sect, according to a theory. Preserved in the Jōdo and Shin sects until the Taisho period. Though it contains some melodies and narration, it is sermon, not public entertainment.

- **Influence to posterity:**

  Fushidan-sekkyō fathered future narrative arts. *Sekkyō-bushi* became the roots of many narrative performing arts such as *rōkyoku*, *kōdan*, *rakugo*, and so on.

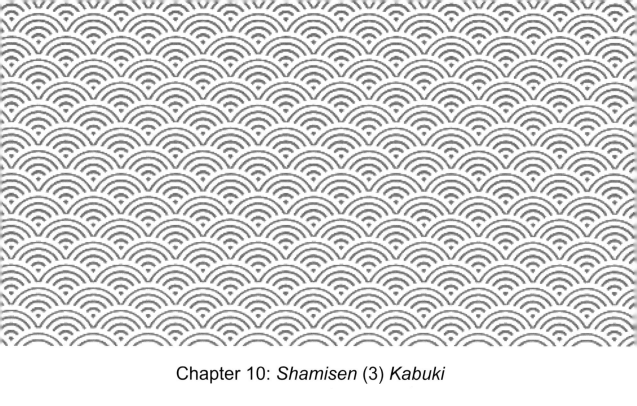

Chapter 10: *Shamisen* (3) *Kabuki*

Kabuki: Japanese Counterpart of Western Revue

It is well-known that Ōgai Mori, the great writer in the Meiji period, saw opera in Europe where he was studying and wrote in a letter "I saw a Western *kabuki*". Both share the same commonality as a theatrical performing art.

Today, the word '*kabuki*' is written with three kanji characters: song (*ka*), dance (*bu*) and art (*ki*). But '*kabuki*' did not originally mean a composite art: it originated from the word '*kabukimono*' meaning an eccentric or abnormal person.

Kabuki, one of the three major traditional performing arts in Japan, has been selected as a World Intangible Cultural Heritage by UNESCO. It is world famous, but in reality, people rarely see it on a live stage today, and the general understanding about it is only limited to some aspects. For example, that it is an old play based on historical events, or is dance accompanied by *shamisen*.

The programs of *kabuki* are roughly divided into two groups: *kabuki-kyōgen* (the drama with speech) and the *kabuki* dance. However, *kabuki-kyōgen* has music and dance and the *kabuki* dance has dramatic elements. For example, one of the most famous scenes of the *kabuki* repertory is the "Ataka no Seki (Barrier Station at Ataka)" from "Kanjinchō", based on the long saga of the Heike and the Genji. Here, Togashi, the barrier keeper, and Benkei, the loyal servant to Yoshitsune of the Genji, argue as fiercely as with clashing and blocking swords. Even though there is exchange in a long speech, "Kanjinchō" is not classified into *kabuki-kyōgen,* but as dance. *Kabuki* is the performing art stylishly and completely integrated with dramas, dances and Japanese traditional music.

There are many differences between *kabuki* and opera. For opera, the music is most important and the name of the composer is ranked higher than that of the librettist. For *kabuki*, because the music is made to accompany the story, the name of the composer does not come to the fore. Dance plays an especially important role in *kabuki*. Moreover, *kabuki* actors hardly sing. Colorful costumes, stylized *kata* (choreographed patterns), star actors, the atmosphere of the Edo city, picturesque stage settings, kaleidoscopic and splendid music...*Kabuki* is indeed a gorgeous revue in the Edo period.

Traditional Japanese Music at a Glance

■*Kabuki*

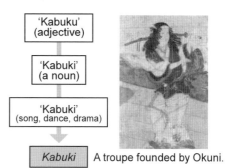

A troupe founded by Okuni.

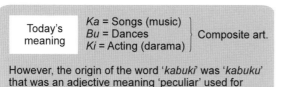

However, the origin of the word '*kabuki*' was '*kabuku*' that was an adjective meaning 'peculiar' used for person, dress, behavior and so on.

●*Kabuki*, a compilation of Japanese arts:

Incorrect definition:
- Classical plays with old subjects
- Dances accompanied by Japanese musical instruments

Correct concept:

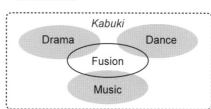

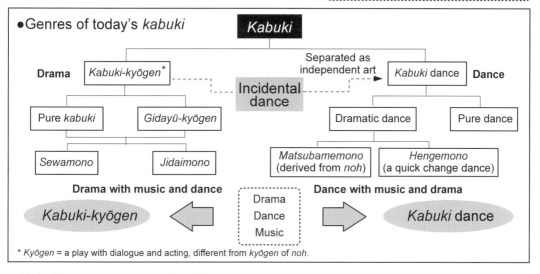

●*Kabuki* as a Japanese theatrical revue

| Characteristics | • Actor basis. A popular actor is required to have a good eye gazing, voice, and a figure, as well as facial make-up.
• Extreme exaggeration and simplification.
• *Kata* (choreographed patterns) and *ma* (space), both Japanese aesthetics.
• Spectacular costume in bright colors and fashionable styles.
• Picturesque and functional stages with *hanamichi* (a passage through audience to stage), sets, and *keren* (stagecraft tricks).
• Drama with fictional and nonfictional ideas.
• Multi-layered Japanese arts and mixture of various public entertainments. |

Kabuki: Hodgepodge Performing Arts

Kabuki-kyōgen (the drama with speech) is divided into two groups: pure *kabuki* and *gidayū-kyōgen*. The pure *kabuki* is an original *kabuki* play and *gidayū-kyōgen* is a copy of a successful *ningyō-jōruri* show adapted to *kabuki*. In *gidayū-kyōgen*, the human actors themselves speak replacing the puppets, and the *jōruri* narrator describes the circumstances as the story unfolds. Everything except the puppets and actors is the same as *ningyō-jōruri*. *Gidayū-kyōgen* is further divided into two groups: *sewamono* and *jidaimono*. *Sewamono* is a contemporary drama dealing with the life of common people in the Edo period and *jidaimono* is a drama that features historical events.

Kabuki dance is divided into two groups: narrative "dramatic dances" and lyrical "pure dances". *Kabuki* dance evolved along with the times. One of the variations was *hengemono* in which the dancer quickly changes his costume. For example, in *shichihenge* (seven changes) the dancer changes his costume seven times in a single performance. *Hengemono* became so popular that it formed a sub-genre in the dance category.

Kabuki has always been susceptible to the latest fashions and flexible to adapt new and advanced ideas. For example, influenced by the New Theatre movement attuned to current trends, *shin kabuki* (new *kabuki*) began in order to pursue the ideal stage in the modernized Meiji period. Such flexibility to adapt new and advanced ideas continues to the present. For example, original new plays have been produced based on modern subjects and introduction of innovative stagecraft tricks, called *keren*, such as the midair stunt. A Western orchestra, in addition to the Japanese traditional ensemble was used in the so-called "super *kabuki*".

The flexibility of *kabuki* is rooted in its unique way for production: the "mixing together" method. It weaves into a single script by using historical events or the lives of well-known people as the warp and the original, new plots, called *shukō*, freely inserted into the storyline based on the ideas of the playwrights as the weft.

It was not surprising that the scholar and playwright Shōyō Tsubouchi compared *kabuki* to the chimera of Greek mythology composed of the parts of multiple animals. *Kabuki* is an unconstrained and "anything possible" world. The actual performance and dramaturgy are also unconstrained. For example, only the highlights of a play, called *mitori-kyōgen*, are ordinarily staged. A wide range of new stagecraft is used to emphasize a climax. *Kabuki* is a performing art as novel as today's modern visual arts.

Traditional Japanese Music at a Glance

■Kabuki Today

◀A scene of a *kabuki* theater by Masanobu Okumura around 1741-44

▶Kabuki-za Theater in Tokyo renovated in 2013

●Categories

Kabuki-kyōgen	Plays with actors' speeches and actions, distinguished from *kabuki-buyō (kabuki* dance). '*Kyōgen*' stands for drama with dialogue, not farce *kyōgen* in *noh*.
Jun-kabuki	Original plays for *kabuki*. '*Jun*' stands for 'pure'.
Gidayū-kyōgen	A complete copy from a *ningyō-jōruri* play to a *kabuki* play.

Jidaimono	Plays that feature historical plots and characters of *samurai* or the nobles.	Found in both *jun-kabuki* and *gidayū-kabuki*.
Sewamono	Contemporary plays, which generally focus on towners and merchants.	

Kabuki-buyō	Dances over music. The word '*buyō*' is a compound noun of *mai* (revolving motions) and *odori* (saltatory movement) which were strictly distinguished each other until the Meiji period.
Dramatic dances	Dances with a story. Some are similar to *kabuki-kyōgen* with actors' speeches.
Pure dances	Dances without a story or speeches used for *michiyuki*, for instance.
Henge dances	Transformation or quick-change dances in which a single actor continuously dances various roles in various costumes and music styles.
Shin-kabuki	New plays written by playwrights other than *kabuki* writers, e.g. Shōyō Tsubouchi and Yukio Mishima. Also transcriptions from foreign novels or plays. This reflects *kabuki*'s enterprising spirit.
'Super' Kabuki	Modern *kabuki* with comtemporary theme, arts and music such as the Western orchestra. The actor En'nosuke Ichikawa began it with his "Yamato Takeru".

●Dramaturgy

Sekai	The fixed framework of a play such as time, historical events, background, and characters.	Blended	Different basic plots (*sekai*) are interwoven into a new plot in *jidaimono* and *sewamono*. The unique writing method of *kabuki* world.
Shukō	Writer's new ideas added to *sekai*.		

●Terms

Kata	*Kata* is choreographed patterns of movements designated for a specific play. It characterises the Edo *kabuki* but *shukō* was more respected in the Kyoto-Osaka area.
Mie	A frozen pose of an actor to emphasize *kata*. Similar to the idea of a facial close-up in movies.
Tsuke	*Tsuke* is the sound effect produced by clappers struck to a wooden board, used for battle scenes and such.
Keren	Unexpected stagecraft tricks such as midair stunt, quick role changes, and collapse of a building by using stage equipment.

●Programming

Tōshi-kyōgen	Full productions of a single play. This was standard in the Edo period.
Midori-kyōgen	A production with select scenes from *jidaimono*, dances, and *sewamono*.

The Birth of *Kabuki*

Kabuki originated from '*kabuki-odori*', a revue with dances and skits performed by a troupe of several female dancers in male attire, called *kabukimono*, meaning peculiar people, and led by the female entertainer Izumo no Okuni (1572- \). In these early stages, this revue was accompanied by *shibyōshi* (four musical instruments: a flute and three drums). It developed into *yūjo kabuki* (prostitutes *kabuki*) and *wakasyū kabuki* (young men *kabuki*). *Shamisen* was added, but the accompaniment music was still not full-blown. After *yūjo kabuki* and *wakasyū kabuki* was abolished due to its moral corruption, *yarō kabuki* (mature men *kabuki*) based on *kyōgen* (drama) prospered. In the Genroku period (1688-1704), with the emergence of the star actors, Danjūrō of Edo and Tōjūrō of the Kyoto-Osaka area, *kabuki* became popular. At this time, the original form of *edo nagauta* and early *geza* (offstage) music as the incidental music began to be used. However, overwhelmed by the popularity of *ningyō-jōruri* by Chikamatsu Monzaemon and Takemoto Gidayū, it completely declined and was even said that *kabuki* barely existed. *Kabuki* then revived by copying the successful shows of its competitor, *ningyō-jōruri*, to *kabuki* plays, that is, by daring to plagiarize.

In the meantime, the dance by *on'nagata* or *oyama* (male actors who impersonate women) began. The dance at that time was a mixture of cheerful early *kabuki* and *noh* dances. *Furi*, the choreographic expressions that would become more dramatic later, sprouted, and *shosagoto*, meaning 'dances' but different from early *kabuki-odori*, was established.

The narrative music, *jōruri*, such as *gidayū-bushi* and *tokiwazu-bushi*, began to be used for the *kabuki* dances. At last, *kabuki* literally became a 'song (*ka*), dance (*bu*) and art (*ki*)' public entertainment. Then, *tachiyaku* (male) dances and *hengemono* (quick change dances) were established, *nagauta* was complete as the music dedicated to *kabuki*, and a brilliant formation, called '*kakeai*', evolved in which two or more different styles, for example, *nagauta* and *jōruri*, were juxtaposed to compete.

New *kyōgen* (dramas) works were produced one after another. *Kabuki* showed off new ideas, such as complicated plots, realistic acting by actors, and skillful and mind-boggling stagecraft. With the emergence of star actors, *kabuki* gained immortal popularity. At the same time, *geza* music performed in a room, called *kuromisu*, at the right side of the stage, was added and became indispensable to *kyōgen*. Dances are placed in the climax of *kabuki*, accompanied by *shamisen* music.

Traditional Japanese Music at a Glance

■Birth and Development of *Kabuki*

Early Stage (-1687): Resistance against oppression with dance

Okuni kabuki	Dance and short plays by female performers in *kabuku* (peculiar) costume.
Yūjo kabuki	Erotic revues by *yūjo* (prostitutes) in splendid costume. Later banned by the government.
Wakashū kabuki	Acrobatic shows by young men. Dance and songs basis. Later banned by the government.

Music of kabuki — Izumo no Okuni

Accompanied by shibyōshi* and dance songs.   * = a flute and 3 drums.

Actors play shamisen onstage.

Shamisen + shibyōshi was called kabuki-bayashi.

Genroku (1688-1704): Style completion and *Tsuzuki-kyōgen* (drama)

Yarō kabuki	*Kabuki* by adult male actors permitted by the government.	*On'nagata*** ** Male actors in female roles.
Aragoto (fighting plays)	By. Ichikawa Danjūrō in Edo.	*Kinpiramono* (based on *kinpira jōruri*)
Wagoto (gentle plays)	By Sakata Tōjūrō in the Kyoto-Ōsaka region.	*Nuregoto* (love scenes) *Yatsushigoto* (scenes with a scion falling)

Chikamatsu Monzaemon

Adoption of jiuta: nagauta (jiuta) & drama songs

Adoption of ko-jōruri

Appearance of Nagauta & kuromisu (geza)

Kyōhō (1716-1736): *Kabuki*'s slump and revival with *gidayū-kyōgen*

Maruhon kabuki	A complete copy of *ningyō-jōruri* plays.
Big hit of "Sugawaradenju Tenaraikagami", "Yoshitsune Senbon Zakura", and "Kanadehon Chūshingura".	
On'nagata shosagoto (dance-drama)	By Segawa Kikunojō, Nakamura Tomijūrō

Chikamatsu Hanji

Takemoto (jōruri) adopted.

Bungo-bushi

Tokiwazu (jōruri) adopted.

Tenmei (1781-1789): Bloom of *Kabuki* and its music

Tachiyaku dances	Dramatic dances. Dances by *tachiyaku* (male actors playing male roles).
Maruhon kabuki	Complete copies of *ningyō-jōruri* plays.
Innovative stages	Revolving stages, stage lifts, and a building collapse. Called *Keren*

Namiki Shōzō

Tomimoto & uta-jōruri adopted.

Nagauta established.

Development of Geza music

Bunka-Bunsei (1804-1829): Realism

Hengemono	An actor plays multiple roles in a single play. E.g. "Musume Dōjōji"	*Hayagawari* (quick change)
Kizewamono	Realistic drama of contemporary life.	*Kabuki-jūhachiban* (repertoire of 18 *kabuki* plays)

Tsuruya Nanboku

Kiyomoto & shin'nai adopted.

Kakeai (juxtaposed music styles) blooms.

End of Edo (1853-1867): A.k.a. '*Saruwaka-machi*' period.

Shiranamimono	Drama depicting the adventures of thieves.
Bloom of *sewamono*	With *semeba* (scenes of torture), *nureba*, and *yusuriba* (scenes of a threat).

Kawatake Mokuami

Geza music completed.

Meiji (1868-1912): Intellectual "New Play Movement"

Shin-kabuki	New plays by playwrights other than *kabuki* writers or adaptation of foreign literature.	
Matsubamemono	Adaptation of *noh* plays such as "Kanjinchō" and "Funa Benkei"	*Katsurekimono* (historical dramas)

Kidō Okamoto

Degatari*** Debayashi***

*** = musicians onstage.

Music of *Kabuki*

Though *kabuki*'s repertoire is divided into two groups, *kyōgen* (dramas) and dances, actually, they have an indivisible relationship. The apprentice of *kabuki* actors begins his practice with dancing. That is because *kata* (choreographed patterns and gestures) of the dance is the basic of acting for the *kyōgen* actors. Most *kabuki* dances have stories with various scenes, from the fighting scene to the dialogue scene, in which the dancers are required to both act and speak a part. These *kyōgen* and dances unfold effectively and smoothly with various types of *kabuki* music. In short, the drama, the dance and the music form a functional connection and if these three factors are not combined perfectly, *kabuki* does not materialize.

Music plays an extensive role in *kabuki*. It includes: dance music, background music, melodious accompaniment to the actor speaking his part, sound effects, and the opening and ending music. In the early stages, *jiuta*, *ko-jōruri* and folk songs were used. At present, in addition to the most important *nagauta*, *takemoto* (the alias of *gidayū-bushi*) and *geza* music for *kyōgen*, and *uta-jōruri* such as *tokiwazu-bushi* and *kiyomoto-bushi* are used for dances. *Katō-bushi* and *ōzatsuma-bushi*, which were frequently used in older *kabuki*, are used only for special scenes now.

For the *kabuki* dances, the musicians line up on the tiered platform set on the stage where the dancers perform. This onstage formation is called *debayashi* for *nagauta* musicians and *degatari* for *jōruri* musicians. For other repertoire, music is mostly played in *kuromisu*, a room at the side of the stage, and this offstage formation is called *kagebayashi*.

Certain plays correspond to particular titles of *kabuki* music and they are determined as illustrated on the right page. This is the usual manner, but occasionally non-*nagauta* music is played for the pure dance and *nagauta* is played for the dramatic dance. This kind of flexibility characterizes *kabuki*. *Geza* music is the essential part of *kabuki* music, whether *kyōgen* or dances.

■Music of *Kabuki*

●Tasks

- Accompanying dances with *nagauta, tokiwazu, kiyomoto,* or *takemoto* (=*gidayū-bushi*), in a single style or *kakeai* (juxtaposition of different styles).
- Accompanying *kyōgen*. Anything other than the narration of *takemoto*.
- Describing scenes and playing background music by the *geza* ensemble (singers and performers).
- Producing sound effects such as rain, winds, battle sounds and supporting *mie* (actor's frozen pose) with pitchless sounds of percussion.
- Giving signals to the audience. The first and second signals by a drum for the beginning of performance and *shagiri* for the end of intermission.

For dances as well as dramas with speeches, music plays an important role. It describes scenes and accompanies the entrance and exit and speeches of actors. That is why *kabuki* is often compared with Western operas and musicals.

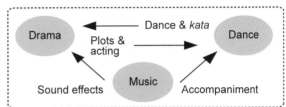

●Type of music

Nagauta	Developed for *kabuki* and used for dances as well as drama.
Geza music	Ensemble of *nagauta* performers (voices, *shamisen* and *narimono*), also called *kuromisu*.
Takemoto	The same as *gidayū-bushi* of *ningyō-jōruri*.

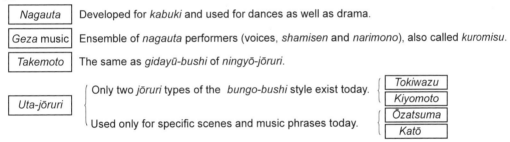

Uta-jōruri:
- Only two *jōruri* types of the *bungo-bushi* style exist today. { Tokiwazu, Kiyomoto }
- Used only for specific scenes and music phrases today. { Ōzatsuma, Katō }

●Terms regarding music

- Performance onstage and on a platform: *Debayashi* and *hinadan* (for *nagauta*), *degatari* and *yuka* (for *takemoto*), and *degatari* and *yamadai* (for *tokiwazu* and *kiyomoto*).
- Performance behind the curtain: *kuromisu* (for *kabuki-bayashi* or *kage-bayashi*), *misuuchi* (for *takemoto*).
- *Okuri-sanjū* (a musical accompaniment to a protagonist's exit).
- *Tsuke* (striking wooden clappers onto the floor) used for *ōzatsuma-bushi*, *okuri-sanjū*, and sound effects.

●Repertoires*

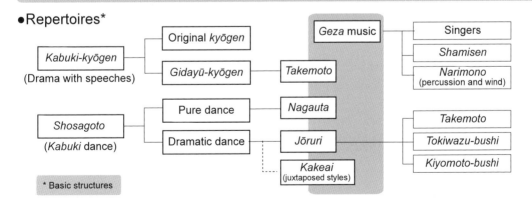

* Basic structures

Diversified *Nagauta*

Nagauta, sung to the accompaniment of *shamisen,* is vocal music developed for *kabuki.* Because purely instrumental works were created in later years, we tend to think that *nagauta* is an independent music genre, but basically, it should be regarded as the core of *kabuki* music.

Kabuki is the compilation of all kinds of public entertainment in Japan, and likewise, *nagauta* is the fusion of the melodic phrases, methods and subject matters of all kinds of Japanese music. Thus, the forms and styles of *nagauta* are so diversified that it seems to be almost impossible to systematically organize and classify them.

In the early stages of *kabuki,* there was no music exclusively for it, and instead, *kouta,* the popular songs at that time, or *hauta* and *nagauta* of *jiuta* (note that this *nagauta* is different from *kabuki*'s *nagauta*) were used for the performance. The drama songs were derived from these songs and then the songs called *nagauta* were formed in the Genroku period (note that this *nagauta* is also different from *kabuki*'s *nagauta*). It began in Edo, developed in the Kyoto-Osaka area, and then came back to Edo. It was occasionally called *ōsaka nagauta* or *kyōto nagauta* according to the birthplace of the musician but *edo nagauta* sung to the accompaniment of 'thin neck' *shamisen* gradually became the standard, absorbing the style of *edo jōruri.* *Edo nagauta* musicians enthusiastically and continuously developed *nagauta.* They established *nagauta-jōruri* by adapting the melodic phrases of *jōruri.* They adapted bold *ōzatsuma-bushi,* contrived the new tunings such as *hon-chōshi* and *uwa-jōshi* suitable for dancing, adapted *tokiwazu-bushi* and *kiyomoto-bushi* for *hengemono* (quick change dances), and contrived *kakeai* in which two or more different styles such as *nagauta* and *uta-jōruri* were juxtaposed to compete. They finally completed *nagauta* dedicated to *kabuki* as heard at present.

Every *shamisen* musician until then sang to his own accompaniment, but the singers and *shamisen* players for *nagauta* were separated. Also four instruments called '*shibyōshi*', a flute and three drums, were added. They created brilliant and cheerful *shamisen* music, loved by the audience.

Nagauta evolved and stimulated the will of the composers and players to create, which resulted in the emergence of professional musicians who abandoned *kabuki* to concentrate on pure music. Such trends encouraged *kabuki* performers, who, in turn, gave *nagauta* musicians the motivation for more improvement. This was how *nagauta* diversified.

■ *Nagauta*: Compilation of Japanese Music

Nagauta is vocal music sung to the accompaniment of *shamisen* and *narimono* (percussion and wind) though some are instrumental music.

- **Tasks**
  - A part of *shamisen* music
  - Accompaniment for *kabuki* drama — **Edo nagauta**: The name of *nagauta* in the early stage
  - Accompaniment for *kabuki* dances — **Edouta**: The collective name of *Edo-jōruri*

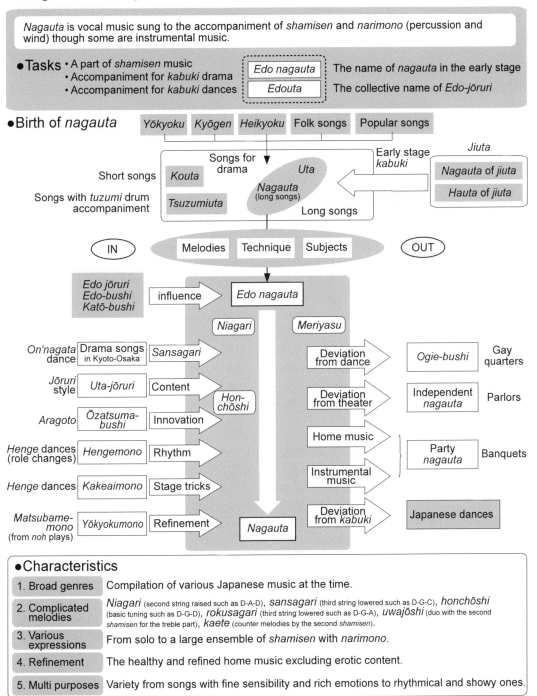

- **Characteristics**

1. Broad genres	Compilation of various Japanese music at the time.
2. Complicated melodies	*Niagari* (second string raised such as D-A-D), *sansagari* (third string lowered such as D-G-C), *honchōshi* (basic tuning such as D-G-D), *rokusagari* (third string lowered such as D-G-A), *uwajōshi* (duo with the second *shamisen* for the treble part), *kaete* (counter melodies by the second *shamisen*).
3. Various expressions	From solo to a large ensemble of *shamisen* with *narimono*.
4. Refinement	The healthy and refined home music excluding erotic content.
5. Multi purposes	Variety from songs with fine sensibility and rich emotions to rhythmical and showy ones.

Nagauta: Orchestra of Japanese Instruments

For the *kabuki* dances, the *nagauta* musicians as well as *narimono* (all instruments other than *shamisen*) players line up on the tiered platform on a red carpet that is stretched over the entire stage. It is simply amazing to see them play *debayashi* (onstage) music in this gorgeous setting.

A *nagauta* ensemble consists of a minimum of one singer and two *shamisen* players. Because of the visual effect and the balance on the very wide stage, it is not rare that there are as many as ten *shamisen* players and ten singers. *Shibyōshi*, four instruments composed of a flute and three drums, line up in the front row of the tiered platform in red but when the *nagauta* musicians are as many as twenty, the four musicians lack punch. In that case, flutes and drums are added. There is no conductor even for this big ensemble. The groups of singers and *shamisen* players split the platform at the center, and the singer and *shamisen* musician at the center are called *tateuta* and *tateshamisen* respectively, are the leaders of each group.

Nagauta stands for a 'long song' because it is long, and a single work is composed of a few sections. *Jo-ha-kyū* (beginning, break, rapid), the compositional concept of *gagaku* and *noh*, was also applied to *jōruri* and *nagauta*. Each section gradually develops from *oki* (an introductory instrumental section) to *chirashi* (a section with a faster tempo), along with *ki-shō-ten-ketsu* (start, continue, change, conclusion) with the story of the dramatic dance.

The *kabuki* dances developed and became more versatile and new styles such as *hengemono* (quick change dances) were established. If the stage settings and dancer's costume change, but the music is unchanged, it would not attract the audience. Thus, in order to make the performance more attractive, '*kakeai*', a competition by two or more different musical styles, was contrived. In *kakeai*, the singers and the *shamisen* players of *tokiwazu-bushi* or *kiyomoto-bushi* in addition to *nagauta* simultaneously line up on the same stage. The stage of 'triple *kakeai*' looks extremely luxurious. In addition to the *nagauta* musicians on the central tiered platform, *tokiwazu* and *takemoto* (= *gidayū-bushi*) musicians line up on the tiered platforms of the left wing and the right wing respectively. Moreover, the *shamisen* tunings, for example, *honchōshi* or *niagari*, and vocalization differ for each genre. The costume and music stands for each genre also differ. As a result, the stage of *kakeai* becomes really gorgeous.

For *kyōgen* (dramas), the *nagauta* musicians play the incidental music in a small off-stage room called *kuromisu*. Unlike the dance with steady rhythm and tempo, the music for a romantic or tragic scene of a drama must be flexible to correspond to the speech and movements of the actors. Such a rendering style is called '*meriyasu*', originated from a Spanish word '*medias*', an elastic knitted fabric.

Structure of *Nagauta*

●Kabuki Ensemble

- The basic ensemble is composed of 2 *shamisen* and 1 singer. Some large scale ensembles contain more than 10 *shamisen* and 10 *narimono* (flute+percussion) or even multiple ensembles.
- The type of *nagauta shamisen* is *hosozao* (thin neck).

Nagauta musicians:
- Utaikata (singers)
- Shamisenkata (*shamisen* players)

Narimono players:
- Hayashikata — Taiko — Ōtsuzumi — Kotsuzumi — Shinobue — **Narimono**

●Seating

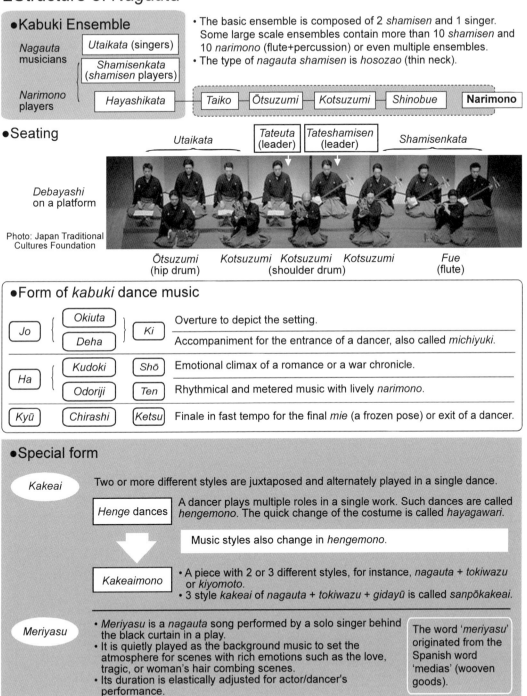

Debayashi on a platform

Photo: Japan Traditional Cultures Foundation

Utaikata | Tateuta (leader) | Tateshamisen (leader) | Shamisenkata

Ōtsuzumi (hip drum) | Kotsuzumi Kotsuzumi Kotsuzumi (shoulder drum) | Fue (flute)

●Form of *kabuki* dance music

Jo	Okiuta	Ki	Overture to depict the setting.
	Deha		Accompaniment for the entrance of a dancer, also called *michiyuki*.
Ha	Kudoki	Shō	Emotional climax of a romance or a war chronicle.
	Odoriji	Ten	Rhythmical and metered music with lively *narimono*.
Kyū	Chirashi	Ketsu	Finale in fast tempo for the final *mie* (a frozen pose) or exit of a dancer.

●Special form

Kakeai: Two or more different styles are juxtaposed and alternately played in a single dance.

Henge dances: A dancer plays multiple roles in a single work. Such dances are called *hengemono*. The quick change of the costume is called *hayagawari*.

⬇ Music styles also change in *hengemono*.

Kakeaimono:
- A piece with 2 or 3 different styles, for instance, *nagauta* + *tokiwazu* or *kiyomoto*.
- 3 style *kakeai* of *nagauta* + *tokiwazu* + *gidayū* is called *sanpōkakeai*.

Meriyasu:
- *Meriyasu* is a *nagauta* song performed by a solo singer behind the black curtain in a play.
- It is quietly played as the background music to set the atmosphere for scenes with rich emotions such as the love, tragic, or woman's hair combing scenes.
- Its duration is elastically adjusted for actor/dancer's performance.

The word '*meriyasu*' originated from the Spanish word '*medias*' (wooven goods).

Jōruri in *Kabuki*

As mentioned already, there was no music dedicated to *kabuki* in its early stages and *jiuta* or other types of songs were used. Among them were *jōruri* (*ko-jōruri*) such as *geki-bushi*, *handayū-bushi*, and *kinpira-bushi* that was diverted to *kabuki* from the beginning.

Kabuki was so overwhelmed by *ningyō-jōruri* that it was once said that it 'rarely existed', but devised a means of pulling back from the brink of extinction. *Kabuki* dramatized the puppet shows as *gidayū-kyōgen* of *kabuki*, which is why *gidayū-bushi* became indispensable music for *kabuki*. *Gidayū-kyōgen* is also called *maruhonmono* meaning the 'entire book', that is, the entire puppet show copied into a *kabuki* play.

Among other *jōruri*, most of *bungo-bushi* types in addition to primary *icchū-bushi* had a close relation with *kabuki* but ultimately only two *jōruri* styles, suitable for dancing, *tokiwazu-bushi* and *kiyomoto-bushi*, remained as the *kabuki* dance music. The two other *jōruri* styles, *ōzatsuma-bushi* and *katō-bushi*, were also used in the early stages. But at present, their performances are limited only to the specific scenes from specific plays, for example, "Yanone" (*ōzatsuma-bushi*) and "Sukeroku" (*katō-bushi*), both of which are included in the "Eighteen Best *Kabuki* Plays".

In *kabuki*, *gidayū-bushi* is called by its alias '*takemoto*', probably because the original name was reserved for the originator, *bunraku* (the present name of *ningyō-jōruri*). In *gidayū-kyōgen* of *kabuki* the actors replaced the puppets and everything else of music was copied from *gidayū-bushi*. *Gidayū-kyōgen* of *kabuki* looks like a complete copy but things are not so simple according to the *kabuki* actors. For example, the *jōruri* narrator of *ningyō-jōruri* recites the speech of the puppets and narrates description of the scene as well as all mentality and emotion of the characters, and the puppets adjust to the music. On the contrary, however, the narrator and *shamisen* players of *kabuki* must adjust to the movements and speech of the human actors.

Adapting *bungo-bushi* types of *jōruri* into *kabuki* resulted in the birth of the "dramatic dance" with a story. Because *furigoto* or *shosagoto*, the specific and meaningful gestures, not abstract gestures, unfolded a story, the *kabuki* dances significantly changed. In this way, *kabuki* adapted other performing arts and developed.

■ *Jōruri* in *Kabuki*

● Musical styles

Location \ Period	Genroku (1688-1704)	Kyōhō (1716-1736)	Meiwa (1764-1772)	Bunka-Bunsei (1804-1829)
Kyoto-Osaka	Icchū-bushi	*Gidayū-bushi	Sonohachi-bushi	Shin'nai-bushi
Edo	Geki-bushi, Handayū-bushi, **Ōzatsuma-bushi, **Katō-bushi	Bungo-bushi	*Tokuwazu-bushi, Tomimoto-bushi	*Kiyomoto-bushi

* Existing in today's *kabuki*.   ** Some used in a specific way.   No marked: No longer used in *Kabuki*.

● *Gidayū* in *kabuki*

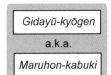

Gidayū-kyōgen a.k.a. Maruhon-kabuki

Jidaimono	Complete copies of popular *ningyō-jōruri* plays such as: "Sugawaradenju Tenarai Kagami", "Yoshitsune Senbon Zakura", "Kanadehon Chūshingura".
Sewamono	"Sonezaki Shinjū", "Natsumatsuri Naniwa Kagami", "Shinjū Ten no Amijima".

- In the Kyōhō period, *ningyō-jōruri* was in its glory so that copying this style was the desperate measure of the declining *kabuki*.

  * The word '*maruhon*' stands for a whole book of *gidayū-bushi*.

- Complete copies of the plots, characters, stage settings, songs, *shamisen* parts, texts, and so on of *ningyō-jōruri*.

Differences

	Characters	Dailogue	Leader	Name
Ningyō-jōruri	Puppets	Tayū (narrator)	Tayū	Gidayū-bushi
Kabuki	Actors	Actors (lines)	Actors (acting)	Takemoto (as a humble name)

● "Bungo's Big Three" styles for dances

- *Ko-jōruri* before the Genroku period and *bungo-bushi* (especially, "Bungo's Big Three" styles) after that were used for dances.

	Tokiwazu-bushi	Kiyomoto-bushi
Lineage	Desciples of Bungonojō, especially the *Bungo's* Big Three	Descendants of the Big-three *bungo* styles and descendents of *tokuwazu* styles
Onset	Meiwa - Tenmei periods (mid-18C)	Bunka-Bunsei periods (early 19C)
Originator	Tokiwazu Mojidayū (1709?-1781)	Kiyomoto Enjudayū (1777-1825)
Usage	*Degatari* (onstage performance) for dances	For dances, drama, and solo *jōruri*
Basic form	3-4 singers and 2-3 *shamisen* players	3-4 singers and 2-3 *shamisen* players
Type of *shamisen*	Chūzao (medium neck) in *honchōshi*, *niagai* and *sansagari*	Chūzao (medium neck) in *uwajōshi* (duo with a second *shamisen* for a treble part)
Vocal style	Natural and monotonous. Middle vocal range for *bungo-bushi*	Technical. Nasal tone in the upper register
Music style	Masculine and heroic	Lively and showy, depending on the period.
Major titles	"Seki no To", "Masakado", "Modoribashi", and "Imoseyama On'na Teikin"	"Kumonimagou Ueno no Hatsuhana", "Yasuna", "Ukare Bōzu"

Geza Music: Sound Effects for Snowfall

The core of *kabuki* is dancing and acting by players. But if they dance and act marvelously, the *kabuki* play would still not succeed without *geza* music. It is like a luxurious car running out of gasoline. The word '*geza*' is a general term and it is called *kuromisu* or *kagebayashi* in the *kabuki* world. *Kuromisu* originally stood for the black bamboo screen enclosing a small room at the left stage, as seen by the audience, where musicians sit and play. Later it also meant the music or the room. The musicians play *kabuki*'s incidental music or produce the sound effects necessary for the scene, while watching the progress on the stage through the black screen.

There are no players dedicated to the *kuromisu* music. It is played by the *nagauta* and *shamisen* musicians as well as players of all kinds of other instruments, called *narimono*. They play *debayashi* (onstage music) sitting on the tiered platform on the stage and *kagebayashi* (offstage music) or *geza* music behind the black screen. Thus, the *kuromisu* music can be thought to be one of the formations of *nagauta* performances.

The *kuromisu* music is in charge of creating and effectively emphasizing an atmosphere of the scenes of dramas and dances. There are various methods, sound effects, and works precisely predetermined for every scene. As shown on the right page, the way to sing and play *shamisen* for each occasion is diversified, from cheerful music by the large number of players to quiet and emotional music by a small number of players. Moreover, there are specific instrumental expressions to symbolically depict a scene or a situation. These expressions or pieces are named, for example, "Tsukuda no Aikata" for a riverside scene, and "Sugagaki" for a cheerful gay quarter scene. They are played before raising the curtain to create an atmosphere of the scene. There are more than 800 such pieces played by the musicians without any score or music.

In addition to basic *shamisen* and *shibyōshi*, many other percussive instruments are used, some of which are beyond our imagination. The sound effects are specifically selected. For example, the eerie sounds of the flute and the drums mean that a ghost appears. Amazingly, even a scene and the atmosphere of silently falling snow are successfully expressed by the remarkable sound effects.

Traditional Japanese Music at a Glance

■*Geza* Music

| *Geza* Music | Background and dance music, or sound effects played by an ensemble seated in a small room behind black screens called *kuromisu*. |

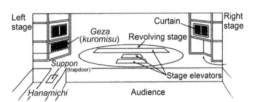

| A.k.a. *Kuromisu* | *Geza* music is also called *kuromisu* after the small room, *kuromisu*, for musicians. | ↑ A small room behind the laticeworked window with black screens at the left side. |

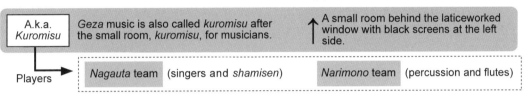

Players → *Nagauta* team (singers and *shamisen*)   *Narimono* team (percussion and flutes)

●Performance styles

- *Shamisens* only: Music between actors' dialogue, etc.
- Singers only: Worksongs such as a boatman's song and a horseman's song.
- A single singer: Songs accompanied by two *shamisens* for a love scene, etc.
- Duet: Two singers with two *shamisen* perform for actor's entrance or *michiyuki* (travels), etc.
- *Noh* chants: 1-3 singers sing *noh*'s chants accompanied by instrumentalists.
- A single *shamisen*: *Shamisen* solo called *shinobi-sanjū* or *taimen-sanjū*, etc.
- *Shin'nai nagashi*: *Shamisen* duo perform *shin'nai* songs.
- *Narimono* only: *Narimono* means any instruments other than *shamisen*. Rain or water effect by large drums or flutes.
- Whole ensemble: Music for stage opening, actor's entrance/exit, or fighting scenes, etc.

●Music for specific scenes

- Some songs are assigned to specific plays and scenes depending on the time and location in the story.
- There are more than 800 handed-down special songs, 60% of which were made in Edo and the rest in the Kyoto-Osaka area.

Jidaimono: (1) palace (2) temples/shrines or cherry-brlossom viewing (3) *samurai* classes (4) fighting scenes (5) active and rhythminc scenes (6) changing clothes (7) dumb shows (8) lift in motion (9) solo *shamisen* (10) miscellaneous

Sewamono: (1) countryside (2) main roads/shores (3) temples/shrines (4) festivals or chivalrous men (5) gay quarters (6) farce (7) fighting scenes (8) wounded characters (9) ghosts (10) solo singing (called *meriyasu*) (11) chorus (12) singing practice (13) miscellaneous

●Instruments of *geza*

Tack-fixed drums: *ōdaiko* (stick drum), *gakudaiko* (*gagaku* drum), *hiramarudaiko* (flat-round drum), *uchiwadaiko* (fan drum)

Shimedaiko (tight drum): *sarugaku* drum, *okedō* drum, double drums, *kakko* drum

Tsuzumi drums: *ōtsuzumi* (large hip drum), *kotsuzumi* (small shoulder drum)

Gong/bells: hand-held gongs such as *atarigane*, *surigane*, *fusegane*, and *matsumushi*; *dora* (gong), *waniguchi* (medal shaped steel drum), temple bell, hand bells, horse bells, *dobyōshi* or *chappa* (hand-held cymbals)

Flutes: *nohkan*, *shinobue*, *shakuhachi*, *charumela* (oboe-like horn), pipes, a cricket whistle

Others: *kokyū*, xylophone, glockenspiel, *kotodoro* (*koto* being out of tune), temple block, *bangi* (suspended board), *shakubyōshi* (clappers), *shakujō* (metal rings), *kinuta* (hammer to beat cloth), *hyōshigi* (wooden/bamboo clappers), keg, fan, *kokiriko* (clapper made from wooden slats connected by a cord)

Modern *Nagauta* as Pure Music

Nagauta is the music developed for and dedicated to *kabuki*. Absorbing the various essence of all preceding Japanese music, it became the most popular and unique *shamisen* music in the Edo period. Its popularity did not stay within the *kabuki* theater and spread to other areas.

Ogie Royū, who was the section leader of *nagauta* at the Ichimura-za theater in Edo, extended his activity to the gay quarters from the theater, and developed *nagauta* as parlor style songs to establish his own style, *ogie-bushi*.

Partly because the great pieces of *nagauta* were produced one after another from the later period of Edo to the Meiji period, *nagauta* got support of a wide range of people from the townsmen to the warrior classes. *Nagauta* became favored by the connoisseurs such as the wealthy merchants, *samurai*, and the literary men who were unrelated to the *kabuki* theater. The boom of this independent *nagauta* stimulated the questioning mind and artistic and creative urge of *nagauta* musicians, the core of which was no longer the singers, but the *shamisen* players who composed music. The *shamisen* players then established a new style for artistic *nagauta*. The three big composers in *shamisen* music, listed on the right page, are still highly evaluated and their excellent masterpieces are played at present.

With this as a turning point, *nagauta* as purely artistic music completely independent from *kabuki* was played in the concerts in the Meiji period. Especially, the recitals of the *shamisen* group, Nagauta Kensei-kai, featuring Kineya Jōkan II and Yoshizumi Kosaburō IV, were so popular that a very long line of attendees allegedly surrounded the concert hall.

Following this successful group, new *shamisen* groups were created, and even Kineya Rokuzaemon, the leading *shamisen* player in the *kabuki* world, was involved. *Nagauta* was no longer the music in the houses of disrepute (theaters and the gay quarters), and its social position improved. It became home music like *sōkyoku*, suitable for children from good homes.

In this trend, Sakichi Kineya IV (1884-1945) of Nagauta Fuyō-kai, one of the *shamisen* groups, developed vocal *nagauta* into instrumental music. He called his music the '*sangen shusōgaku*' and pioneered the new world of *shamisen*. In this way, *nagauta* which had been subordinate to *kabuki* started its new life as instrumental and purely artistic music.

Traditional Japanese Music at a Glance

■Modern *Nagauta*

Note: all names are written with the family name followed by the given name.

●Integrated to *kabuki* plays

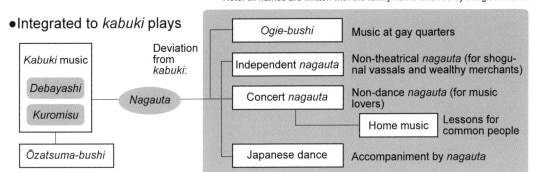

●Non-theatrical *nagauta*

Ogie-bushi	Ogie Royū I brought *nagauta* into gay quarters around 1750-1770. *Shamisen* was subordinate to singing without skillfull phrases of *nagauta*.
Independent *nagauta*	During 1815-1868, intellectuals, wealthy merchants and feudal lords who favored *nagauta* and *kabuki* enjoyed performances by *nagauta* musicians at their estates or parlors. Many masterworks were composed.
Concert *nagauta*	During the Meiji period, purely artistic *nagauta* deviated from *kabuki* dance were performed in concerts. The goup, Nagauta Kensei-kai, successfully organized concert series followed by other new groups.
Home music	During the Meiji and Taisho periods, *nagauta* was welcomed by families, no longer music for gay quarters. Daughters of cultured families began to learn *nagauta* as well as *koto* music.
Japanese dance	In 1804-1830, dancing became popular in towns. At the end of Edo period there were 21 schools with many training rooms in towns. Professional dancers appeared and used *nagauta*.

●Groups of concert *nagauta* performers and their founders

Kensei-kai	Fuyō-kai	Kakumei-kai	Kineroku-kai	Okayasu-kai
Yoshizumi Kosaburō IV Kineya Jōkan II	Kineya Sakichi II	Kineya Eizō III Fujita Otozō V	Kineya Rokuzaemon VI Yoshizumi Kosahachi	Okayasu Kisaburō VI

●Modern *nagauta* masters: Singers became *shamisen* players

------ Big-3 composers in mid-Meiji period: ------

- Kineya Kangorō III: "Tsunayakata", "Hashibenkei", "Kishū-dōjōji", "Shiki no Yamanba", "Mochizuki"

- Kineya Katsusaburō II: "Funabenkei", "Miyakodori", "Goshiki no Ito", "Kuramayama", "Shiguresaigyō"

- Kineya Shōjirō III: "Ume no Sakae", "Tsuchigumo", "Renjishi", "Kagamijishi", "Genroku Hanamiofori"

------ Big-8 *nagauta* masters at the ------
end of Meiji-Taisho periods

Singers: Yoshimura Ijūrō VI, Fujita Otozō V
Yoshizumi Kosaburō IV, Matsunaga Wafū IV

Shamisen players:
Kineya Rokuzaemon XII, Kineya Kangorō V
Kineya Jōkan II, Kineya Rokuzaemon XIII
Kineya Katsutarō IV, Kineya Eizō IV
Kineya Sakichi IV, Kineya Mitarō V

Japanese Dances

The present Japanese dance, or *buyō*, as an independent genre of the performing art, originated from *kabuki* dances. Japanese dance is not a commercial success in contrast to *kabuki*. It developed after the middle of the Edo period. In the early stages, it probably began at dance schools opened by the choreographers of *kabuki* in the city, to teach people from *geisha* to the children from good homes. Now, since fewer people learn it and the audience is smaller today, it is not financially successful. Even so, there are more than two hundreds schools (styles) and the genre is still a large family.

Japanese dance is characterized by *furi* (or *furigoto*), the choreographic and meaningful expressions developed in *kabuki*. In the wide sense, the Japanese dance includes the *kabuki* dance but in the narrow sense, it refers to '*edo* dance' in Edo and '*kamigata* dance' in the Kyoto-Osaka area. These two styles are quite different from each other. Though influenced by *kabuki*, the *kamigata* dances were based on the performing arts such as *noh* dances and *kusemai* favored at parlors in the gay quarter. As its alias '*jiuta* dance' suggests, *kamigata* dances are accompanied by *jiuta*. The music for the '*edo* dances' is basically *nagauta*, *tokiwazu-bushi* and *kiyomoto-bushi* as well as *katō-bushi* and *ogie-bushi*, similar to *kabuki*. The Japanese dances derived from the *kabuki* dances, use the costume and *furigoto* similar to that of *kabuki* but unlike the male dominant *noh* and *kabuki* worlds, the female roles are played by female dancers, not *on'nagata* (or *oyama*) who are male. Also, more female musicians play the *nagauta* or other accompaniment music for the dance than for *kabuki*. That is probably because there were female performers who taught dancing and music at the shogun's harem and in the cities.

There are so many schools (styles) as said "a school per dancer" that the lineage of Japanese dance is extremely complicated. At present, Japanese dance is diversified from the creative avant-garde dance to the democratic dance. For the democratic dance, popular music and folk songs, rather than purely artistic music, are often used.

■*Kabuki* Dance and *Nihonbuyō* (Japanese Dance)

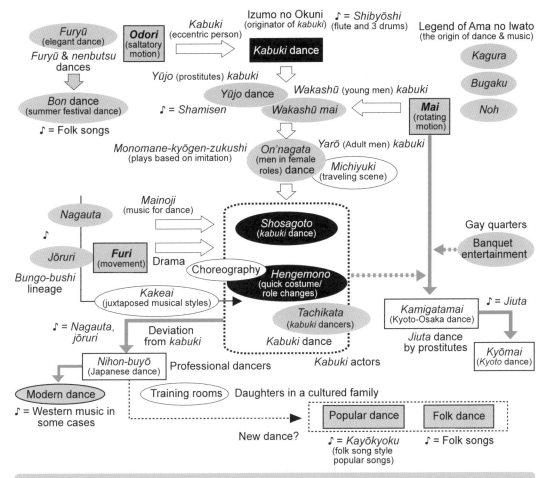

- ●Schools of Japanese dance
  - Many shools of Japanese dance are private. There are more than 200 schools today.
  - 21 schools were listed in a ranking list of *okyōgenshi** in 1872: Bandō, Nakamura, Fujima, Nishikawa, Mizuki, Iwai, Matsuga, Hirokawa, Ichiyama, Seyama, Sawamura, Matsumoto, Azuma, Ichikawa, Tomoe, Fujimoto, Hanayagi, Shigayama, Katsumi, Tonegawa, Ōnishi.
  - Big-five Japanese dance shools: Fujima-ryū, Nishikawa-ryū, Hanayagi-ryū, Wakayagi-ryū, Bandō-ryū.
  - Each *ryū* (schools) splits to *ha* (factions): e.g. Kan'emon-ha, Kanjūrō-ha, Monzaburō-ha, and Murasaki-ha of Fujima-ryū.
  - Classification based on the type of the school and founder:

Choreographers:	Fujima-ryū, Nishikawa-ryū, Ichiyama-ryū, Hanayagi-ryū, Wakayagi-ryū
Kabuki actors:	Bandō-ryū, Nakamura-ryū, Mizuki-ryū, Iwai-ryū, Ichikawa-ryū
Okyōgenshi*:	Matsumoto-ryū, Matsuga-ryū, Azuma-ryū, Hirokawa-ryū, Sawamura-ryū
Kyoko-Osaka styles:	Yamamura-ryū, Yoshimura-ryū, Shinozuka-ryū, Inou'e-ryū

  * *Okyōgenshi* = female dancers/actresses who gave performance or lessons at the palaces of shogun or feudal lords.

Chapter 11: *Shamisen* (4)—Short Songs

Popular Songs at the End of the Edo Period

Shamisen music developed through interacting with various kinds of public entertainment. It established itself as the music for the theaters and the parlors of the gay quarters. Then, professional performers who made a living with *shamisen* came about. At the same time, songs with short lyrics, such as *ryūtatsu-bushi* and *rōsai-bushi*, became popular among the common people.

Fashionable *hauta*, different from formal *kumiuta*, was born in *jiuta* in the Kyoto-Osaka region. It became popular and developed into *edo hauta* in Edo. This *hauta* (=*edo hauta*) was so popular that it was adapted in *kabuki* music and was also sung as short love songs in vaudeville, which was more familiar than the theaters to common people. As a result, it penetrated people's lives and became overwhelmingly favored as the popular songs. This is how the joyful songs for people established themselves, not only to be listened to, but also widely sung. Groups of song lovers soon formed under the guidance of female instructors who were retired *geisha*, the performers at the parlors of the gay quarters. Those groups were called *ren* (company) and consisted of *samurai* warriors, farmers, craftsmen, and merchants, breaking the class system of the four social ranks of Japanese feudal society. *Ren* was a unique social phenomenon at the end of the Edo period.

The higher the musical level of *hauta* groups became, the more profound, graceful and magnificent songs such as *icchū-bushi* were sought and a new style, called *utazawa*, was soon established and became a role model. This *utazawa* rose to be the core of *hauta*, while the original *hauta* was confined to the art of *geisha* at the parlors of the gay quarters and declined among common people. The name of *utazawa* originated from the name of the group led by Osawa, a female *hauta* instructor. There were two factions, but they are called *utazawa* as a whole.

In the Meiji period, a 16-year-old girl, Kiyomoto Oyō composed a song more concise than *hauta*, titled "Chiru wa Uki". This was the first *kouta*. Sung to the accompaniment of *shamisen* plucked by a finger nail, not a plectrum, this intimate and stylish song could easily be sung by anybody, and so won more popularity than *utazawa*.

After World War II, when jazz and pop songs were introduced from the Western countries, the popularity of *kouta* boomed, but because of internal strife concerning the head family of the school, it ruined its own success.

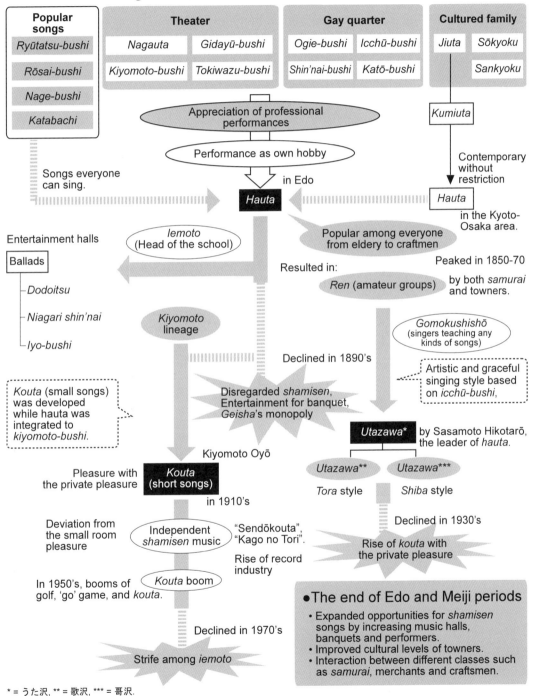

Refined Aesthetic Sense of Edo

When, for the first time, we hear the women in traditional *kimono* sing *hauta*, *utazawa* or *kouta* to the accompaniment of *shamisen*, we do not readily know how these songs differ. It is natural that these three types resemble each other and are classified in the same category of "*shamisen* short songs" since they are only named differently depending on their process of development. More than half of all songs have the same titles among *hauta*, *utazawa* and *kouta*, for example, "Sakura Miyotote (To See Cherry Blossoms)".

The only difference among them, if we must say, is that *hauta* is accompanied by other instruments in addition to *shamisen* and is generally rhythmical and cheerful because it is a party song at parlors. For *utazawa*, the same titled songs as *hauta*'s are sung in the lower register and at a slower tempo than *hauta*'s and sound grave and kind of sullen, like *jōruri* songs. On the other hand, *kouta* is modest, sung in the comparatively high register with quiet and whispering, not intensive, voice. *Hauta* is generally associated with the male patrons dancing to the instrumental accompaniment performed by a group of *geisha* at the parlor. It is comprised of *utazawa* with a *geisha* who sings to her own *shamisen* accompaniment sitting in front of the gilt folding screens at the parlor, and *kouta* with a male patron singing together with a *geisha* in an intimate room.

These are the subtle differences in the musical styles based on the places where they were played in Edo. In short, these songs represent the Edo culture developed in the parlor of the gay quarters. These songs and the lyrics give us a glimpse of the aesthetic sense of the sophisticated townspeople; that is, the stylish concept of well-informed and knowledgeable city dwellers tactful with handling of things and with understanding of human feelings and nature.

Strolling *shin'nai* performers shows the true worth of this culture. The intermittent sounds of *shamisen* duo and melancholic melodies in the high register in the quiet of night well represent the Edo atmosphere and the gay quarter's culture. These songs were played at vaudeville as lightly humorous ballads, showing a well-cultivated taste, as well. The *ukiyoe* (colored woodblock prints) depicting the scene of lessons of the refined instructor and the pupil facing each other really stirs our imagination of the urban life in Edo.

■*Shamisen* Songs of Edo Culture

●Popular songs among towners in Edo

Hauta	Songs for banquets in gay quarters in Edo. *Shamisen* is as important as singing. *Hauta* is lively songs with the simple rhythm and meter, accompanied by *shamisen*, drums, hand gongs and flutes.
Utazawa	Graceful songs based on *hauta*. Singing, similar to narration, is more important than *shamisen*. *Utazawa* is grave songs in a low register, complicated rhythm and slow tempo.
Kouta	Quiet songs based on *hauta*. *Shamisen* takes the initiative. *Kouta* is songs in a higher register, fast tempo and simple rhythm and meter. *Shamisen* was plucked by a finger nail.

Zokkyoku (ballads)	Songs performed in the places like a variety hall. Mainly popular *hauta* or *kouta* songs such as *dodoitsu*, *kappore*, *niagari-shin'nai*, and *yakko-san*. They were sung between regular narrative entertainment.

●Similarity and confusion among *shamisen* songs

- *Shamisen* songs were established in the Edo period. Many *hauta*, *utazawa*. and *kouta* share the same title. *Hauta* songs with a unique title were composed in the Kyoto-Osaka region. Some titles of *hauta* and *utazawa* are not found in *kouta* bacause the *shamisen* part did not fit the *kouta* style.
- All *shamisen* short songs created in the Showa period are *kouta*.

●Edo culture as the gay quarter culture

- The plays, literature and arts in the Edo period were closely related in the gay quarters.
- The qay quaters in the Edo period were also the places to socialize without prostitution until the Meiji period when the brothels took over.
- In the qay quaters, everyone was treated equally and people interacted with different classes.
- The unique aesthetic was established in Edo, e.g. *iki* (chic, stylish) and *tsū* (highly cultivated).

●*Gomokushishō*

The performers, former *gaisha*, who taught various performing arts such as *hauta*, *kouta*, *nagauta*, *jōruri* and even dance, were called '*gomokushishō*'. They offered private lessons and became very popular. Each town had at least one *monokushishō*.

●Stylish performers other than *jōruri* singers

Shin'nai	*Shin'nai* performers who strolled in the gay quarters and performed for clientele were called *shin'nai nagashi*. They were a duo of two *shamisen* players and sang *shin'nai-bushi* in the very high register to their own accompaniment.

Evolution of *Shamisen* Music

For three hundred years, from its introduction to the beginning of the Meiji period, *shamisen* music evolved on the theatrical stages and in the parlors of the gay quarters. Many new musical genres and styles were established influencing each other with constant musical merger and separation so that *shamisen* has become regarded as one of the most typical of Japanese musical instruments.

However, due to the Europeanization policy of the Meiji Restoration and the cultural tide idealizing Western music, *shamisen* music, the flower of the Edo culture, was despised by iconoclasts as vulgar music of the gay quarters. Rapidly becoming popular, Western music influenced Japanese traditional music, especially *koto* music first, and a new *koto* style, called *Meiji shinkyoku* (Meiji new songs), arose with adaptation of the system of Western music. *Koto* was followed by *shamisen* in deviating from the Edo culture. Beginning with the new "concert *nagauta*", *jōruri* music, such as *tokiwazu-bushi* and *kiyomoto-bushi,* tried to differ from theatrical music style and establish its identity as pure music. In *gidayū*, the new style deviating from narrative music, called *toyomoto-bushi*, was established. In *jiuta-sōkyoku*, Michio Miyagi with other musicians immediately began the music activity called '*shin nihon ongaku* (new Japanese music)'.

Those who were in the business circles and knowledgeable about music proposed a new musical style with new vocalization and with ensembles, and so on, based on the traditional *shamisen* music. For example, Hiroshi Hiraoka, a leader of the railroad industry, founder of baseball in Japan, established the Tōmei School of Samisen Music, *tōmeigaku*. Kishichirō Ōkura, the second generation of the Ōkura financial combine, established *yamatogaku*.

In the meantime, folk songs, which used to be unaccompanied and sung in the private parlors, were turned into party songs sung to the accompaniment of *shamisen* in such places. *Shamisen* became very important for folk songs. Among *shamisen* for folk songs, *tsugaru shamisen* of northern Japan developed a unique performing style and technique and became a solo instrument. In addition, *naniwabushi* (or *rōkyoku*), that is narrative singing and more storytelling than music, was inseparable from *shamisen* to the extent that it cannot exist without *shamisen*.

■Other *Shamisen* Music
●*Shamisen* music after the Meiji Restoration

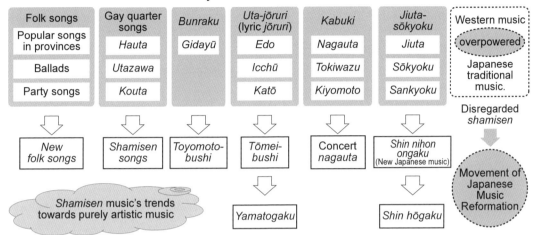

●Modern *shamisen* music

Tōmei-bushi	Established, based on the combination of *icchū-bushi* and *yōkyoku* (*noh* chants), in 1910 by Hiroshi Hiraoka, who had left a great achivement in reviving *katō-bushi*. It is skillful, ornate, sensitive, and varied with rich modulation.
Yamatogaku	Established in 1933 by Kishichirō Ōkura who invented *ōkraulo* (*shakuhachi* with key pads). This new *shamisen* music adopted Western style singing. Works for *shamisen*, *koto*, bass *koto*, *narimono* and even Western instruments were composed.
Toyomoto-bushi	Established in 1954 by Matsunosuke of *bunraku*. Its lyrical character was derived from narrative *gidayū-bushi*. Used for dance as well. Voice is always paired with the *shamisen* part.

●Other genres derived from *shamisen* music:

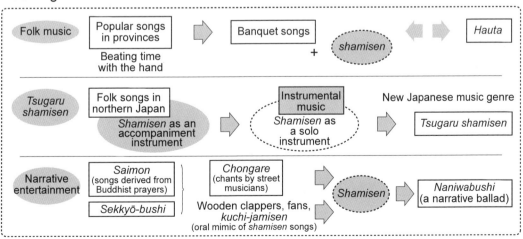

Music of Townspeople: Brief History of *Shamisen* Music

The Okinawan *sanshin*, from which *shamisen* originated, was introduced to Japan just before the beginning of the Edo period. Naturally, *shamisen* and its music developed in the Edo period.

About half a century after its introduction, *sanshin* transformed into *shamisen*, as used at present by *biwa-hōshi* (*biwa* minstrels), and *shamisen-kumiuta* of *jiuta*, the earliest works for *shamisen* were created. In addition, *ko-jōruri* (the early stages of *jōruri*) and *kabuki* dances adapted *shamisen*. As for *koto* music in the same period, *koto-kumiuta* was established by Yatsuhashi Kengyō.

These events coincided with the establishment of the Tokugawa Shogunate in Edo. As illustrated on the right page, the music culture in Edo prospered and was diversified like many flowers blooming in profusion. During the peaceful Edo period following the Middle Ages made unstable by civil wars, and despite an existing feudal system, the main cultural bearers shifted from the warrior class to the merchant class. As a result, elegant music was favored over less refined music of common people

Unlike the *noh* theater which was patronized by the warrior class, public entertainment which prospered in the Edo period did not have sponsors. The entertainers gave performances to the public to make a living. Since the taste of the merchant class changed quickly, innovation and constant improvement of the cultural activity and of the public entertainment were always necessary. The actors and performers who made a living with performances had to always work to better their art or they went out of business if they did not meet the expectations of the public. They tried hard to improve themselves and developed new *shamisen* music as well as its collateral culture to satisfy the sophisticated townspeople of Edo. The number of performers and expert playwrights and their masterpieces greatly increased. *Shamisen* music was at its peak during the Meiji period and began its decline when Western music was introduced.

Music in Japan was generally introduced from foreign countries and influenced by other cultures. But, because of the national isolation during the Edo period, *shamisen* music, supported by the common townspeople, evolved domestically and became unique and pure Japanese music.

Traditional Japanese Music at a Glance

■History of *Shamisen* Music

Momoyama (1573-1603)
- *Shamisen* introduced (ca. 1560).   • *Tsukushi-goto* invented by Kenshin (end of 16C).
- *Heikyoku* performers turn to *jōruri* (mid-16C).
- *Shamisen* accompanies *jōruri* (ca. 1580).   *Ningyō-jōruri* begins (1595).

Edo (1603-1868)
- Battle of Sekigahara (1600).
- Jiuta *shamisen-kumiuta* established (ca. 1600).   • Okuni begins *kabuki dance* (1603).
- *Noh* designated as the ceremonial music of the government (1610).
- Sugiyama Tangonojō begins *jōruri* in Edo (1615).   • Satsuma Jōun begins *jōruri* in Edo (1626).
- Yatsuhashi Kengō composes 13 *koto-kumiuta* (1630).
- *Yūjo-kabuki* banned (1652).   • *Wakashū-kabuki* banned (1653).   • *Yarō-kabuki* begins (1653).
- Ichikawa Danjūrō begins the rough '*aragoto*' style (1673).
- Sakata Tōjūrō begins the soft '*wagoto*' style (1678).
- *Tōdōza* monopolizes *koto/shamisen* (17C).
- Gidayū founds *Takemoto-za* (1684).   *Sōkyoku* and *jiuta* unite (17C).
- Ikuta Kengyō establishes Ikuta School (1695).   Revenge of the 47 Ronin (1702).
- Chikamatsu's *sewamono*, e.g. "Love Suicides at Sonezaki" becomes popular (1703).
- *Edo nagauta* appears (1704).   *Katō-bushi* begins (1717).
- Miyakoji Bungonojō moves to Edo (ca. 1730).
- *Shosagoto* established (ca. 1730).   *Bungo-bushi* oppressed (1739).
- *Nagauta* established (1730's).   • 3-puppeteer system of *bunraku* (1734).
- "Sugawaradenju Tenarai Kagami", "Yoshitsune Senbon Zakura", and "Kanadehon Chūshingura" performed (1746-8).
- *Maruhon kabuki* begins (1746).   *Tokiwazu-bushi* begins (1747).
- *Tomimoto-bushi* begins (1748).   *Tsuruga-bushi* begins (1751).
- "Kyō Kanokomusume Dōjō-ji" premiered (1753). *Henge* dance blooms.
- *Ogie-bushi* begins (1768).   • Theater *Takemoto-za* closed (1772).
- *Geza music* established (early 19C).   • Yamada School begins (1777).
- *Bunraku-za* established (1811).   *Kiyomoto-bushi* begins (1814).
- *Hauta* blooms (1800's).   • *Bakumatsu shin sōkyoku* (mid-19C).
- *Shamisen* as a major accompaniment instrument for folk songs.
- Meiji Restoration (1868).

Meiji (1868-1912)
- *Tōdō* system and Fuke Sect abolished (1871).
- *Jiuta* musician groups established → Tōdō Ongakukai (1875).
- Ongaku Torishirabegakari (Institue of Music) established in Ministry of Education (1879).
- *Utazawa* begins (1895).   • *Sōkyoku* and *shakuhachi* open to public.
- *Sankyoku* of *koto*, *shamisen* and *shakuhachi* booms (early 20C).
- Nagauta Kenseikai established (1902).   • Sakichi Kineya begins *sangen syusōgaku* (1902).
- *Kouta* becomes popular (1900's).

Taisho (1912-1926)
- Michio Miyagi begins "Shin Nihon Ongaku" movement (1920), and composes "Haru no umi" (1929).
- *Shin hōgaku* begins (ca. 1930).

Showa-Heisei (1926-)
- *Hōgaku* (Japanese Music) Department established in Tokyo University of Arts where Miyagi and Nakanoshima teach (1950).   • NHK Hōgaku Ikuseikai established (1955).
- *Tsugaru shamisen* becomes popular in Tokyo (1960's).

Chapter 12: Folk Songs

Songs of the Countryside

Folk songs are long-lived songs created and sung by the public, and passed on by oral tradition. Folk songs are called '*min'yō*' today, but since they were created and passed down in the remote provinces, they were called '*inakauta* (countryside songs)', '*riyō* (provincial songs)' or '*zokuyō* (secular songs)' until the Meiji period. Folk songs of big cities such as Kyoto, Osaka, Nagoya and Edo were rare.

Some think that the category of the folk songs includes the traditional children's songs and lullabies. But according to the classification of the ethnomusicology at present, folk songs classified as folk music are distinguished from traditional children's songs, based on the purpose, circumstances, and the meaning of the lyrics of the songs.

The folk songs that are songs passed down for generations meet six conditions as illustrated on the right page: the spontaneity, the oral tradition, the migration, the collectivity, the artlessness and the locality. However, today's well-known folk songs do not necessarily meet these conditions. Initially sung unaccompanied or occasionally sung to handclaps, they were brought into banquets and private parlors where they were transformed into *shamisen* music as drinking and parlor songs with the accompaniment of *shamisen* and other instruments. They were passed along into cities and evolved into the refined *shamisen* music such as *hauta*, *kouta* and *zokkyoku* (ballads) at the gay quarters.

Soon some folk songs became a fixed model called '*seichō*', a standardized melody. As a result, those refined popular songs lost their original nature such as the oral tradition, the locality and the artlessness as the "ever-changing" folk songs. This is what we know as folk songs today.

Before and after World War II, there were a few folk song booms that triggered professional folk song singers to appear. The recordings of their songs were released and placed as "folk songs" in the popular song category. Folk songs in the rural regions, unknown until then were discovered and released as the popular songs and "new folk songs" by the professional musicians were created during these booms. These new folk songs led the later Japanese traditional songs.

Traditional Japanese Music at a Glance

■Folk Songs

Folk songs = popular or provincial songs created and sung by the public.

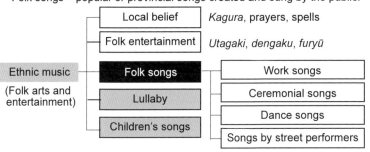
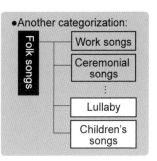

● Another categorization:

●*Min'yō* (folk songs)

After the Meiji period, the word '*min'yō*' referred to folk songs. Until then, folk songs were called seculer songs, provincial songs, popular songs, unsophisticated songs, and so on.

● Ringai Maeda's definition:
("Collections of Japanese Folk Songs", 1907)

Min'yō (folk songs)	Songs in rural areas made of melodies in free tempo, free dynamics, and free form without instrumental accompaniment.
Riyō (provincial songs)	Songs sung in the dialect in a specific area in free form without instrumental accompaniment.
Zokuyō (secular songs)	Songs in forms with instrumental accompaniment. Often taught by instructors.

Folk entertainment

Songs or performance by street performers. They were not regarded as artistic music but entertainment for common people.

■Attributes of folk songs

Natural generation	A song generated and spread of itself.
Oral Tradition	Songs transmitted and gradually developed through oral tradition without any musical notation system.
Migration	Songs carried and transplanted by people into an another local area.
Collectivity	Songs created for and by the local people, not by an individual.
Simplicity	Songs to express our fundamental life without musical sophistication.
Provincial	Songs with unique characteristics such as rhythm or texts of the local areas.

●Ever-changing folk songs

Originally folk songs were for labor classes.

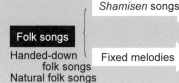
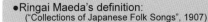

Work Songs

The total number of folk songs is probably 58,000, ranked after the top 70,000 or more school songs among Japanese songs. Since many folk songs were changed in the oral tradition process or renamed in the other regions where they were passed along, differently titled songs could be the same or could have originated from the same one. The number of folk songs includes those duplicated songs.

There are several classification methods of folk songs. This book uses the three category system shown on the right page. The first group is the work (labor) song that seems to account for 80-90 percent of all the folk songs in Japan. Playing music in a working place, for example, the background music in manufacturing plants has proven to improve performance of workers. In the past it was manual labor by a team of workers in the agriculture, forestry, fishery, mining and construction industries, and the work songs and the interjected (usually meaningless) shouts to mark time or of encouragement, seem to be necessary for concentration on the job and improvement of performance. That is why there are so many work songs. Among work songs, the agricultural songs, specifically rice-producing songs, are minutely subdivided according to the working process. The process of rice production in those days can even be compiled in a manual by collecting these songs. Farmers and fishers worked in the same way nationwide and the same titled work songs existed in each village. Today's changes of mechanization and modernization in the manufacturing system have affected the work songs. Songs related to the abolished working process disappeared in large numbers.

The second group is the ritual song. The festive dance songs to pray for a good harvest and ancestor worship or songs for the wedding celebration belong to this group. Religious services are often accompanied by songs and dances. Probably, people's prayer and gratitude to gods and Buddha were expressed as dance songs.

The last group is the entertainment song by strolling entertainers. Among them, especially the songs and stories by the blind female entertainers, called *goze*, or blind male entertainers, called *zatō*, who sang or played *shamisen* for a night's lodging and a meal, were one of the biggest pastimes for the public at the time. The entertainers who strolled from a village to another passed the songs unique to the area to other areas.

Traditional Japanese Music at a Glance

■Scenes and Purpose of Folk songs

Folk songs can be categorized based on where and for what they are sung.
(Categorization by the Agency for Cultural Affairs and the scholars, Kunio Yanagida and Kashō Machida.)

●How many folk songs in Japan?

There are approx. 58,000 folk songs, 80-90% of which are work (labor) songs. Work songs are sung during the work or break in the farms, mountains, seas and homes in order to:
- Conduct a task (often coordinate timing), and
- Improve labor efficiency.

As our life styles and society change, old work songs directly related to them are disappearing.

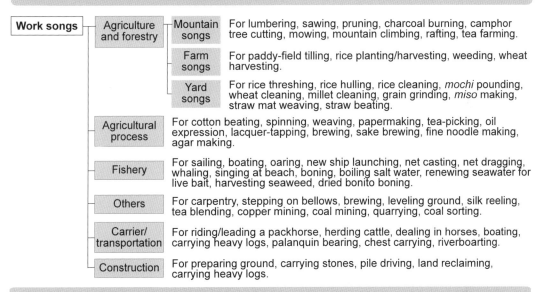

Work songs		
	Agriculture and forestry	Mountain songs: For lumbering, sawing, pruning, charcoal burning, camphor tree cutting, mowing, mountain climbing, rafting, tea farming.
		Farm songs: For paddy-field tilling, rice planting/harvesting, weeding, wheat harvesting.
		Yard songs: For rice threshing, rice hulling, rice cleaning, *mochi* pounding, wheat cleaning, millet cleaning, grain grinding, *miso* making, straw mat weaving, straw beating.
	Agricultural process	For cotton beating, spinning, weaving, papermaking, tea-picking, oil expression, lacquer-tapping, brewing, sake brewing, fine noodle making, agar making.
	Fishery	For sailing, boating, oaring, new ship launching, net casting, net dragging, whaling, singing at beach, boning, boiling salt water, renewing seawater for live bait, harvesting seaweed, dried bonito boning.
	Others	For carpentry, stepping on bellows, brewing, leveling ground, silk reeling, tea blending, copper mining, coal mining, quarrying, coal sorting.
	Carrier/ transportation	For riding/leading a packhorse, herding cattle, dealing in horses, boating, carrying heavy logs, palanquin bearing, chest carrying, riverboating.
	Construction	For preparing ground, carrying stones, pile driving, land reclaiming, carrying heavy logs.

●Religious songs for Shinto rituals, events, and lives

People in the community or region mutually aid and enjoy songs, dance and banquets.

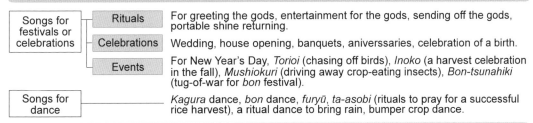

Songs for festivals or celebrations	Rituals	For greeting the gods, entertainment for the gods, sending off the gods, portable shine returning.
	Celebrations	Wedding, house opening, banquets, aniverssaries, celebration of a birth.
	Events	For New Year's Day, *Torioi* (chasing off birds), *Inoko* (a harvest celebration in the fall), *Mushiokuri* (driving away crop-eating insects), *Bon-tsunahiki* (tug-of-war for *bon* festival).
Songs for dance		*Kagura* dance, *bon* dance, *furyū*, *ta-asobi* (rituals to pray for a successful rice harvest), a ritual dance to bring rain, bumper crop dance.

●Songs by entertainers

Songs by street or roaming performers were great pleasure for people in the rural areas. Such songs settled in the local areas and became the province songs.

Songs by street or roaming performers	Narrative songs	*Goze* songs, *zatō* songs, *kudoki-bushi*
	Celebrative songs	*Manzai*, *harugoma*, *daikoku-mai* by street performers and *gan'ninbōzu*.

Folk Songs of Early Modern Age

It is difficult to analyze the characteristics of the folk songs in a scholarly and scientific fashion since an enormous number of songs and a great variety of styles exist. The rhythmic and melodic structure of Japanese folk songs is so unique that the Western notation system is only partially applied. If we try to transcribe the melodies of the folk songs into the staff notation, the resulting scores are incomplete, like a foreign language written in English. Though not perfect, transcribed music of folk songs is useful for our research. The characteristics based on analyses are summarized on the right page.

The first factor is the syllable meter of lyrics. Nearly ninety percent of the folk songs have the seven-seven-seven-and-five syllable meter. This syllable meter is not found in the songs older than the early modern age, namely the Edo period (1603-1868). This means that the majority of folk songs existing now appeared or changed in or after the early modern age.

As for the scale, the *min'yō* scale (anhemitonic pentatonic scale: mi-so-la-ti-re) is mostly used, followed by the *miyakobushi* scale (hemitonic pentatonic scale: mi-fa-la-ti-do). The folk songs in other scales are usually unique to the specific region with local colors, for example, *okinawa* scale (hemitonic pentatonic scale: do, mi, fa, so, ti) in Okinawa, and *ritsu* scale (anhemitonic pentatonic scale: re, mi, so, la, ti) in the mountain regions and islands.

The rhythmic structure is classified into two contrasting groups: the *yagibushi* style of a fixed rhythm (or a metrical rhythm) and the *oiwake* style of the free rhythm (or non-metrical rhythm).

As for the singing style, basically, a solo singer sings. Occasionally there are the antiphony style (a call and response style) and the *ondo* style (a leader and others style), but singing together in chorus seems to rarely exist, except for the interjected shouts. There is no harmony.

When the work songs, which account for the great part of the folk songs, became independent of labor and were sung at drinking parties, their purpose changed to pleasure rather than work efficiency. As a result, the accompaniment of an instrument such as *shamisen* was added and the keys or scales changed. The tuning system of *shamisen* also changed from *honchōshi* (basic tuning, for example, D-G-D) to *niagari* (the second string raised, for example, D-A-D) and *sansagari* (the third string lowered, for example, D-G-C). The rugged tone was refined, and the stiff mood was replaced with showy, cheerful, stylish and sexy one reflecting the trend of the times. The character of work songs completely changed to that of the parlor songs.

Traditional Japanese Music at a Glance

■Musical Structure of Folk Songs

●Texts: 80-90 % of texts are in the 7-7-7-5 syllable pattern found in most of modern *kouta*.

- Most of today's folk songs were created after the Edo period.
- The texts are often improvised.
- Some are in the patterns shown below:

> The 5-3-5-3 syllable pattern found in "Hōhaibushi" of Aomori Prefecture.
> The 5-7-5 syllable pattern found in "Naniyatoyara" of Iwate Prefecture.
> The repeated 5-7-5 syllable pattern found in "Saitarōbushi" of Miyagi Prefecture.
> The continuously repeated 7-7 syllable pattern found in "Yagibushi" of Gunma Prefecture.

For example, "Kudokibushi", a poetic epic song, is in this style.

●Scales: Mostly '*min'yō* scale'

Min'yō scale	• Found in the entire Japan but less found in southern Kyushu and Okinawa.
Miyakobushi scale	• Modern urban popular songs migrated to the rural areas and settled as province folk songs.
Okinawa scale	• On the contrary to the above two scales, this is found in Okinawan folk songs.
Ritsu scale	• Not so common but found in isolated areas such as mountain villages or islands all over Japan.
Miyakobushi variant	• The scale has the lowered mid tone of the *miyakobushi* scale found in the urban songs sung by professional folk song singers.

●Rhythm: *Yagibushi* and *oiwake* rhythms

Yagibushi style	To coordinate timing for a group: 　　For dance songs, seine net songs, ground-pounding songs, children's songs. 　　In the metrical or divisive rhythm independent from dynamics. 　　Syllabic melodies accompanied by drums and *shamisen*.
Oiwake style	For an individual: 　　Packhorse riding songs, sawyer songs, boat songs, lullabies. 　　In the free rhythm and accompanied by *shakuhachi*. 　　Melismatic melodies with texts mainly placed at the beginning.

●Singing: Folk songs show the character of Japanese music.

- Mostly sung by a solo singer or a chorus in unison following a leader's solo part.
- Occasionally an antiphon style is found but no harmony is created by multiple parts.
- No absolute pitches for singing in antiphon or unison. Even accompaniment is in heterophony composed of a single melodic line.

●*Shamisen*: The song is characterized by the tuning.

		Tendency		
Honchōshi	Grave and calm		Work songs	Folk songs gradually became more sophisticated and standardized to become concert music.
Niagari	Gay and lively	↓	Banquet songs	
Sansagari	Erotic and stylish		Gay quarter songs	

Accompaniments for Folk Songs

Before refined into party or parlor songs, folk songs, mostly work songs, were sung unaccompanied by instruments but with human shouts to mark time or encouragement. Soon, handclapping joined the singing during the happy circle in a recess from work or the reveling after work. We can imagine people had an enjoyable time.

In the late Edo period, work songs were brought into brothels and the gay quarters in various places, where *geisha* and maids who served clients and worked as prostitutes sang to their own *shamisen* accompaniment. Work songs became the parlor songs to be sung, listened to, and enjoyed.

At present the accompaniment instruments for the folk songs include most of the traditional Japanese musical instruments: strings, pipes, and percussion. Among them, *shamisen* is the most important. *Tsugaru shamisen* is used in the northern region, and *sanshin* in Okinawa. Packhorse driver's songs and boatman's songs, characterized with a singer's sonorous voice, are more accompanied by *shakuhachi* than *shamisen*. Some songs are sung to the accompaniment of *shamisen* and *shakuhachi* along with a wide range of traditional Japanese percussive instruments such as *shime-daiko* (small drum played with sticks). The uncommon instruments used for folk songs include a wooden cask for "Yagi-bushi" and "Niigata Jinku", and *kokyū* (two or three stringed fiddle) for "Echizen Ohara-bushi".

The rhythmical, interjected chants or shouts, called '*kakegoe*', are indispensable for the unaccompanied folk songs. In other words, there is no folk song without interjected chants or shouts. As illustrated on the right page, some songs have interjected chants longer than the song lyrics. For the folk songs in Aomori (Tsugaru) and Akita (Nanbu) regions, six meaningless characters, 'a, i, u, e, o, and n', are prolonged and chanted in the melismatic style, similar to scats in jazz. Though the words are meaningless, the melismatic melody is an integral part of the song.

Since these various, characteristic interjected chants or shouts make the personality of the song, some are even named after the *kakegoe*. What is good about folk songs is that we can feel as if we sing the song only by participating in the interjected chants and we don't have to be a good singer. One of the pleasures about singing a folk song is, unlike the *karaoke*, there is no restriction such as fixed pitches or tempo.

■Accompaniment of Folk songs
●A cappella folk songs
Originally folk songs were not accompanied by any instruments but only with hand clapping. Gay quarter songs derived from folk songs were accompanied mainly by *shamisen*.

String instruments	• *Shamisen*: Main accompaniment instrument for all folk songs in any style and location. • *Tsugaru shamisen*: For folk songs in northern Japan, especially Aomori Prefecture and Hokkaido. • *Ryūkyū shamisen*: For folk songs in southern Japan, especially Okinawa and southern Kyushu. • *Kokyū*: Used only for folk songs in the Hokuriku region (Japan Sea side of Japan).
Flutes	• *Shakuhachi*: For *oiwake-bushi* and *magouta* style songs, both packhorse rider's songs. • *Shinobue*: Always for *bon* (summer festival) dance songs and rice planting songs.
Percussion	• *Shime-daiko* (tightened drums) of a horizontally placed short body type: For older songs such as rice planting and gay quarter songs. • *Byōuchidaiko* (tack-fixed drums) of a horizontally placed short body type: Used mainly in the northern part of Japan. • *Ōdaiko* (large drums) of a longitudinally placed long body type: Essential to *bon* dance songs. • Waist drums or *kakko* of a keg body type: Held and struck by dancers.
Others	• Hand-held gongs such as *shōko*: Various types in various sizes. • Others: Kegs, wooden clappers, *dobyōshi* (hand cymbals), *kokiriko*, conch shell horn.

●*Hayashi-kotoba*

Hayashi-kotoba (meaningless words in a song for rhythm), integral parts for folk songs, are used in order to:

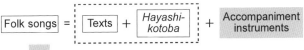

Folk songs = Texts + *Hayashi-kotoba* + Accompaniment instruments

- Coordinate timing of a group of workers,
- Herd cattle and horses, or steer a boat or a raft,
- Assist a song or cheer singers, and
- Fill the space rhythmically without texts.

●Some songs are titled after *hayashi-kotoba*. (The *hayashi-kotoba* represents the song.)

For example:
"Sōranbushi", "Yosarebushi", "Yosakoibushi", "Hōhaibushi", "Donpanbushi", "Aiyabushi", "Okosabushi", "Kanchororin".

●**Boatman's songs:** They have longer *hayashi-kotoba* in general.
- "Kaigarabushi" of Tottori Prefecture has shouts of seamen who came from foreign countries:
   "Yasahō-o-e-e-ya, ho-o-e-ya, ē-e-e, yoiyasano, sassā, yansano, ē-e, yoiyasano, sassā."
- "Mogamigawa-funauta" of Yamagata Prefecture, probably derived from boatmen's shouts around Sakata Port.
   "Yō-i, sanomagashō, en'yakoramā-gasē, e-en'yaa,ē-eyaa, ē-e, ē-eyaa, ē-do, yō-i, sanomagā-shō, en'yakoramā-gasē."
   The longer the hayashi-kotoba are, the shorter the texts.

●**Horse driver's songs:** *Kakegoe* by drivers/keepers of a horse or cattle are not long in general.
- The *kakegoe* against a horse or cattle are variations of "hai hai" or "hāi hai".

●**Folk songs of northern Japan:** Some songs in Aomori and Akita have very long *hayashi-kotoba*.
- In many cases, because the vowels of the texts are prolonged in the melismatic style, the transition between the texts and the *hayashi-kotoba* is not clear.
- E.g. "Tsugaru Yosarebushi", "Tsugaru Sansagari", "Akita Oiwake", "Akita Oharabushi".
- *Hayashi-kotoba* is made of a single vowel such as 'a, i, u, e, o, or n (n is regarded as a vowel), not words.

●***Bon* dance songs:** The meaningless words are close to *kakegoe*, rather than *hayashi-kotoba*.
   Yoiyoi, dōshitadōshita, dokkoisho

Diffusion of Folk Songs

Folk songs were handed down locally with time, of course, but many of them spread to other places, sometimes far from their homes.

The folk song titles of the northern Japan including southern part of Hokkaido (Esashi), Aomori (Tsugaru) and Akita (Nanbu) are listed on the right page. Note that "Ai-yabushi", "Yosarebushi", "Oharabushi", "Magouta (packhorse driver's song)", "Kobikiuta (sawyer's song)" and "sansagari (*shamisen*'s third string lowered)" are common titles with a prefix of a place name such as Esashi, Tsugaru and Nanbu and so on. The common title prefixed with a place name is not unique to these northern regions but is found everywhere in Japan. In the Edo period, traveling to other regions was restricted and the means of the transportation and communication were not well developed. Then, how did the folk songs spread to the whole country in those days?

The answer is "the carriers of the songs existed". The Tokugawa shogunate employed a system that demanded a feudal lord to reside in the Tokugawa castle at Edo for periods of time, alternating with residence at his own castle, while his wife and heir remain in Edo as hostages. It led to the improvement of communications between each domain and Edo and the development of a commercial economy along the route of the procession to Edo. The procession was a long trip staying at many posting towns. For example, the procession of the Tsugaru feudal clan had to go through ninety posting towns to arrive at Edo. When the procession took the seaway or crossed a river, it experienced confinement for a few days depending on the weather. As a result, the posting towns and harbors became bigger and the brothels and the gay quarters in them prospered. Here the local folk songs were brought in, changed, and refined, and then spread nationwide.

The peddlers, the itinerant entertainers, and the ordinary pilgrims in addition to the procession stayed at posting towns, where the packhorse drivers, the palanquin bearers, and the maids, who served clients and worked as prostitutes, also helped travelers. Those people were "the carriers of the songs" and played a part in changing and spreading the songs. This is how folk songs spread, changed in nature, and established new identities and characteristics through migration and passage of time.

■Diffusion of Folk Songs

- **Temporal transmission (vertical axis) vs. Geographic transmission (horizontal axis)**
  ↓
  Transformation in transmission
  ↓
  Diffusion
  In the new location, songs find a new identity.

> **Migration of songs:**
> Songs migrate adopting the manners, customs, and dialect in the new location and settle as the provincial songs.

- **Song carriers:**
  - Warriors and servants for *daimyo*'s alternating Edo residence
    Post towns, gay quarters
  - Boatmen, seamen, packhorse riders, horse dealers
    Ports, *kitamaesen* (cargo ships that sailed the Japan Sea), *taru-kaisen* (cargo ships)
  - Peddlers
    Candy, medicine, and oil
  - Traveling entertainers
    Goze, zatō, kadozuke, gan'ninbōzu
  - Seasonal laborers
    Toji (a sake brewer), fishermen, sawyers
  - Pilgrims
    Ise Shrine or Mt. Daisen

> The common folk songs have been adopted and modified in the new location. Each region name such as Esashi (Hokkaido), Tsugaru (Aomori), Nanbu (Akita+Iwate), Echigo (Niigata), and Sōma (Fukushima) were prefixed to the common title.

Nanbu Ushioiuta
Nanbu Ushikatabushi
Nanbu Umakatabushi
Nanbu Komabikiuta
Nanbu Dōchūumakatabushi
Nanbu Kobikiuta
Nanbu Aiyabushi
Nanbu Isobushi
Nanbu Komoriuta
Nanbu Sakayamotosuriuta
Nanbu Jinku
Nanbu Sumōjinku
Nanbu Taueuta
Nanbu Daikokumai
Nanbu Chayabushi
Nanbu Nagayabushi
Nanbu Nikatabushi
Nanbu Bonuta
Nanbu Mochitsukiuta
Nanbu Yosharebushi

Esashi Oiwake
Esashi Okesa
Esashi Sansagari
Esashi Jinku
Esashi Funakatabushi
Esashi Magouta
Esashi Mochitsukibayashi
Hamagoya Okesa
Matsumae Iwaiuta
Matsumae Oiwake
Matsumae Oharabushi
Matsumae Kenryōbushi
Matsumae Sansagari
Matsumae Nikatabushi
Tsugaru Aiyabushi
Tsugaru Oharabushi
Tsugaru Ondo
Tsugaru Kazoeuta
Tsugaru Gan'ninbushi
Tsugaru Kobikiuta
Tsugaru Sansagari
Tsugaru Jonkarabushi
Tsugaru Jinku
Tsugaru Tantobushi
Tsugaru no Komoriuta
Tsugaru Bayashi
Tsugaru Bon'uta
Tsugaru Yamauta
Tsugaru Yosarebushi

- **Transportation in the Edo period**
  - At post towns of land routes: Packhorse riders, palanquin bearers, maids (prostitutes) at an inn were the song carriers.
  - At ports of sea routes: Boatmen and seamen had to stay long waiting for good weather and transmitted songs to prostitutes at gay quarters.
  - Songs were transmitted:
    - Slowly on the land route village to village with oral tradition.
    - At a bound to another port on sea routes.

Land routes:
■ Five main highways:
- Tōkaidō (53 post towns)
- Nakasendō (69 post towns)
- Nikkō Kaidō (21 post towns)
- Ōshū Kaidō (90 post towns)
- Kōshū Kaidō (35 post towns)

■ Other highways:
Iseji, Hokkoku Kaidō, Chūgokuji, Mikuni Kaidō, Sadoji, Minoji, Mitoji, Nagasakiji

Sea routes:
■ Ten main ports (*tsu*) and harbors (*minato*):
- Ano-tsu (Tsu, Mie)
- Hakata-tsu (Hakata, Fukuoka)
- Sakai-tsu (Sakai, Osaka)
- Mikuni-minato (Sakai, Fukui)
- Motoyoshi-minato (Hakusan, Ishikawa)
- Wajima-minato (Wajima, Ishikawa)
- Iwase-minato (Toyama, Toyama)
- Imamachi-minato (Jōetsu, Niigata)
- Tsuchizaki-minato (Akita, Akita)
- Tosa-minato (Goshogawara, Aomori)

Haiyabushi: Main Body of Folk Songs

Many folk songs spread to various places away from their homes, among which the lineage of "Haiyabushi" spread the most widely and in the largest numbers. The current state of its lineage is illustrated on the page on the right.

The "Haiyabushi" variants are characterized by an opening word '*haiyaē*' (or han'yaē) from which the song title was derived. With the texts in the seven-seven-seven-and-five-syllable-meter, and the accompaniment of *shamisen* tuned in *niagari* (for example, D-A-D) as well as loud drums, this party song is played in a fast tempo with dances in general. After spreading to various places, the opening word and the song title changed from '*haiya*' to '*han'ya*' or '*aiya*' reflecting the dialect of the local area.

The word '*haiya*' originated from the word '*hae*' referring to a south wind, used by the fishermen in Amakusa, the southern islands. Though the song spread nationwide, the original song is thought to be "Ushibuka Haiyabushi" of Kumamoto, the southern part of Japan, based on the line "sailing with the south wind" in the text. This song is dotted about along the coast line of Sea of Japan. Starting at Ushibuka, it was probably brought north because the sailors of the cargo ships that sailed the Japan Sea during the Edo period passed it from harbor to harbor. The brothels and gay quarters at each harbor probably gave the sailors an ideal opportunity to spread the song while they spent time for loading and unloading and waiting for a favorable wind and tide.

The famous folk song "Sado Okesa" is thought to be a lineage of "Haiyabushi". Probably "Haiyabushi", brought into the Sado Island, was combined with the lyrics of the old, local folk song "Okesa". This theory is convincing because the song is a dance song with a similar opening word and the syllable-meter type as "Haiyabushi". On the hand, another famous folk song of the Sado Island, "Awa Odori", does not have the characteristics of "Haiyabushi". That is because the song, that had once been the authentic "Haiyabushi" in the late Edo period. It disappeared in the Meiji period and was restored during the Taisho period with the original dancing and *shamisen* accompaniment and a completely different song, "Yoshikonobushi" of Nagoya, from which *dodoitsu* songs were later derived.

Traditional Japanese Music at a Glance

■Haiyabushi: An Example of Diffusion via Sea Routes

- "Haiyabushi", or "Aiyabushi", found in various places are variants of "Ushibuka Haiyabushi" of Ushibuka Port in Amakusa, Kumamoto.

  - The song starts with the *hayashi-kotoba* (meaningless words), 'haiyāē' or 'aiyāē'.
  - The word 'haiya' was derived from 'hae (the south winds)' used by fishermen at Ushibuka.
  - The variants of "Haiyabushi" exist and spread more and broader than any other folk songs in Japan.
  - The locations, mainly along the coast of the Sea of Japan and skipping from one port to another, show the characteristics of the sea route migration.

Location	Titles
(1) Kumamoto:	Ushibuka Haiyabushi, Amakusa Haiyabushi
(2) Kagoshima:	Kagoshima Han'yabushi, Rokuchō, Akune Haiyabushi
(3) Nagasaki:	Tasuke Haiyabushi, Gotō Haiyabushi, Ikitsuki Haiyabushi, Kabashima Haiyabushi
(4) Saga:	Yobuko Haiyabushi
(5) Yamaguchi:	Han'nya Odori
(6) Hiroshima:	Mihara Yassabushi
(7) Shimane:	Hamadabushi
(8) Tokushima:	Awa Odori
(9) Kyoto:	Miyazu Aiyae Odori
(10) Nara:	Hase Okesa
(11) Fukui:	Miyama Haiyabushi
(12) Ishikawa:	Kaga Haiyabushi, Shiramine Haiyabushi
(13) Nagano:	Otari Okesa
(14) Niigata:	Sado Han'yabushi (Yamada no Han'ya), Sado Okesa (Aikawa Okesa, Senkōba Okesa), Ogi Okesa, Akadomari Okesa, Niigata Okesa, Teradomari Okesa, Izumozaki Okesa, Kashiwazaki Okesa, Sanjō Okesa, Yakata Okesa, Shiozawa Okesa, Jizōdō Okesa

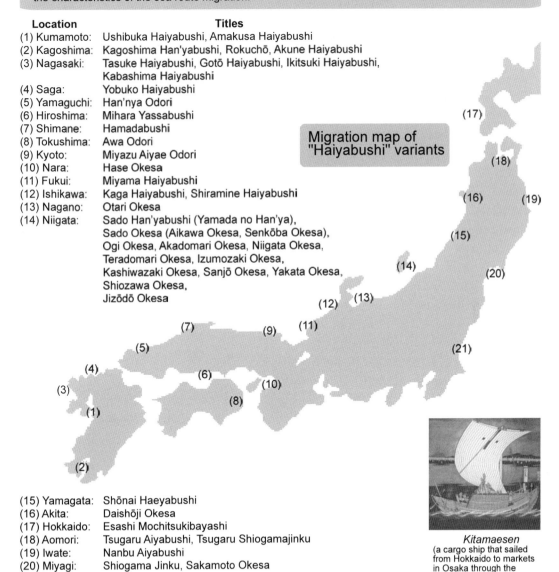

Migration map of "Haiyabushi" variants

(15) Yamagata:	Shōnai Haeyabushi
(16) Akita:	Daishōji Okesa
(17) Hokkaido:	Esashi Mochitsukibayashi
(18) Aomori:	Tsugaru Aiyabushi, Tsugaru Shiogamajinku
(19) Iwate:	Nanbu Aiyabushi
(20) Miyagi:	Shiogama Jinku, Sakamoto Okesa
(21) Ibaraki:	Itako Jinku

Kitamaesen
(a cargo ship that sailed from Hokkaido to markets in Osaka through the Japan Sea)

Esashi Oiwake: More Than a Folk Song

"Oiwakebushi" (or simply "Oiwake") spread through various parts of Japan where it transformed and took root in a similar manner to "Haiyabushi". Among its variants, the most famous is "Esashi Oiwake", the melody of which is so refined and artistically magnificent that we think it is wasteful to sing it at a drinking party. According to an established theory, "Oiwakebushi" originated from a packhorse driver's song called *magouta* at the Oiwake inn in Nagano Prefecture where main highways meet. Some advocate that a packhorse driver's song in Mie Prefecture was passed to Gifu Prefecture where it became "Kiso Umakatabushi", which became "Komurobushi" in Nagano Prefecture, and then became "Oiwakebushi" at the Oiwake inn. This theory has not been established. "Shinano Oiwake", the "Oiwakebushi" in Nagano Prefecture, was passed to distant Hokkaido by the carriers of the song who were, probably, *goze* or *zatō* roaming on a land route unlike "Haiyabushi" on the sea route. However, this song did not only take a one-way traffic to Esashi but was passed back to south on a Japan Sea route from Matsumae of Hokkaido to Akita Prefecture and became "Honjo Oiwake".

    The variants of "Oiwakebushi" are not always in the *magouta* style like "Esashi Oiwake". Generally, *magouta* in the free rhythm is sung to the accompaniment of *shakuhachi*, not *shamisen*. "Shinano Oiwake" and "Oki Oiwake" were originally parlor songs sung to the accompaniment of *shamisen*, while "Echigo Oiwake" and "Izumo Oiwake" are more like a packhorse driver's song in the "Esashi Oiwake" style. Even "Esashi Oiwake" was concurrently sung in the two styles, the *magouta* style with the *shakuhachi* accompaniment and the parlor song style with the *shamisen* accompaniment, until the early years of the Meiji period. In 1909 the home town of the song established "Seichō (standardized) Esashi Oiwake" as we hear it today. At present, there are more than two hundred 'so-and-so *bushi*' national contests specifically for a famous folk song and the "Esashi Oiwake Contest" is the earliest example of that kind. Since the contestants are evaluated for the established details of the fixed melody, "Seichō Esashi Oiwake" might have deviated from the definition of a folk song. In its generating process, "Esashi Oiwake" adapted "Matsuzaka Kuzushi", the celebration song sung by *goze*, and "Kenryōbushi" sung by the *zatō*, Matsuzaki Kenryō. The complexity of the generating and propagating process gave the song inexpressible subtlety and mystique.

Traditional Japanese Music at a Glance

■Oiwakebushi: An Example of Diffusion via Land Routes

- **"Oiwakebushi" (or "Oiwake")** found in various locations are variants of "Magouta" (a packhorse rider's song) of Shinano Oiwake, Nagano.

  - The packhorse riders and palanquin bearers at Oiwakeshuku and Komoro (or Komuro), Nagano, the post towns.
  - The traveling entertainers such as *goze*, *zatō*, and *kadozuke*.
  - Two styles were generated and spread simultaneously.
  - The routes were both the southward and northward.

  } Transmitted "Oiwake" to various places, even via sea routes.

Woodblock "Oiwakeshuku" by Keisai Eisen (1790-1848)

■Esashi Oiwake
□Natsumae Sansagari
□Tsugaru Sansagari
■Akita Oiwake
□Nanbu Sansagari
□Honjo Oiwake
■Sakata Oiwake
■Ogi Oiwake
■Echigo Oiwake
□Gokayama Oiwake
□Katashina Oiwake
□Shinano Oiwake
□Oki Oiwake
■Izumo Oiwake
□Hase Oiwake
□Asa no Dekake

■ = "Magouta" style
□ = "Sansagari" (*shamisen*) style

- **Two styles of "Oiwakebushi": "Magouta" and "Sansagari (with *shamisen*)"**

| *Magouta* style | Slow and flexible free rhythm |

- Originated from "Magouta" at Komoro (or Komuro) and Usui Pass, Nagano. Another song "Komurobushi"

- Settled as "Matsumaebushi" or "Echigo Oiwake" in Niigata

- Packhorse riders and seasonal workers carried "Tsumikiishibushi" and "Hamagoyabushi".

| *Sansagari* style | Fast and metered rhythm |

- Accompanied by *shamisen* tuned in *sansagari* (third string lowered)
  "Umakata Sansagari" or "Shinano Oiwake"

- Became "Tsugaru Sansagari" and "Nanbu Sansagari" in northern japan.

- Fishermen and sailors carried "Esashi Sansagari" and "Shinchibushi" with: Shakuhachi and Maeuta (prelude).

Standardized in 1909 in the *niagari* tuning as:

"Seichō (standardized) Esashi Oiwake"

In "Seichō Esashi Oiwake", not only the melody but also all grace notes are fixed which, some think, makes it no longer a folk song.

257

Children's Songs

The definition (or the category) of the folk songs differs whether or not to include traditional children's songs. Traditional children's songs are artless songs spontaneously generated, passed down by the oral tradition, and developed in a manner similar to that of folk songs.

Though they are traditional, the children's songs are a little different from adults' folk songs since children's fertile imagination and creativity routinely alter and improvise the lyrics, melodies and the way to play with the song. Since children's play, such as beanbag juggling, hopscotch, and traditional rope skipping are disappearing at present, the various play-songs listed on the right page also hang by a thread.

Often regarded similar to traditional children's songs, modern Japanese children's songs are the songs written for the children by adult composers and lyricists after the Taisho period (1912-26). They did not spontaneously generate and are fundamentally different from the traditional children's songs.

A lullaby is a song usually sung by a mother, to calm a child while putting it to sleep. Japanese traditional lullabies were often also sung by young children who were put into service, for example to baby-sit. As a result, some advocate that the traditional lullabies are a sort of children's songs. In those days peasants would often sell their children into service to reduce the number of mouths they had to feed. It should have been hard for the children who were still at a playful age but had to baby-sit for another family. Thus, it is possible to think that the lullaby is not the kind of the traditional children's song but a work song among the folk songs. A lullaby sung by a baby-sitter, carrying a baby on his/her back is not necessarily a soothing song. For example, popular "Takeda Lullaby", "Itsuki Lullaby" and "Shimabara Lullaby" were a sort of lament songs to moan about a hard job like baby-sitting or one's misfortune, and "Hakata Lullaby" is a cynical song to call the master of the family names. Once we know the true meaning hidden behind the rustic dialect words, we feel gloomy about the terrible circumstances of the baby-sitters in those days. Apart from the songs, it is a good thing that such baby-sitters do not exist anymore.

Traditional Japanese Music at a Glance

■Children's Songs and Lullabies

Children's songs are songs that young children invent, alter, and share among themselves.

Children's songs in folk songs are not songs for children created by adults.

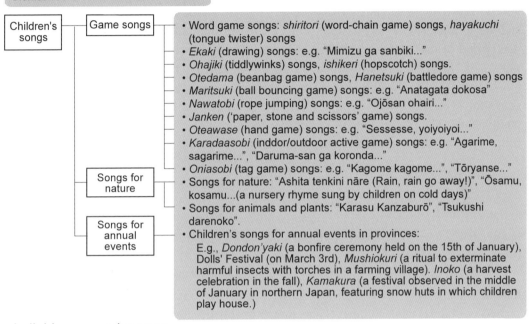

- Word game songs: *shiritori* (word-chain game) songs, *hayakuchi* (tongue twister) songs
- *Ekaki* (drawing) songs: e.g. "Mimizu ga sanbiki..."
- *Ohajiki* (tiddlywinks) songs, *ishikeri* (hopscotch) songs.
- *Otedama* (beanbag game) songs, *Hanetsuki* (battledore game) songs
- *Maritsuki* (ball bouncing game) songs: e.g. "Anatagata dokosa"
- *Nawatobi* (rope jumping) songs: e.g. "Ojōsan ohairi..."
- *Janken* ('paper, stone and scissors' game) songs.
- *Oteawase* (hand game) songs: e.g. "Sessesse, yoiyoiyoi..."
- *Karadaasobi* (inddor/outdoor active game) songs: e.g. "Agarime, sagarime...", "Daruma-san ga koronda..."
- *Oniasobi* (tag game) songs: e.g. "Kagome kagome...", "Tōryanse..."
- Songs for nature: "Ashita tenkini nāre (Rain, rain go away!)", "Ōsamu, kosamu...(a nursery rhyme sung by children on cold days)"
- Songs for animals and plants: "Karasu Kanzaburō", "Tsukushi darenoko".
- Children's songs for annual events in provinces:
  E.g., *Dondon'yaki* (a bonfire ceremony held on the 15th of January), Dolls' Festival (on March 3rd), *Mushiokuri* (a ritual to exterminate harmful insects with torches in a farming village). *Inoko* (a harvest celebration in the fall), *Kamakura* (a festival observed in the middle of January in northern Japan, featuring snow huts in which children play house.)

● Lullabies as work songs
- Lullabies sung by children who served as a nurse for master's baby are regarded as work songs rather than children's songs.
- Some *asobaseuta* (songs to amuse toddlers) are regarded as both work and children's songs.

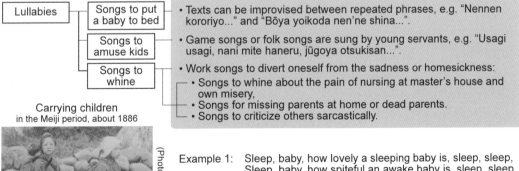

- Texts can be improvised between repeated phrases, e.g. "Nennen kororiyo..." and "Bōya yoikoda nen'ne shina...".
- Game songs or folk songs are sung by young servants, e.g. "Usagi usagi, nani mite haneru, jūgoya otsukisan...".
- Work songs to divert oneself from the sadness or homesickness:
  - Songs to whine about the pain of nursing at master's house and own misery,
  - Songs for missing parents at home or dead parents.
  - Songs to criticize others sarcastically.

Carrying children
in the Meiji period, about 1886

(Photo by Kimbei Kusakabe)

Example 1: Sleep, baby, how lovely a sleeping baby is, sleep, sleep,
Sleep, baby, how spiteful an awake baby is, sleep, sleep.
A spiteful baby shall be put on a chopping block,
And chopped like vegetables, sleep, sleep.

Example 2: My master gave me a broken umbrella spitefully,
As a result, his beloved baby girl is soaked to the skin.

Example 3: My mistress looks like a sweet fruit,
But she tastes bitter.

New Folk Songs

Folk songs are defined as long-lived songs created and sung by the public, and passed on by oral tradition, but there are nonstandard folk songs written by known lyricists and composers. Such songs include "Takedabushi" in Yamanashi, "Chakkiribushi" in Shizuoka, and "Tenryū Kudareba" in Nagano. They are called *shin min'yo* and created during a limited period of the Taisho and Showa periods. The lyricists and composers were sympathizers of "Shin Min'yo Movement" who reconsidered the excessive Westernization in music after the Meiji Restoration. They are basically commercial songs to attract tourists or songs for events in a specific region and are accompanied by instruments, even Western instruments. The public, however, consider the newly created folk songs to be traditional folk songs and we should not persist in the definition of folk songs in this case.

The songs were created not only in big cities with few folk songs but also local areas with plentiful folk songs. In the northern and southern parts of Japan, regarded as the goldmines of folk songs, not so many new folk songs were created. That is because these regions could not afford to commission the artists to write new songs, not because they did not need new ones. As a result, old folk songs were revived and arranged in a new style in these regions.

Nagano prefecture, the cradle of "Oiwakebushi", has nine new folk songs even though it has plenty of famous folk songs. All nine songs were composed by the star composer of those days, Shinpei Nakayama, probably because Nagano was his home town.

The Shin Min'yo Movement ended in the Showa period. After WWII, *kayōkyoku* or *enka*, Japanese pop songs in the half‑Japanese and half‑Western style, bloomed. Some of them targeted a specific province. In a way, the pop songs with a regional theme succeeded the new folk song movement.

■New Folk Songs

From the end of the Taisho period to the Showa period, there was a movement called "Shin Min'yō (New Folk Songs) Movement".

Members
Poets:
  Hakushū Kitahara
  Ujō Noguchi
  Yaso Saijō
Composers:
  Shinpei Nakayama
  Kashō Machida
  Kiyomi Fujii

↓ Westernization reconsidered
↓ New provincial songs in the folk songs style were composed.

Deviation from the general definition of folk songs.

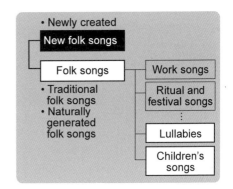

●New folk songs created by song writers

Title (Prefecture, Year)	Lyricist	Composer	Purpose
Takedabushi (Yamanashi, 1955)	Aishi Yoneyama	Kyōsei Akemoto	A hometown song for everyone.
Chakkiribushi (Shizuoka, 1927)	Hakushu Kitahara	Kashō Machida	A tourist attraction song for Shizuoka Railroad.
Tokyo Ondo (Tokyo, 1932)	Yaso Saijō	Shinpei Nakayama	A *bon* dance songs, originally called "Marunouchi Ondo".
Tenryū Kudareba (Nagano, 1934)	Mikihiko Nagata	Shinpei Nakayama	A tourist attraction song for Tenryu-kyo Valley.
Shirahama Ondo (Chiba, ...)	Ryūji Namioka	Ryūji Namioka	There was no folk song in Chiba until this new one.
Hamadabushi (Shimane, 1916)	...	Kichi Tani	Written to promote the the bank protection works in Hamada, Shimane.
Shinano Yoitoko (Nagano, 1934)	Kunio Kobayashi	Kashō Machida	The winning song of the contest sponsored by Shinano Mainichi Newspaper.
Chaguchagu Umakko (Iwate, 1957)	Kinjiro Ono	Naoyoshi Ozawa	A promotion song for Iwate National Sports Festival.
Higashimurayama Ondo (Tokyo, 1949)	Tadashi Tsuchiya	Jun'ichi Hosokawa	An anniversary song for the establishment of a municipal system.

●Fewer folk songs in big cities

- Big cities such as Tokyo, Nagoya, Kyoto, and Osaka have fewer folk songs than do the provinces.
- Party and drinking songs in the cities → *hauta*, *kouta*, parlor songs with *shamisen* derived from local folk songs.
- Northern Japan, the northern regions on Japan Sea side, the middle region of Shikoku, and Kyushu are rich repository of folk songs → Old folk songs have been revised in the new folk song style.
- Forgotten songs → Revived through the media such as records.

●Shinpei Nakayama, the composer

His new folk songs were mostly written for Nagano.
Tokyo: "Tokyo Ondo"
Fukushima: "Iizaka Kouta"
Gunma: "Jōshū Kouta"
Niigata: "Niigata Kouta" and "Tōkamachi Kouta"
Saitama: "Ōmiya-odori"
Nagano:
  "Suzaka Kouta", "Ryūkyō Kouta",
  "Osuwabushi", "Nakano Kouta", "Misasa Kouta", "Mochizuki Kouta", "Chikuma Kouta", "Asamabushi", "Nozawaonsen Kouta"
- There are many famous folk songs in Nagano where "Shinano Oiwake" was born.

●Demand for new folk songs

New folk songs were sought in the regions with few folk songs for tourist attraction and celebrations.

The New Folk Song Movement ended after WWII.

↓ However,

New *enka*, pop songs in the Western and Japanese mixed style, **titled after specific places:** → such as → Tourist spots, Amusement quarters, Big cities, and Hometown.

Instrumental Music Derived From Folk Songs

For folk songs, singing is the core. Until the middle of the Edo period, they were rarely accompanied even by handclaps. Some musical instruments which were subordinately used for the folk songs became independent and established new genres: *tsugaru shamisen* and Japanese drums.

Tsugaru shamisen developed as the door-to-door or street performance by the beggars or strolling musicians in the Tsugaru (present Aomori Prefecture) region, the northern part of Japan. Altered from thick neck *shamisen*, *tsugaru shamisen* uses a very heavy string for low notes, an improved bridge to make higher notes resound well, and a smaller plectrum for faster and acrobatic pounding movements to make its sounds loud and penetrating in the noisy marketplaces. Tsugaru folk songs with the accompaniment of *tsugaru shamisen* and additional drums are so rhythmical and unique that they outclass all the others.

The Tsugaru folk song has an introductory part performed by a *shamisen* player where he can display his unique improvisation and virtuosity before a singer starts. This showy, introductory part became so popular among the young people that it became independent as the instrumental music, '*tsugaru shamisen*'. Recorded or live performances by young "star" players are broadcast from TV stations, more often than by singers of Tsugaru folk songs.

Another modern genre is new drum music. The Japanese drums used for the folk entertainments have a longer history at various places than folk songs. Recently, drum music became independent of the folk entertainments, and the ensembles exclusively composed of Japanese drums, have emerged. Sometimes, surrounding a *miya-daiko* drum, a big drum with a long body which is more than three feet across in diameter, a group of players in costume beat drums and handle the drum sticks skillfully in choreographic or acrobatic motion or in perfect coordination. The performance with thunderous sounds has won popularity as the new and visually delightful shows in foreign countries as well. The number of new drum companies including female only ensembles or groups of cute children is rapidly increasing. Contests are also getting popular and there are many Japanese drum festivals all over the country.

Because most of the works played by those companies are newly created, they are not regarded as traditional Japanese music today. But the drum music represents the Japanese culture, without a doubt.

Traditional Japanese Music at a Glance

■Instrumental Music Derived from Folk Songs

●*Tsugaru shamisen*

Based on the door-to-door performance by *bosama* (blind male entertainers), *tsugaru shamisen* was began by Nitabō of Kanbara Village, Aomori (Tsugaru).

- Thinner *bachi* (plectrum)
- Louder and powerful sounds
- *Suri* (glissando) technique
- Rapid tempo
- Plucking → Beating

Chikuzan Takahashi

Disciples:
- Kinobō ── Shōei Kidarin (robust style)
- Chōsakubō ── Chikuzan Takahashi (elegant style)
- Gunpachirō Shirakawa (left hand's *kamashi* technique)

→ Beating technique

⇒ Many private schools & factions

• **Ever-changing *tsugaru shamisen***

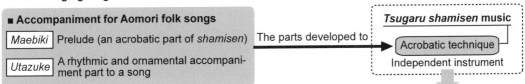

■ Accompaniment for Aomori folk songs	
Maebiki	Prelude (an acrobatic part of *shamisen*)
Utazuke	A rhythmic and ornamental accompaniment part to a song

The parts developed to → *Tsugaru shamisen* music
- Acrobatic technique
- Independent instrument

↓ *Tsugaru shamisen* music we hear today.

Big-3 *Tsugaru* works:
"Tsugaru Jonkarabushi", "Tsugaru Yosarebushi", "Tsugaru Oharabushi"
Big-5 *Tsugaru* works:
Bog-3 works + "Tsugaru Aiyabushi", "Tsugaru Sansagari"

●*Taiko* (drums)

■ Traditional drums

Used for:
- Rituals at temples/shrines
- War drums
- Festivals or *bon* dances
- Folk entertainment

Secondary role ⇒ Primary role

Modern drums

Kumidaiko (a drum ensemble) and newly composed drum works.
- Drum groups.
- Exciting and colorful sounds.
- Performance in sync.
- Choreographic and acrobatic motions.
- Delightful showmanship.

Well-known drum music	Description
Osuwa *daiko*	Originated from war drums of Kawanakajima Battle by Takeda Shingen (1521–1573). Today, it is used for grand *kagura* and *kobu* (drum dance) at Suwa Grand Shrine.
Gojinjo *daiko*	Originated from the legend that Uesugi Kenshin (1530-1578) attacked Wajima. Villagers in demon mask, beating war drums, drove away his army. A drum is struck by a pair of drummers.
Kokura Gion *daiko*	Hosokawa Tadaoki (1563-1646) who rebuilt Kokura Castle established Kokura Gion Festival adopting Gion Festival of Kyoto. A drum placed sideways is struck from both sides. Famous in the movie "Rickshaw Man".
Edo Sukeroku *daiko*	The *bon* dance drum music revived after the end of WWII, based on the drum music preserved at Yushima Tenjin, Tokyo. It is regarded as the first kumidaiko (a drum ensemble) which is extremely popular now.

●Popularity of Japanese drum music

- There are 600-800 drum groups in the Osuwa *daiko* style alone.
- The traditional style drum music in the local areas has been preserved and developed.
- Countless *kumidaigo* drum groups have been established.
- The drum festivals promote the drum music everywhere.
- New works have been composed, stimulating performers.

A live concert of modern *kumidaiko* (Fukushima Taiko Festival 2013)

Songs since the Age of Gods: Summary of Folk Songs

We do not know when the folk songs or folk entertainments began. We can trace them back to the mythology "Amano Iwato (or Amano Iwayato)" that depicts the earliest singing and dancing in Japanese history. In ancient times, there was *utagaki*, a gathering of men and women who sang courtship songs to each other and danced, though no melodies of such songs were left. We may assume that the songs were daily necessities of life in those days, based on many *waka* poems by the public found in the "Kojiki (Records of Ancient Matters)", the oldest extant chronicle in Japan dated from the early 8th century, and other regional chronicles. Soon, *kagura* songs of religious services and rituals as well as *saibara* of *gagaku* and *azuma-asobi* appeared. Those songs not only included songs of the noble and warrior classes but also a large number of songs sung by common people.

In the Heian period, the songs regarded as the original form of the later work songs, such as a rice crop song, already existed among the public and so did popular or secular songs called *imayō* or *fuzoku-uta*. The public entertainment such as *dengaku* and *sarugaku* were originated from those work songs and folk entertainments related to farm work.

When the *shamisen* was introduced and developed in the Edo period and the songs and dances evolved as the performing arts such as *jōruri* and *kabuki*, the quality improved and style of the songs varied. However, only big cities could enjoy them and the folk entertainment in the countryside developed based on the models from the cities. Derived from the work songs, the folk songs, as a part of public entertainment in the countryside, became party songs with the accompaniment of *shamisen* at the gay quarters in the local cities, the posting towns and the harbors. They spread all over the country along the major domestic trade routes and musically evolved influencing each other with other early modern popular songs.

Though the Westernization policy at the Meiji Restoration alienated many types of traditional Japanese music, folk songs survived the cultural and social changes and became indispensable to at drinking parties and gatherings. The prosperous record industry in the Taisyo period triggered a folk song boom and encouraged musicians to create new songs or discover songs in various local regions, which further accelerated the popularity of the folk songs. At the same time, pop songs, called *kayōkyoku*, appeared and fused with the folk songs. They held an established position in the pop culture.

Traditional Japanese Music at a Glance

■History of Folk Songs

Ancient Times	Legend of Amano Iwato. • Ancient songs already exist. • A clay dancing figurine (the origin of *bon* dance?) excavated (ca 3C).
Nara (710-794)	*Utagaki* appear in "Kojiki (The Record of Ancient Matters)". *Azumauta* appears. • Ancient songs appear in the books ("Kojiki", "The Chronicles of Japan", and "Collection of Ten Thousand Leaves", and "Fudoki") (ca 8C).
Heian (794-1185)	*Kagura* songs, *saibara* & *fuzoku-uta* appear (early Heian). *Gagaku* established (894). • Work songs such as boat songs and rice crop songs appear in tales and chronicles ("Tale of Genji", "The Pillow Book", and "Tosa Diary") (10C). • *Imayō* & *dengaku* appear (11C). • *Imayō* songs become popular among the nobles, warriors and the commoners (11-13C). • "Ryōjin Hishō (Collection of *Imayō* Songs)" compiled (1179).
Kamakura (1185-1333)	• "Shin Kokin Wakashū (New Collection of Poems Ancient and Modern)" compiled (1205). • *Imayō*, public entertainment, and *dengaku* contain work songs related to rice farming.
Nanbokucho (1336-1392)	• *Sarugaku-noh* & *dengaku-noh* become popular (14C). • Medieval *kouta* becomes popular among the nobles (ca 14-15C).
Muromachi (1336-1573)	• "Kanginshū (Collection of Japanese Songs and Ballads)" compiled (1518). *Shamisen* introduced (ca.1558-69). • *Kouta* in the folk song style appear. • "Tauezōshi (Collection of Rice Farming Songs)" archives work songs in the old language and tunes.
Momoyama (1573-1603)	• *Shamisen* accompanies *jōruri* (ca 1580). *Ningyō-jōruri* begins (1595). • *Nenbutsu* and *furyū* dances become popular.
Edo (1603-1868)	• Jiuta *shamisen-kumiuta* established (ca. 1600). • Okuni begins *kabuki* dance (1603). • *Shamisen* becomes a standard accompaniment for songs including *kabuki* (17C). • Ryūtatsu-bushi, the origin of modern *kouta*, are popular (16-17C). • *Kitamaesen* (cargo ships that sailed the Japan Sea) begin (mid-Edo period). • *Shamisen*'s popular songs such as *ryūtatsu*, *rōsai*, *katabachi*, and *nage-bushi* in the gay quarters become home music for towners. • Provincial songs such as dance, folk and children's songs in the local areas appear. • *Nagauta* established (1730's). • *Tokiwazu* begins (1747). • *Hauta* blooms (1800's). • *Shamisen* becomes a standard accompaniment for folk songs. (Folk songs diffuse and become banquet songs.) **Meiji Restoration** (1868).
Meiji (1868-1912)	• *Tōdō* system and Fuke Sect abolished (1871). • *Shakuhachi* opens to public. • Ongaku Torishirabegakari (Institue of Music) established in Ministry of Education (1879). • *Kouta* becomes popular (1900's). *Utazawa* begins (1895). • "Seichō Esashi Oiwake" established (1909).
Taisho (1912-1926)	• A "Yagibushi" record released for the first time (1915). • Folk songs in the local areas are revived. • Folk songs bloom as popular songs. • New folk songs such as "Chakkiribushi" appear (1927).
Showa-Heisei (1926-)	• Records of major folk songs released (1937). They spread everywhere but lost their locality. • NHK (Japan Broadcasting Corporation) begins a radio show "Amateur Singing Contest". • *Kouta* blooms (1950's). • The 2nd folk song boom and folk song training schools, bars, contests, and singers appear. • *Tsugaru shamisen* becomes popular in Tokyo (1960's).

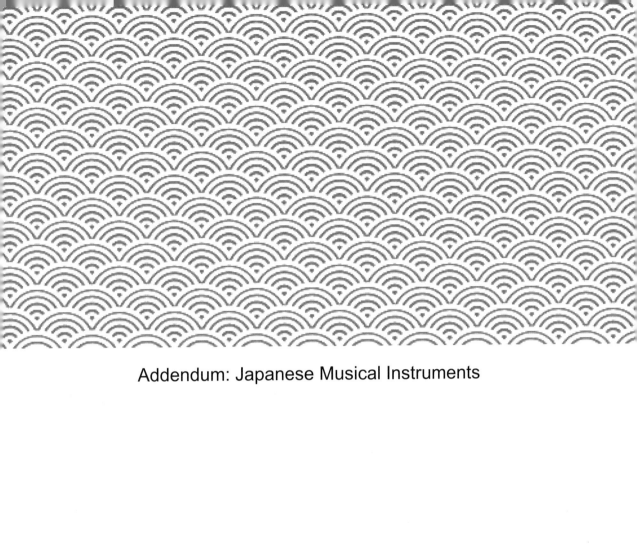

Addendum: Japanese Musical Instruments

Classifications of Japanese Musical Instruments

According to the descriptions in "Kojiki (Records of Ancient Matters)" (Japan's oldest historical record) and "Nihonshoki (Chronicles of Japan)" (Japan's oldest chronicles), it is clear that the musical instruments such as *koto*, flutes, and drums, existed from ancient times in Japan. However, the origins of most of the traditional Japanese musical instruments as we see today were introduced from the continent and adapted to the Japanese climate.

Those instruments, including *shamisen* representative of Japanese musical culture, were transformed not only for adjusting them to the musical tastes of people at the time, but also for adapting them to the highly humid Japanese climate or substituting the materials difficult to obtain with commonly found ones in Japan. When a player of a Japanese traditional instrument performs abroad, more often than before, he must be extremely careful of his instrument's maintenance. For example, the skin of *shamisen*, the wooden body of *biwa*, or the bamboo tube of *shakuhachi*, could break or crack if the climate, especially the humidity, of the country is different from that of Japan.

In the Edo period, the general term for musical instruments was '*narimono*' which was grouped into *hikimono* (strings), *fukimono* (wind), and *uchimono* (percussion). Strictly speaking, *hikimono* includes plucked and bowed types, and *uchimono* includes struck, shaken, and rubbed types. At present, the musical instrument classification in the ethnomusicology is based on the source objects of the vibration of the sound: chordophones, aerophones, diophones, membranophones and electrophones. The elegant names such as *hikimono* and *fukimono* seem more suitable for Japanese music than the Western classification.

The matrix on the right page shows musical instruments and the musical genres for which they are used. We can see that traditional Japanese musical instruments, except for *biwa*, are used for any genres without restriction, overall.

Recently, the borders among global music and musical genres are disappearing and *hichiriki*, *biwa* or *shakuhachi*, for example, are increasingly used in Western style music. In the future, the classification of the traditional Japanese and Western musical instruments may disappear.

Traditional Japanese Music at a Glance

■Musical Instruments and Genres

The Japanese musical instruments are categorized into three groups:
1. *Hikimono* (strings),
2. *Fukimono* (pipes), and
3. *Uchimono* (percussion).

● = the genre in which the instrument is used.

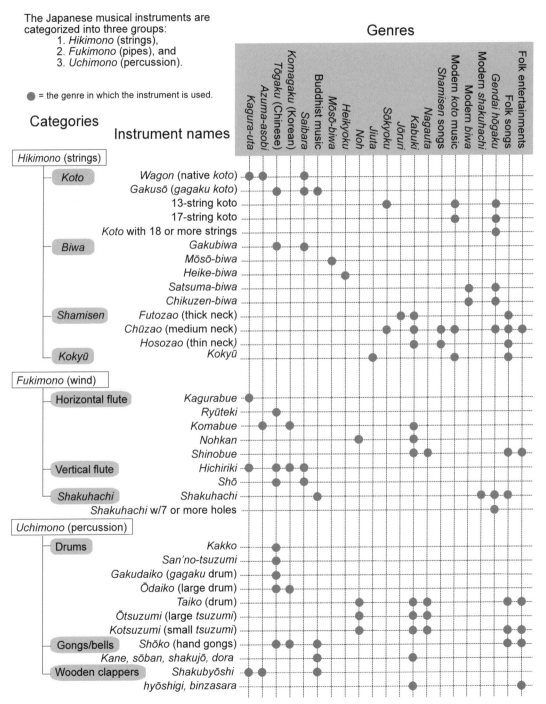

Types of *Shamisen*

Shamisen are basically classified into three types: *futozao* (thick neck), chūzao (medium neck), and *hosozao* (thin neck). However, since the structure, shape and length of these three types are almost identical, they are hardly distinguishable. The major difference among the three is the thickness of the neck and the minor difference is the size of the drum, called '*dō*'.

The *shamisen* type and the music type for which it is used are fixed: the thick neck for *gidayū*, the medium neck for *jiuta*, and the thin neck for *nagauta*. However, *shamisen* players of *jiuta* or Yamada School *sōkyoku* chose the thickness of their instruments as they like.

The more *shamisen* music developed and expanded its boundary, the more diversified timbre, register and loudness were sought. In order to meet the demands, the types of *shamisen* today increased from the basic three to more than a dozen. For example, the thick neck *shamisen* is subdivided to *gidayū shamisen* and *tsugaru shamisen*, which produce very different sounds as if they are different varieties.

Shamisen can be tuned in several ways. The tuning is called '*chōshi*' and there are six types of it. But the main types are three: *honchōshi* (basic tuning such as D-G-D), *ni-agari* (the second string raised such as D-A-D) and *sansagari* (third string lowered such as D-G-C).

The tuning is set according to the song title. But sometimes it is changed in the middle of the song. It is common to see a *shamisen* player adjust a peg in the middle of a performance. He could adjust the loosened string or could change the tuning. A skillful player can do it using only his left hand without interrupting a performance. The tuning is not based on the absolute pitches but relative pitches between strings. That is because singing is the core of *shamisen* music and the instrument is tuned according to the register of the singer's voice.

Similar to *biwa*, *shamisen* structurally produces unique buzz sounds or noise, containing high overtones, on the lowest string. The structure or the buzz sounds are called '*sawari*'. *Shamisen* has no fret like the guitar and is plucked with a big plectrum.

Types of *Koto*: Ever Changing Music for Unchanged Instruments

There are many types of the *koto* (*sō*) family with bridges (written with a kanji character '箏'). *Wagon*, a native *koto* used in a *gagaku* ensemble and different from *gakusō* (*gagaku koto*), has a kanji character '琴' which refers to bridgeless *koto* (*kin* or *gon*), but it has bridges and belongs to the *koto* (*sō*) family with bridges. The music of the *koto* (*sō*) family is called *sōkyoku*. Since *wagon* and *gakusō* are *gagaku* instruments, most people do not have an opportunity to see them in a live performance. Besides, *wagon* is exclusively used for *kuniburi no utamai*, the songs and dances based on the old Japanese music, and *gakusō* is exclusively used for *gagaku kangen*, the instrumental ensembles, thus the general public rarely see them. Thirteen-string *koto* is the most familiar among modern *koto*.

Koto is generally classified into three groups: *gakusō* for *gagaku*, *tsukushi-goto* for Tsukushi School music, and *zokusō* (secular *koto*) of early modern *sōkyoku* after Yatsuhashi Kengyō. In the modern times, *sōkyoku* developed so significantly that a wider register of the instruments was sought. Structurally *koto* has one note per string. In order to meet the demand for a wider register or a different register, strings were added or the body was lengthened. In addition to standard 13-string *koto*, there are more-than-thirteen-string varieties. These include 15-string *koto* (developed by Kin'ichi Nakanoshima), 17-string *koto* often called 'bass *koto*' (invented by Michio Miyagi), 21-string *koto* (developed by Shōin Yamase), 25-string *koto* (developed by Keiko Nosaka), and impractical 80-string *koto* (developed by Michio Miyagi).

However, even though many varieties have been created in the hundreds of year history since its introduction from the continent, the basic structure of *koto* has not changed so much. Though some details, for example, the shape of bridges and plectra, the way to tie strings, and finishing touches of the body, changed, the basic structure of *koto* is unchanged, whether it is *koto* for *gagaku* or *koto* for the contemporary music.

On the one hand, *koto* music changed significantly. In ancient *gagaku*, *koto* took charge of rhythm as a rhythmical instrument, not as a melodic instrument. On the other hand, in the modern times, various new techniques were adapted from the techniques of the Western instruments: for example, the melody lines, vibratos, portamentos, chords plucked by both hands, glissandos, tremolos, and so on.

The reason why various playing methods are possible is because *koto*'s basic structure is simple. That is why *koto* is flexible and capable to respond to new ideas, including new varieties of tuning. Anything is possible for *koto*, whether it is for solo or ensembles, instrumental or vocal music, or classical or modern works.

Types of *Biwa*

There are six varieties of *biwa* used for the *biwa* music at present including *gakubiwa* and *nishiki-biwa*.

Gakubiwa, the largest among *biwa*, is a *gagaku* instrument. The player sits cross-legged, holds the instrument on his lap almost horizontally, and plucks strings with a plectrum in a pushing motion.

Heike-biwa used for *heikyoku* is very similar to *gakubiwa* in shape, structure and holding style. That is probably because Fujihara Yukinaga who established *heikyoku* was a *gagaku* musician. The only difference between the two is *heike-biwa* is smaller than *gakubiwa*. That is probably because the *biwa* minstrels who traveled to perform *heikyoku* preferred the smaller and lighter instrument for easy carrying.

Mōsō-biwa is smaller than *heike-biwa*, about viola size. It is said that the blind monk made his own instrument and probably wanted it small for calls at the homes of the parishioners. His reciting of sutra and playing *biwa* are very rhythmical and fast in tempo.

Satsuma-biwa is characterized by a dynamic performance suitable for heroic tales. Because the player, holding a large *biwa* almost vertically, plays with a striking motion against the ventral board with a big, fan-shaped plectrum, the body of the instrument is made of very solid and robust material such as mulberry or birch wood. The player shows off his virtuosity with skillful handling of the plectrum.

All *gakubiwa*, *heike-biwa*, *mōsō-biwa*, and *satsuma-biwa* are four-stringed and *chikuzen-biwa* and *nishiki-biwa* discussed below are five-stringed. Some *chikuzen-biwa* are four-stringed but most instruments manufactured today are five-stringed. The ventral board of *chikuzen-biwa* is made of paulownia wood to produce soft and elegant sounds.

Nishiki-biwa was derived from *satsuma-biwa* and *tsuruta-biwa* of Tsuru School was derived from *nishiki-biwa*. *Ji* (frets) was improved to play melodious music and the "scratching strings" technique was invented. The music of *chikuzen-biwa* and *nishiki-biwa* is more instrumental than the others and sounds like almost different kinds compared with *heikyoku*. Tsuru School performers, especially, often play together with Western style ensembles and are active as instrumentalists.

The *biwa* music seems to still be in transition influenced by other types of music, for example, the melodious performing style of increasingly popular Chinese *pipa*.

Varieties of *Shakuhachi*

Modern *shakuhachi* is the descendant of *fuke shakuhachi* and no two instruments are the same. A professional *shakuhachi* player usually personalizes his instrument. Therefore, there is no standard and, as a result, various types and sizes exist.

The biggest difference between *fuke shakuhachi* and modern *shakuhachi* is the way to finish the inside of the bamboo stalk. For *fuke shakuhachi*, all seven nodes of a bamboo stalk are roughly removed without being finished, which is called "non-fabricated pipe", while for modern *shakuhachi*, all seven nodes of a bamboo stalk are removed and then the inside of the pipe is smoothed with white pigment and finished with lacquer. Therefore, *fuke shakuhachi* produces natural but sometimes softer sounds with more noise (some speculate that its sounds can reach farther than that of modern *shakuhachi*). That is why *fuke shakuhachi* is harder to play than modern versions. At present, the conservative Myōan schools still use non-fabricated pipes.

The best material of *shakuhachi* is the root end of four or five year old *madake* (Japanese timber bamboo). But because it is difficult and costly to manufacture *shakuhachi* with homogeneous quality by processing and finishing the natural bamboo roots, maple wood is used recently for beginners' *shakuhachi*. Cheap plastic versions are also made for school children.

Since *shakuhachi* have no reed, it is hard to produce sounds. In addition, the shape and angles of the blowing hole differ for the Kinko School and Tozan School. For school children who cannot produce sounds with *shakuhachi*, an adaptor to the blow holes was invented to make it easier.

The name *shakuhachi* is derived from the length of one foot (*shaku*) and eight (*hachi*) tenths foot but there are various sized instruments. They cover the range from alto to bass and are used in *shakuhachi* ensembles of modern works. *Shakuhachi* with extra finger holes to enable playing halftones are used for modern folk songs.

In order to solve the difficulty of fingering and blowing of *shakuhachi*, a new pipe with keys like the Boehm flute and a *shakuhachi*-style mouthpiece was invented by Baron Kishichirō Ōkura (1882-1963). It was named Ōkuraulo after his name and a Greek fife 'aulos'. But because it was too remote from *shakuhachi*, it became obsolete.

Varieties of Pipes

Pipes existed in Japan from the distant past. They were mostly transverse flutes. It is said that the pipes in China were generally end-blown flutes in the old times and the transverse flutes were contrived after the Han Dynasty.

Japanese transverse flutes are *kagurabue* (*kagura* flute), *ryūteki* (dragon flute) and *komabue* (Korean flute) used for *gagaku*, *nohkan* used for *noh*, and *shinobue* widely used for traditional rites and folk entertainments.

In *gagaku*, which one of the three types mentioned above is used is determined by the title of the work. The three resemble each other in form in spite of some differences such as length. *Ryūteki* has six finger holes and the rest seven finger holes.

Though similar to *ryūteki* in form and size, *nohkan* is uniquely structured: a short pipe called a '*nodo* (throat)' is embedded inside the pipe between the blowing hole and the finger hole. This unique device has the effect of increasing the peculiar sounds of the blown air, like screaming shrill voice, called '*hishigi*'.

Shinobue is made of unprocessed bamboo. The decorative finish is also simple. Structurally, it is the same as other transverse flutes. However, thirteen pipes differing in length based on the twelve tones are prepared in order to accommodate the register of the singer and *shamisen*. Pipe pitch becomes higher by halftone increments and the shortest one is an octave higher than the longest.

There are two end-blown pipes: *hichiriki* and *shō*. *Hichiriki* is used for most of the works of *gagaku* and plays the main melody. It is small in size but produces loud sounds with unique portamentos. Uniquely shaped *shō* is a necessary instrument in *gagaku*. This free reed musical instrument with seventeen bamboo pipes can produce chords. The sound production principle is the same as a reed organ and accordion. The combination of *hichiriki* and *shō* is familiar with us as the solemn music for the wedding ceremony at a Shinto shrine.

Varieties of Percussion

The Japanese traditional percussion instruments are called '*uchimono*', meaning "struck instruments". Recently some ethnomusicologists advocate that the rubbed instruments such as *suri-shō* (rubbed small gong) and the shaken instruments such as hand-held bells should be classified into a different group or sub-grouped within *uchimono*. Moreover, we had better think that the temple bells and the fish-shaped wooden temple drums are Buddhist altar equipment rather than musical instruments though they are used as common percussion.

In this section, we will focus on two kinds of struck instruments: *taiko* (drums) and *tsuzumi* (hand drums). In Japan, *taiko* and *tsuzumi* are customarily distinguished. *Taiko* is struck with drumsticks and *tsuzumi*, which has a very slim body, is tapped with the tips of the fingers. Actually, the difference of the two is not clear.

Most Japanese *taiko* drums are skinned on both ends which are generally the same in size and shape. The *taiko* drums are divided into two types based on the body shape and the way of fitting the skin: *shime-daiko* (rope-tensioned drums) and *byōdome-daiko* (tack-fixed drums). *Shime-daiko* is further divided into two: framed *shime-daiko* and frameless *shime-daiko*. For framed *shime-daiko* the skin is fixed to the iron frame before it is fitted.

The *taiko* drums are only related to the music genres such as *gagaku*, *noh* or *kabuki*. Since the *taiko* drums are the core of festivals and Buddhist ceremonies, the folk entertainments, and *geza*, there are tens of kinds of drums. The *gagaku* drums are basically simple except for the colorful decorations on the skin, body and stands.

The *tsuzumi* drums used for *noh* are assembled with the body, two framed skin pieces, and laces for each performance. The skin for *ōtsuzumi* (large *tsuzumi*, hip drum) is toasted and dried for an hour and a half with a charcoal fire to tighten the tension before being assembled. On the contrary, *kotsuzumi* (small *tsuzumi*, shoulder drum) is loosely tightened. A *kotsuzumi* player places a small piece of wet rice paper over the drum skin or puffs on it in order to moderately humidify it. In general, if the musical instruments have the same structure, the larger they are in size, the lower sounds they produce. But because of the way of fitting the skin, the larger *tsuzumi* produces higher pitches than the smaller one.

Though a kanji character '*ko* (drum)' is used for the percussion instrument '*shōko*', actually it is not a drum but a small gong.

Index

13-string *koto*
　十三弦箏, 269, 271
17-string *koto*
　十七弦箏, 269, 271
21-string *koto*
　二十一弦箏, 271
25-string *koto*
　二十五弦箏, 271
5 keys
　五調子, 62, 63
5-character quatrain
　五言絶句, 125
7 notes
　七声, 63
80-string *koto*
　八十弦箏, 166, 271
ado
　アド, 101, 102
agemaku
　揚幕, 89
ai-kyōgen
　間狂言, 72, 86, 100, 101
Aiyabushi
　あいや節, 252
Akashi Kakuichi
　明石覚一, 114
Amano Iwato
　天岩戸, 22, 23, 72, 264
aragoto
　荒事, 202, 217
ashirai-buki
　アシライ吹き, 99
ashirai-byōshi
　アシライ拍子, 99

ashirai-uchi
　アシライ打チ, 98, 99
Awa Ningyō-jōruri
　阿波人形浄瑠璃, 207
Awaji Ningyō-jōruri
　淡路人形浄瑠璃, 206, 207
awase-uchi
　合セ打チ, 98, 99
azuma-asobi
　東遊, 32, 33, 40, 264
bakumatsu shinsōkyoku
　幕末新箏曲, 154, 155, 157
ban'e-shōzoku
　蛮絵装束, 40, 41
banbayashi
　番囃子, 85
banshikichō
　盤渉調, 62, 63
betsu-shōzoku
　別装束, 40, 41
bettō
　別当, 170
big-3 *Tsugaru* works
　津軽三ツ物, 263
binan-kazura
　美男鬘, 104
binzasara
　びんざさら, 269
biwa songs
　琵琶歌, 118, 122, 123
biwa-hōshi
　琵琶法師, 68, 112
bokkaigaku
　渤海楽, 26

276

bonbai
　梵唄, 54
bongosan
　梵語讃, 56
Buddhist chants
　仏教歌謡, 56
Buddhist music
　仏教音楽, 69
bugaku
　舞楽, 18, 29, 30, 34
bun'ya-bushi
　文弥節, 194
bungo-bushi
　豊後節, 194, 204
Bungo's Big 3
　豊後三流, 204
bunraku
　文楽, 162, 190, 191, 192, 206
Bureau of Song
　大歌所, 46
byōdome-daiko
　鋲留太鼓, 275
carriers of songs, 253, 256
carriers of the songs, 252
chi
　徴, 63
Chikamatsu Monzaemon
　近松門左衛門, 196, 198
Chikuho School
　竹保流, 136
chikuzen mōsō-biwa
　筑前盲僧琵琶, 112
chikuzen-biwa
　筑前琵琶, 112, 118, 269, 272
chirashi
　チラシ, 223
chobo
　ちょぼ, 206
Chōsan
　張参, 134, 135
chūkyoku
　中曲, 42, 43, 62
chūnori
　中ノリ, 96, 97
chūzao
　中棹, 269, 270
concert *nagauta*
　演奏会長唄, 229, 238
continental *bugaku*
　大陸系舞楽, 29
continental dance and music
　大陸系舞楽, 19
Coronation Banquet
　大嘗祭, 33
daishōmono
　大小物, 99
danmono
　段物, 152, 156, 157, 177
debayashi
　出囃子, 218, 226, 229
degatari
　出語り, 218
deha
　出端, 202, 223
dengaku
　田楽, 74
dengaku-noh
　田楽能, 74, 76
Dōami
　道阿弥, 76
dodoitsu
　都都逸, 237, 254
dongxiao
　洞簫, 128
dora
　銅鑼, 269
dot system
　胡麻譜, 13
drinking songs
　酒盛歌, 244, 245
early modern *sōkyoku*
　近世箏曲, 153, 155, 156, 157, 160,

Index

182, 271
Ecchū Owarabushi
越中おわら節, 184
edo nagauta
江戸長唄, 176, 216, 217, 220
Edo short songs, 172
Edodayū Katō
江戸太夫河東, 204
eikan-bushi
永閑節, 194
einori
詠ノリ, 97
en'nen
延年, 68
En'nin
円仁, 54, 66, 144
enka
演歌, 260
entertainment song
芸事歌, 246
erhu
二胡, 184
Esashi Oiwake
江差追分, 140, 256
Etenraku
越殿楽, 36, 37, 44, 152
Etenraku songs
越殿楽謡物, 152, 153, 164
five compulsory subjects
五学問, 54
five-stringed *biwa*, crafted with mother-of-pearl
螺細紫檀五絃琵琶, 110
fue
笛, 94, 95, 99
Fujiike School
藤池流, 160
fujimatsu-bushi
富士松節, 204
Fuke sect
普化宗, 130, 131, 132, 133, 134, 135,

136, 137, 140, 144, 162
fuke shakuhachi
普化尺八, 130, 131, 139, 144, 273
fukimono
吹物, 39, 268, 269, 274
furi
振, 216, 224, 230, 231
fushi
節, 94, 95
fushidan-sekkyō
節談説教, 68, 69
Fūshi-kaden
風姿花伝, 78
futozao
太棹, 196, 269, 270
fuzoku-uta
風俗歌, 264
gagaku
雅楽, 10, 18, 19, 20, 21, 26, 28, 30, 32, 34, 38
Gagaku Bureau
宮内省雅楽局, 44
雅楽寮, 47
gagaku kayō
雅楽歌謡, 28, 30, 36
gagaku score
雅楽の総譜, 44
Gagakuryō
雅楽寮, 26, 46, 47
gaikyoku
外曲, 136, 140, 141
gakubiwa
楽琵琶, 38, 110, 111, 120, 269, 272
gaku-byōshi
楽拍子, 43
gakudaiko
楽太鼓, 38, 269
gakuke
楽家, 46
gakuso
楽所, 46

278

gakusō
楽箏, 38, 44, 45, 269, 271
gayageum
伽耶琴, 149
geki-bushi
外記節, 194, 224
gendai hōgaku
現代邦楽, xii, 138, 155, 162
genzai-noh
現在能, 76, 78
geza
下座, 184, 194, 216, 218, 219, 226, 227, 275
gidayū-bushi
義太夫節, 6, 172, 177, 190, 191, 194, 196, 200, 202, 204, 206, 218, 222, 224, 225
gidayū-kyōgen
義太夫狂言, 206, 213, 214, 224
gigaku
伎楽, 24, 26, 46, 48, 74
gin'ei
吟詠, 122, 123, 138
gobandate
五番立て, 78, 82, 83
goeika
御詠歌, 58
goin-hakase
五音博士, 62, 63
gon
琴, 148, 149
gottan
ゴッタン, 174
gozeza
瞽女座, 170
Gregorian chant, 12, 62
gyosan shōmyō
魚山声明, 54
gyoyū
御遊, 26, 36, 46
hade

破手, 176, 178
hadegumi
破手組, 182, 183
Haiyabushi
ハイヤ節, 254, 255
hakama-noh
袴能, 84, 85
hakase
博士, 12, 13, 62, 63
handayū-bushi
半太夫節, 194
han-noh
半能, 84, 85
hashigakari
橋掛かり, 88, 89
Hatano Kawakatsu
秦河勝, 46, 72
hauta
端唄, 172, 234, 236, 237, 244
hauta in Kyoto-Osaka
端歌, 176
hautamono
端歌物, 179
hayashi
囃子, 94, 95, 98
hayashikata
囃子方, 86, 223
hayashi-kotoba
囃子詞, 251
Heian Gagaku-kai
平安雅楽会, 48
Heike Monogatari
平家物語, 114, 116
heike-biwa
平家琵琶, 112, 120, 269, 272
Heike-mabushi
平家正節, 116, 117
heikyoku
平曲, 68, 114, 116, 117, 120, 164, 170, 192

hengemono
　変化物, 214, 220, 221, 222
hichiriki
　篳篥, 38, 44, 268, 269, 274
hiji
　秘事, 116, 117
hikimono
　弾物, 39, 268, 269
hiramono
　平物, 116, 117
hiranori
　平ノリ, 96, 97
Hiraoka, Hiroshi
　平岡煕, 238
hishigi
　ヒシギ, 98, 274
Historical Views of Kinko School Shakuhachi
　琴古流尺八史観, 134
hitamen
　直面, 86, 90, 91
hitoyogiri
　一節切, 130, 131
hizen-bushi
　肥前節, 194
hōe
　法会, 60, 61, 68
hōe gagaku
　法会雅楽, 68, 69
hole number system
　孔名譜, 13
honbutai
　本舞台, 89
honchōshi
　本調子, 222, 248, 249, 270
honde
　本手, 176
hon-kyōgen
　本狂言, 72, 73, 82, 101
honkyoku
　本曲, 136, 140, 141, 184

hon-shōmyō
　本声明, 58
hōshi-uta
　法師歌, 177
hosozao
　細棹, 269, 270
hōyō
　法要, 60, 61
hu-yue
　胡楽, 21
hyōbyaku
　表白, 58
hyōjō
　平調, 34, 62, 63
hyōshi
　拍子, 10, 42
hyōshi-ai
　拍子合, 96, 97
hyōshi-awazu
　拍子不合, 96, 97
hyōshigi
　拍子木, 269
hyūga mōsō-biwa
　日向盲僧琵琶, 112
icchū-bushi
　一中節, 154, 156, 194, 204, 224
Ichigatsu-ji Temple
　一月寺, 132, 133, 134
Ichigen-kin
　一絃琴, 166
Ichikata School
　一方流, 114
ichikotsu
　壱越調, 34, 62, 63
iemoto
　家元, 14, 15, 86, 194
Ikuta Kengyō
　生田検校, 154, 155, 156, 160, 164, 186
Ikuta School
　生田流, 154, 155, 158

Ikuta-ryū *sōkyoku*
　生田流箏曲, 160
imayō
　今様, 58, 68, 81, 152, 264
independent *nagauta*
　鑑賞用長唄, 221, 228
Ishikawa Kōtō
　石川勾当, 179
Ishimura Kengyō
　石村検校, 174, 176, 178, 179, 182
Izumo no Okuni
　出雲の阿国, 176, 213, 216
izumo-goto
　出雲琴, 166
Japanese dance
　日本舞踊, 230
ji
　地, 200, 201
　柱, 148
jidaimono
　時代物, 198, 200, 202, 213, 214
jinbun
　神分, 58
jiuta
　地歌, 150, 151, 154, 158, 170, 172, 176, 178, 180, 182
jiuta dance
　地歌舞, 230
jiutai
　地謡, 86, 94, 97
jiuta-sōkyoku
　地歌箏曲, 150, 180
jobyōshi
　序拍子, 43
jo-ha-kyū
　序破急, 42, 43
jōmen
　尉面, 91
jōruri
　浄瑠璃, 114, 170, 172, 176, 178, 190, 191, 193
jueju
　絶句, 124, 125
jun-taikyoku
　准大曲, 42, 43
jushisarugaku
　呪師猿楽, 74
kabuki
　歌舞伎, 8, 34, 68, 80, 100, 114, 116, 120, 162, 172, 176, 178, 184, 190, 192, 196, 202, 204, 206, 212, 213, 214, 216, 218, 220, 224, 226
kabuki dance
　歌舞伎舞踊, 100, 202, 204, 212, 213, 214, 215, 218, 222, 224, 230, 240
kabuki ensemble
　歌舞伎囃子, 223
kabuki odori
　かぶき踊, 176
kabuki-jōruri
　歌舞伎浄瑠璃, 190, 191, 202
kabuki-kyōgen
　歌舞伎狂言, 100, 206, 212, 214, 215, 219
kabuku
　傾く, 213
kada
　伽陀, 58, 64
kaede
　替手, 136, 156, 176
kaete
　替手, 136
kagami-ita
　鏡板, 88, 89
kagebayashi
　陰囃子, 218, 226
kagura songs
　神楽歌, 32, 264
kagurabue
　神楽笛, 38, 269, 274
kagurauta
　神楽歌, 29, 33

kakeai
　掛合, 216, 220, 222
kakeaimono
　掛合物, 221
kakegoe
　掛声, 94, 250, 251
kakko
　鞨鼓, 30, 38, 269
kaku
　角, 63
kakudayū-bushi
　角太夫節, 194
Kakushin
　覚心, 134, 135
kamigatamai
　上方舞, 184, 231
Kan'ami
　観阿弥, 76
Kanadehon Chūshingura
　仮名手本忠臣蔵, 196, 206
Kanchō
　寛朝, 54, 66
kangen
　管絃, 26, 28, 29, 30, 36, 37, 38, 40, 152, 164, 271
kangosan
　漢語讃, 56
kanjin-noh
　勧進能, 82
kanshi
　漢詩, 124
Kanze School
　観世流, 76, 86
kappore
　かっぽれ, 237
kari
　カリ, 142, 143
kasane-shōzoku
　襲装束, 40, 41
Kasuga Gagaku-kai
　春日雅楽会, 47

Kasuga Wakamiya Shrine Festival
　春日若宮御祭, 100, 106
kata
　型, 90, 94, 212, 215, 218
katarimono
　語り物, 2, 6, 7, 172, 190, 200
katō-bushi
　河東節, 154, 156, 194, 204, 218, 224, 230
kazura-noh
　鬘能, 82, 83
kazuraoke
　鬘桶, 104, 105
keigoto
　景事, 198
kendate hōe
　顕立法会, 61
kengyō
　検校, 170
Kenjun
　賢順, 152, 164
keren
　ケレン, 214, 215
Kiami
　喜阿弥, 76
Kichiku Zenshi
　虚竹禅師, 134
Kikuoka Kengyō
　菊岡検校, 181
kin
　琴, 148, 149
Kineya Jōkan II
　稀音家浄観（二世）, 228
King Lanling
　蘭陵王, 40, 48
Kinko School
　琴古流, 136, 137, 138, 139, 273
kinpira-bushi
　金平節, 194, 224
kinpira-jōruri
　金平浄瑠璃, 192, 193

Kinpū School
錦風流, 138, 139

Kinshin School
錦心流, 118

kinutamono
砧物, 156, 157

kiri-noh
切能, 82, 83

Kishichirō Ōkura
大倉喜七郎, 238, 273

Kitajima Kengyō
北島検校, 152, 154, 160

Kiyomoto Enjudayū
清元延寿太夫, 204

Kiyomoto Oyō
清元お葉, 234

kiyomoto-bushi
清元節, 6, 204, 218, 219, 220, 222, 224, 225, 230, 238

Kobikiuta
木挽唄, 252

kodai shakuhachi
古代尺八, 128, 129

ko-jōruri
古浄瑠璃, 177, 190, 191, 193, 194

kōken
後見, 86

Kokū
虚空, 134, 140

kōkurigaku
高句麗楽, 24

kokyū
胡弓, 170, 180, 184, 185, 269

komabue
高麗笛, 34, 38, 269, 274

komagaku
高麗楽, 26, 28, 29, 34, 42

komosō
薦僧, 132, 133

komusō
虚無僧, 130, 131, 133

ko-omote
小面, 90, 91

kōshiki
講式, 61

koto
箏, 琴, 38, 148

kōtō
勾当, 170

kotoba
詞, 94, 95, 200, 201

koto-kumiuta
箏組歌, 154, 155, 156, 177, 178, 240

kotsuzumi
小鼓, 94, 95, 98, 269, 275

kouta
小唄, 14, 172, 220, 234, 235, 236, 237, 244

kōwakamai
幸若舞, 76, 81, 192

Ko-Yatsuhashi-ryū
古八橋流, 160

kudoki
クドキ, 6, 94, 202, 203, 223

kugutsu
傀儡, 74

kumeuta
久米歌, 29, 32, 33

kumiuta
組歌, 68, 152, 158, 164, 178, 183, 234

kuniburi no utamai
国風歌舞, 28, 29, 30, 32, 36, 271

Kurokawa-noh
黒川能, 106

kuromisu
黒御簾, 216, 218, 226, 227, 229

Kurosawa Kinko
黒澤琴古, 136, 137

kusemai
曲舞, 76, 230

kuzure
くずれ, 118

kyōgen
  狂言, 72, 82, 86, 100, 101, 102, 104, 106
kyōgen actors
  狂言方, 87
kyōgen props
  狂言の小道具, 104, 105
kyōgen-ashirai
  狂言アシライ, 102, 103
kyōgen-utai
  狂言謡, 102, 103
kyōke
  教化, 58
kyokusetsu
  曲節, 116
kyōmai
  京舞, 231
Kyorei
  虚鈴, 140
Kyotaku Denki Kokujikai
  虚鐸伝記国字解, 135
Kyoto style *tegotomono*
  京風手事物, 178, 179, 181, 183
kyū
  宮, 63
left side
  左方, 28
location system
  勘所譜, 13
Lucun
  呂才, 129
lullaby
  子守唄, 244, 245, 258, 259
lushi
  律詩, 125
lute, 111
lyric *jōruri*, 190
ma
  間, 10, 11
machifū-biwa
  町風琵琶, 118

maebiki
  前弾き, 263
Magouta
  馬子唄, 252, 257
mai
  舞, 231
maruhon-kabuki
  丸本歌舞伎, 206, 207, 225
maruhonmono
  丸本物, 224
Matsuura Kengyō
  松浦検校, 181
Meiji Sentei-fu
  明治撰定譜, 45
meiji shinkyoku
  明治新曲, 154, 155, 157
melismatic, 10
melodic songs, 2, 6, 7, 172, 202
meri
  メリ, 142, 143
meriyasu
  メリヤス, 222, 223
metsuke-bashira
  目付柱, 88, 89
meyasu-hakase
  目安博士, 62
Mibu-*kyōgen*
  壬生狂言, 106
michiyuki
  道行, 198
midori-kyōgen
  見取狂言, 215
mie
  見得, 215
mikagura
  御神楽, 32
mikagura no gi
  御神楽之儀, 32
min'yō
  民謡, 244, 245

min'yō scale
　民謡音階, 10, 11, 248, 249
Minezaki Kōtō
　峰崎勾当, 181
mitsudate hōe
　密立法会, 61
Mitsuhashi Kōtō
　三ツ橋勾当, 179
Mitsuzaki Kengyō
　光崎検校, 154, 164, 181
Miyagi, Michio
　宮城道雄, 162, 164
Miyagi-kai
　宮城会, 160
miyakobushi scale
　都節音階, 10, 11, 248, 249
Miyakodayū Icchū
　都太夫一中, 204
Miyakoji Bungonojō
　宮古路豊後掾, 204
miyazono-bushi
　宮薗節, 204
modern biwa
　近代琵琶, 112, 118
modern sōkyoku
　現代箏曲, 157, 162, 164
Momijiyama Gakuso
　紅葉山楽所, 46, 47
monogurui-noh
　物狂能, 78
more-than-thirteen-string koto
　多弦箏, 271
mōsō-biwa
　盲僧琵琶, 110, 111, 269, 272
mōsōza
　盲僧座, 170
Motoori, Nagayo
　本居長世, 162
mugen-noh
　夢幻能, 76, 78
Mukaiji

霧海篍, 134
muromachi-kouta
　室町小歌, 76
music for gagaku dance
　舞譜, 44
music of Baekje
　百済楽, 24
Myōan lineage
　明暗各派, 137
Myōan Society
　明暗教会, 136
Myōan-ji temple
　明暗寺, 132, 133
nagauta
　長唄, 172, 216, 218, 219, 221, 222,
　　228, 229
nagauta (long songs)
　長歌, 長哥, 178, 221
Nagauta Fuyō-kai
　長唄芙蓉会, 228, 229
Nagauta Kensei-kai
　長唄研精会, 228, 229
nagautamono
　長歌物, 179
Nakanoshima, Kin'ichi
　中能島欣一, 162
Nakao Tozan
　中尾都山, 136, 137
Nakayama, Shinpei
　中山晋平, 260, 261
nami-byōshi
　並拍子, 98, 99
Namiki Sōsuke
　並木宗輔, 196
naniwabushi
　浪花節, 208, 238, 239
Nanto Gakuso
　南都楽所, 47
Nanzan-shinryū
　南山進流, 54, 64

Nara *shōmyō*
奈良声明, 54
naraimono
習物, 116, 117
narimono
鳴り物, 222, 226, 268
narrative songs
語り物, 2, 6, 7, 172, 190, 200, 202
netori
音取り, 30, 42
neumatic notation, 12, 62
new drum music
創作太鼓音楽, 262
new folk songs
新民謡, 260, 261
new music
新楽, 42
niagari
二上り, 222, 248, 249, 254, 270
niagari-shin'nai
二上り新内, 237
nigen-kin
二絃琴, 166
Niiname Festival
新嘗祭, 33
ningyō
人形, 177
ningyō-jōruri
人形浄瑠璃, 176, 190, 192, 196, 200, 202, 206
nishiki-biwa
錦琵琶, 118, 272
nodo
喉, 98, 274
noh costume
能装束, 92, 93
noh props
能の小道具, 90, 91
nohgaku
能楽, 72, 73
nohkan

能管, 98, 269, 274
non-fabricated pipe
地無し管, 273
nori-byōshi
ノリ拍子, 98, 99
norigata
ノリ型, 96
notation system
記譜法, 12, 13, 44, 45, 136, 142
nuoxi
儺戯, 74
ōdaiko
大太鼓, 38, 40, 269
odori
踊, 231
odoriji
踊り地, 202, 203
ogie-bushi
荻江節, 8, 9, 14, 228, 229, 230
Oharabushi
おはら節, 252
oiwake styles
追分様式, 10, 248, 249
Oiwakebushi
追分節, 256, 257
Okamoto Bun'ya
岡本文弥, 204
Okina
翁, 82, 98, 100, 106
okina masks
翁面, 90, 91
okina-sarugaku
翁猿楽, 74
okinawa scale
沖縄音階, 10, 11, 248, 249
okiuta
置唄, 223
okuni-kabuki
阿国歌舞伎, 217
Ōkuraulo
オークラウロ, 273

old music
　古楽, 42
ōmi-sarugaku
　近江猿楽, 74, 76
omote
　表, 10
　面, 90
on'nagata
　女形, 216
ōnaobiuta
　大直日歌, 29, 33
ondo
　音頭, 248
ōnori
　大ノリ, 96, 97
oral transmission
　口伝, 12, 13
ōshikichō
　黄鐘調, 62, 63
oshirabe
　お調べ, 88
Osuwa daiko
　御諏訪太鼓, 263
ōtsuzumi
　大鼓, 94, 95, 98, 269, 275
Ōuchi Gakuso
　大内楽所, 47
oud, 110, 111
ōuta
　大歌, 29, 33
Ōutadokoro
　大歌所, 46, 47
oyama
　女形, 216
ōzatsuma-bushi
　大薩摩節, 6, 194, 218, 219, 220, 224
parlor jōruri
　座敷浄瑠璃, 202
parlor song
　座敷歌, 244
party nagauta
　宴会用長唄, 221
pattern system
　曲節法, 13
pipa
　琵琶, 110, 272
poetry reading
　歌披講, 36, 123
puppet operators
　傀儡師, 193
qijue
　七絶, 124
Ranryōō
　蘭陵王, 40, 48
reform of the musical system
　楽制改革, 20, 26, 28, 34
Reihō-ji
　鈴法寺, 132, 133
rhythmic notation
　粒付譜, 13
right side
　右方, 26, 28, 30
rinyūgaku
　林邑楽, 24
ritsu scale
　律音階, 10, 11, 248, 249
ritual song
　神事歌, 246, 247
riyō
　俚謡, 244
Roan
　蘆安, 130, 131, 132, 134
rōei
　朗詠, 26, 29, 30, 37
rongi
　論議, 58
rubbed instruments
　擦り物, 275
ruika
　誄歌, 29, 32, 33
Ryōnin
　良忍, 54, 66

287

ryōtō-shōzoku
　裲襠装束, 40, 41
ryūteki
　龍笛, 34, 38, 269, 274
sahō
　左方, 30
sahō no mai
　左方舞, 30
saibara
　催馬楽, 26, 30, 39
saimon
　祭文, 58, 64
Sakichi Kineya IV
　杵屋佐吉（四世）, 162, 228
sakumono
　作物, 178, 179, 182
san'no-tsuzumi
　三ノ鼓, 38, 39
sangaku
　散楽, 72, 74
sangen shusōgaku
　三絃主奏楽, 162, 228
sangyō
　三業, 198
sankangaku
　三韓楽, 24
sankyoku
　三曲, 138, 139, 140, 150, 181, 185, 186, 187
sankyoku gassō
　三曲合奏, 172, 184, 187
Sanpō Gakuso
　三方楽所, 46, 47
sansagari
　三下り, 248, 249, 252, 257, 270
sanshin
　三線, 174
santan
　讃嘆, 58
sarugaku
　猿楽, 72, 73, 74, 76

sarugaku-noh
　猿楽能, 68, 74, 81
sashi-byōshi
　サシ拍子, 98, 99
sashinori
　サシノリ, 97
satokagura
　里神楽, 32
satsuma mōsō-biwa
　薩摩盲僧琵琶, 112
satsuma-biwa
　薩摩琵琶, 112, 118, 269, 272
Satsuma-Yatsuhashi-ryū
　薩摩八橋流, 160
sawari
　サワリ, 174, 270
Sawazumi Kengyō
　沢住検校, 170, 181, 194
se
　瑟, 149
seichō
　正調, 244, 245, 256, 257
Seien School
　西園流, 137
Seiha Hōgaku-kai
　正派邦楽会, 160
sekkyō-bushi
　説経節, 192, 208, 209
Semimaru
　蝉丸, 112, 170
seven-seven-seven-and-five syllable meter
　七七七五調, 248
sewamono
　世話物, 196, 198, 200, 214
shaken instruments
　振り物, 275
shakubyōshi
　笏拍子, 38, 269
shakuhachi
　尺八, 128, 130, 132, 134, 136, 138,

288

140, 142, 144, 162, 184, 186, 250, 251, 269

shakuhachi w/7 or more holes
多孔尺八, 131, 269

shakujō
錫杖, 269

shamisen
三味線, 150, 162, 170, 172, 174, 176, 178, 186, 190, 192, 212, 219, 220, 223, 226, 228, 234, 237, 238, 240, 248, 250, 251, 254, 269

shamisen short songs
三味線小歌曲, 236

shamisen-kumiuta
三味線組歌, 174, 176, 177, 178, 182, 240

shibaiutamono
芝居歌物, 179

shibyōshi
四拍子, 94, 95, 98, 102, 216, 220

shichibongosan
四智梵語讃, 56

shichigen-kin
七弦琴, 148, 149

shichikangosan
四智漢語讃, 56

Shichiku Shoshin-shū
糸竹初心集, 186

shifū-biwa
士風琵琶, 118

shigetayū-bushi
繁太夫節, 194

shigin
詩吟, 122, 123

shikisanban
式三番, 83, 99

shimai
仕舞, 84, 85

shime-daiko
締太鼓, 250, 275

shin hōgaku
新邦楽, 138, 162

shin kabuki
新歌舞伎, 214, 215

shin nihon ongaku
新日本音楽, 138, 140, 154, 155, 162, 238

shin'nai-bushi
新内節, 204, 237

Shinanono Zenji Yukinaga
信濃前司行長, 114

shingi shōmyō
新義声明, 54

Shingon *shōmyō*
真言声明, 54

Shingon *Shōmyō*
真言声明, 54

shinobue
篠笛, 269

Shinpō School
真法流, 137

shiori
シオリ, 90

shiragigaku
新羅楽, 24

shite
シテ, 76, 78, 86, 88, 90, 94, 96, 101, 102, 106

shitekata
シテ方, 86

shitsu
瑟, 149

shō
商, 63
笙, 38, 269, 274

Shōbutsu
生仏, 114

Shōchō School
松調流, 139

shōdan
小段, 94, 95

shōga
    唱歌, 12, 44
shōko
    鉦鼓, 38, 269, 275
shōkyoku
    小曲, 43
shōmyō
    声明, 48, 54, 56, 58, 61, 62, 63, 65, 67, 68, 69, 114
shosagoto
    所作事, 216, 231
shōsōin shakuhachi
    正倉院尺八, 128, 129
shura-noh
    修羅能, 83
sō
    箏, 148
sōban
    双盤, 269
Sōetsu School
    宗悦流, 136, 137
sōga
    早歌, 76
sōjō
    双調, 62, 63
sōkyoku
    箏曲, 148, 150, 151, 154, 155, 164
sōkyoku transcribed from *jiuta*
    地歌移曲箏曲, 156, 181
solmization, 12
Sonezaki Shinjū
    曽根崎心中, 198
songs and dance native to Japan
    国風歌舞, 19
songs by entertainers
    芸事歌, 247
sonohachi-bushi
    薗八節, 204
straight-neck *biwa*
    直頸楽琵琶, 111
string name system
    弦名譜, 13
strolling *shin'nai* performers
    新内流し, 236
su-bayashi
    素囃子, 85
Sugawara Denju Tenarai Kagami
    菅原伝授手習鑑, 196, 206
suizen
    吹禅, 132, 133
suma-goto
    須磨琴, 149, 166
Sumiyama School
    隅山流, 160
super *kabuki*
    スーパー歌舞伎, 214, 215
su-utai
    素謡, 84, 85
syllabic, 10, 11
syllabic system
    唱歌譜, 13
Tachibana-kai
    橘会, 118
Tachibana-ryū
    橘流, 118
taiko
    太鼓, 98, 269
taikomono
    太鼓物, 99
taiku
    大曲, 42, 43
taishō-goto
    大正琴, 166
taishō-koto
    大正琴, 166
Taizan School
    対山流, 137
Takeda Izumo II
    竹田出雲（二世）, 206
takemoto
    竹本, 206, 218, 219, 222

Takemoto Gidayū
　竹本義太夫, 190, 194, 204
Takemoto-za
　竹本座, 196, 206
Tale of Princess Jōruri
　浄瑠璃姫物語, 176, 177
Tarō-kaja
　太郎冠者, 100, 104
tateshamisen
　立三味線, 222, 223
tateuta
　立唄, 222, 223
tauta
　田歌, 29, 33
tegoto
　手事, 156
tegotomono
　手事物, 178, 179, 180
Ten'nō-ji Gakuso
　天王寺楽所, 46, 47
Ten'nō-ji Garyō-kai
　天王寺雅亮会, 47
Tendai *shōmyō*
　天台声明, 54
Tengyōshōrei
　転経唱礼, 54
tenpuku
　天吹, 130, 131
Tenpyō Biwa-fu
　天平琵琶譜, 44
theatrical music
　劇場音楽, 2, 8, 68, 238
three orthodox *honkyoku*
　三虚霊, 140
three-man puppet manipulation
　三人遣い, 196
tōdō
　当道, 150, 152, 154, 162, 164, 170
tōdōza
　当道座, 112, 118, 120, 164, 170
tōgaku
　唐楽, 24, 26, 29
Tokiwazu Mojidayū
　常磐津文字太夫, 204
tokiwazu-bushi
　常磐津節, 172, 204, 225
tōkyoku
　当曲, 43
tōmei-bushi
　東明節, 239
tōmeigaku
　東明楽, 238
Tomimoto Buzen'nojō
　富本豊前掾, 204
Tomimoto Buzendayū
　宮本豊前太夫, 204
tomimoto-bushi
　富本節, 204
toragaku
　度羅楽, 24
tōshii-kyōgen
　通し狂言, 215
Toyomi Shigetayū
　豊美繁太夫, 204
toyomoto-bushi
　豊本節, 238, 239
Toyotake Wakadayū
　豊竹若太夫, 196
Toyotake-za
　豊竹座, 206
Tozan School
　都山流, 137, 138, 139, 273
triple *kakeai*
　三方掛合, 222
tsugaru shamisen
　津軽三味線, 238, 239, 250, 262, 263
Tsugaru-Ikuta School
　津軽郁田流, 160
tsuke
　ツケ, 215
Tsukushi School
　筑紫流, 152, 153, 157

tsukushi-goto
  筑紫箏, 68, 152, 271
tsuridaiko
  釣太鼓, 38
Tsuru School
  鶴派, 118, 272
tsuruta-biwa
  鶴田琵琶, 272
tsuyogin
  ツヨ吟, 96, 97
tsuzumi
  鼓, 86, 98, 99, 275
u
  羽, 63
uchimono
  打物, 39, 268, 275
Ueda School
  上田流, 137
Uemura Bunrakuken
  植村文楽軒, 190, 206
uhō
  右方, 30
uhō no mai
  右方舞, 30
ura
  裏, 10
Urasaki Kengyō
  浦崎検校, 179
Ushibuka Haiyabushi
  牛深はいや節, 254, 255
utagaki
  歌垣, 22, 23, 264
utai
  謡, 78
utaikata
  唄方, 223
utaimono
  歌い物, 2, 6, 7, 68, 172
  謡物, 179
uta-jōruri
  歌浄瑠璃, 190, 191, 202, 204, 218, 219
Utamai no Tsukasa
  うたまいのつかさ, 26
utazawa
  うた沢, 234, 235, 236, 237
uwa-jōshi
  上調子, 220
Uzume
  天鈿女命, 23
wagon
  和琴, 38, 44, 148, 149, 269, 271
wagoto
  和事, 217
wakashū kabuki
  若衆歌舞伎, 217
waki
  ワキ, 86, 94
waki-kyōgen
  脇狂言, 100
waki-noh
  脇能, 83
work songs
  仕事歌, 245, 246, 247, 248, 249, 250
wujue
  五絶, 124
Yaezaki Kengyō
  八重崎検校, 181
yagibushi style
  八木節様式, 248, 249
yakumo-goto
  八雲琴, 166
Yamada Kengyō
  山田検校, 154, 156
Yamada School
  山田流, 156, 158, 164
yamatogaku
  大和楽, 238, 239
yamato-sarugaku
  大和猿楽, 74
yamatouta
  倭歌, 29, 33

大和歌, 29, 32, 33
Yanagawa Kengyō
　柳川検校, 178, 179, 181, 183
Yanagawa School
　柳川流, 182, 183
yanyue
　燕楽, 21, 24
yarō kabuki
　野郎歌舞伎, 216, 217
Yasaka School
　八坂流, 114
Yasumura School
　安村流, 160
Yatsuhashi Kengyō
　八橋検校, 152, 160, 181
yōkyoku
　謡曲, 62, 95, 96
Yosarebushi
　よされ節, 252
Yoshitsune Senbon Zakura
　義経千本桜, 196
Yoshizawa Kengyō
　吉沢検校, 154, 156
Yoshizumi Kosaburō IV
　吉住小三郎（四世）, 228
yowagin
　ヨワ吟, 96, 97
yūjo kabuki
　遊女歌舞伎, 216, 217
yuri
　ユリ, 143
yushan
　魚山, 54
Yūzaki-za
　結崎座, 76
zashiki music
　お座敷音楽, 8
zashiki song
　座敷歌, 172
zashiki-jōruri
　座敷浄瑠璃, 190, 202, 203, 204
zatō
　座頭, 170
zatsu-noh
　雑能, 83
zatsu-shōmyō
　雑声明, 56
Zeami
　世阿弥, 42, 76, 78, 80
zekku
　絶句, 124
Zhenzhou Puhua
　普化禅師, 134, 135
zokkyoku
　俗曲, 244
zokusō
　俗箏, 152, 271
zokuyō
　俗謡, 244

About the Authors

Dr. Kenji Tanaka 田中健次 was born in Wakayama, Japan, in 1954, and received D.Lit. at Osaka University in 1998, and M.A. at Kunitachi College of Music in 1980. After working with musical business companies such as Casio Ltd., he taught at Saga University until 2002. Currently he is Professor at Ibaraki University. He has taught, as a lecturer and a visiting professor, at many schools in Japan and abroad, including Waseda University, Kunitachi College of Music, Yokohama National University, National Taiwan University, National Hsinchu University of Education, and Universiti Putra Malaysia. In 1995 he was awarded The First Roland Electronic Music Foundation Prize for developing software for music education. He is the member of Musicological Society of Japan, Music Education Society of Japan, International Society for Music Education, and International Computer Music Association. He has written and co-authored many books on music. His publications include: "Zukai Nihon Ongakushi (Illustrated History of Traditional Japanese Music)" 2008, Tokyodo Shuppan); "Hitome De Wakaru Nippon Ongaku Nyumon (Introduction to Traditional Japanese Music at a Glance)" (2003, Ongaku No Tomo Sha); "Denshi Gakki Sangyo Ron (On the Electronic Musical Instrument Industry)" (1998, Tokyo Kobundo); and "Ongaku Kyoshi No Tame No Konpyuta Hando Bukku (A Handbook of Computer for Music Teachers)" (1995, Kyoiku Geijutsu Sha).

Dr. Takashi Koto 小藤隆志, born in Tokyo in 1946, received his Ph.D. in Music from Harvard University, his M.M. in Composition from the New England Conservatory, and his B.M. in Musicology/Theory from Kunitachi College of Music in Tokyo. In 1983 he won the Irino Prize for his "Like Flickering Light" for violin and piano. He was editor for a musical journal "Ongaku Geijutsu" in Japan and has written extensively on musical matters and translated articles and books into Japanese. His translations of full texts into Japanese include the latest book "Sonic Design" by Robert Cogan and Pozzi Escot, "Molto Agitato" by Johanna Fiedler, "Stravinsky" by Robert Craft, "Evenings with Horowitz" by David Dubal, and "The Memory of All That" by Joan Peyser. He is integrally involved in Japanese musical activities in Boston, such as the Portsmouth Peace Treaty Concert Series "JAPAN DAY" 2005. He has been the music director of the "Afternoon of Shakuhachi and Koto Music". He has composed many chamber and orchestral works, including his double concerto for *shakuhachi* and *koto* and three *koto* concertos premiered in Massachusetts. In 2015, he composed the anthem "Hokkaido Pioneers" and a work for brass orchestra and chorus based on the anthem to celebrate the 25th Anniversary of the sister state relationship between Massachusetts and Hokkaido, Japan.